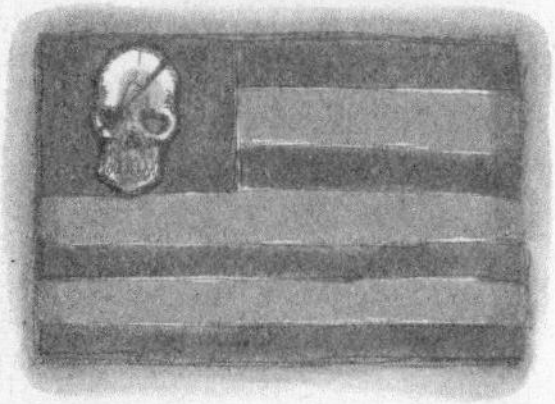

I went to America for work. San Diego. I appeared at an event called Comic-Con and met a lot of my American fans. I saw some local cosplay and I did a lot of interesting interviews. There were some who lined up the night before to hear me speak. It was all fresh and fun. I'm proud that my first overseas trip was a trip to meet my American fans.

-Tite Kubo

Bleach is author Tite Kubo's second title. Kubo made his debut with *ZOMBIEPOWDER.*, a four-volume series for *Weekly Shonen Jump*. To date, *Bleach* has been translated into numerous languages and has also inspired an animated TV series that began airing in the U.S. in 2006. Beginning its serialization in 2001, *Bleach* is still a mainstay in the pages of *Weekly Shonen Jump*. In 2005, *Bleach* was awarded the prestigious Shogakukan Manga Award in the *shonen* (boys) category.

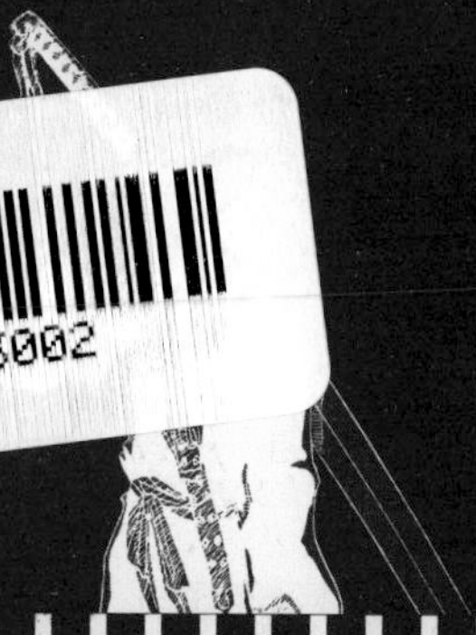

BLEACH
Vol. 35: HIGHER THAN THE MOON
SHONEN JUMP Manga Edition

This volume contains material that was originally published in English
in SHONEN JUMP #99–102. Artwork in the magazine may have been
altered slightly from what is presented in this volume.

STORY AND ART BY
TITE KUBO

English Adaptation/Lance Caselman
Translation/Joe Yamazaki
Touch-up Art & Lettering/Mark McMurray
Design/Sean Lee, Yukiko Whitley
Editors/Alexis Kirsch, Yuki Takagaki

BLEACH © 2001 by Tite Kubo. All rights reserved. First published
in Japan in 2001 by SHUEISHA Inc., Tokyo. English translation rights
arranged by SHUEISHA Inc.

Printed in the U.S.A.

Published by VIZ Media, LLC
P.O. Box 77010
San Francisco, CA 94107

10 9 8 7 6 5 4 3 2 1
First printing, June 2011

PARENTAL ADVISORY
BLEACH is rated T for Teen and is recommended
for ages 13 and up. This volume contains
fantasy violence.
ratings.viz.com

Born and then fall
Is the same as death

BLEACH 35

HIGHER THAN THE MOON

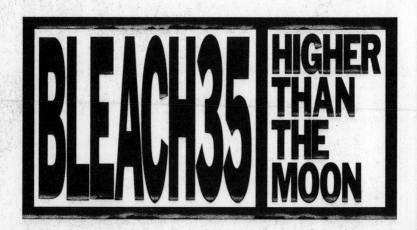

STARS AND

Orihime Inoue

Mayuri Kurotsuchi

Ichigo Kurosaki

plot

When high school student Ichigo Kurosaki meets Soul Reaper Rukia Kuchiki his life is changed forever. Soon Ichigo is a soul-cleansing Soul Reaper too, and he finds himself having adventures, as well as problems, that he never would have imagined. Now Ichigo and his friends must stop renegade Soul Reaper Aizen and his army of Arrancars from destroying the Soul Society and wiping out KarakuraTown as well.

Having penetrated the enemy's stronghold Las Noches to rescue Orihime, Ichigo and his allies must face the powerful Espadas. Just as Ichigo faces a hopeless crisis, reinforcements from the Soul Society arrive and begin their counterattack! Kenpachi joins their battle against Nnoitora, Byakuya saves Rukia, and Mayuri drives his cold blade into Szayelaporro!

BLEACH ALL

ネリエル

Nelliel

更木剣八

Kenpachi Zaraki

Nnoitora

ノイトラ

STORIES

BLEACH 35

HIGHER THAN THE MOON

Contents

306. Not Perfect is GOoD

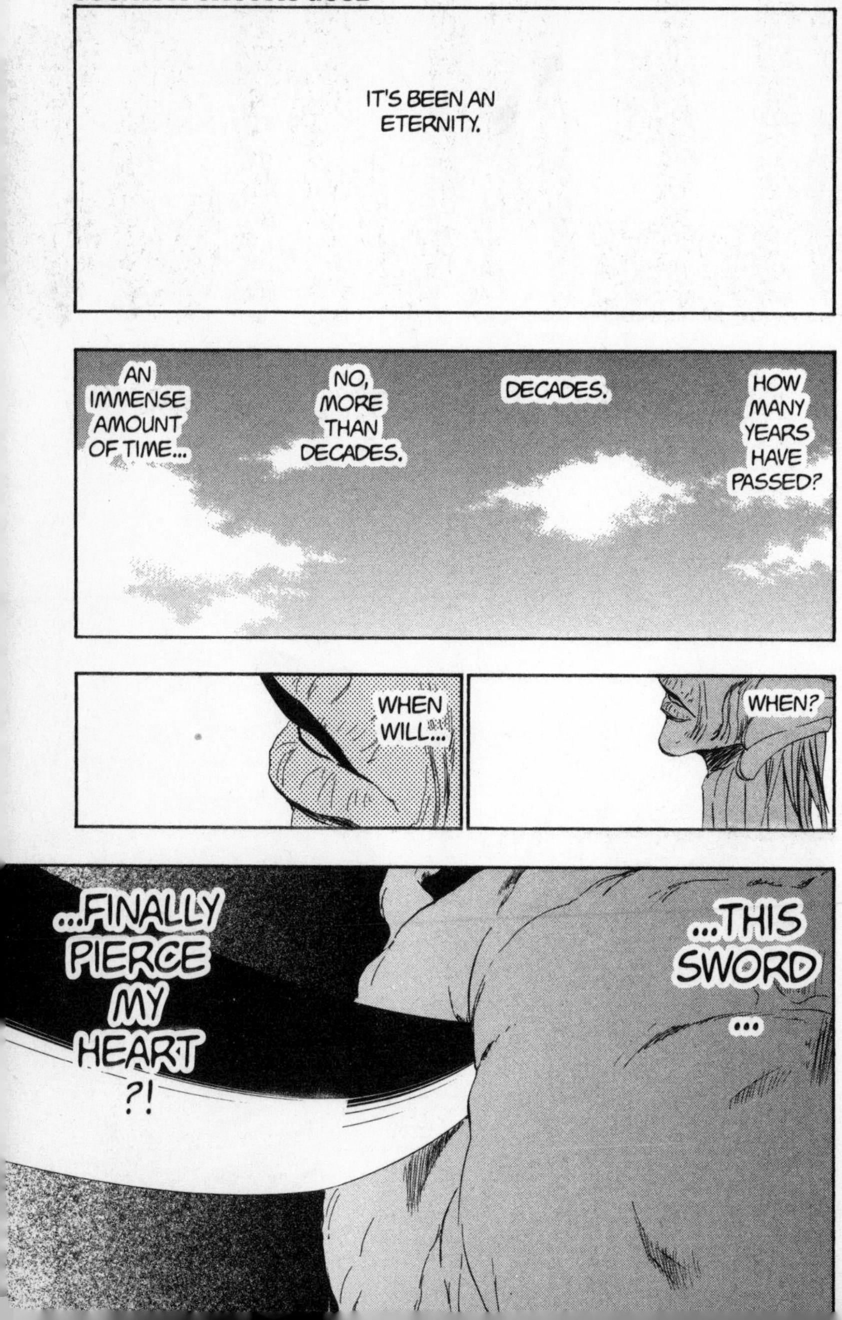
IT'S BEEN AN ETERNITY.
HOW MANY YEARS HAVE PASSED?
DECADES.
NO, MORE THAN DECADES.
AN IMMENSE AMOUNT OF TIME...
WHEN?
WHEN WILL...
...THIS SWORD ...
...FINALLY PIERCE MY HEART ?!

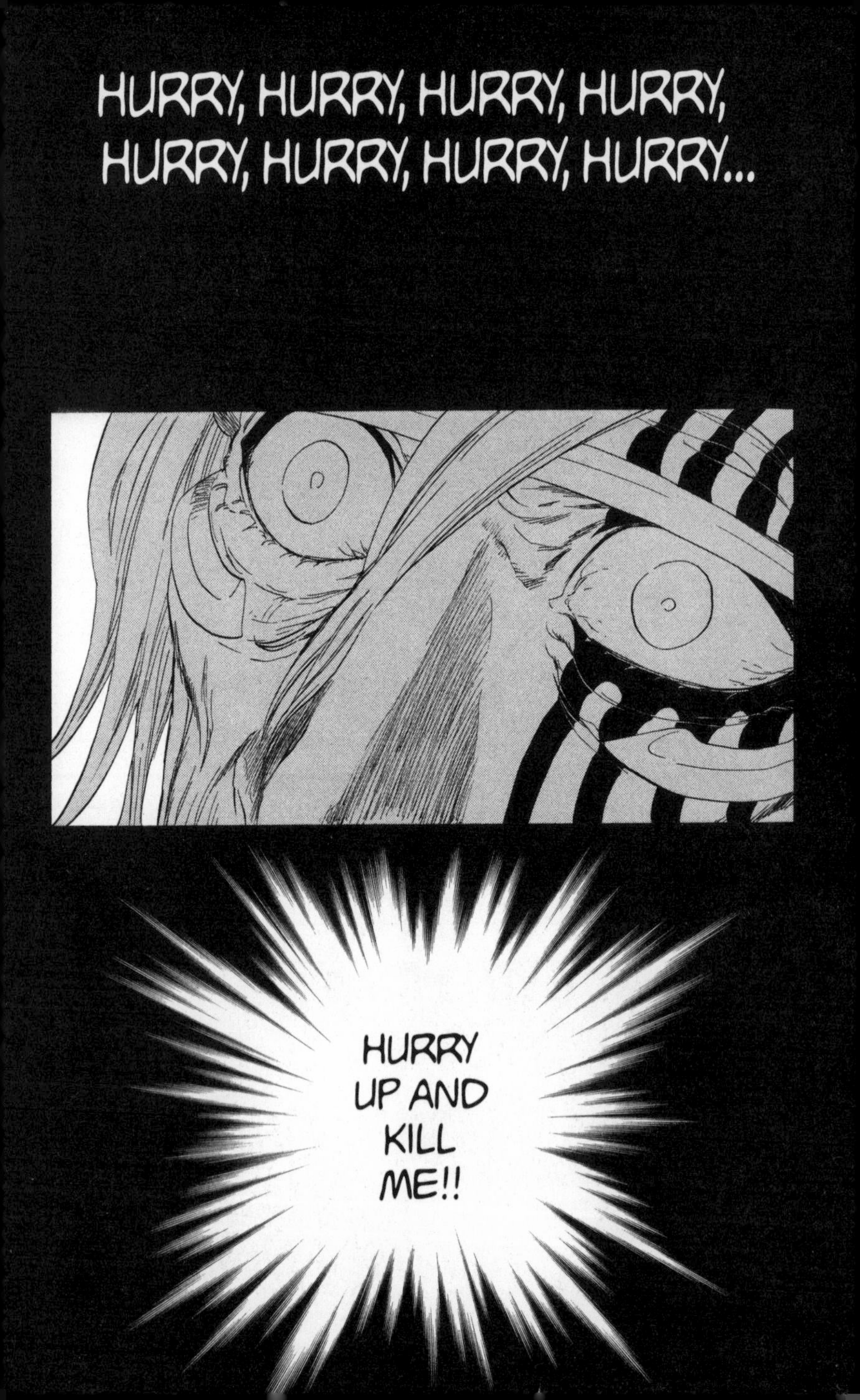
HURRY, HURRY, HURRY, HURRY, HURRY, HURRY, HURRY, HURRY...
HURRY UP AND KILL ME!!

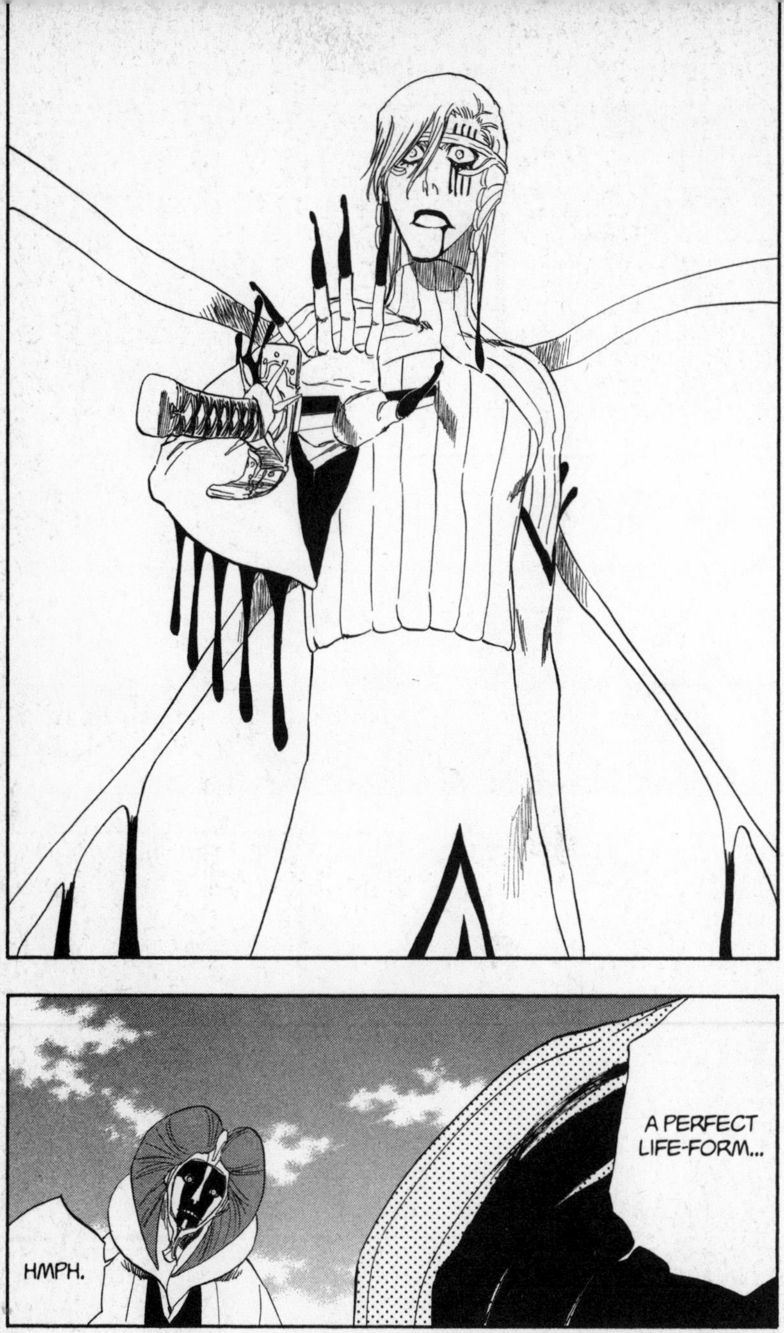
A PERFECT LIFE-FORM...
HMPH.

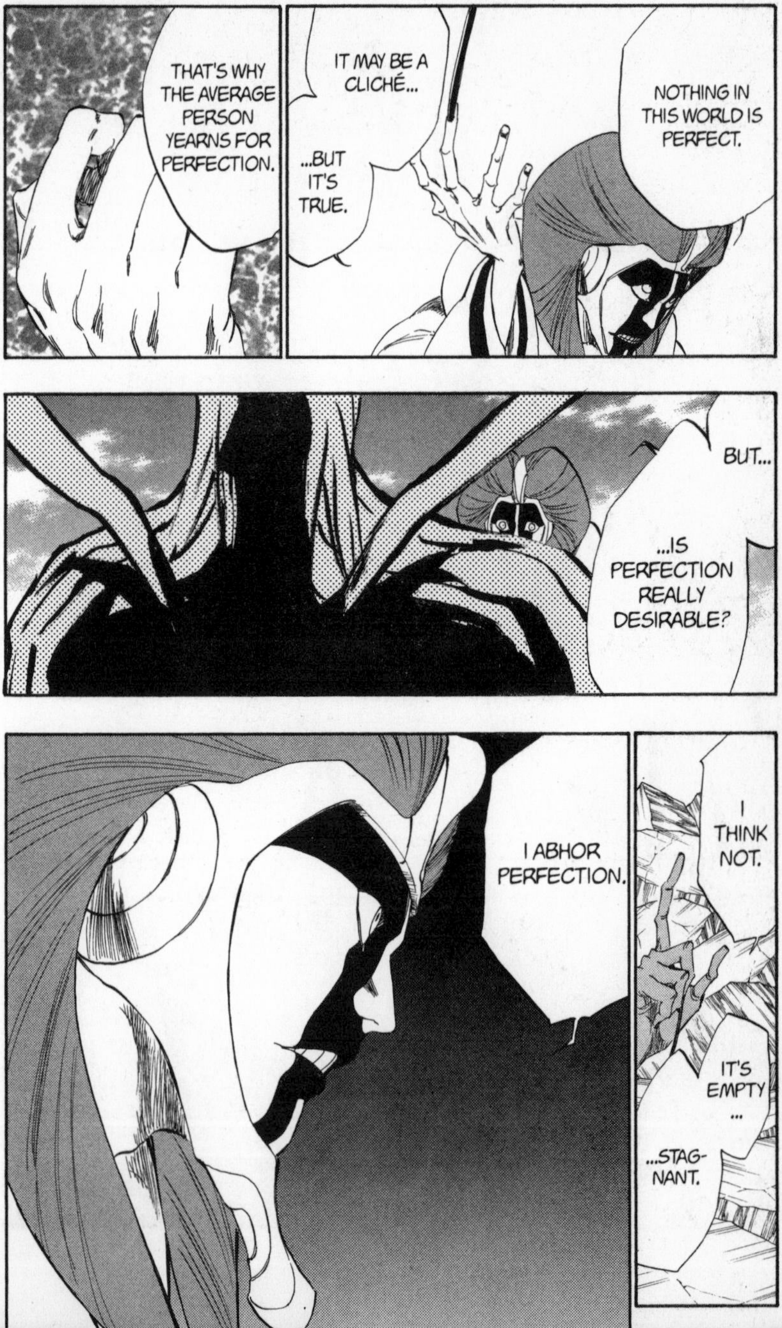
NOTHING IN THIS WORLD IS PERFECT.
IT MAY BE A CLICHÉ...
...BUT IT'S TRUE.
THAT'S WHY THE AVERAGE PERSON YEARNS FOR PERFECTION.
BUT...
...IS PERFECTION REALLY DESIRABLE?
I THINK NOT.
IT'S EMPTY...
...STAG-NANT.
I ABHOR PERFECTION.

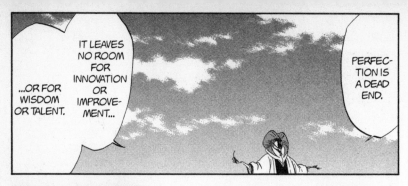

PERFECTION IS A DEAD END.
IT LEAVES NO ROOM FOR INNOVATION OR IMPROVEMENT...
...OR FOR WISDOM OR TALENT.
DO YOU UNDERSTAND?
FOR US SCIENTISTS ...
...PERFECTION MEANS...
...DESPAIR.
BE GREATER THAN ALL THAT'S COME BEFORE...
...BUT...
...NEVER BE PERFECT.
SCIENTISTS ALWAYS STRUGGLE WITH THAT CONTRADICTION...
...BUT THEY MUST ALSO FIND PLEASURE IN IT.
IN OTHER WORDS ...

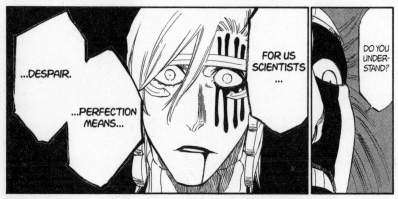

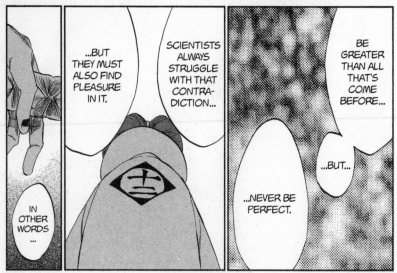

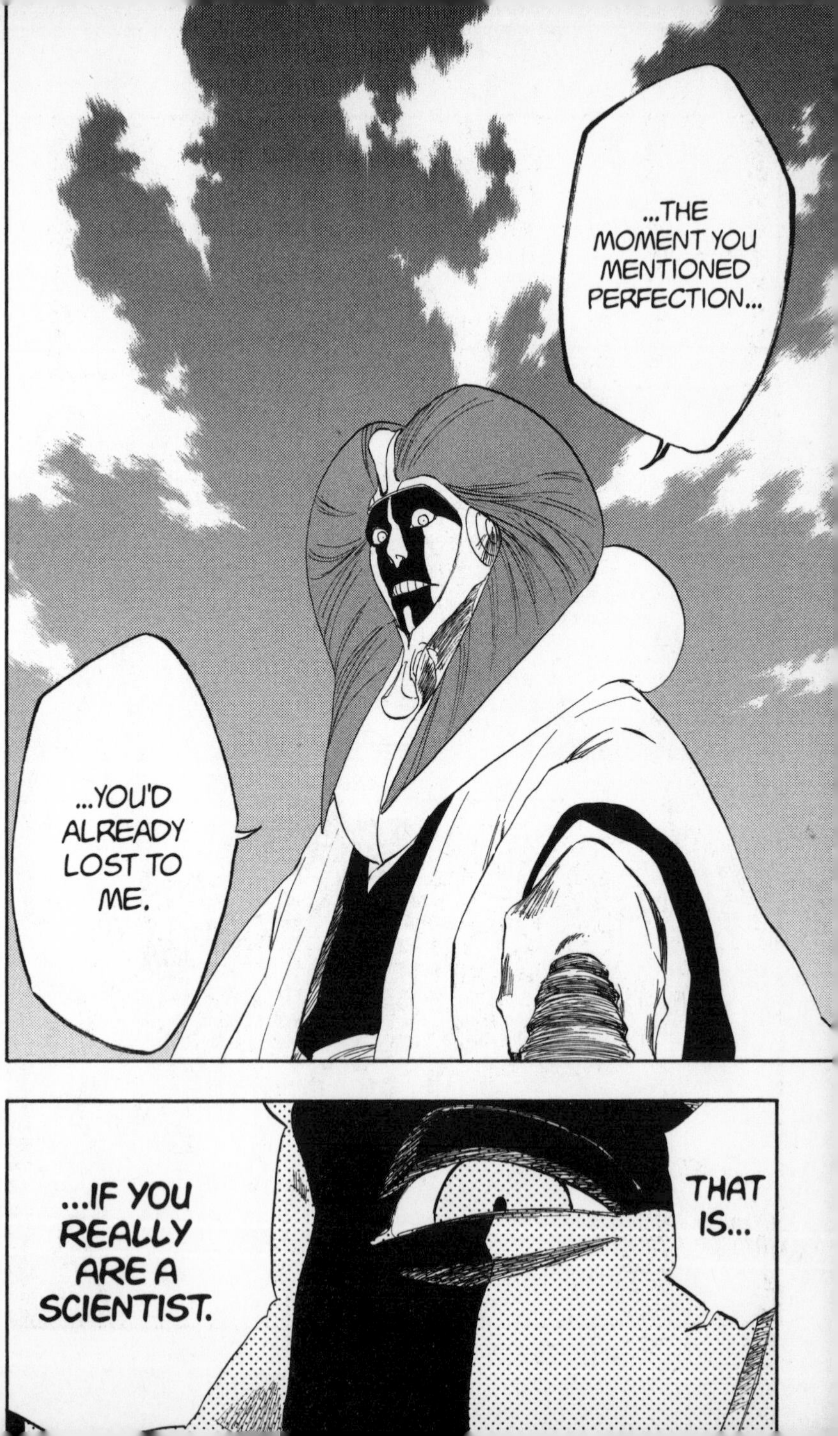
...THE MOMENT YOU MENTIONED PERFECTION...
...YOU'D ALREADY LOST TO ME.
THAT IS...
...IF YOU REALLY ARE A SCIENTIST.

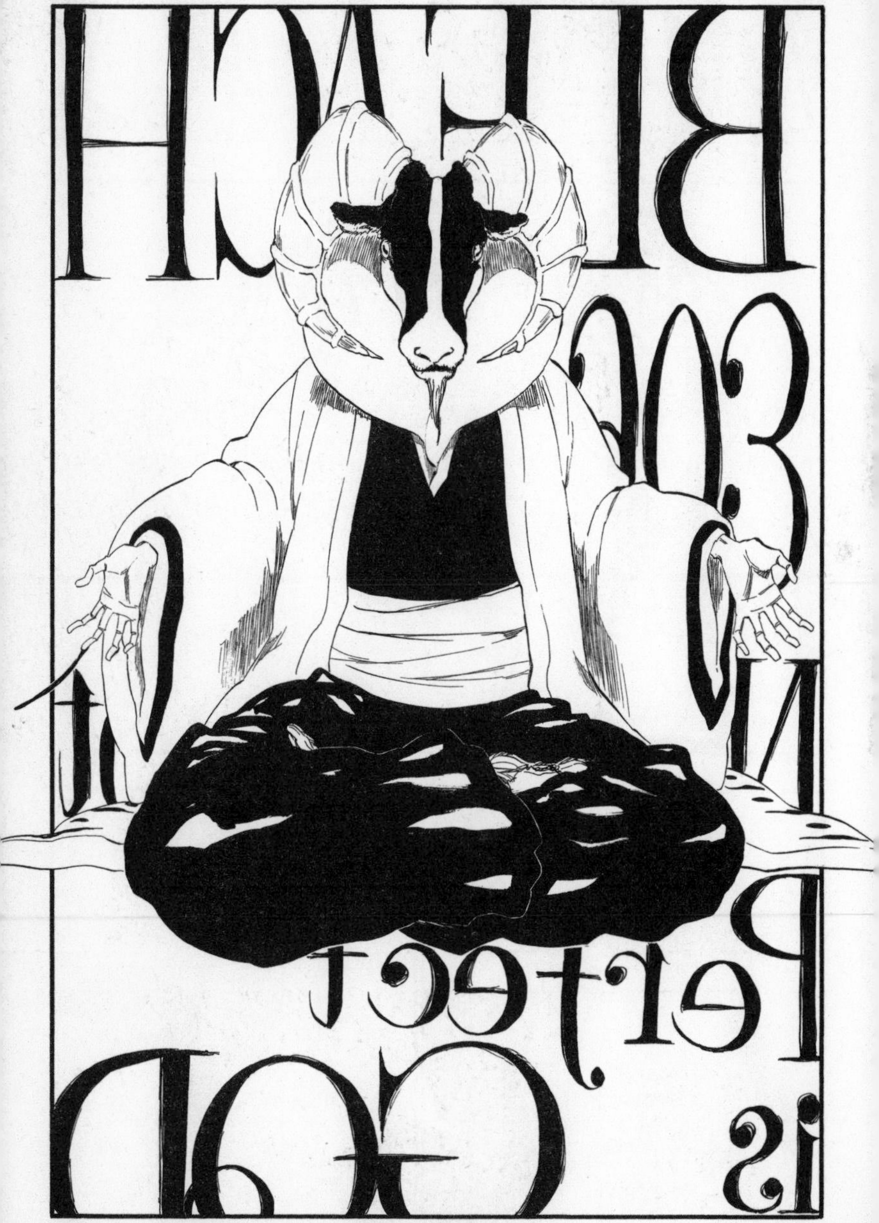

BLEACH 306. Not Perfect is GOoD

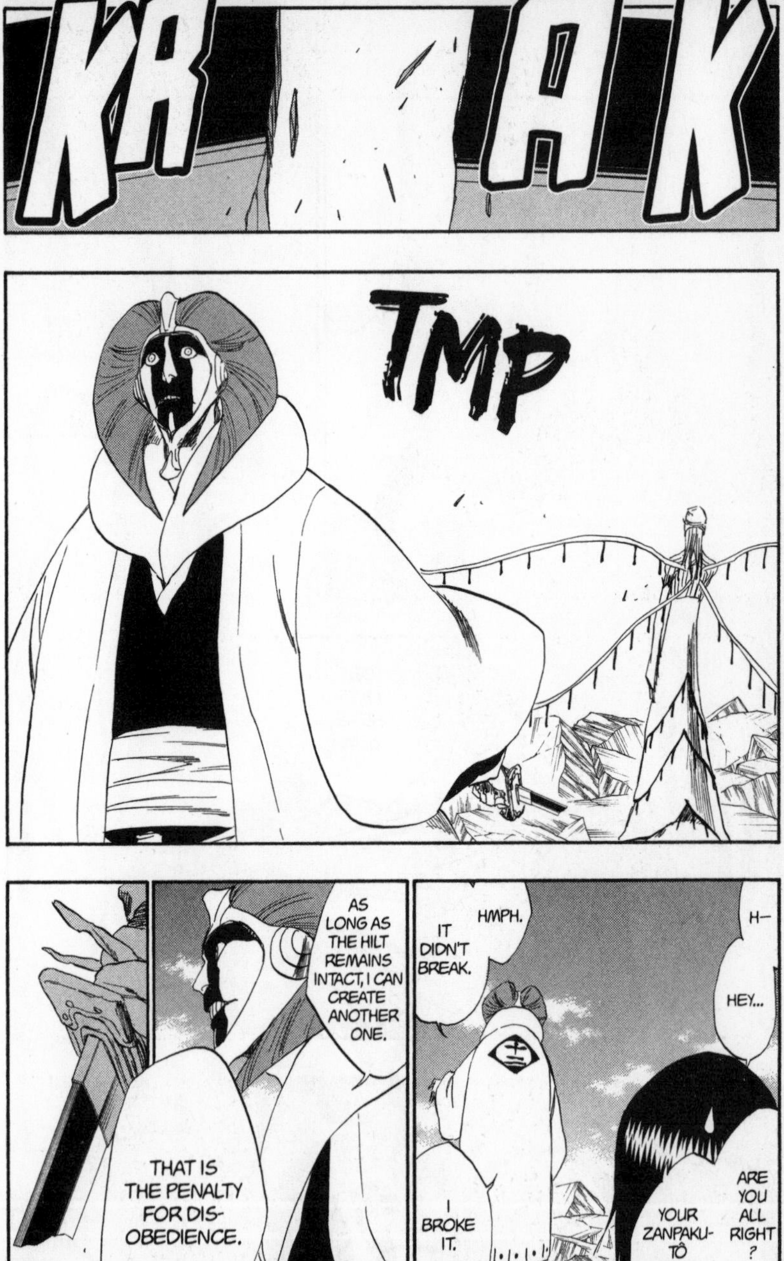
KRAK
TMP
H—
HEY...
ARE YOU ALL RIGHT?
YOUR ZANPAKU-TÔ BROKE.
HMPH.
IT DIDN'T BREAK.
I BROKE IT.
AS LONG AS THE HILT REMAINS INTACT, I CAN CREATE ANOTHER ONE.
THAT IS THE PENALTY FOR DIS-OBEDIENCE.

...

WIP WIP

WHAP

GET OVER HERE, NEMU!

NEMU!

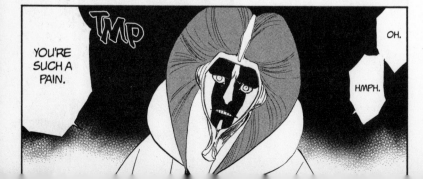

TMP

YOU'RE SUCH A PAIN.

OH.

HMPH.

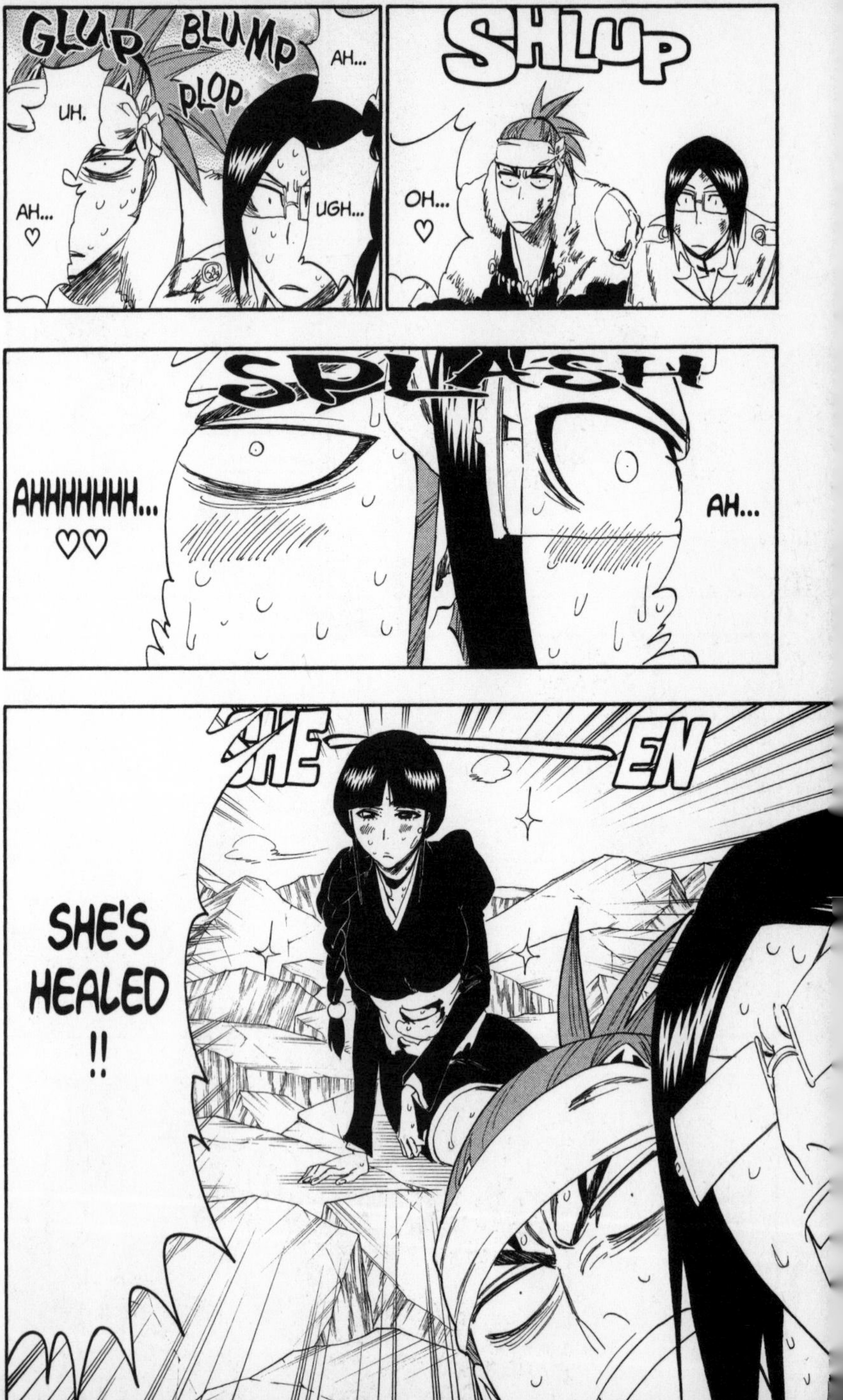
SHLUP
OH... ♡
AH...
BLUMP
GLUP
PLOP
UH.
UGH...
AH... ♡
SPLASH
AH...
AHHHHHHH... ♡♡
SHE—EN
SHE'S HEALED !!

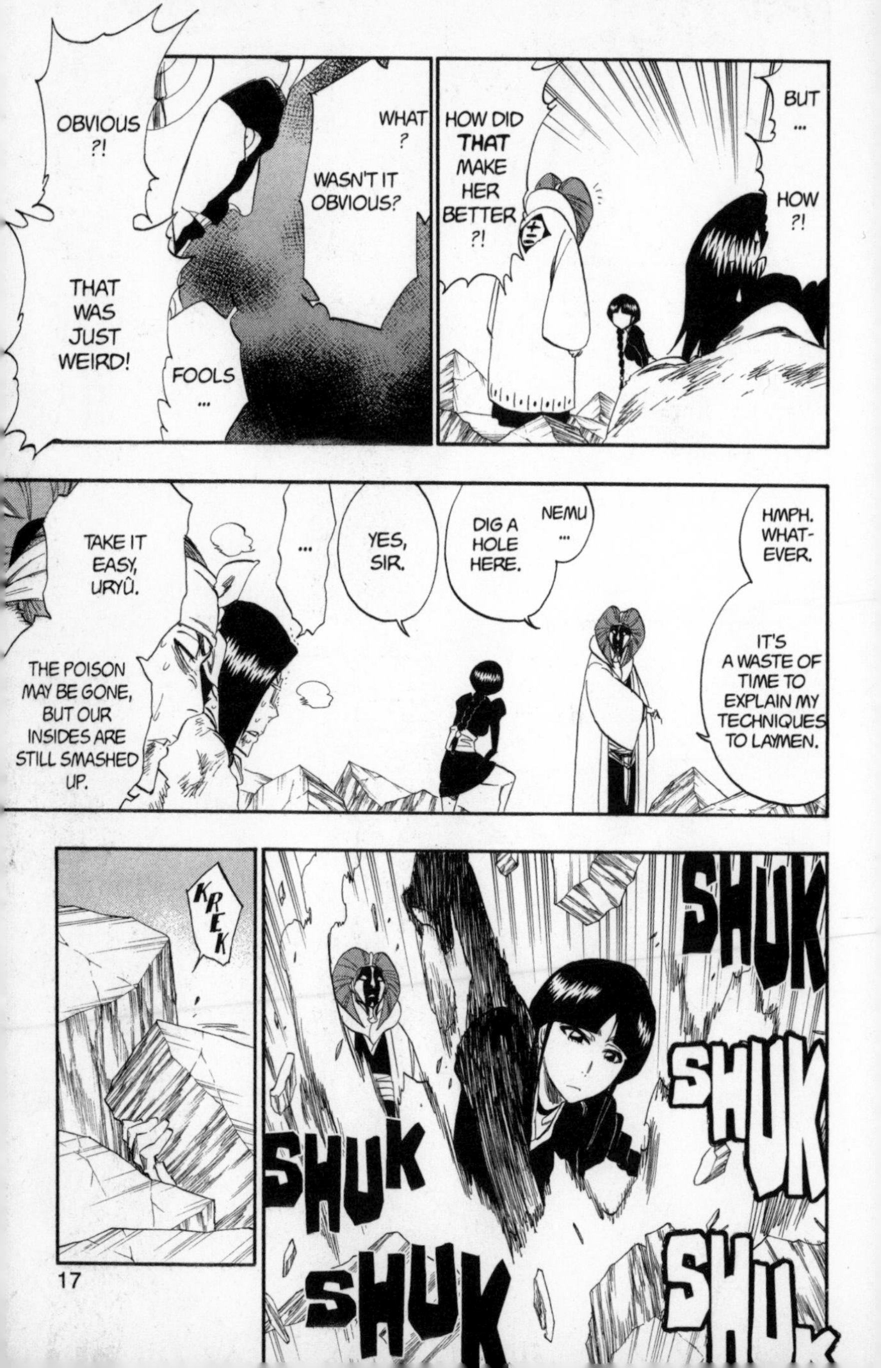

BUT ...
HOW ?!
HOW DID THAT MAKE HER BETTER ?!
WHAT ?
WASN'T IT OBVIOUS?
FOOLS ...
OBVIOUS ?!
THAT WAS JUST WEIRD!
HMPH. WHATEVER.
IT'S A WASTE OF TIME TO EXPLAIN MY TECHNIQUES TO LAYMEN.
NEMU ...
DIG A HOLE HERE.
YES, SIR.
...
TAKE IT EASY, URYÛ.
THE POISON MAY BE GONE, BUT OUR INSIDES ARE STILL SMASHED UP.
SHUK
SHUK
SHUK
SHUK
SHUK
KREK

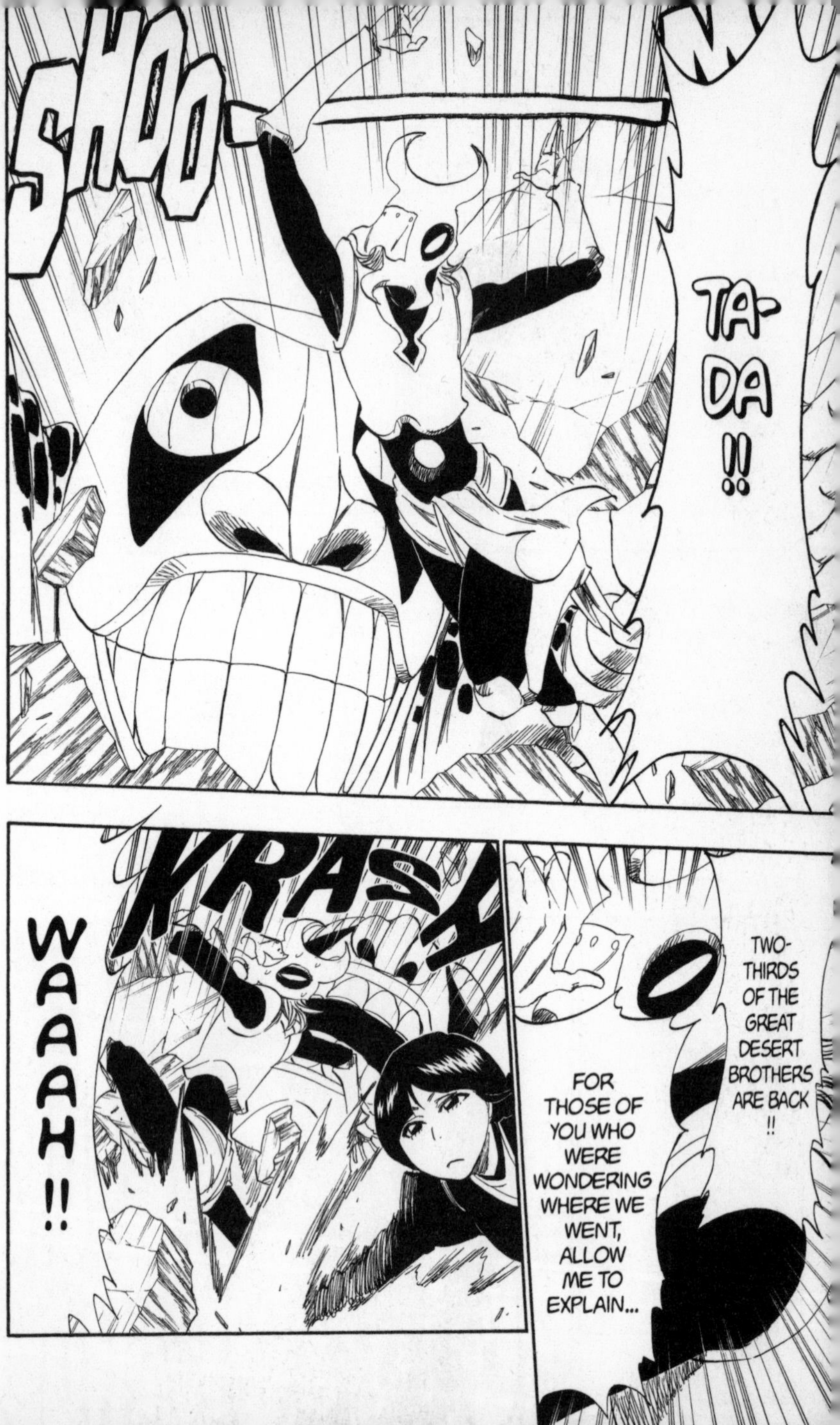
TA-DA!!
SHOO-
TWO-THIRDS OF THE GREAT DESERT BROTHERS ARE BACK!!
FOR THOSE OF YOU WHO WERE WONDERING WHERE WE WENT, ALLOW ME TO EXPLAIN...
KRASH
WAAAAH!!

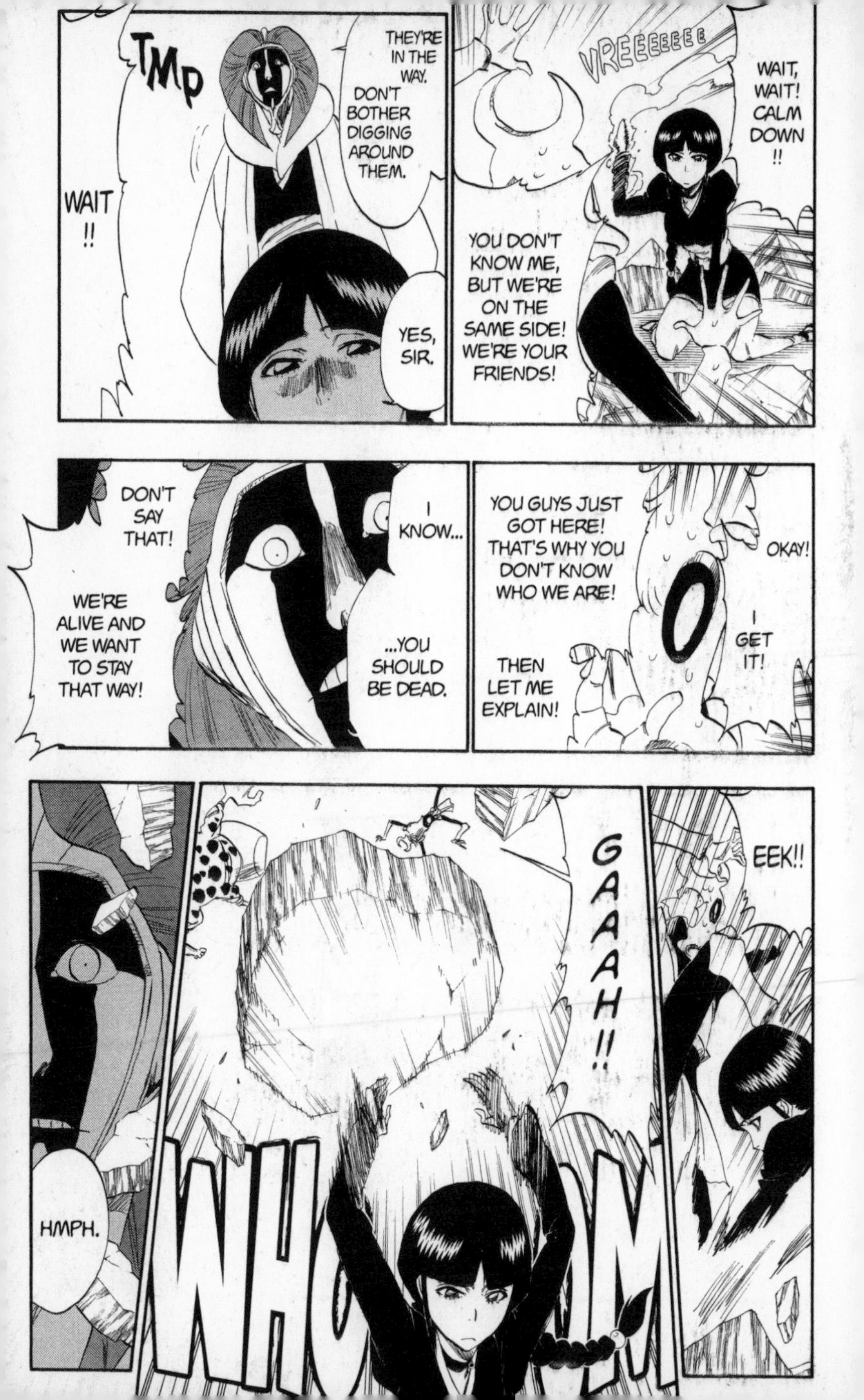
VREEEEEEEE
WAIT, WAIT! CALM DOWN !!
YOU DON'T KNOW ME, BUT WE'RE ON THE SAME SIDE! WE'RE YOUR FRIENDS!
THEY'RE IN THE WAY.
DON'T BOTHER DIGGING AROUND THEM.
TMP
WAIT !!
YES, SIR.
OKAY!
I GET IT!
YOU GUYS JUST GOT HERE! THAT'S WHY YOU DON'T KNOW WHO WE ARE!
THEN LET ME EXPLAIN!
I KNOW...
...YOU SHOULD BE DEAD.
DON'T SAY THAT!
WE'RE ALIVE AND WE WANT TO STAY THAT WAY!
EEK!!
GAAAAH!!
WHOOM
HMPH.

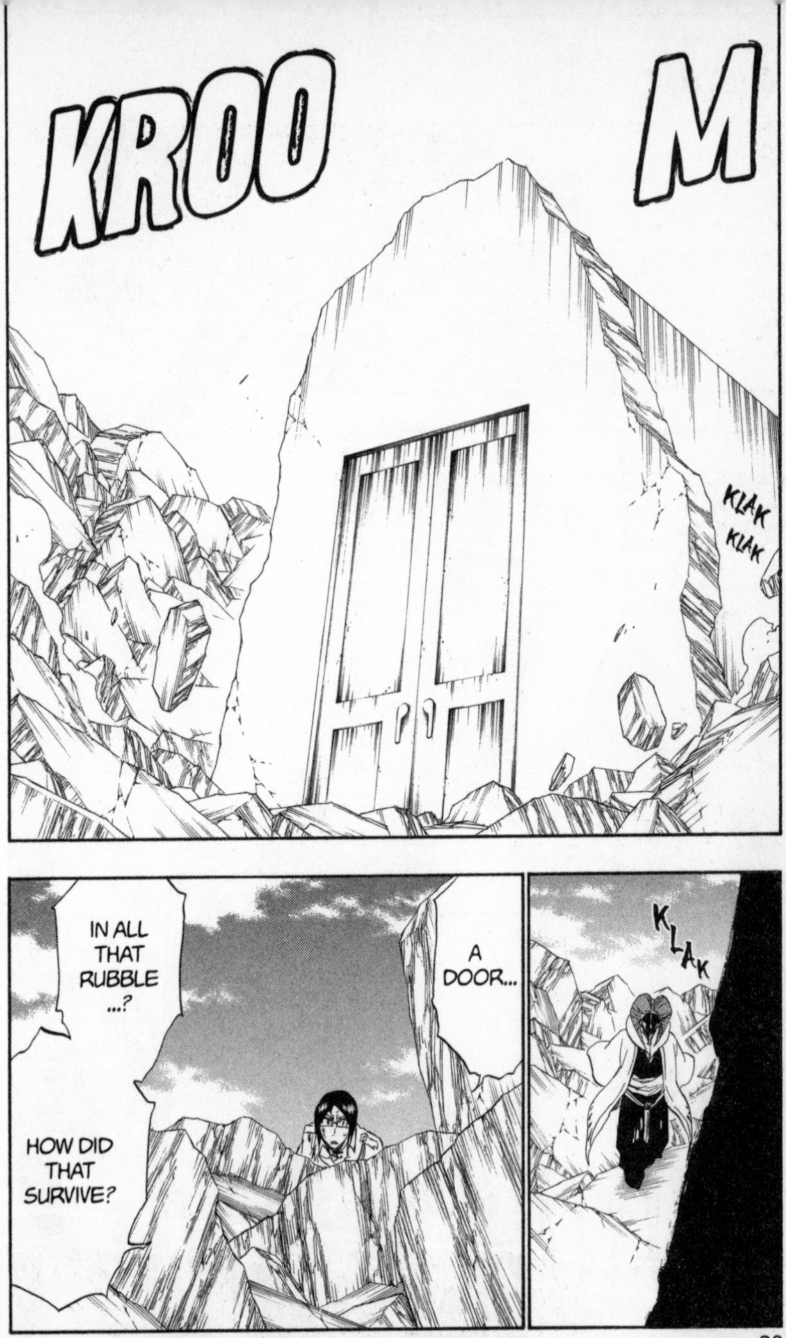
KROOM
KLAK KLAK
KLAK
A DOOR...
IN ALL THAT RUBBLE ...?
HOW DID THAT SURVIVE?

READ THIS WAY

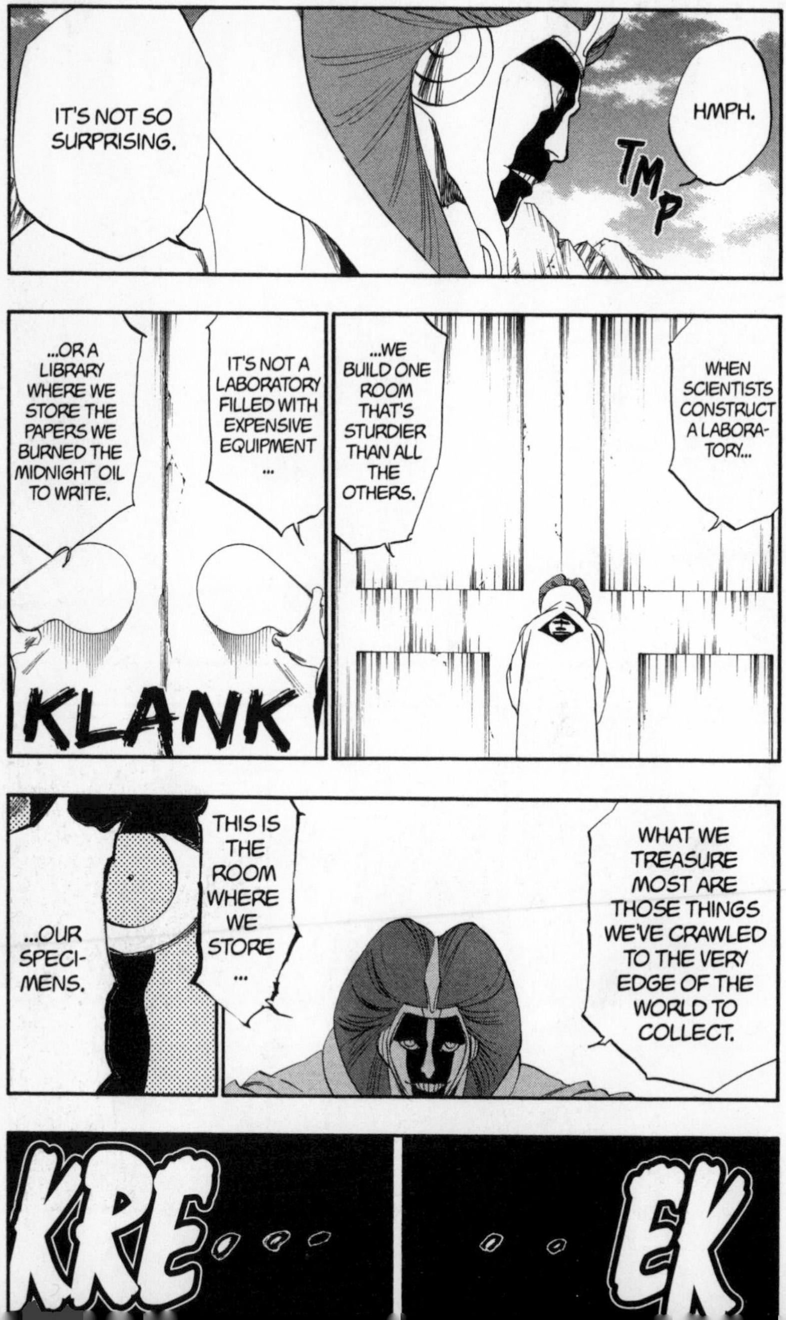
HMPH.
TMP
IT'S NOT SO SURPRISING.
WHEN SCIENTISTS CONSTRUCT A LABORATORY...
...WE BUILD ONE ROOM THAT'S STURDIER THAN ALL THE OTHERS.
IT'S NOT A LABORATORY FILLED WITH EXPENSIVE EQUIPMENT...
...OR A LIBRARY WHERE WE STORE THE PAPERS WE BURNED THE MIDNIGHT OIL TO WRITE.
KLANK
WHAT WE TREASURE MOST ARE THOSE THINGS WE'VE CRAWLED TO THE VERY EDGE OF THE WORLD TO COLLECT.
THIS IS THE ROOM WHERE WE STORE...
...OUR SPECIMENS.
KRE... ...EK

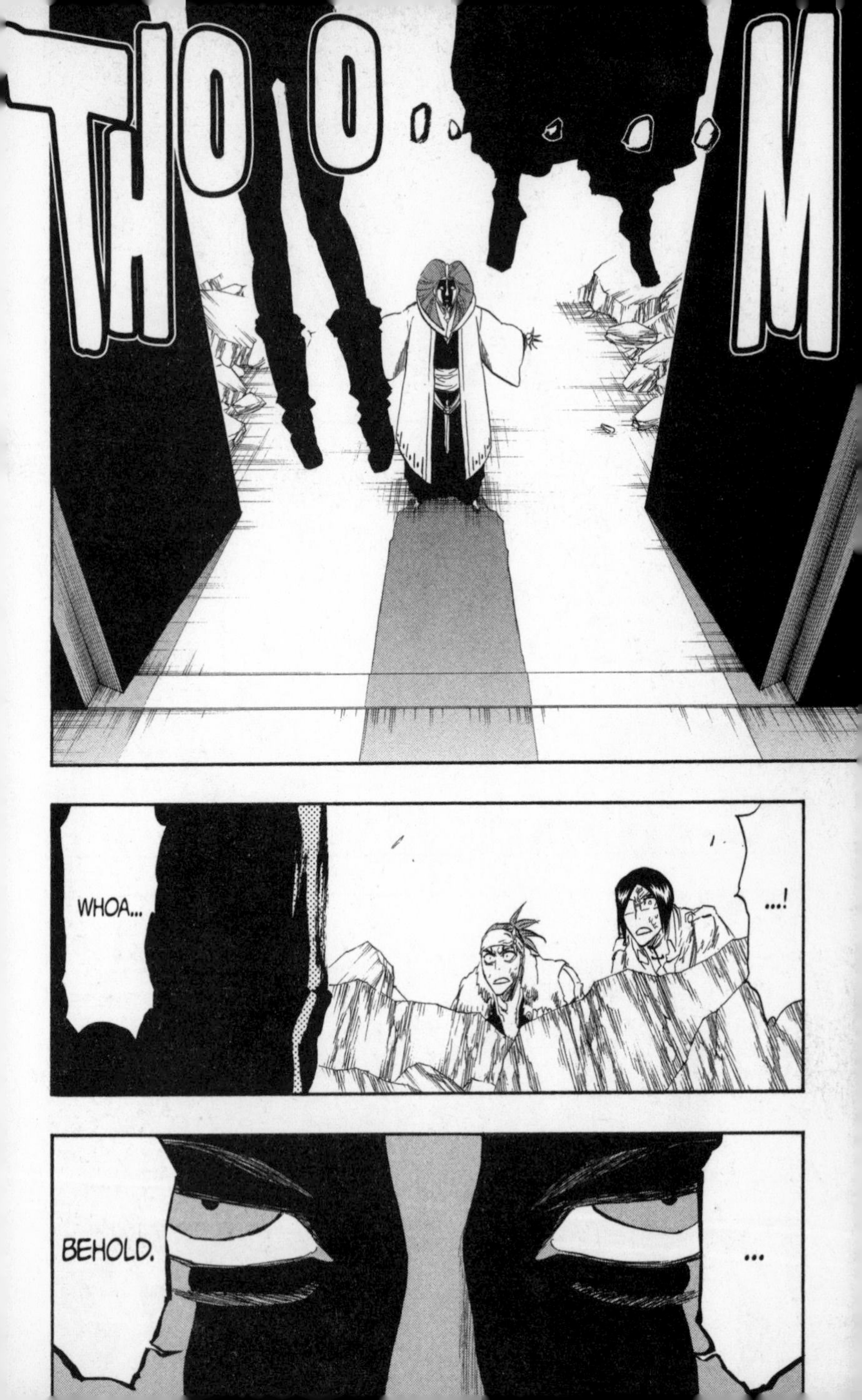
THOOOOM
...!
WHOA...
...
BEHOLD.

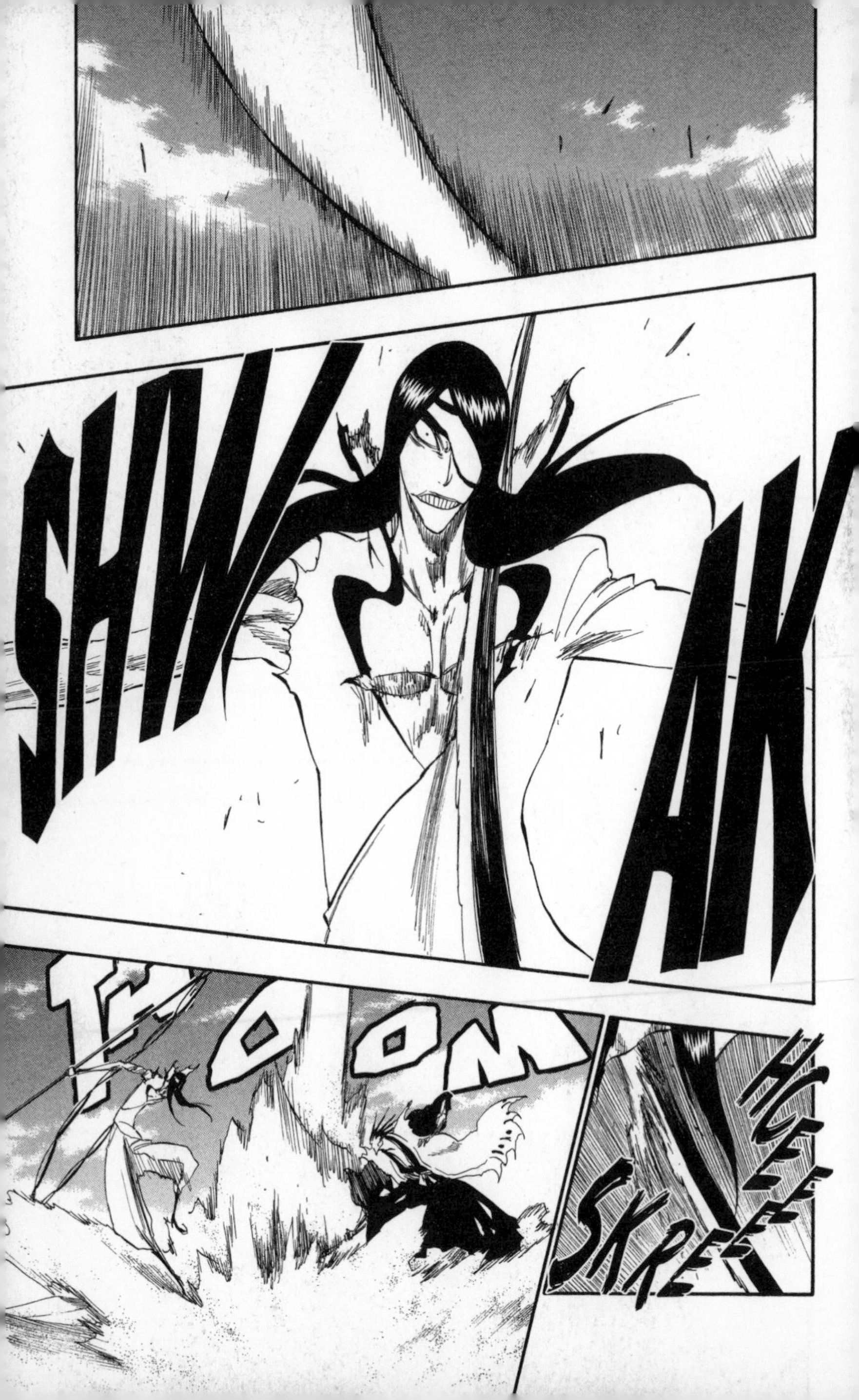
SHW
AK
HCEEEE
SKREE
THOOM

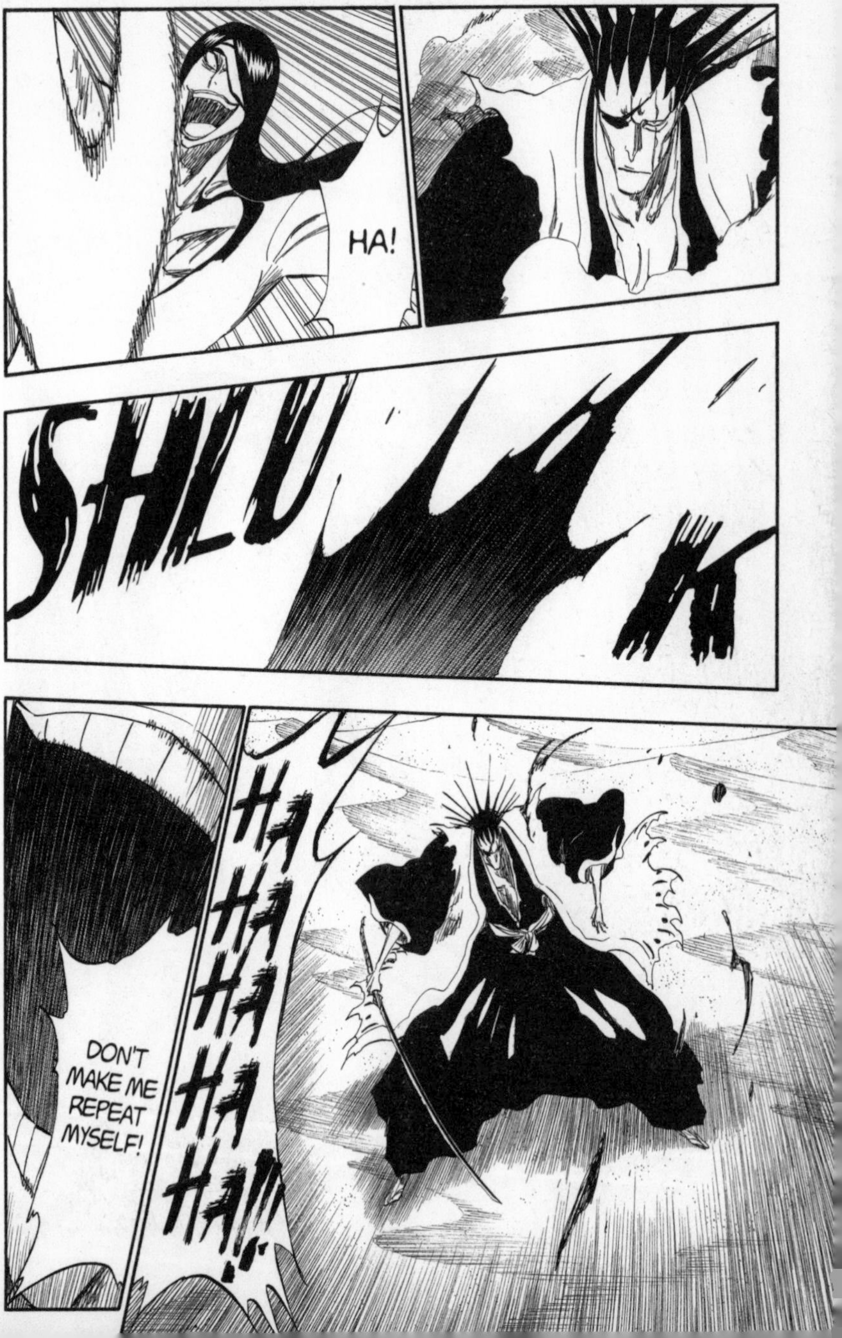
HA!
SHLUUUK
HAHAHAHAHA!!
DON'T MAKE ME REPEAT MYSELF!

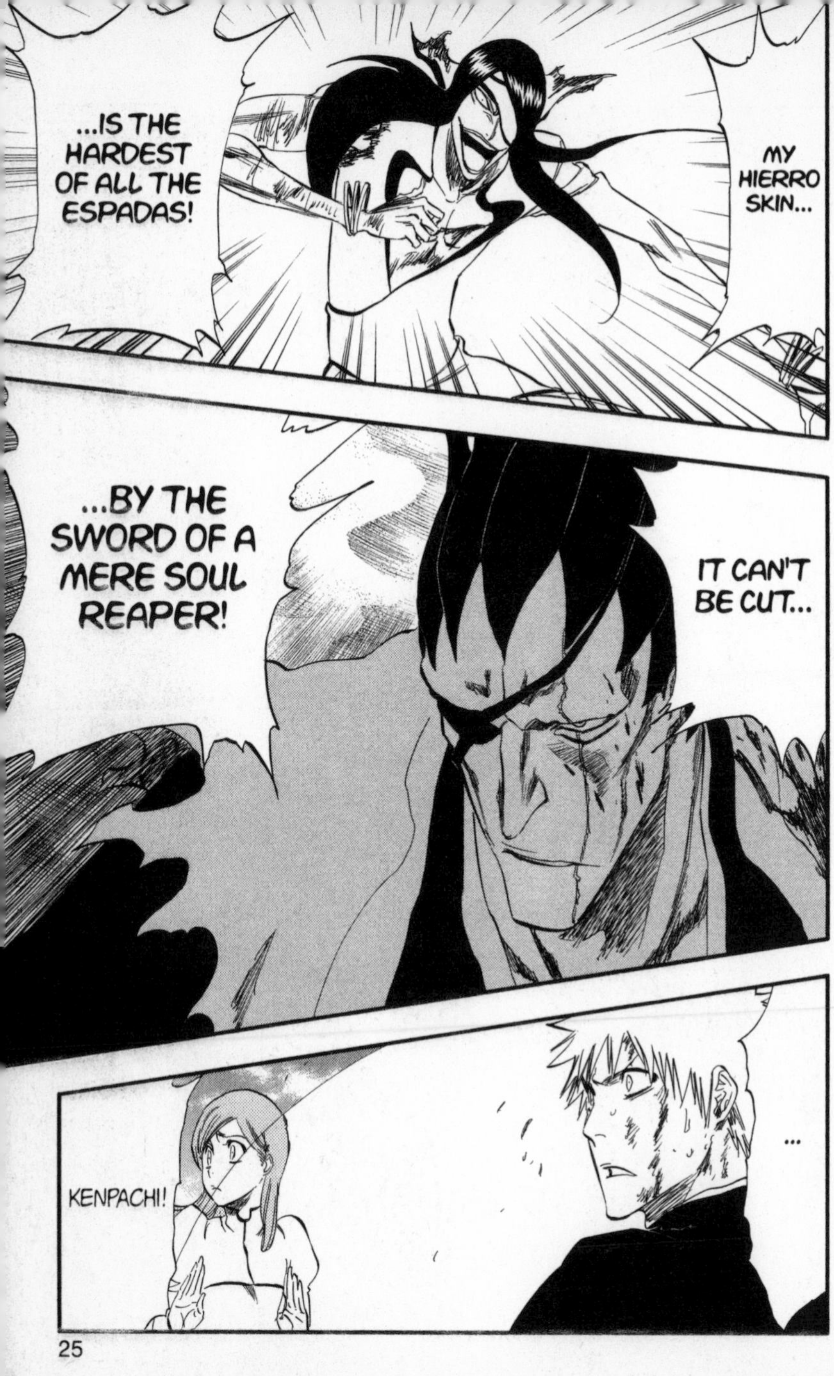
MY HIERRO SKIN...
...IS THE HARDEST OF ALL THE ESPADAS!
IT CAN'T BE CUT...
...BY THE SWORD OF A MERE SOUL REAPER!
...
KENPACHI!

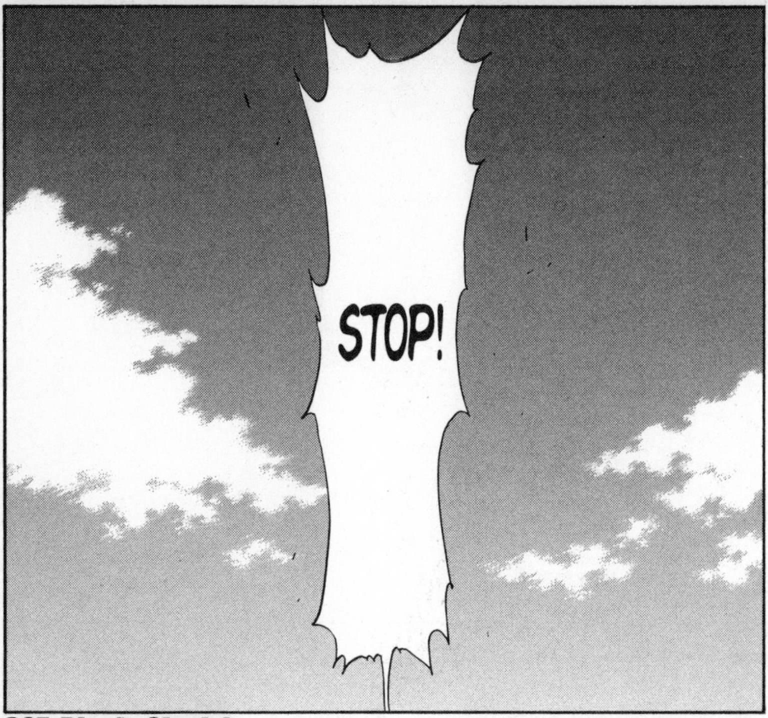
STOP!

307. Bite it, Slash it

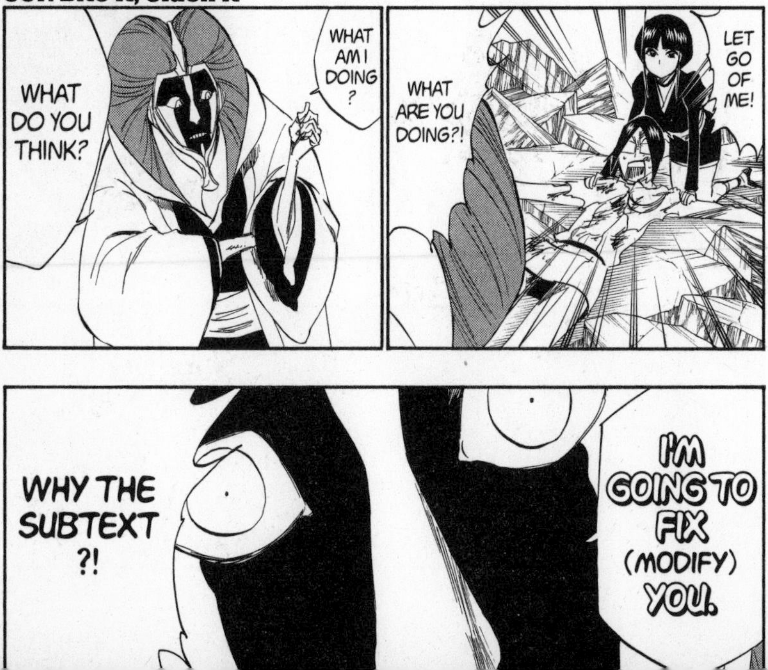
LET GO OF ME!
WHAT ARE YOU DOING?!
WHAT AM I DOING?
WHAT DO YOU THINK?
I'M GOING TO FIX (MODIFY) YOU.
WHY THE SUBTEXT?!

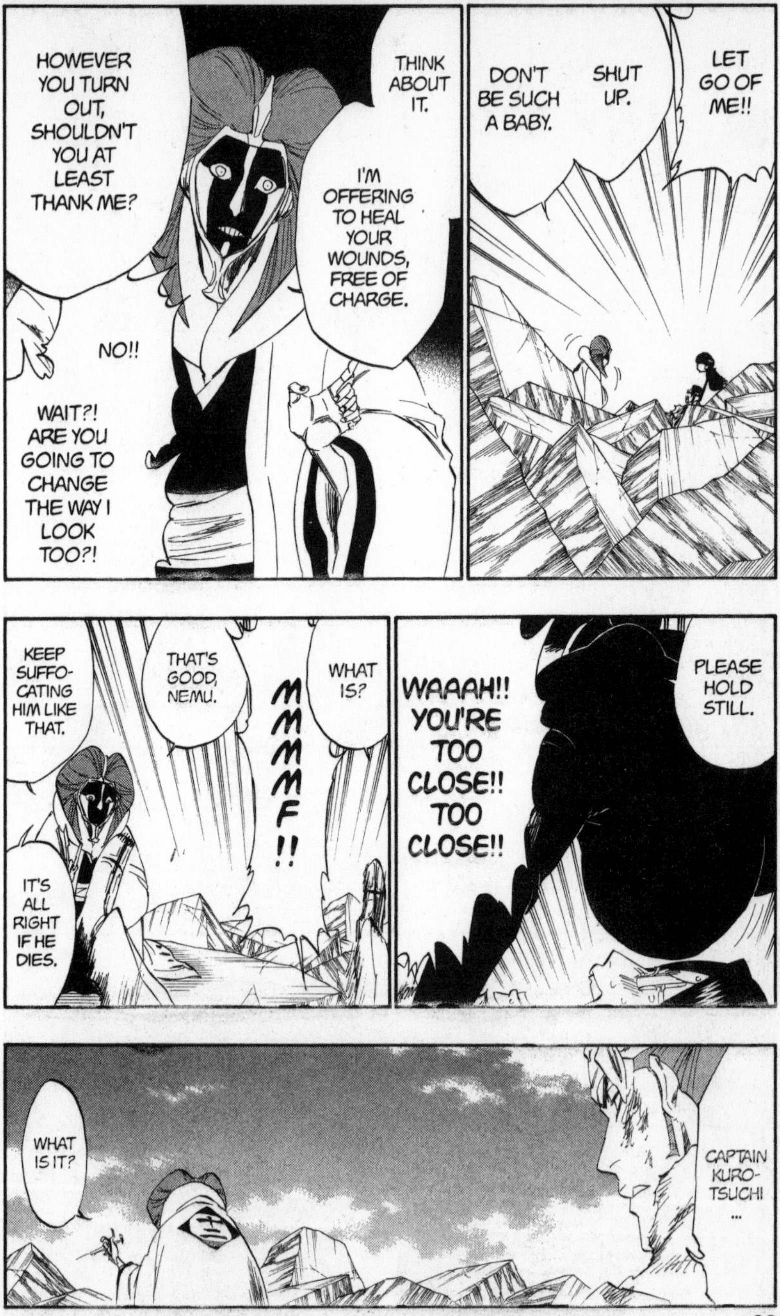
LET GO OF ME!!
SHUT UP.
DON'T BE SUCH A BABY.
THINK ABOUT IT.
I'M OFFERING TO HEAL YOUR WOUNDS, FREE OF CHARGE.
HOWEVER YOU TURN OUT, SHOULDN'T YOU AT LEAST THANK ME?
NO!!
WAIT?! ARE YOU GOING TO CHANGE THE WAY I LOOK TOO?!
PLEASE HOLD STILL.
WAAAH!! YOU'RE TOO CLOSE!! TOO CLOSE!!
WHAT IS?
MMMMMF!!
THAT'S GOOD, NEMU.
KEEP SUFFO-CATING HIM LIKE THAT.
IT'S ALL RIGHT IF HE DIES.
CAPTAIN KURO-TSUCHI ...
WHAT IS IT?

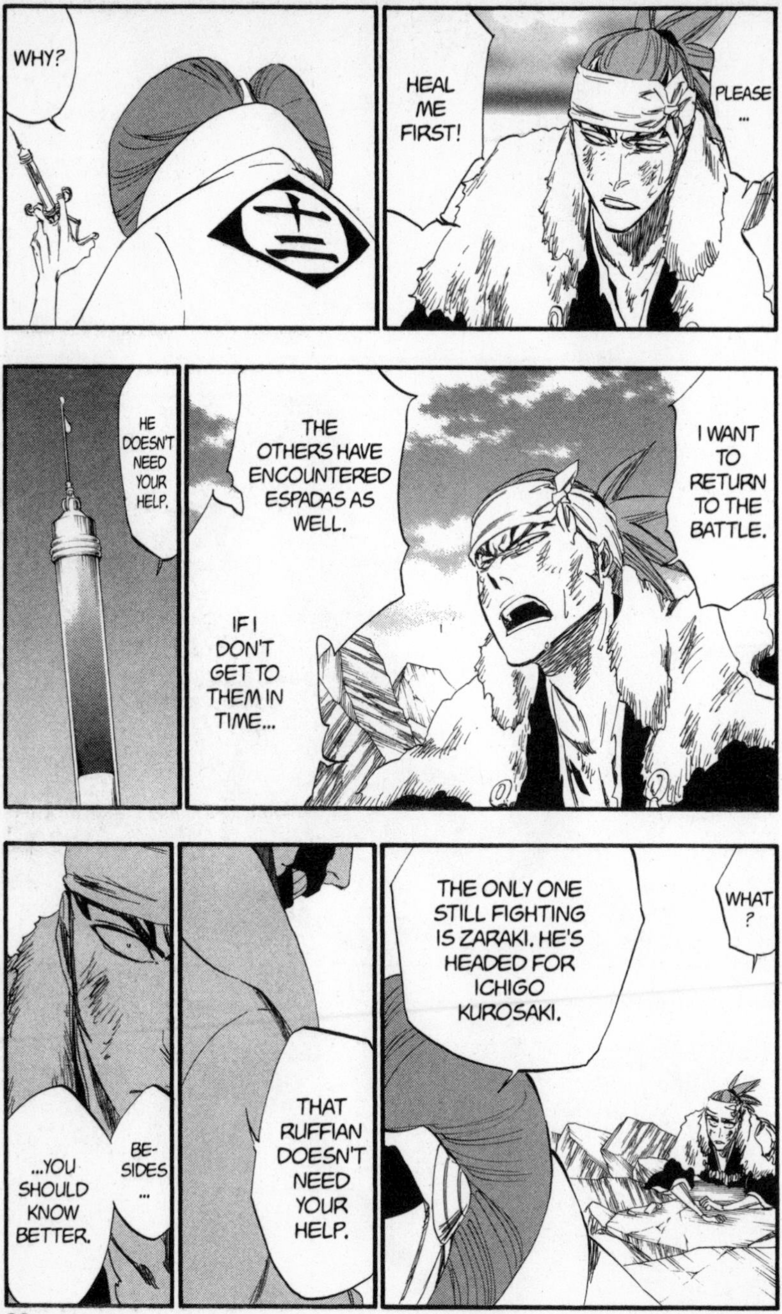
PLEASE...
HEAL ME FIRST!
WHY?
I WANT TO RETURN TO THE BATTLE.
THE OTHERS HAVE ENCOUNTERED ESPADAS AS WELL.
IF I DON'T GET TO THEM IN TIME...
HE DOESN'T NEED YOUR HELP.
WHAT?
THE ONLY ONE STILL FIGHTING IS ZARAKI. HE'S HEADED FOR ICHIGO KUROSAKI.
THAT RUFFIAN DOESN'T NEED YOUR HELP.
BE-SIDES...
...YOU SHOULD KNOW BETTER.

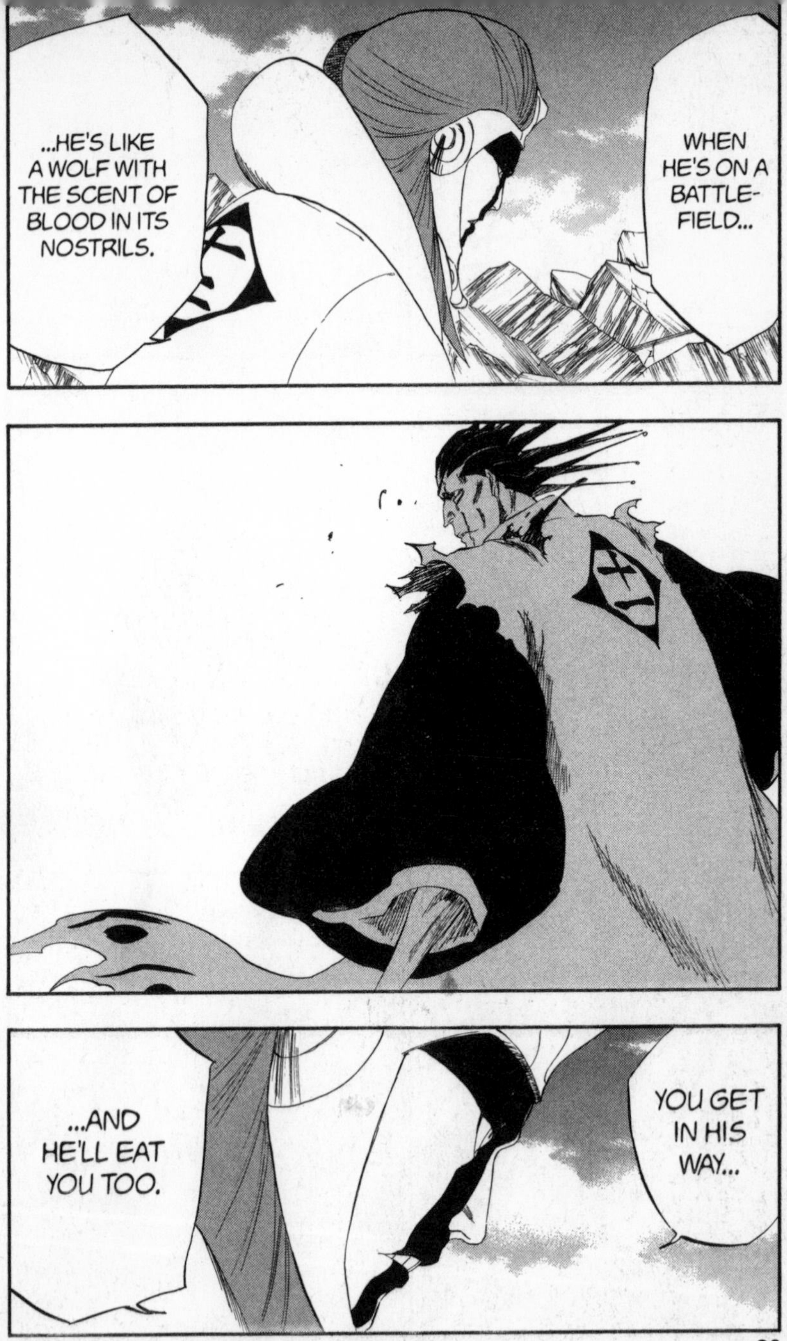
WHEN HE'S ON A BATTLE-FIELD...
...HE'S LIKE A WOLF WITH THE SCENT OF BLOOD IN ITS NOSTRILS.
YOU GET IN HIS WAY...
...AND HE'LL EAT YOU TOO.

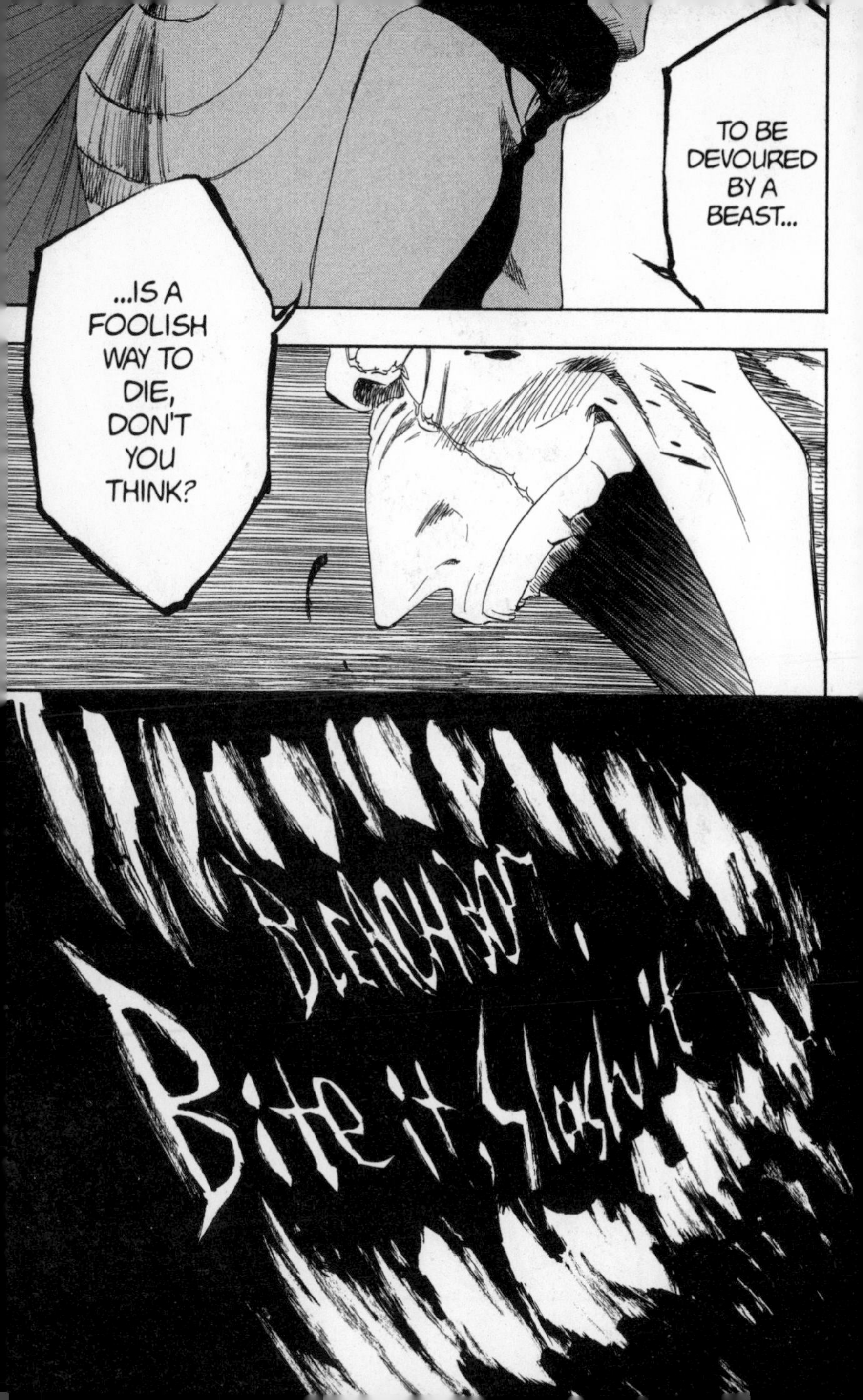
TO BE DEVOURED BY A BEAST...
...IS A FOOLISH WAY TO DIE, DON'T YOU THINK?
BLEACH 307
Bite it, Slash it

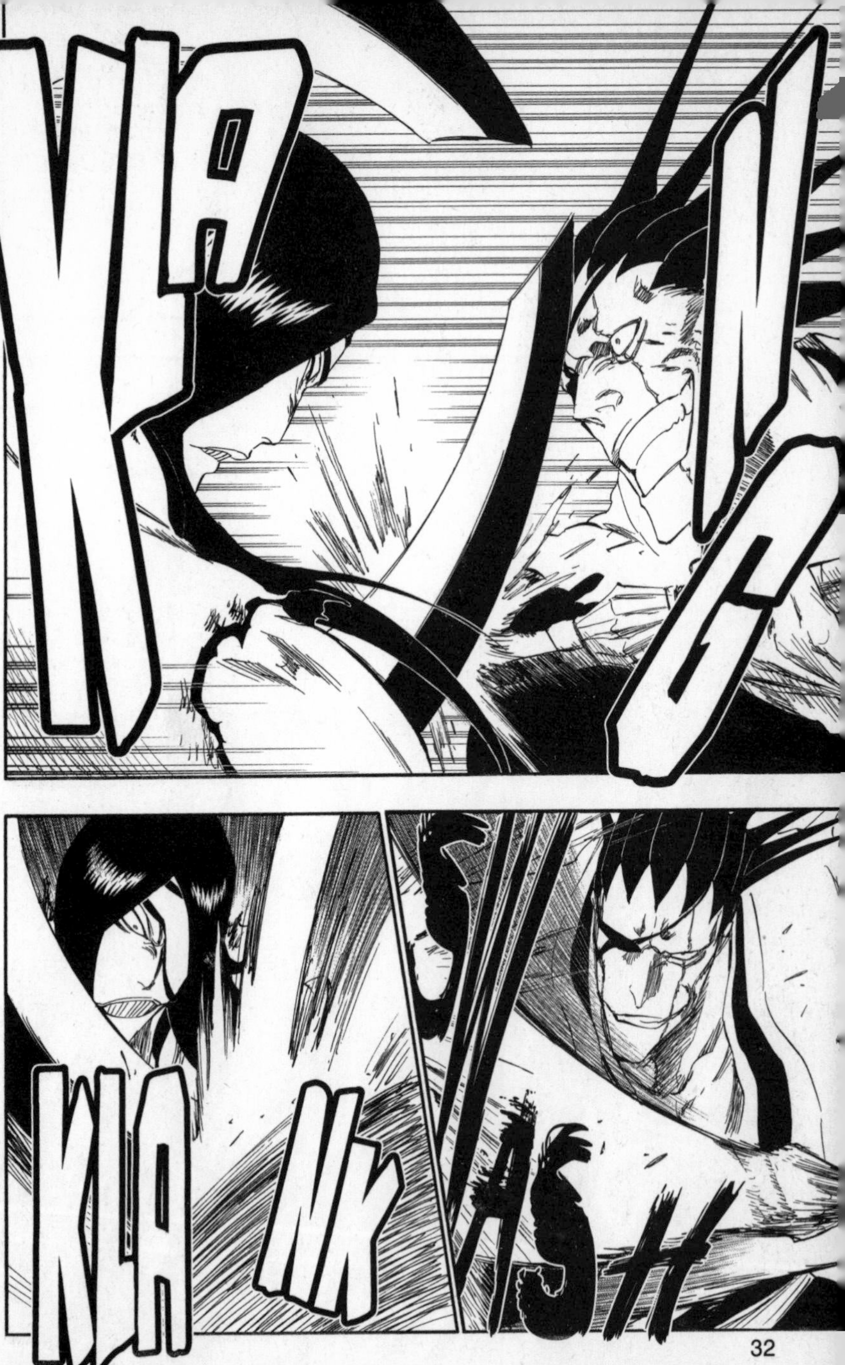
KLANK

READ THIS WAY

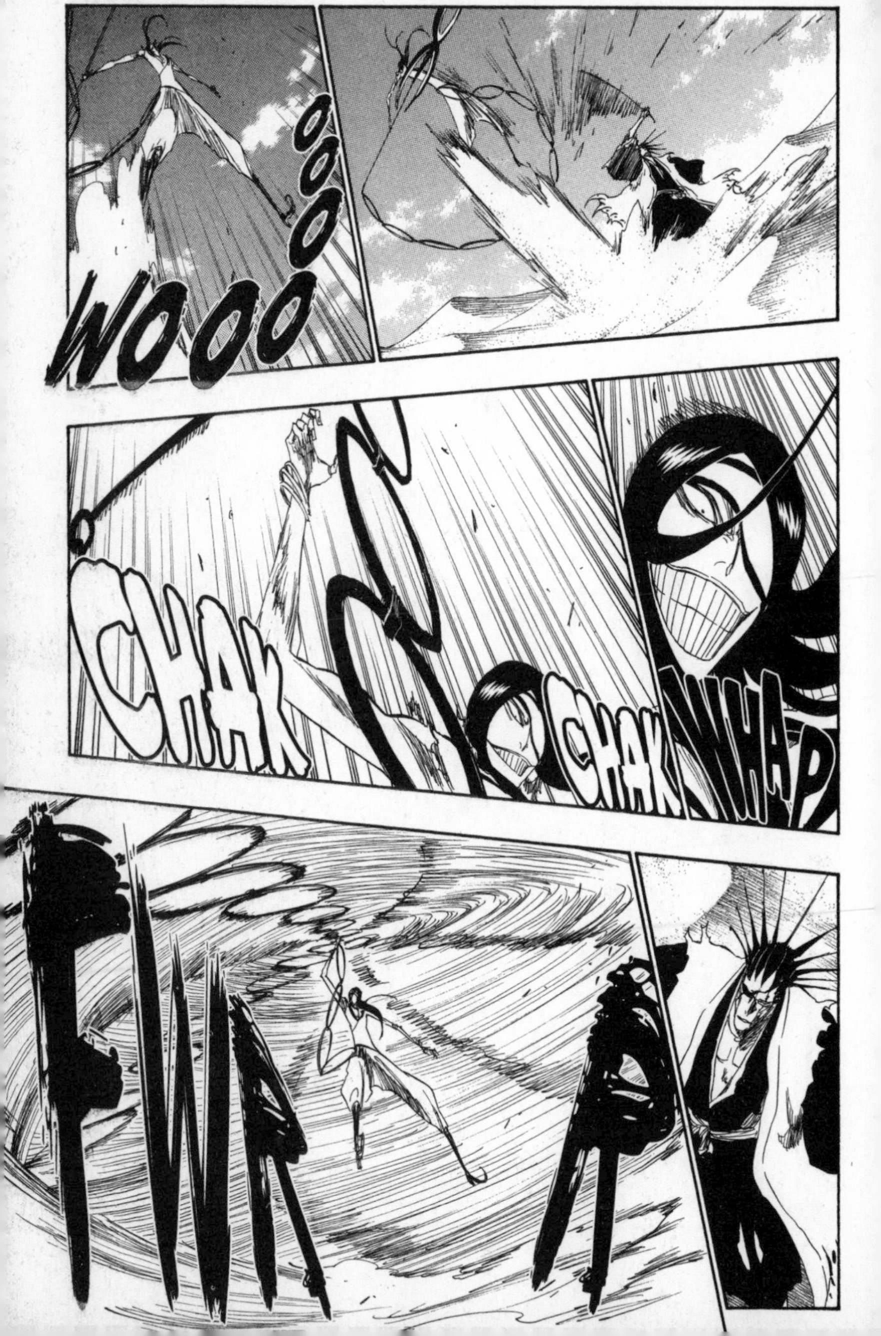
WOOOOOOOO
WHAP
CHAK
CHAK
FWAP

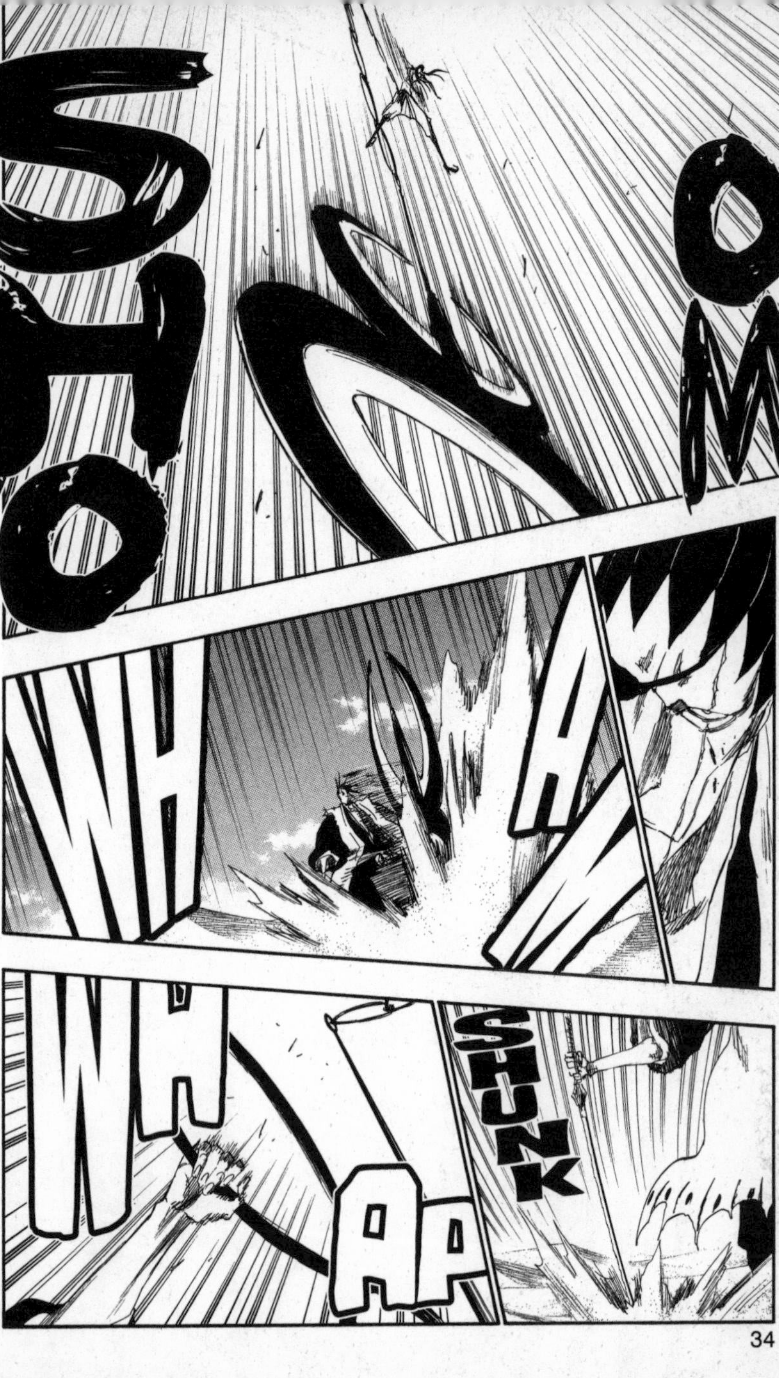
SHOOOM
WHAM
SHUNK
WHAP

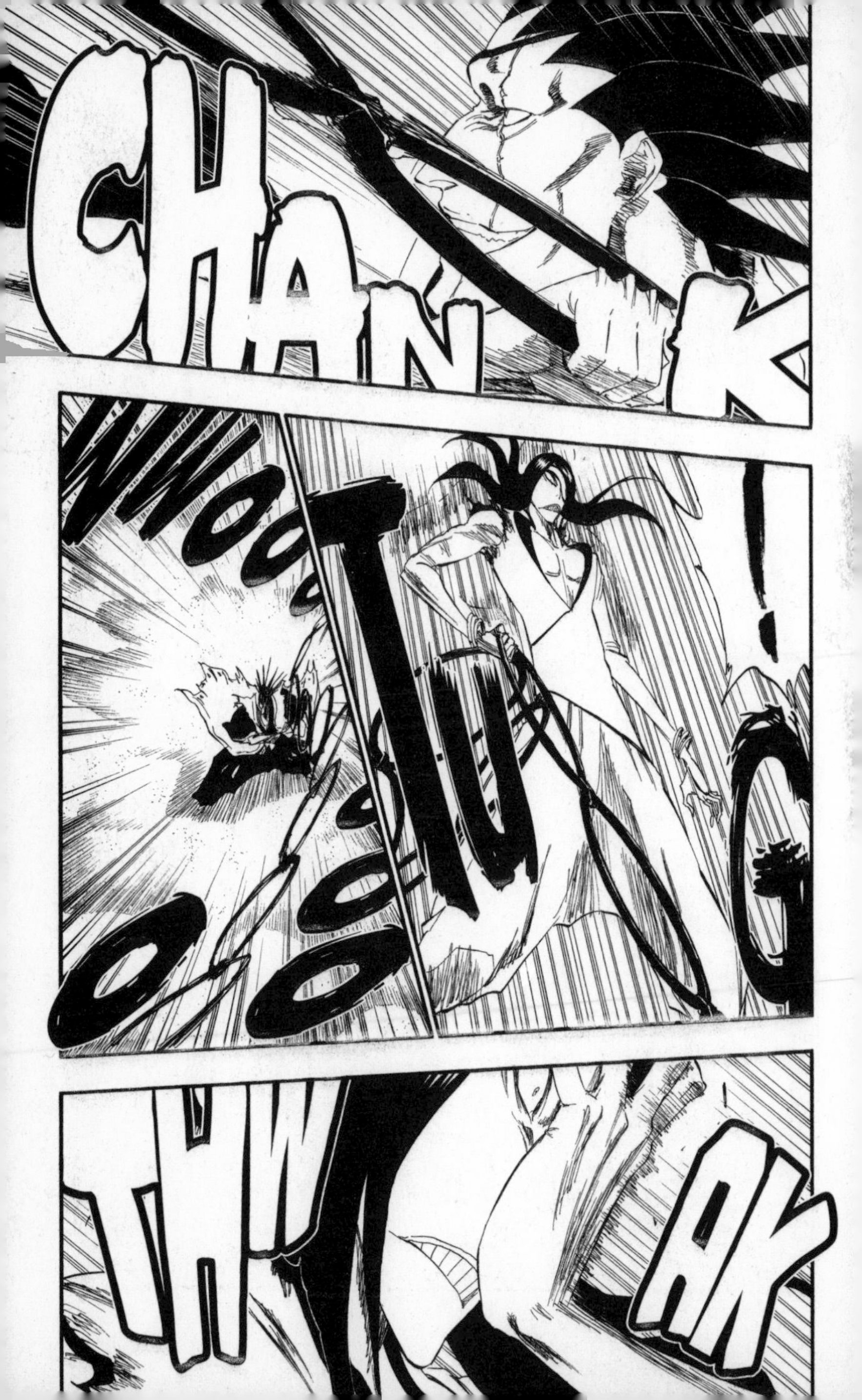
CHANK
!
TUG
WOOOOOOO
THWAK

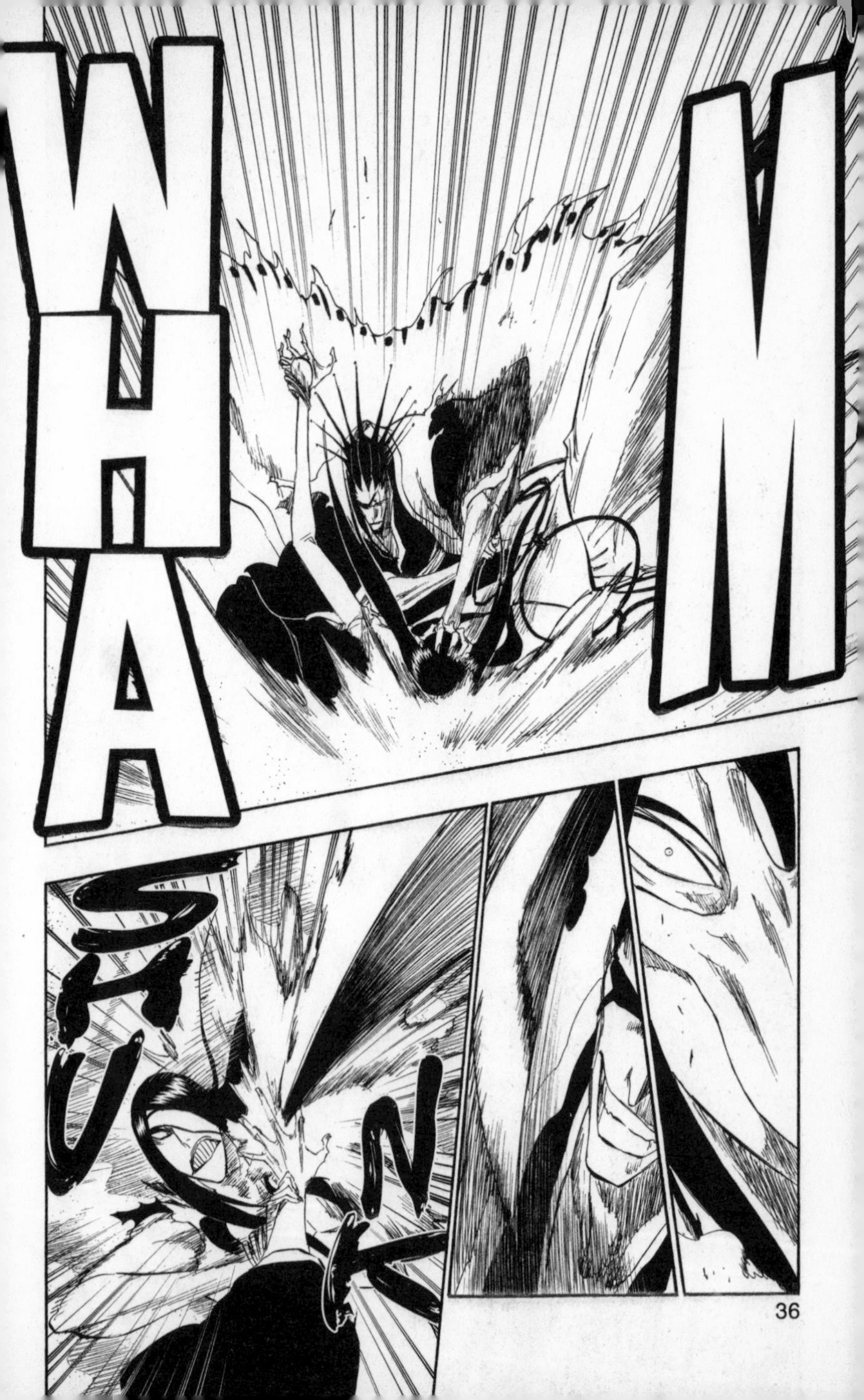
WHAM
SHUN

READ THIS WAY

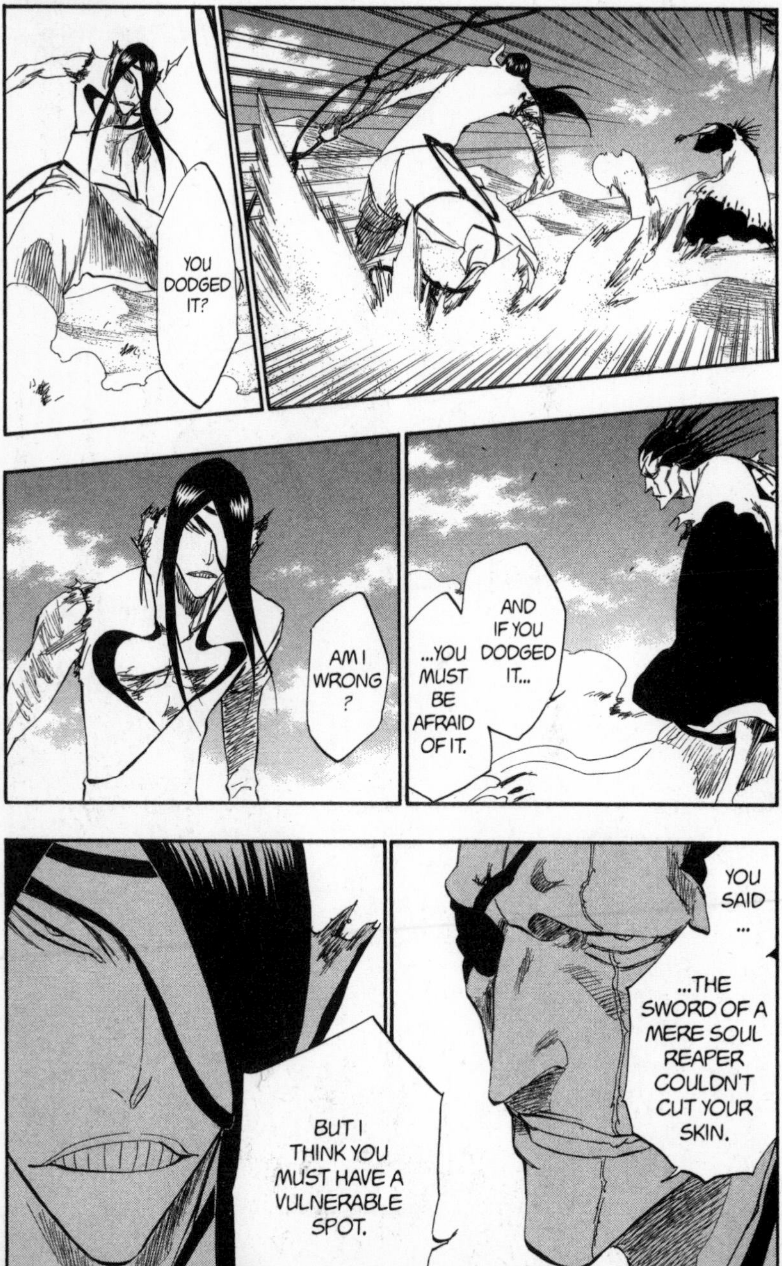
YOU DODGED IT?
AND IF YOU DODGED IT...
...YOU MUST BE AFRAID OF IT.
AM I WRONG?
YOU SAID...
...THE SWORD OF A MERE SOUL REAPER COULDN'T CUT YOUR SKIN.
BUT I THINK YOU MUST HAVE A VULNERABLE SPOT.

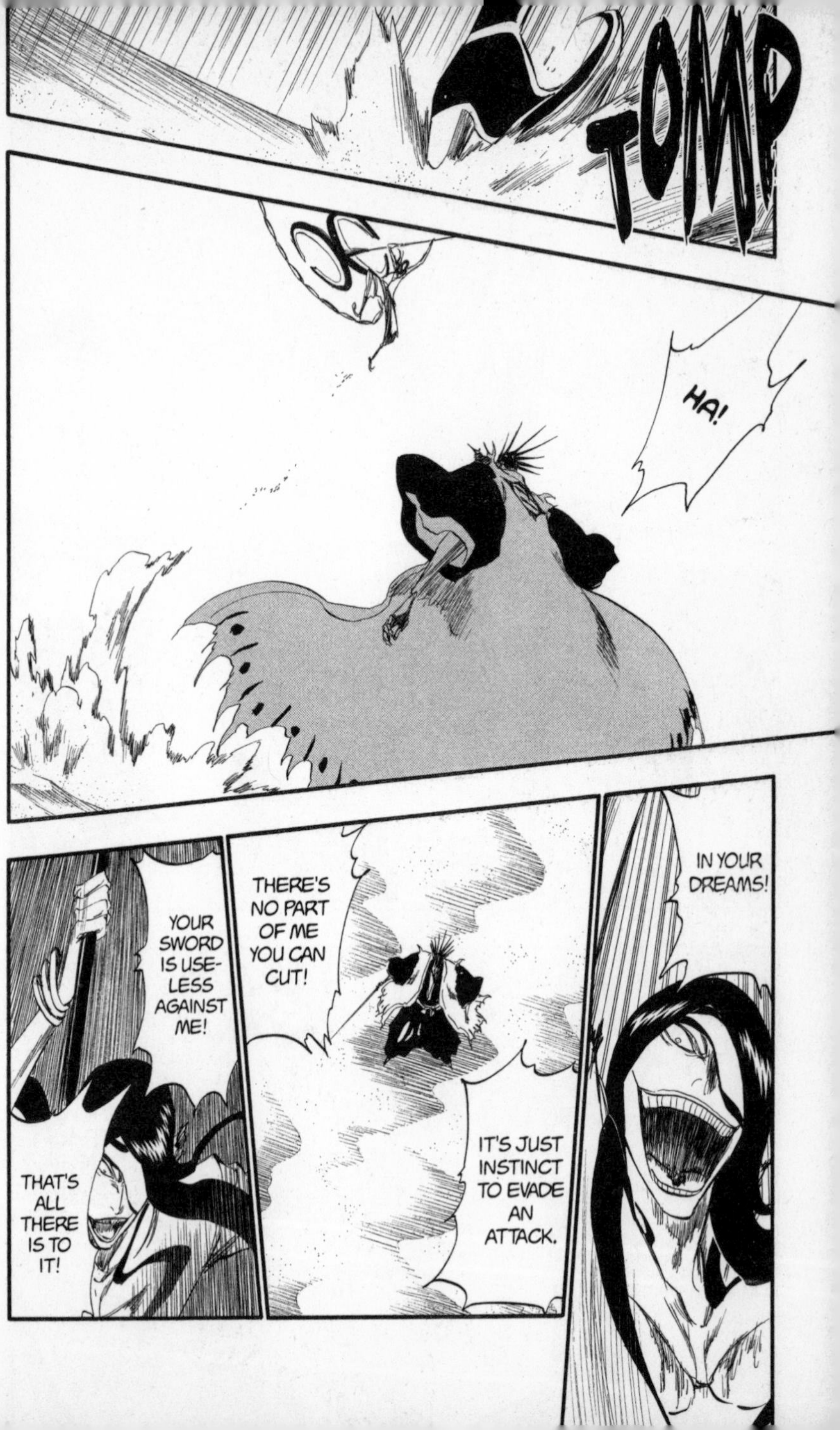
TOMP
HA!
IN YOUR DREAMS!
THERE'S NO PART OF ME YOU CAN CUT!
IT'S JUST INSTINCT TO EVADE AN ATTACK.
YOUR SWORD IS USE-LESS AGAINST ME!
THAT'S ALL THERE IS TO IT!

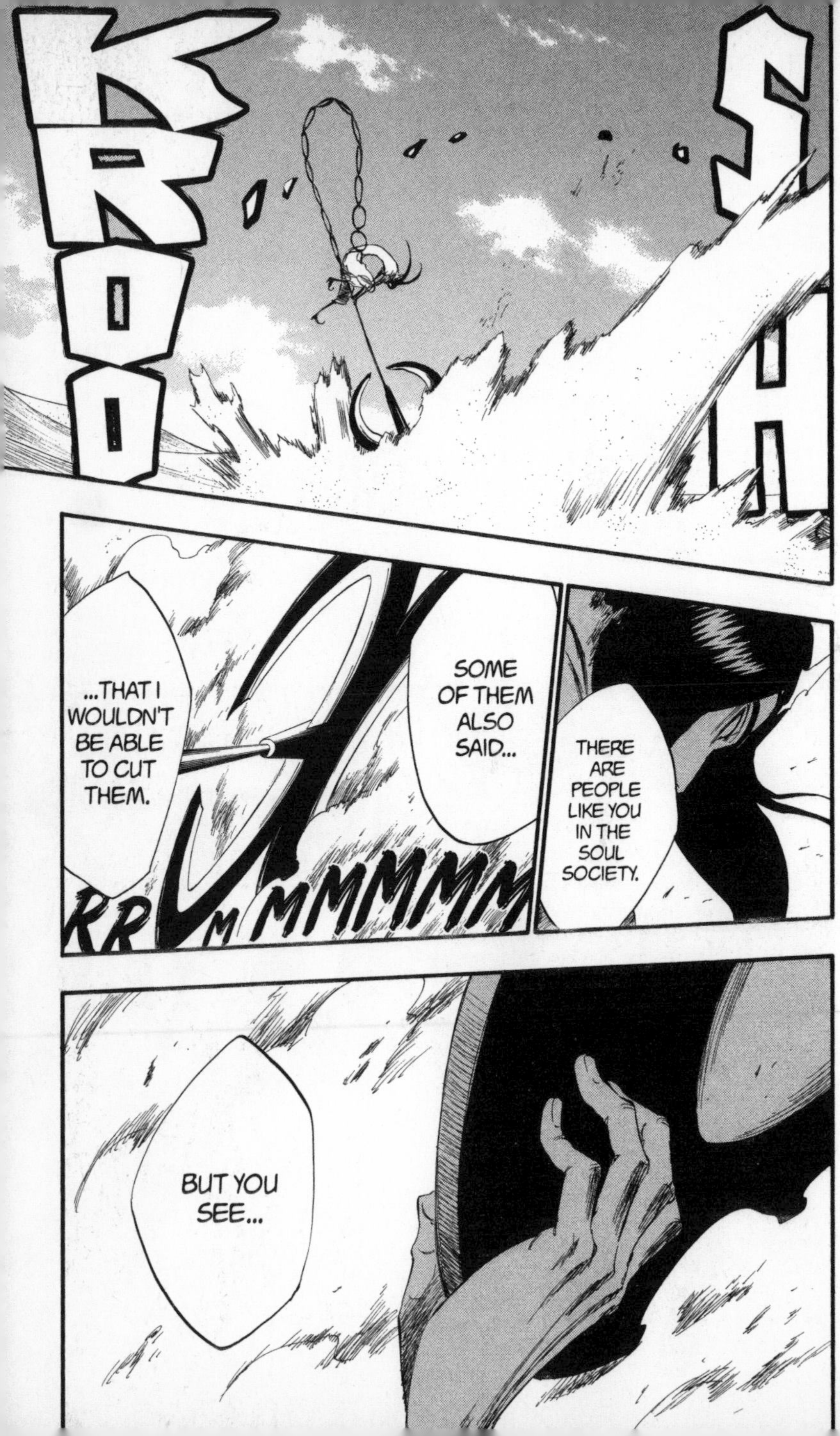
KROOSH
THERE ARE PEOPLE LIKE YOU IN THE SOUL SOCIETY.
SOME OF THEM ALSO SAID...
...THAT I WOULDN'T BE ABLE TO CUT THEM.
RRMMMMMMMM
BUT YOU SEE...

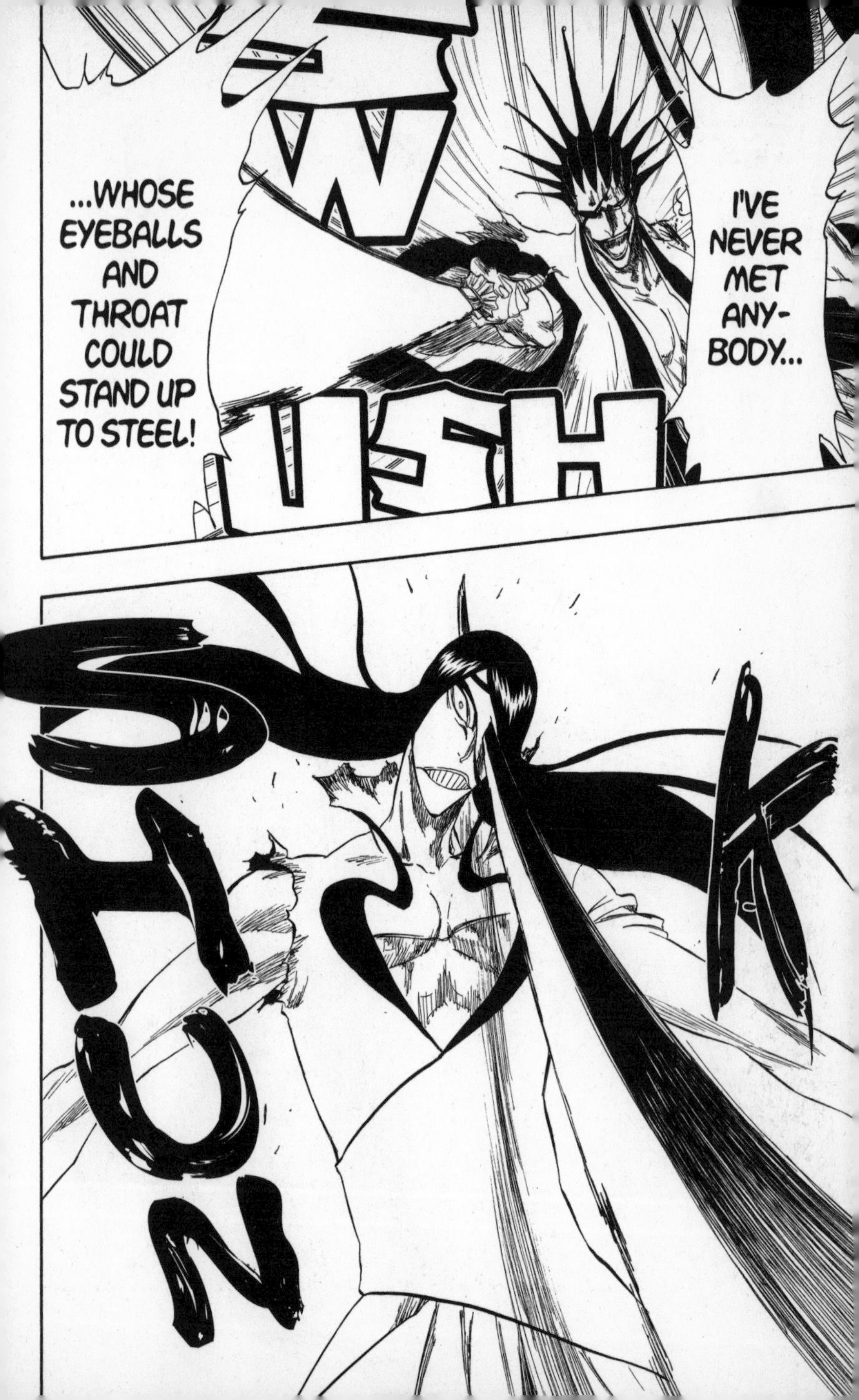
I'VE NEVER MET ANYBODY...
...WHOSE EYEBALLS AND THROAT COULD STAND UP TO STEEL!
SHUNK

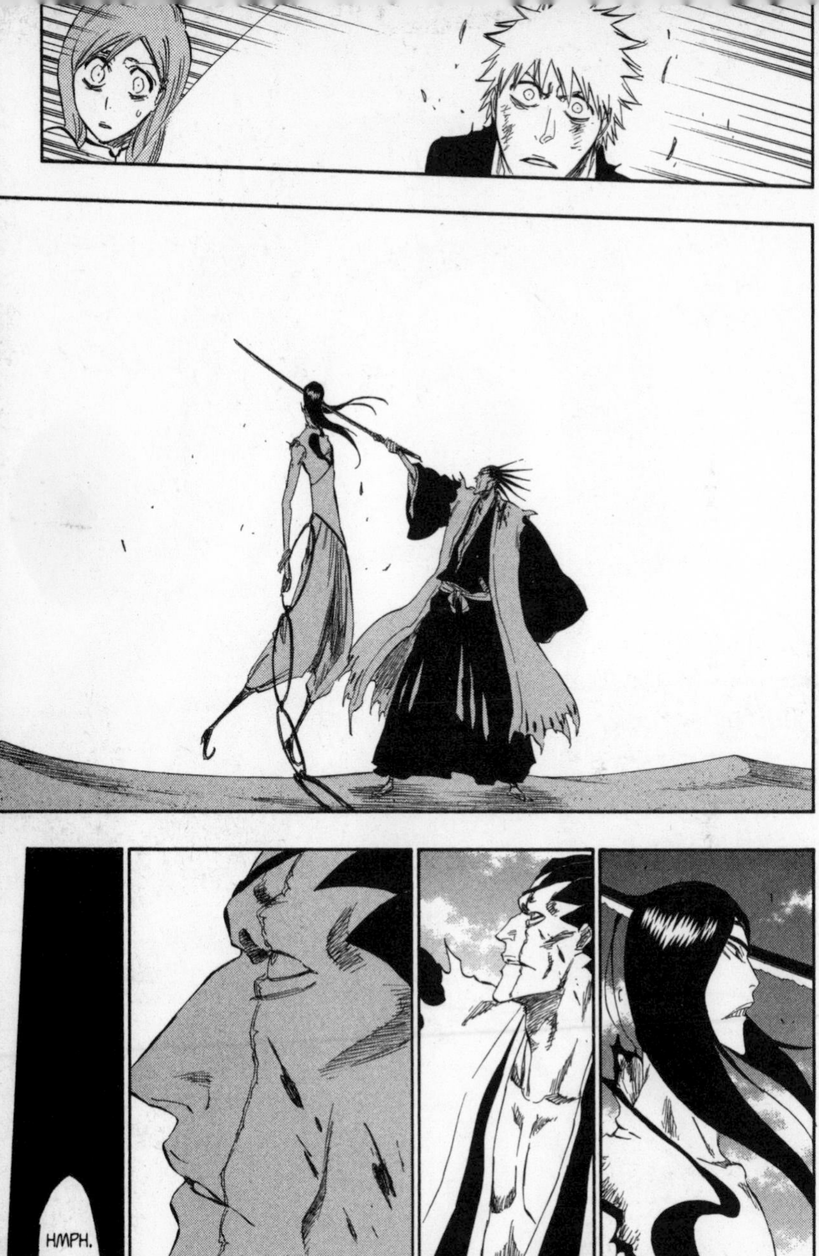
HMPH.

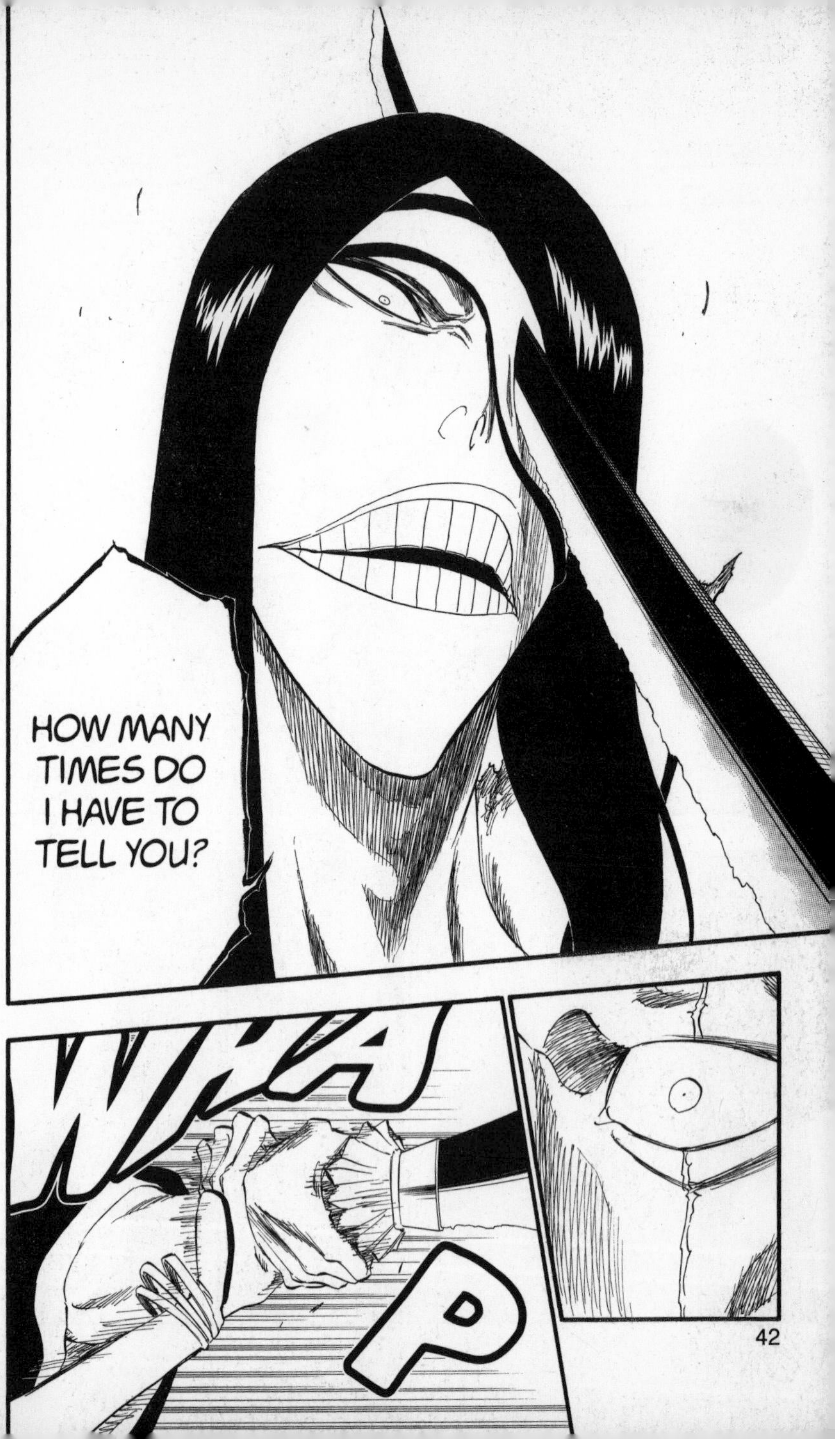
HOW MANY TIMES DO I HAVE TO TELL YOU?
WHAP

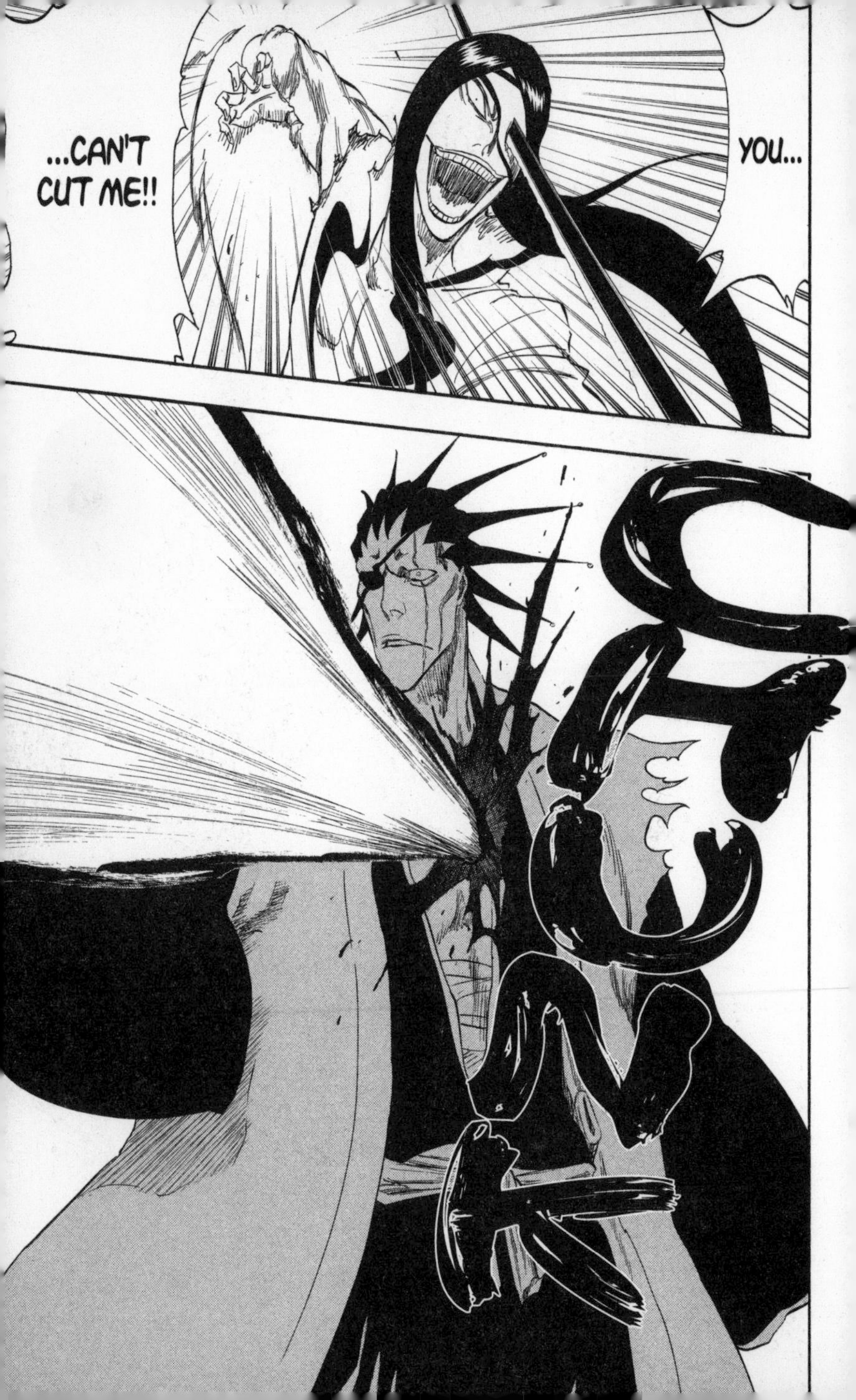
YOU...
...CAN'T CUT ME!!

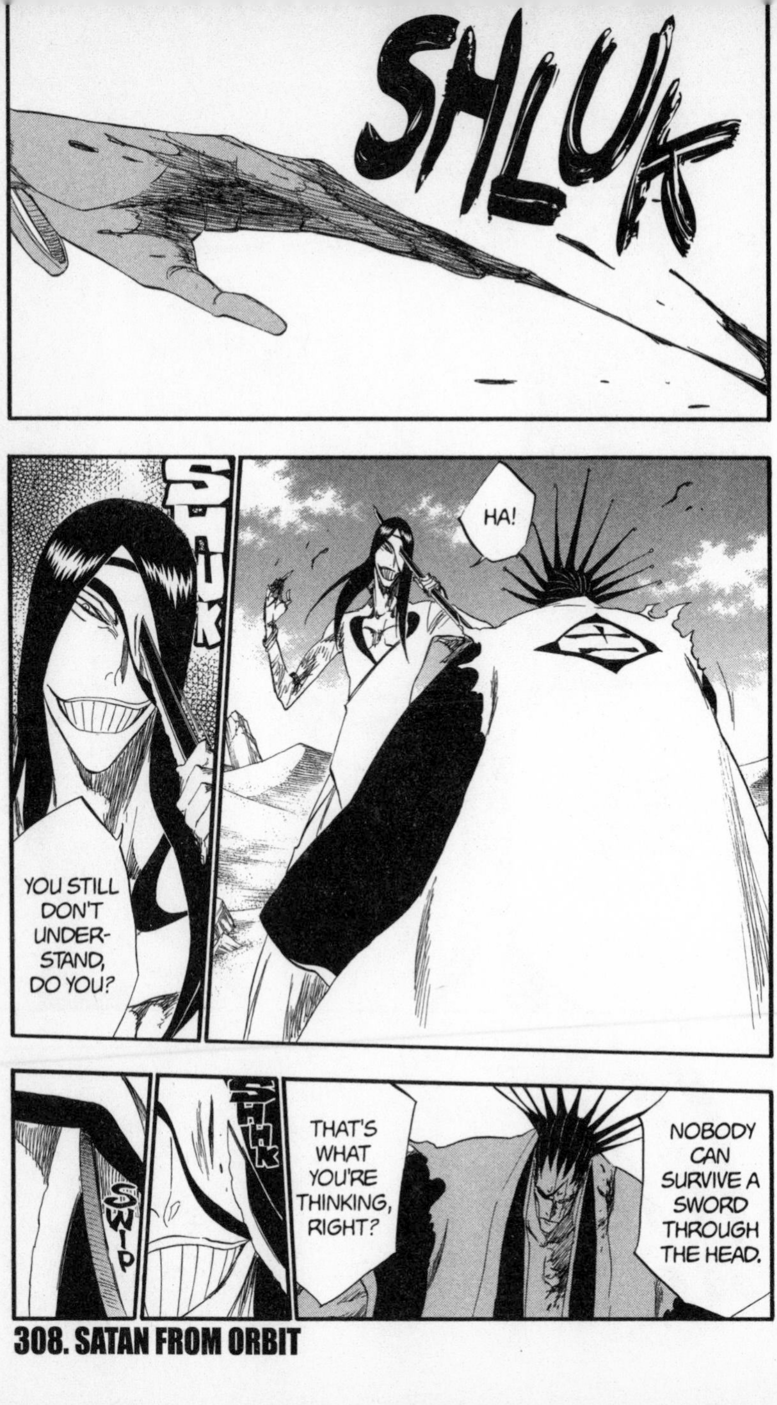
SHLUK
HA!
SHUK
YOU STILL DON'T UNDER-STAND, DO YOU?
NOBODY CAN SURVIVE A SWORD THROUGH THE HEAD.
THAT'S WHAT YOU'RE THINKING, RIGHT?
SHHK
SWIP

308. SATAN FROM ORBIT

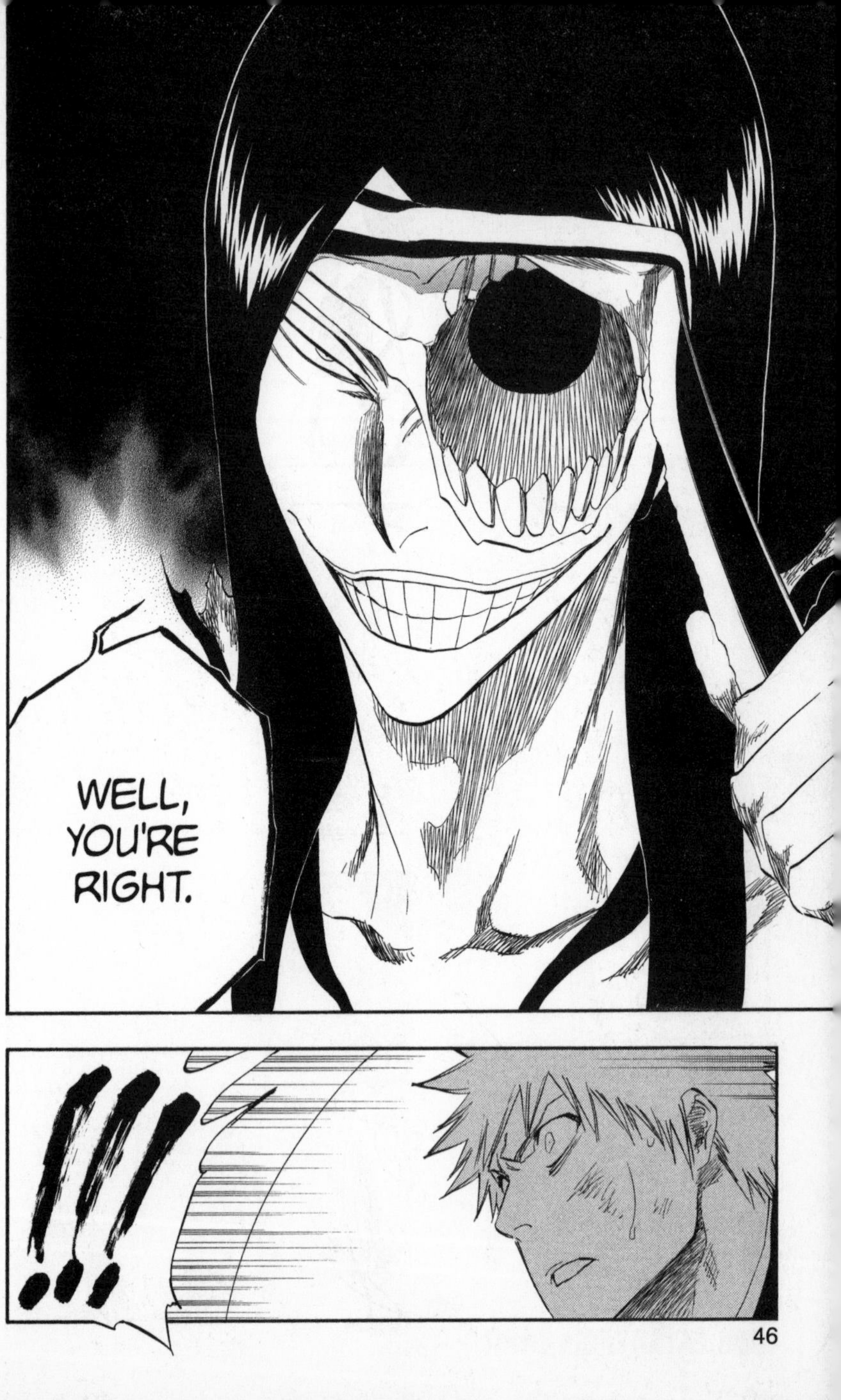
WELL, YOU'RE RIGHT.
!!!

NOBODY CAN SURVIVE A SWORD THROUGH THE HEAD.

BUT YOUR SWORD DIDN'T PIERCE MY HEAD.

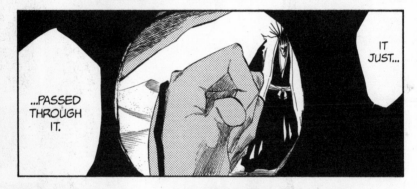

IT JUST...

...PASSED THROUGH IT.

...YOUR MATCH...

UNDER-STAND?

YOU'VE MET...

...SOUL REAPER.

WHAT?

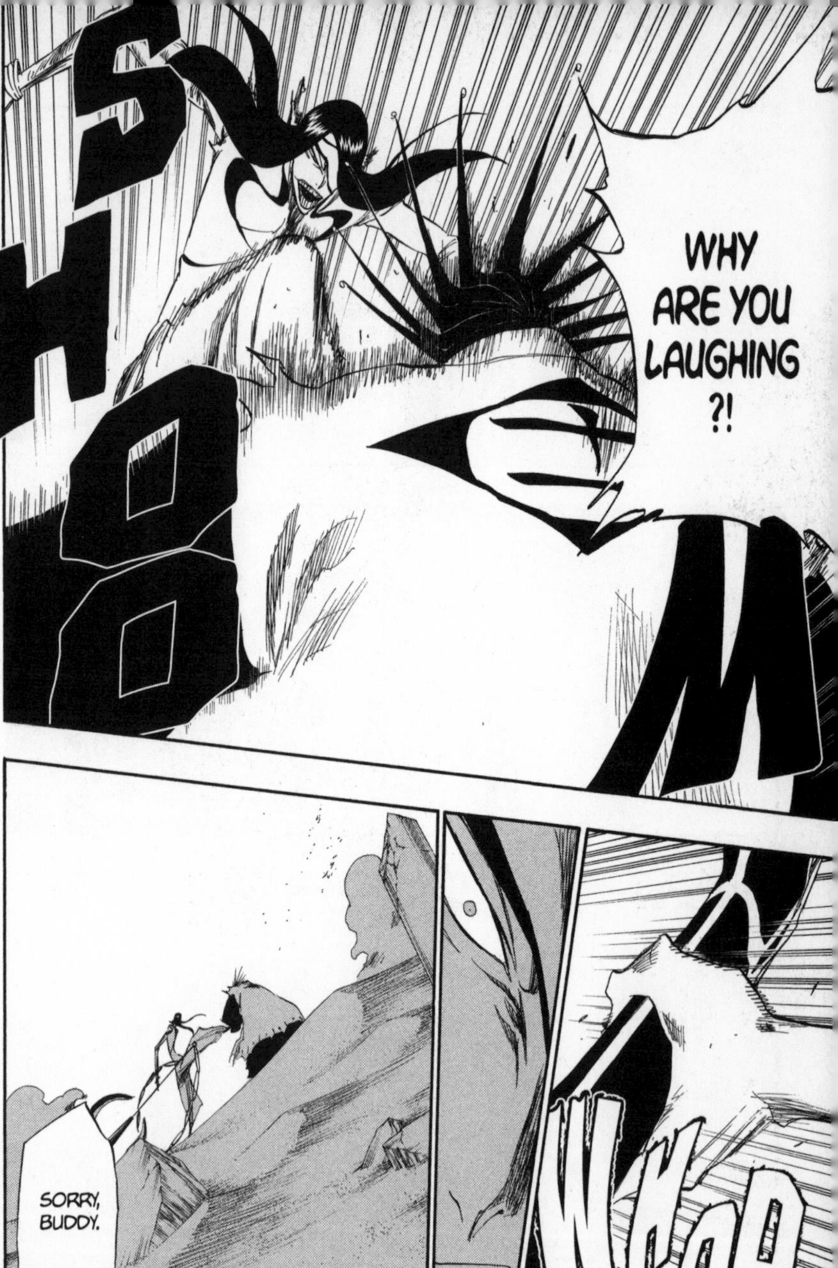
WHY ARE YOU LAUGHING ?!
SHOOM
WHAP
SORRY, BUDDY.

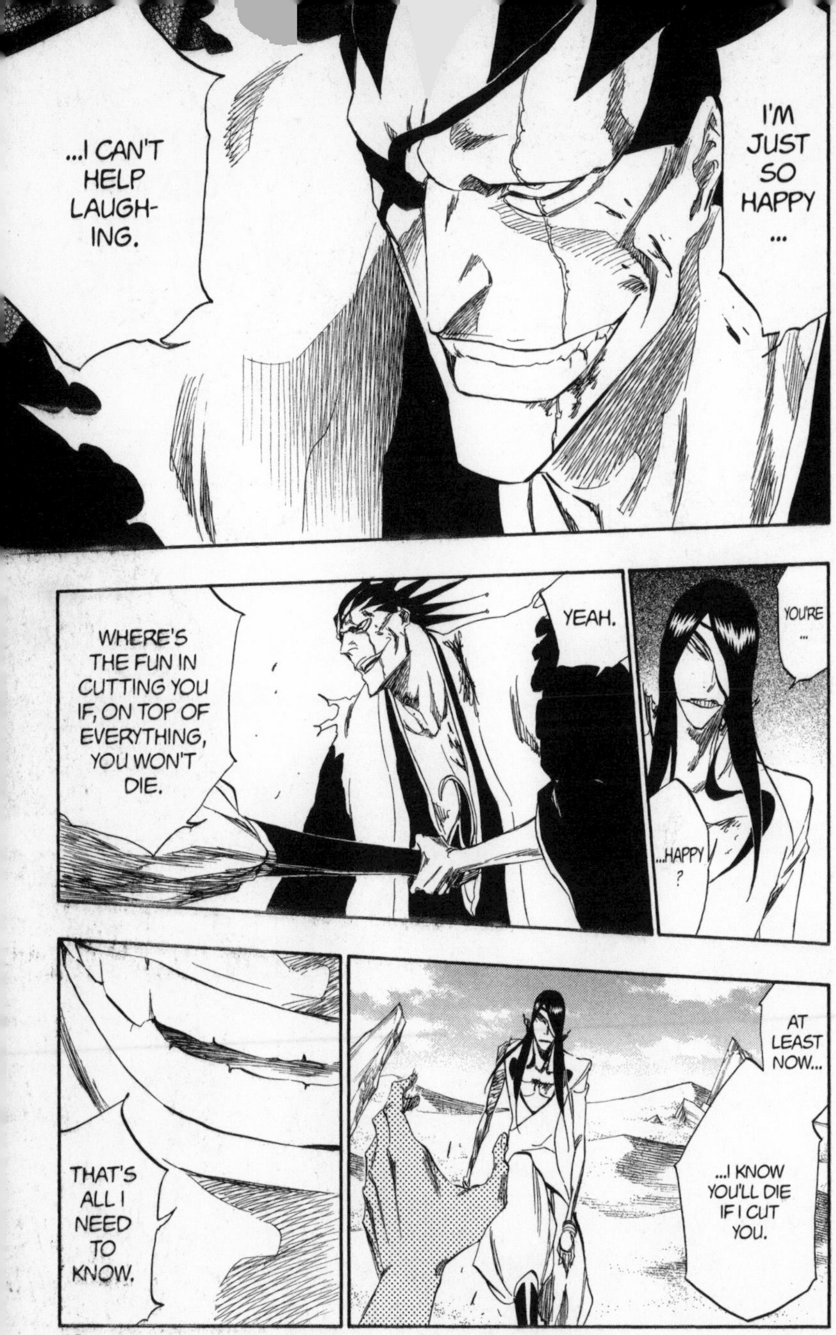
I'M JUST SO HAPPY...
...I CAN'T HELP LAUGHING.
YOU'RE ...
...HAPPY ?
YEAH.
WHERE'S THE FUN IN CUTTING YOU IF, ON TOP OF EVERYTHING, YOU WON'T DIE.
AT LEAST NOW...
...I KNOW YOU'LL DIE IF I CUT YOU.
THAT'S ALL I NEED TO KNOW.

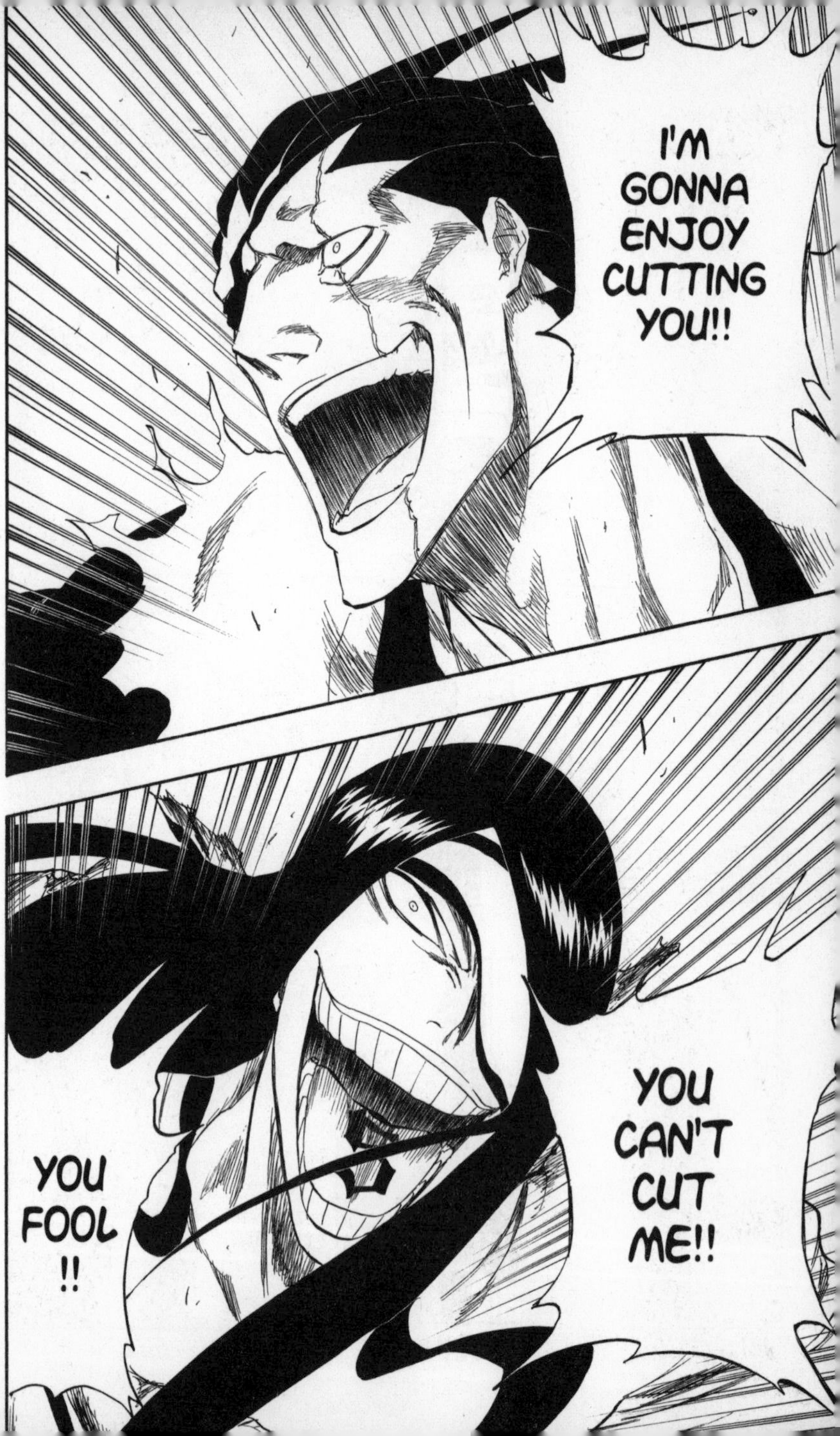
I'M GONNA ENJOY CUTTING YOU!!
YOU CAN'T CUT ME!!
YOU FOOL!!

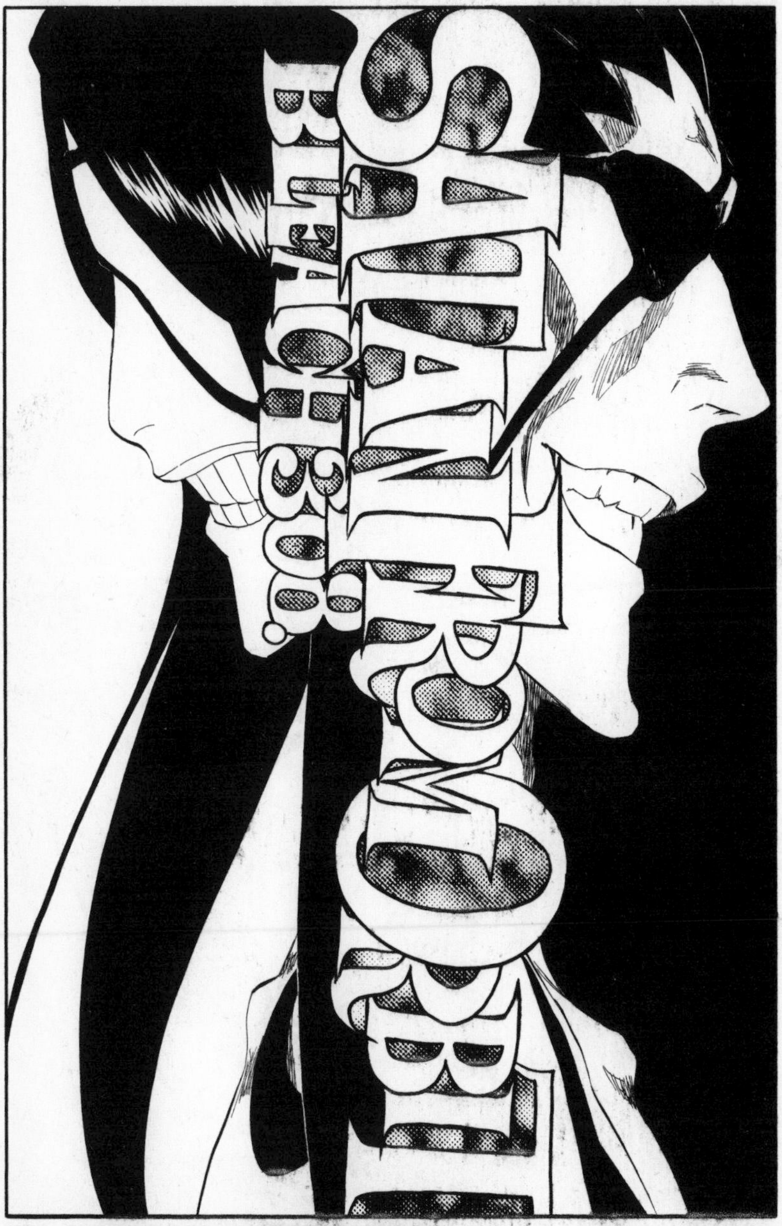
BLEACH 308.
SATAN FROM ORBIT

BLEACH 308. SATAN FROM ORBIT

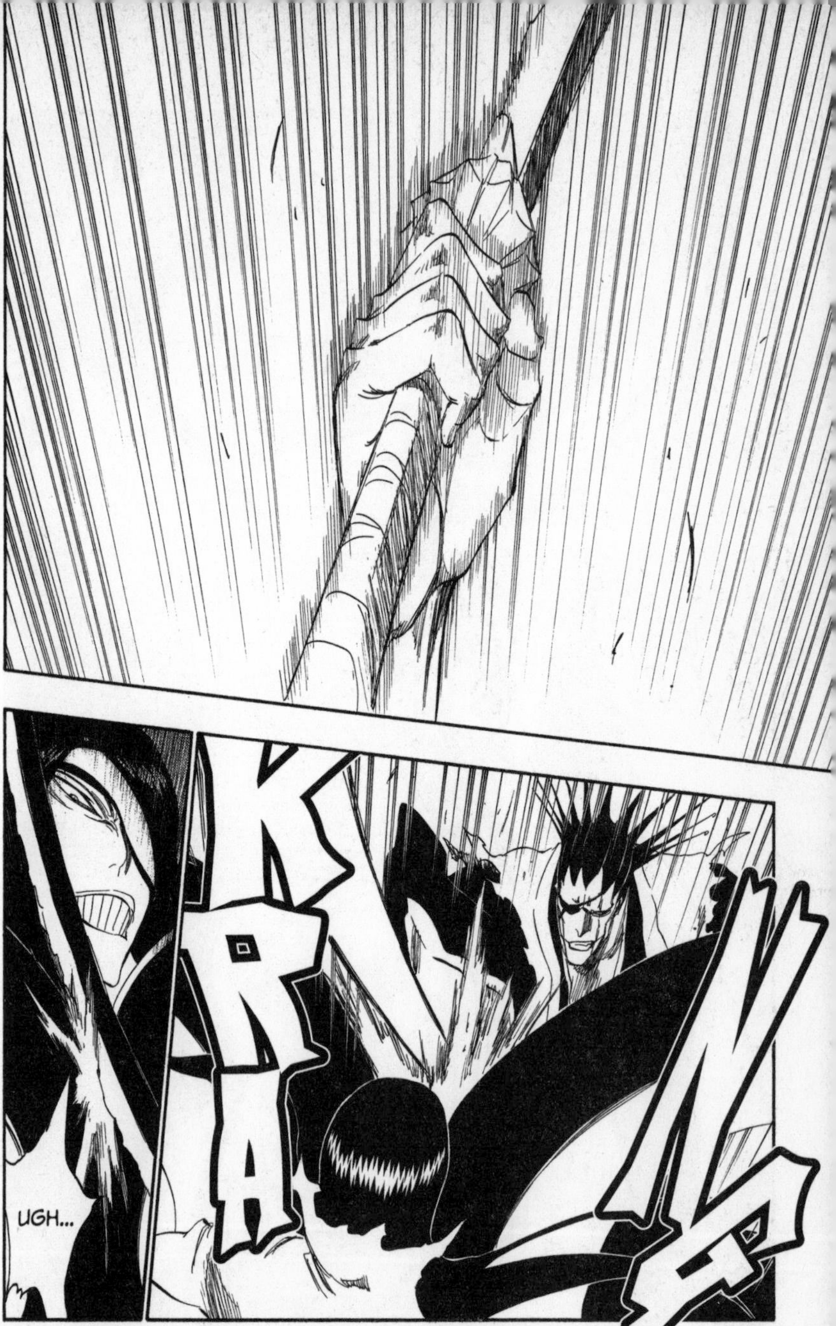
UGH...

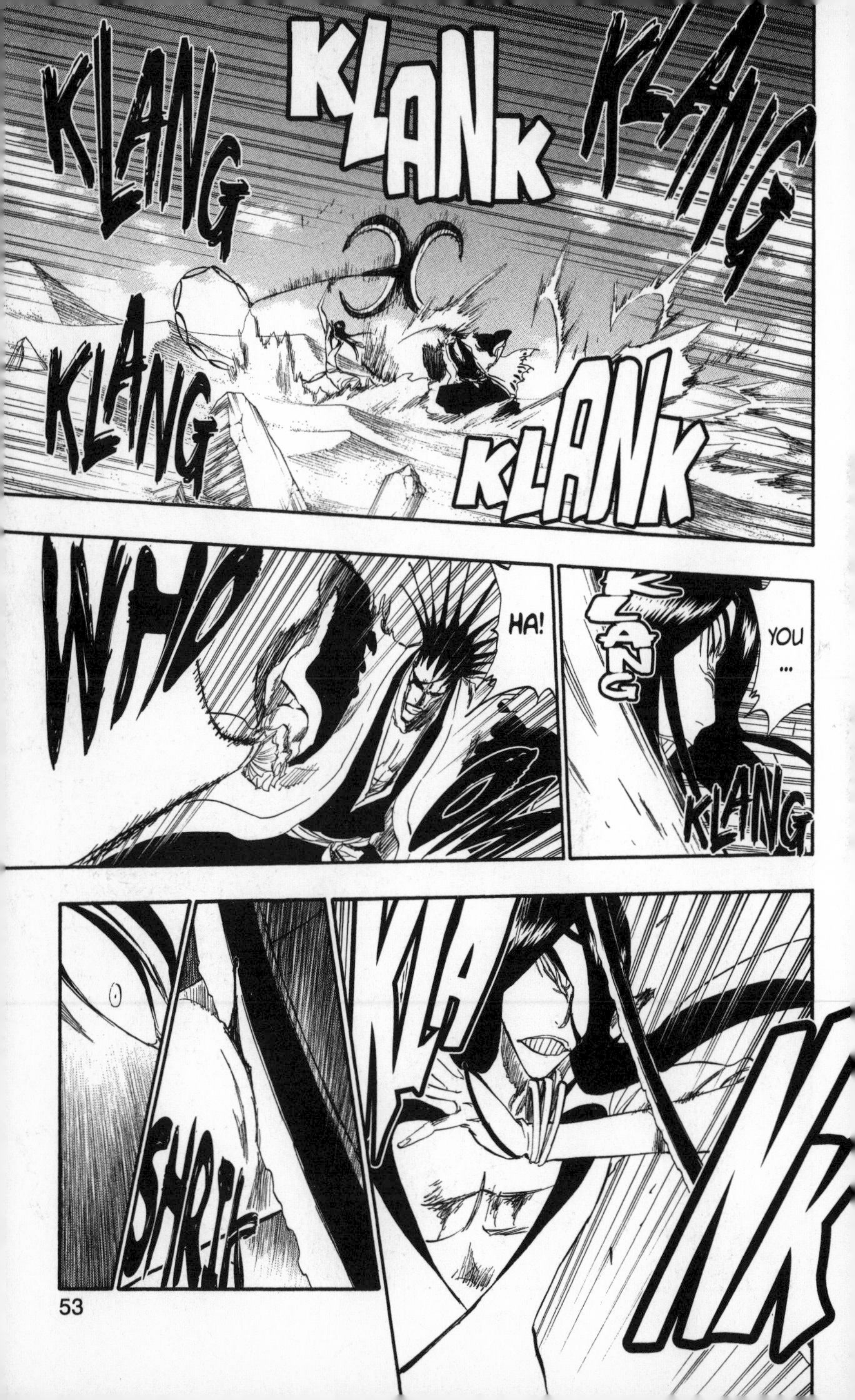
KLANG
KLANK
KLANG
KLANK
KLANG
KLANG
YOU ...
KLANG
HA!

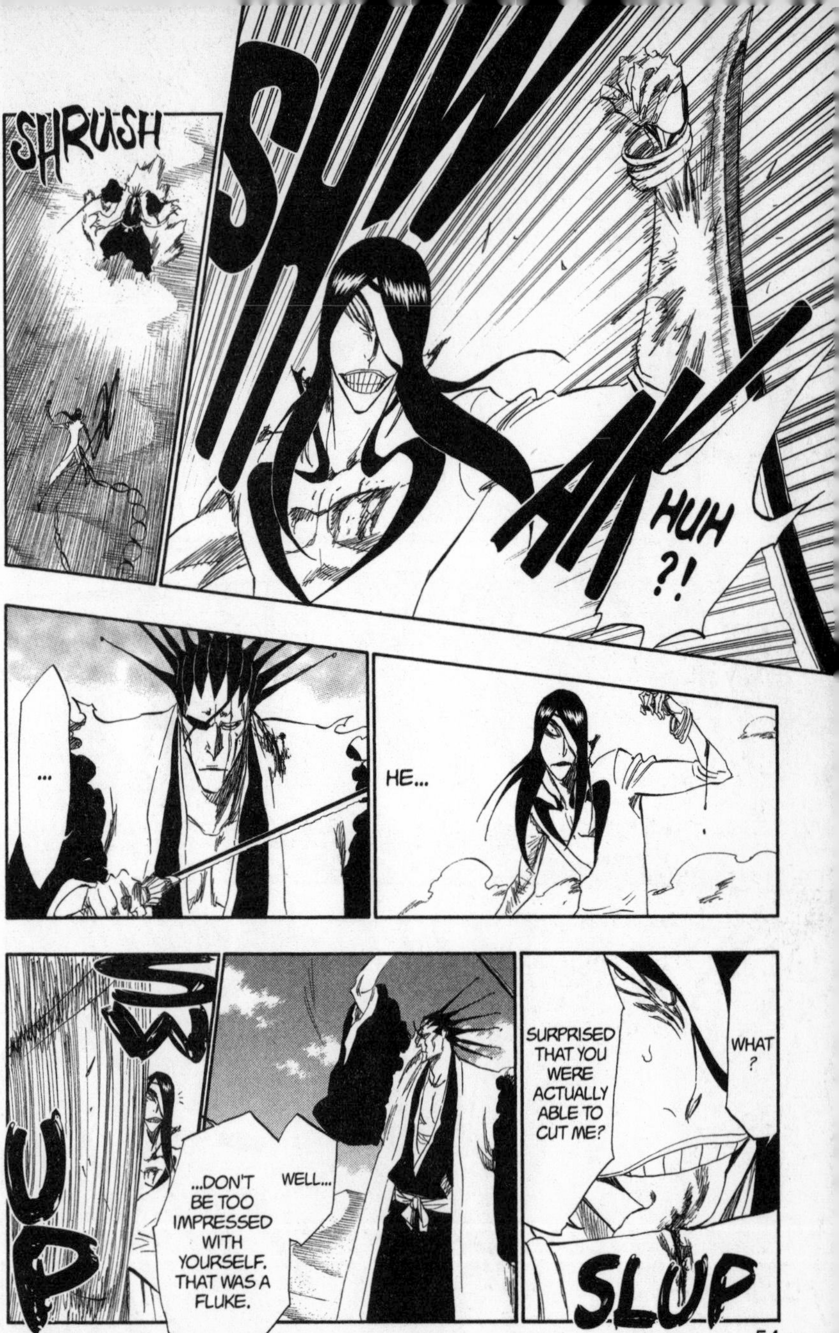
SHWISHAK
HUH?!
SHRUSH
HE...
...
WHAT?
SURPRISED THAT YOU WERE ACTUALLY ABLE TO CUT ME?
SLUP
WELL...
...DON'T BE TOO IMPRESSED WITH YOURSELF. THAT WAS A FLUKE.
SWUP

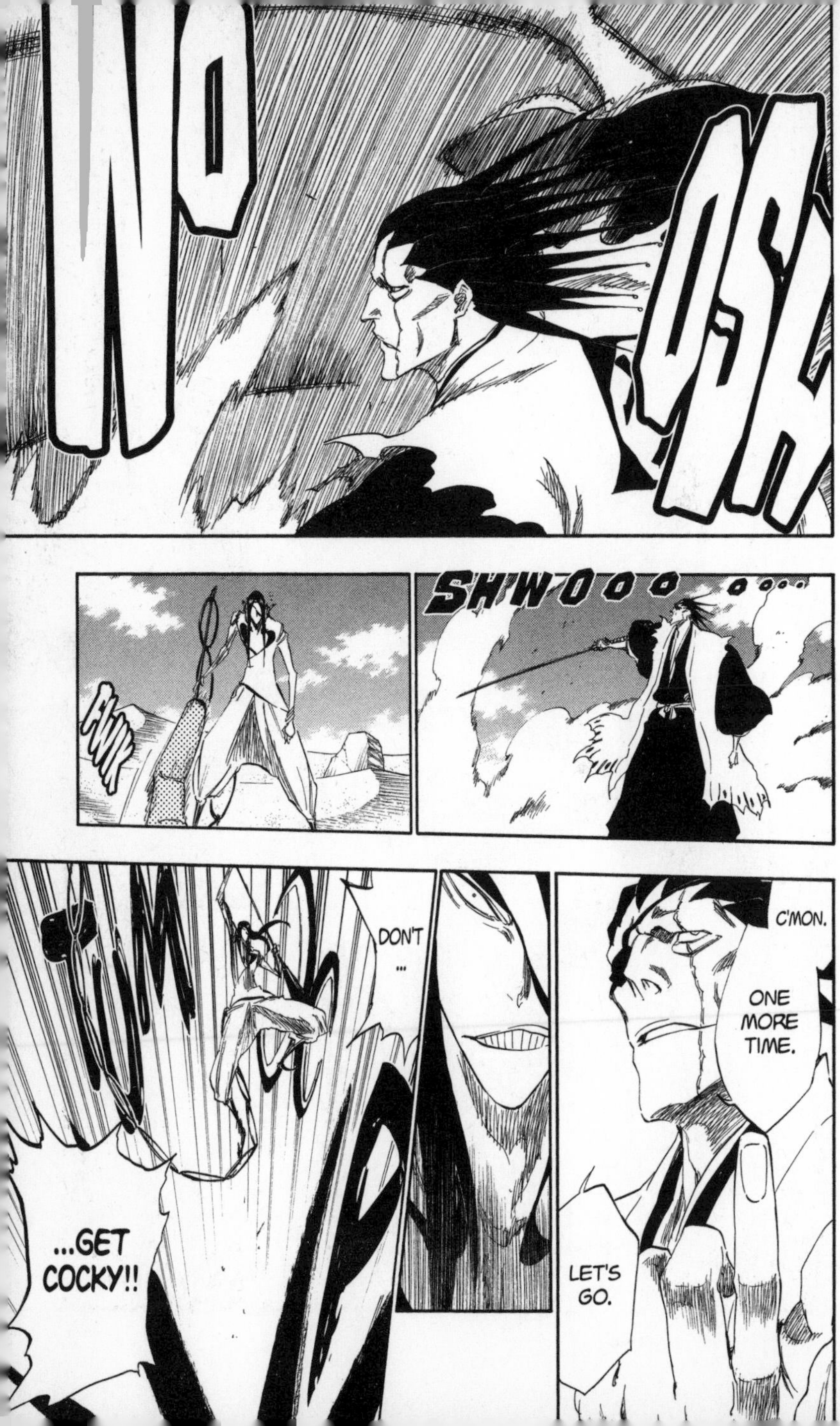
SHWOOOO OOO...
C'MON.
ONE MORE TIME.
LET'S GO.
DON'T ...
...GET COCKY!!

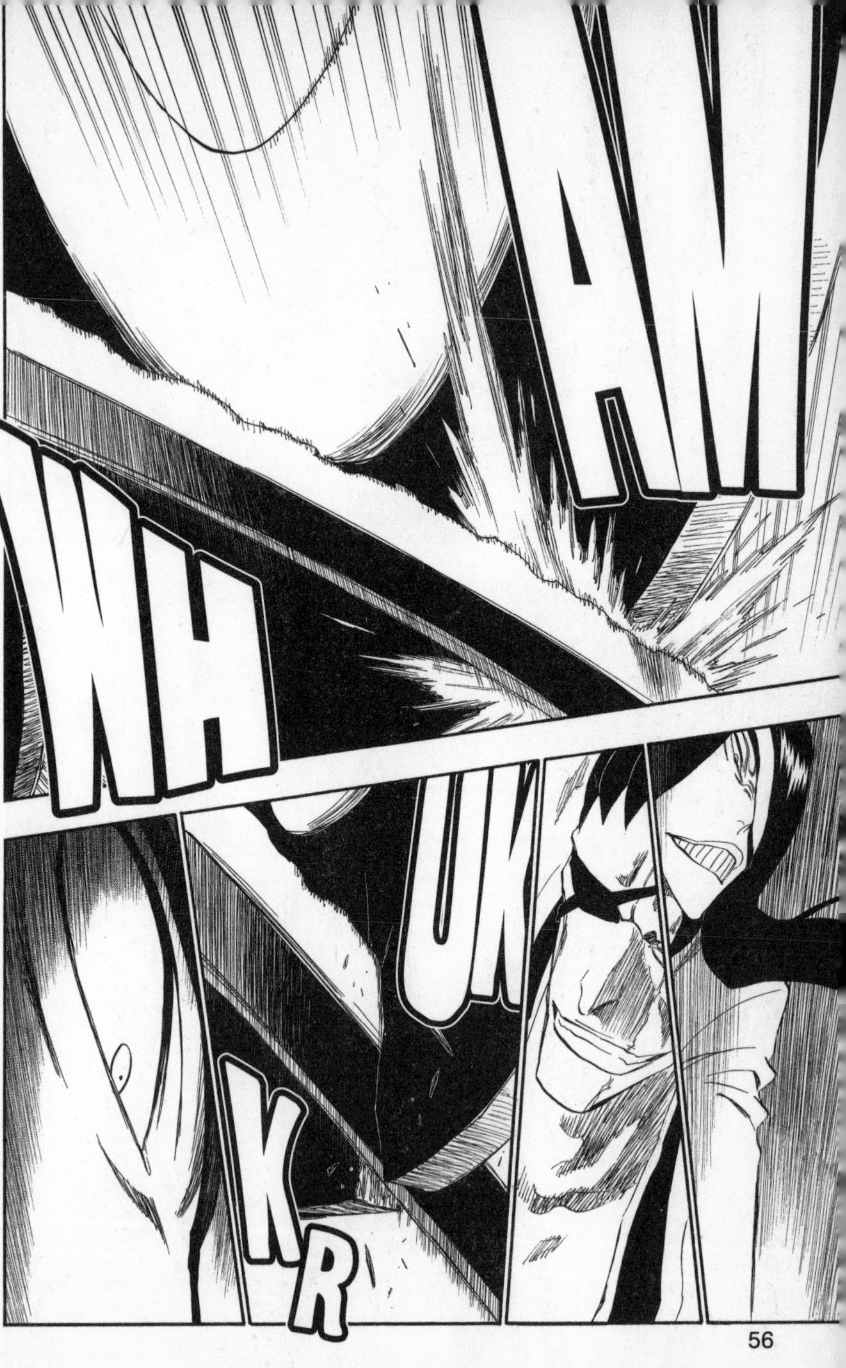
WHAM
KRUNK

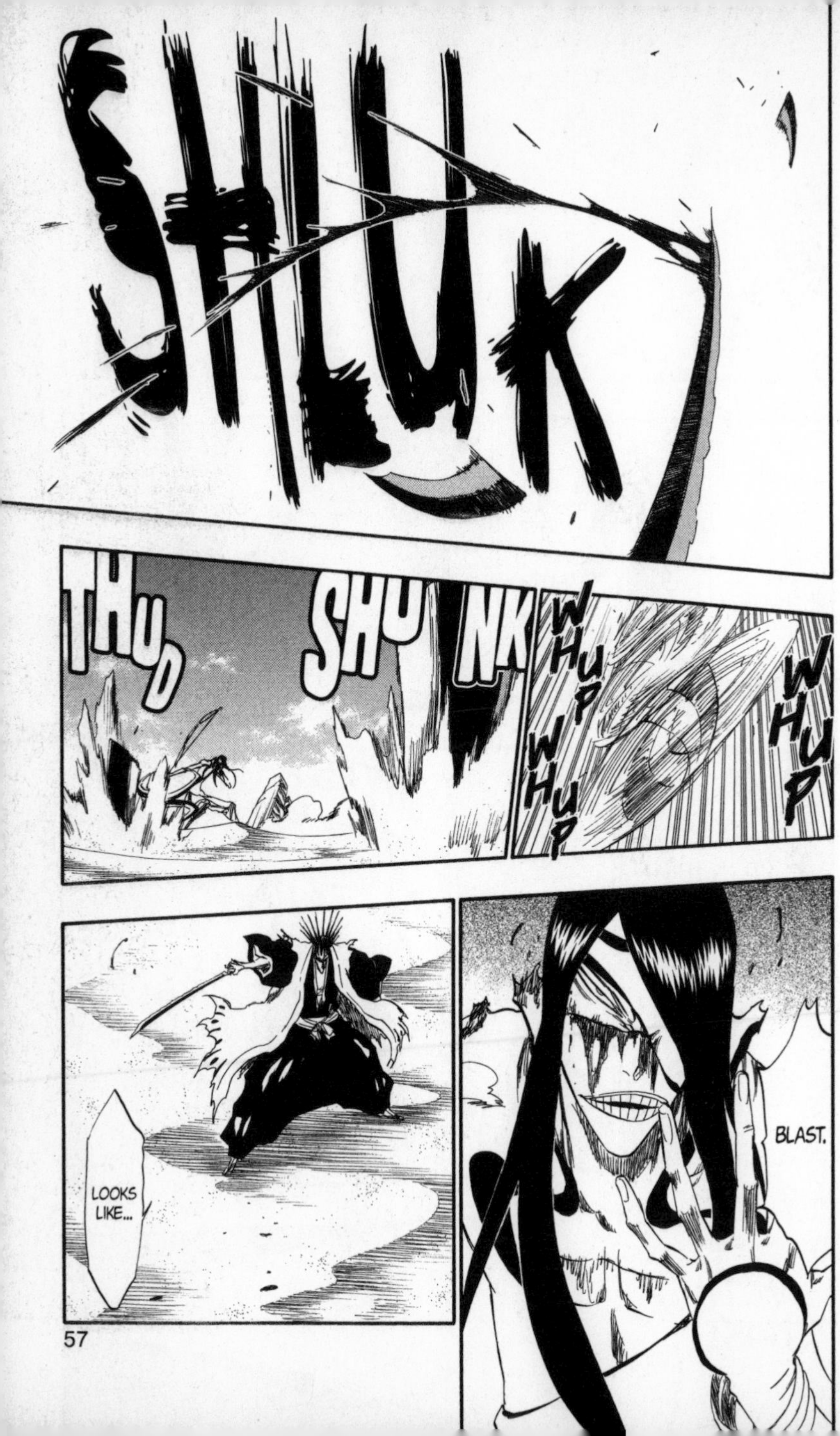
SHUK
WHUP
WHUP
WHUP
SHUNK
THUD
BLAST.
LOOKS LIKE...

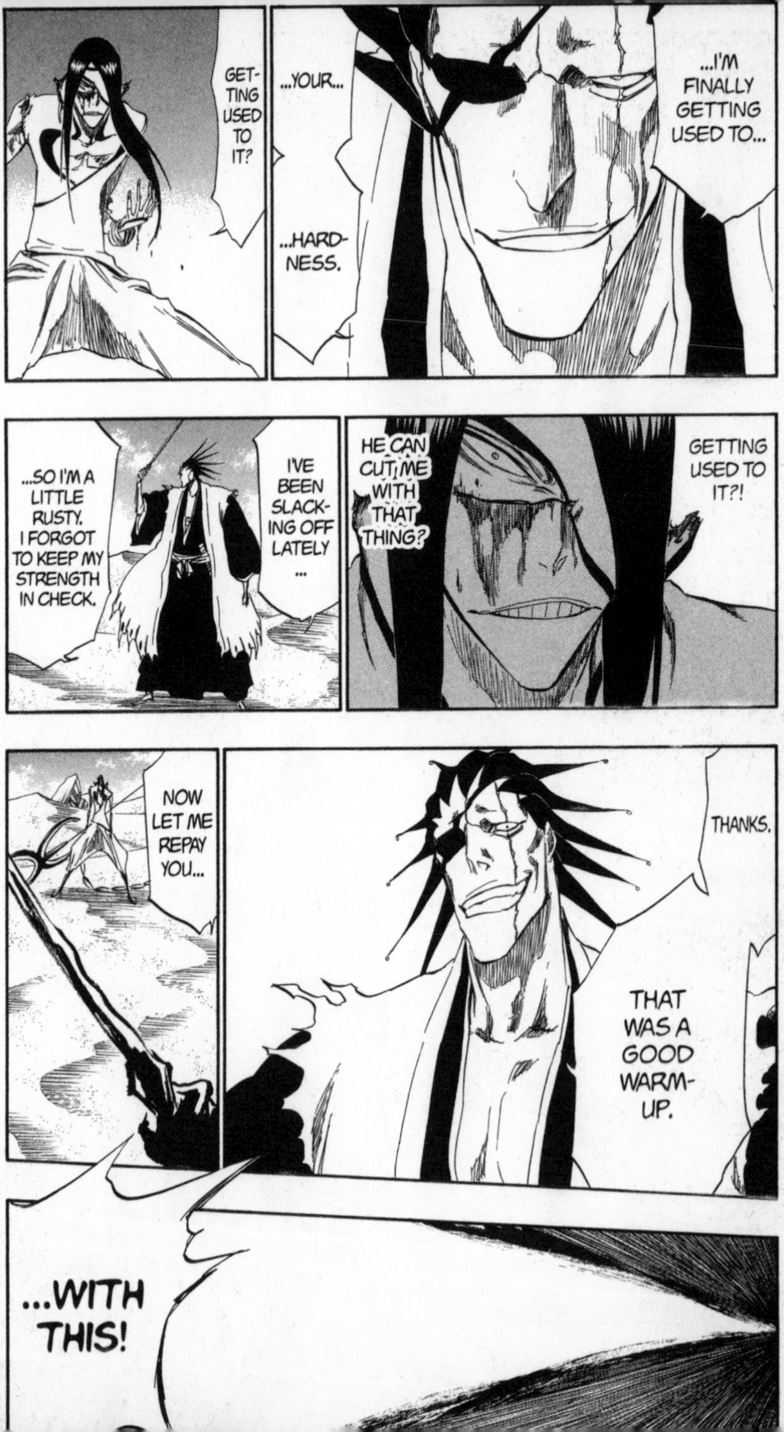
...I'M FINALLY GETTING USED TO...
...YOUR...
...HARDNESS.
GETTING USED TO IT?
GETTING USED TO IT?!
HE CAN CUT ME WITH THAT THING?
I'VE BEEN SLACKING OFF LATELY...
...SO I'M A LITTLE RUSTY. I FORGOT TO KEEP MY STRENGTH IN CHECK.
THANKS.
THAT WAS A GOOD WARM-UP.
NOW LET ME REPAY YOU...
...WITH THIS!

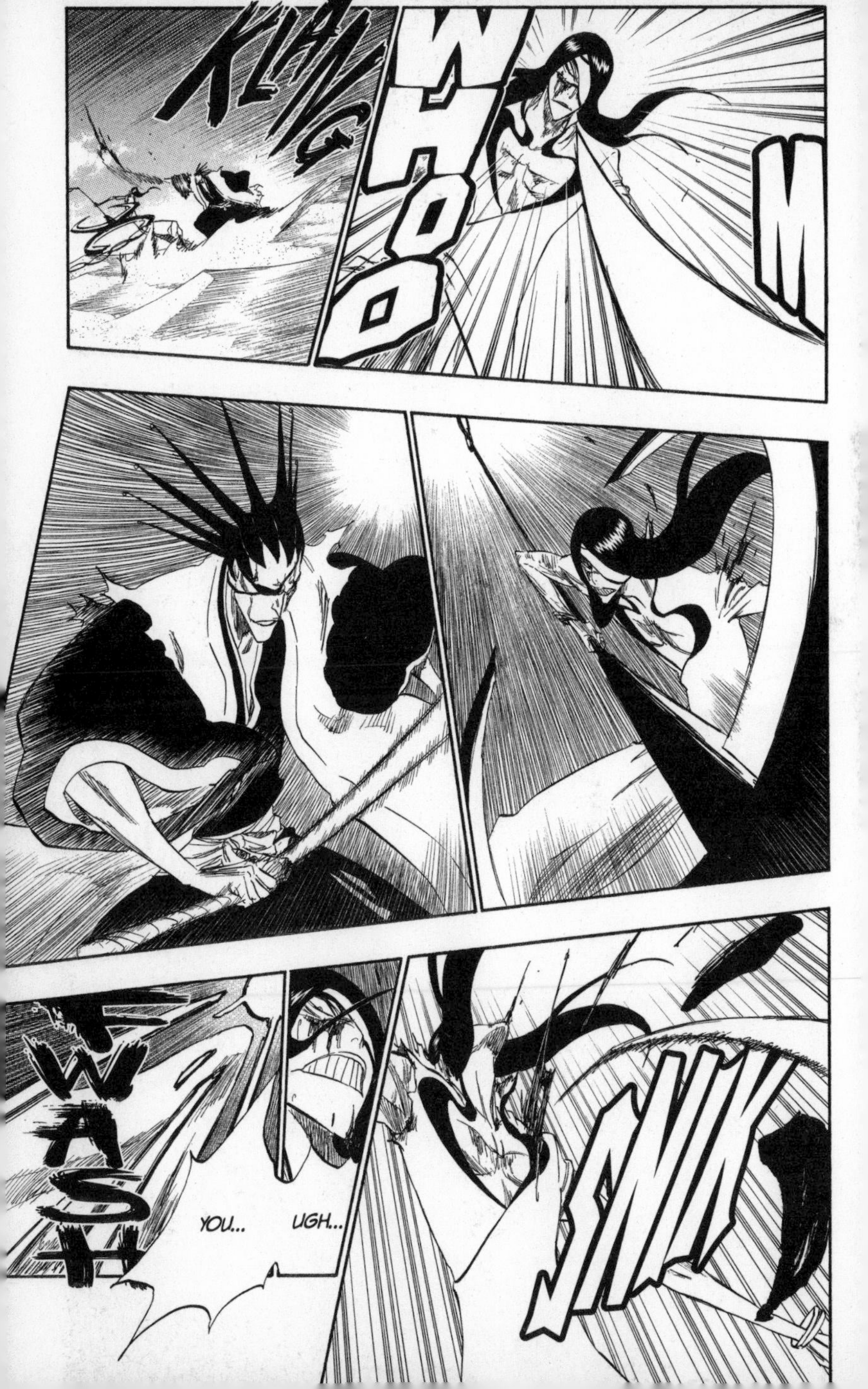
WHOOM
KLANG
UGH...
YOU...
FWASH

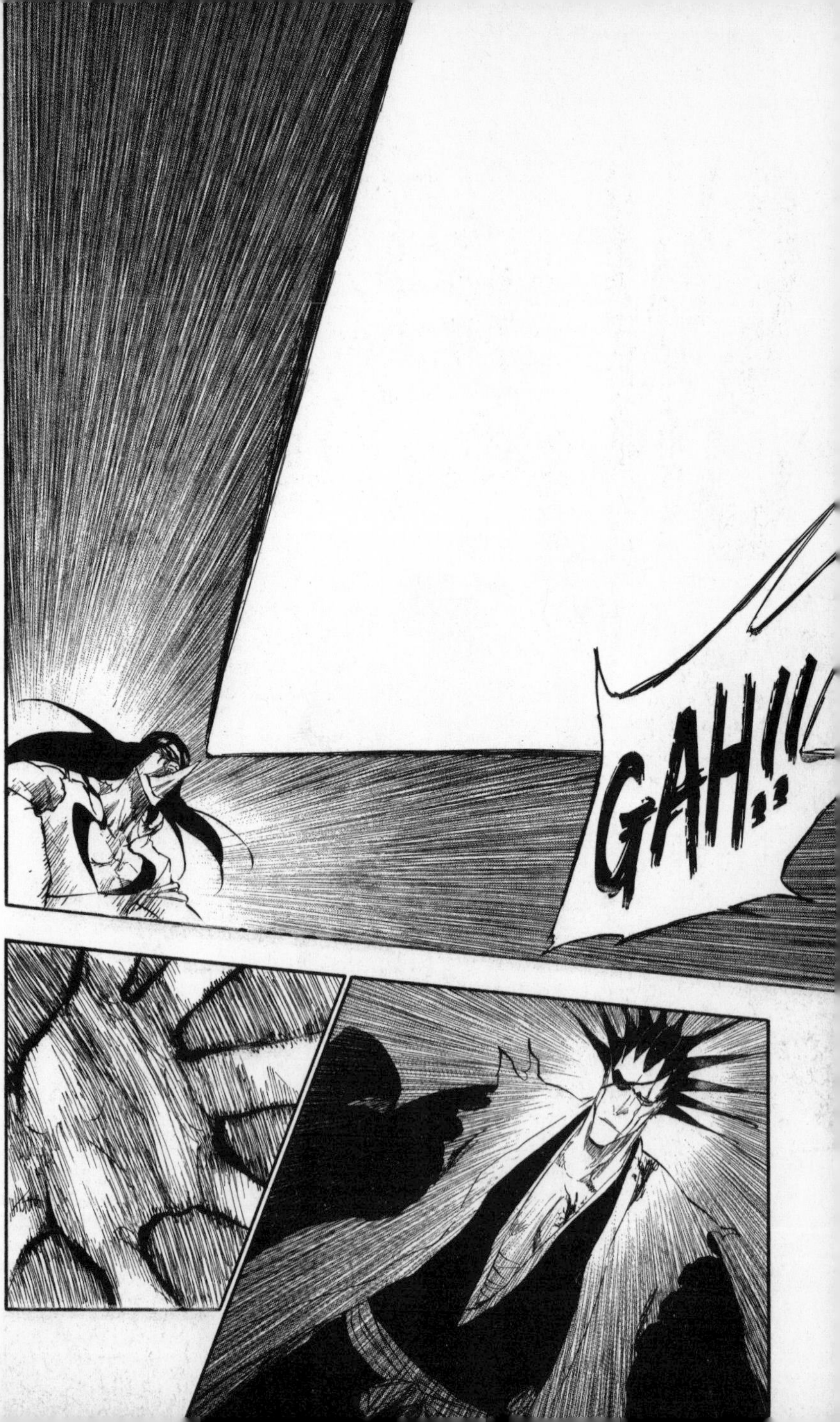
GAH!!

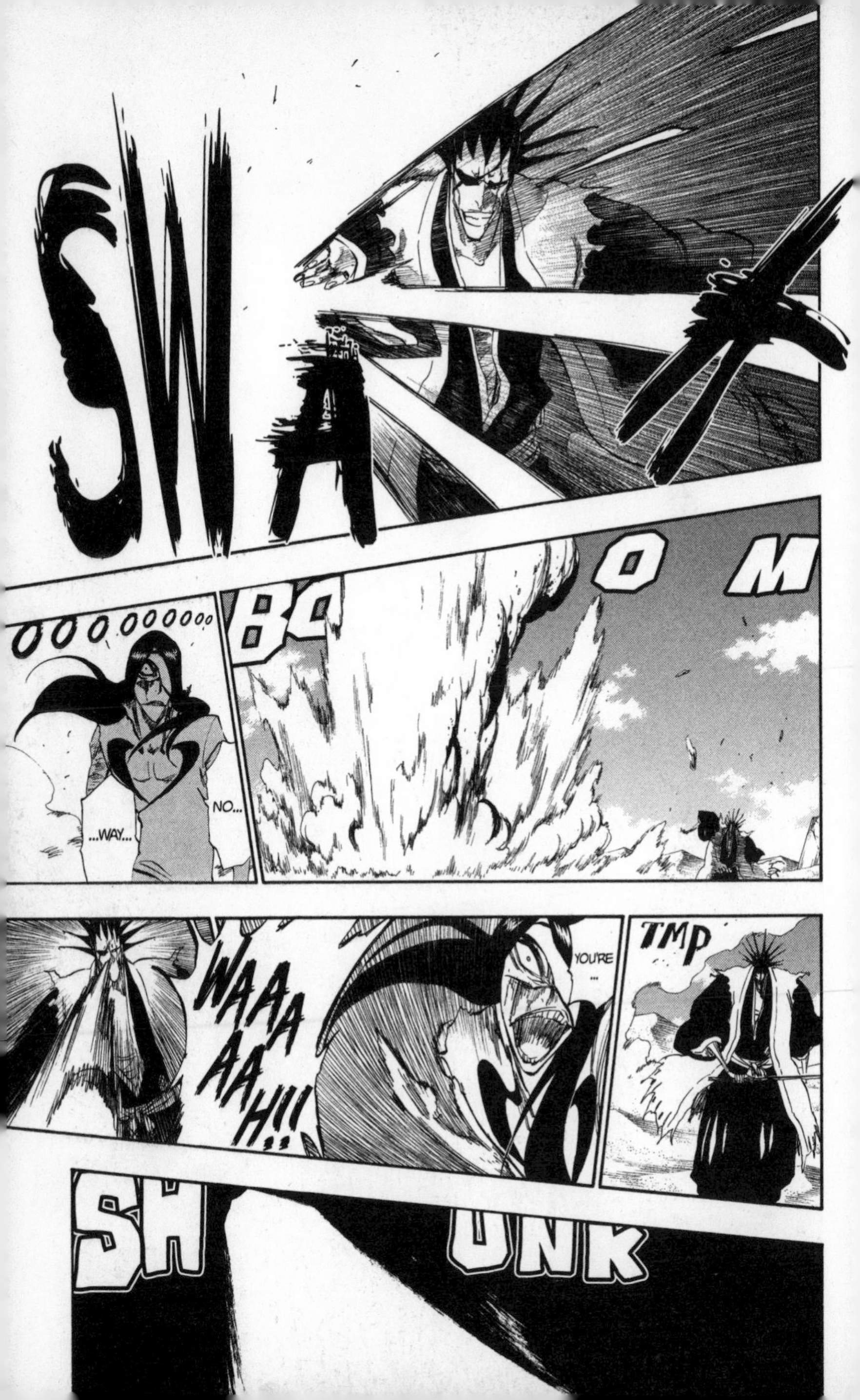
SWA
BOOM
OOOOOOOOOO
NO...
...WAY...
TMP
YOU'RE ...
WAAAAAAH!!
SHUNK

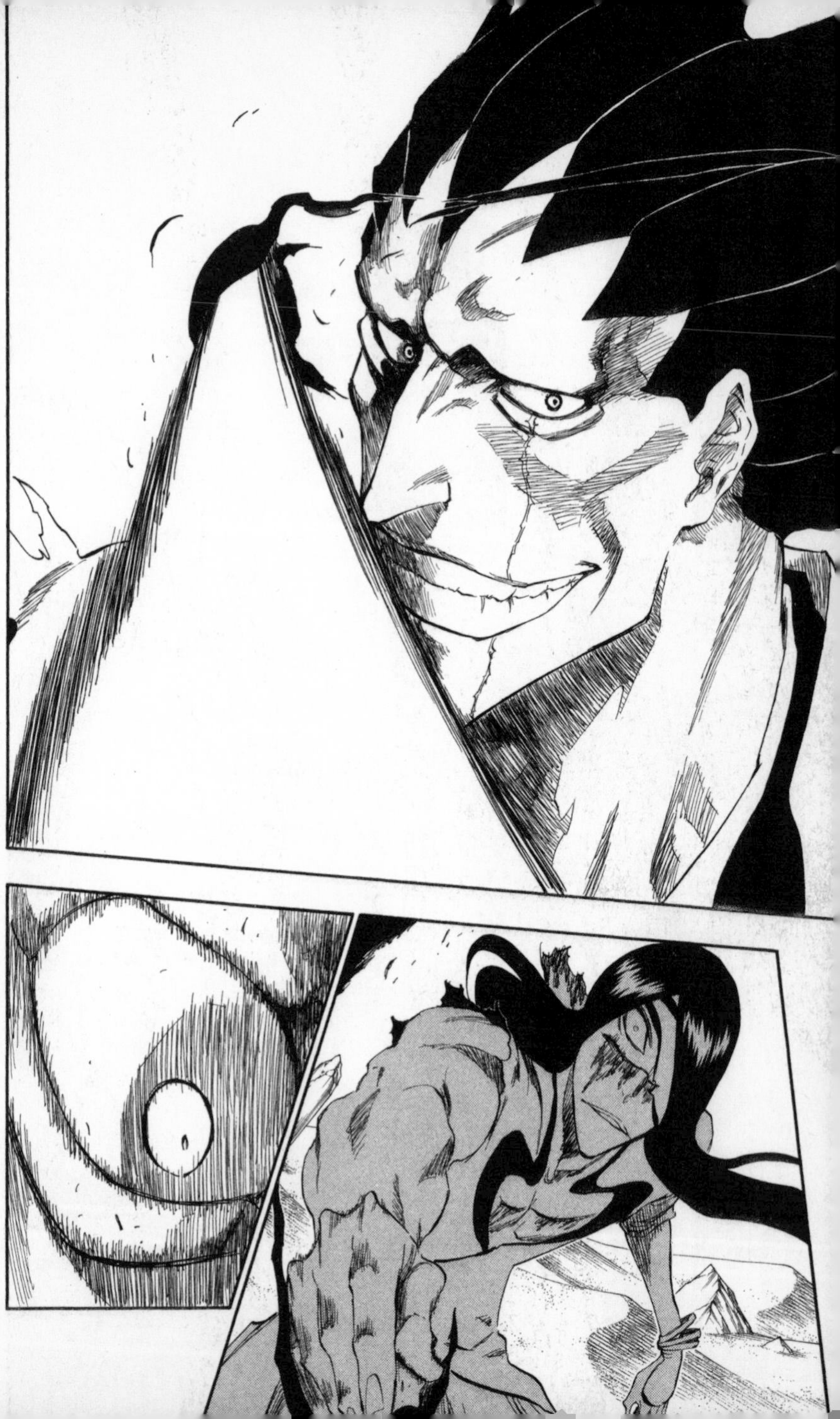

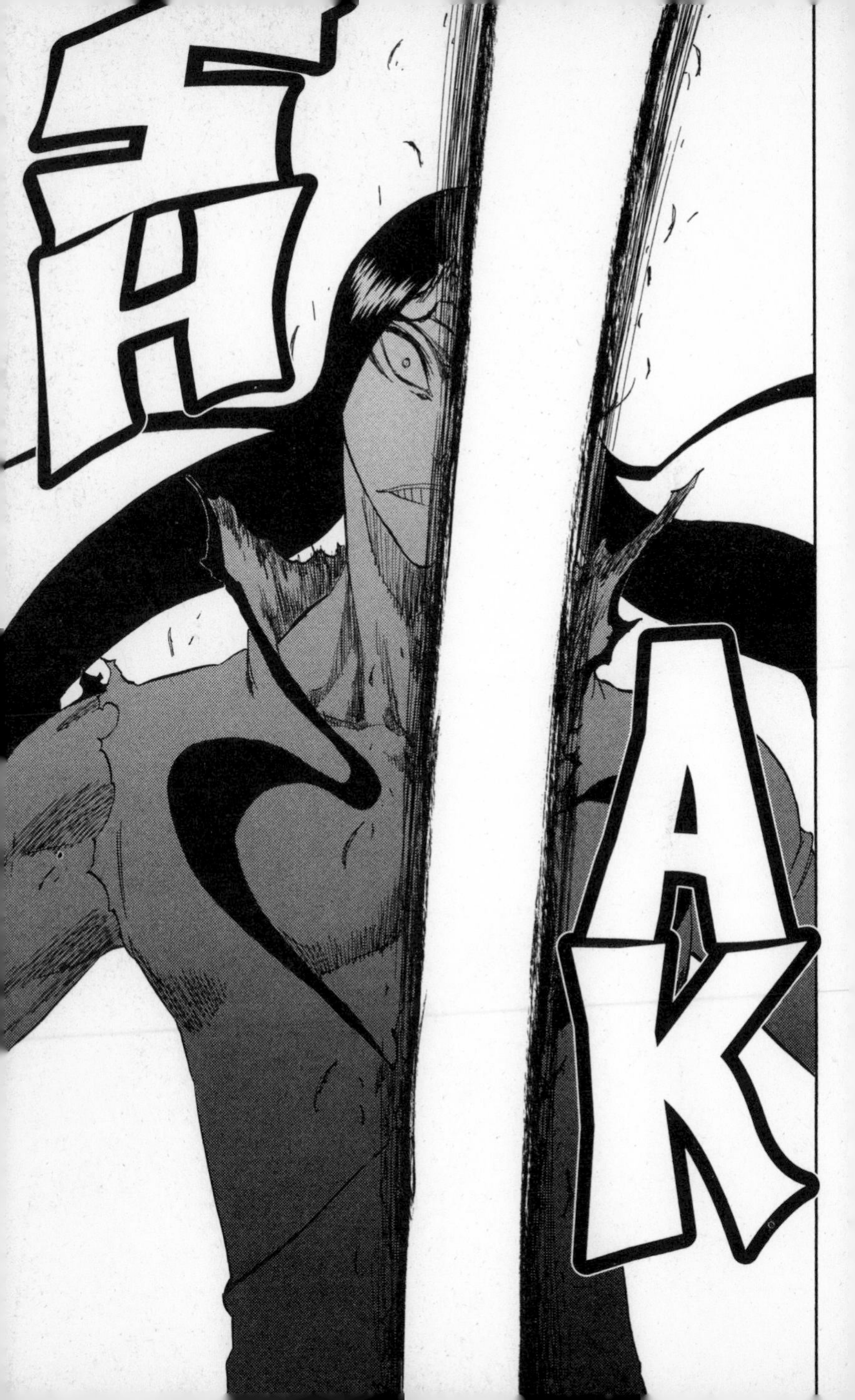
CHAK

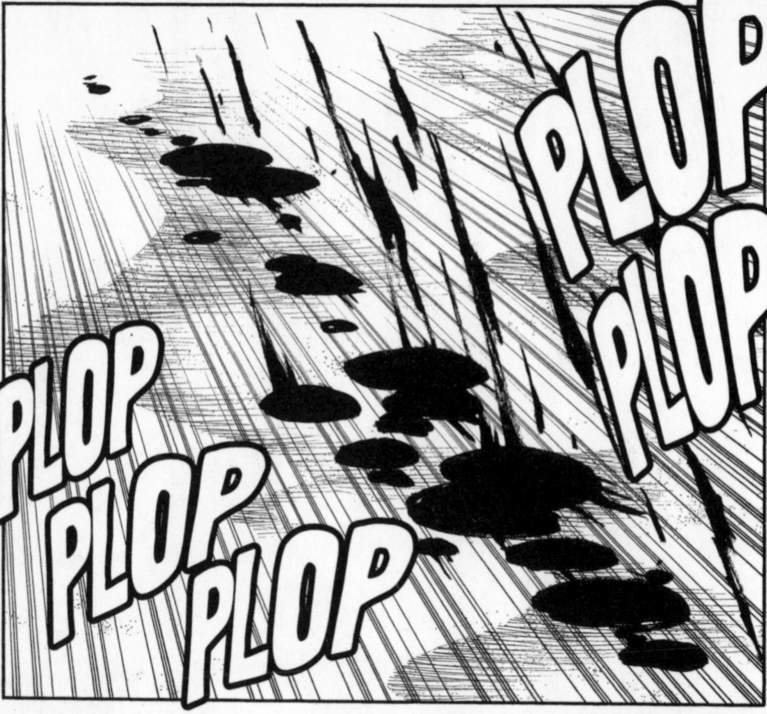
PLOP
PLOP
PLOP
PLOP
PLOP

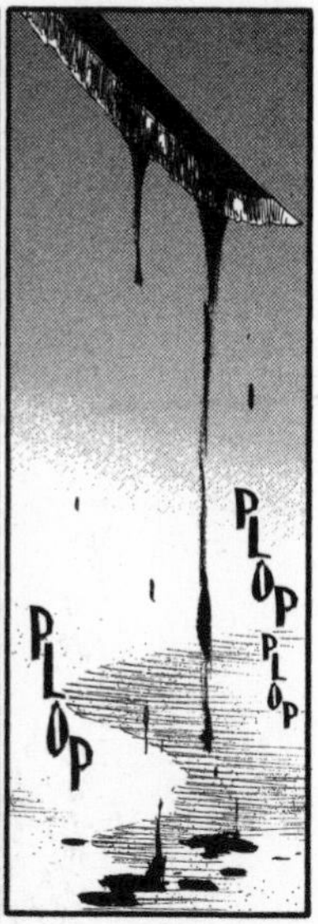
PLOP
PLOP
PLOP

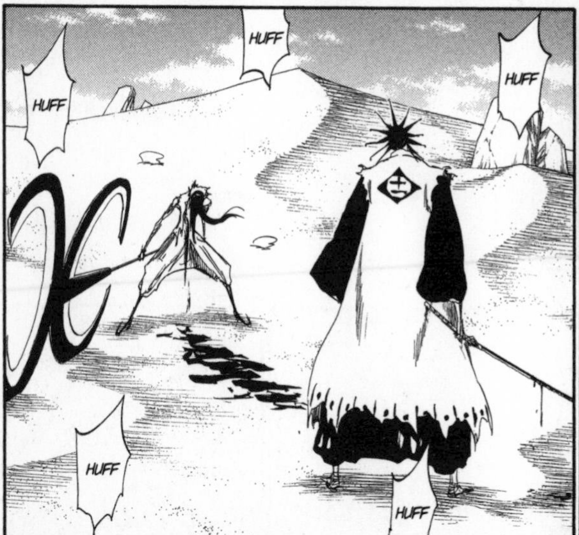
HUFF
HUFF
HUFF
HUFF
HUFF

309. Pray for the Mantis

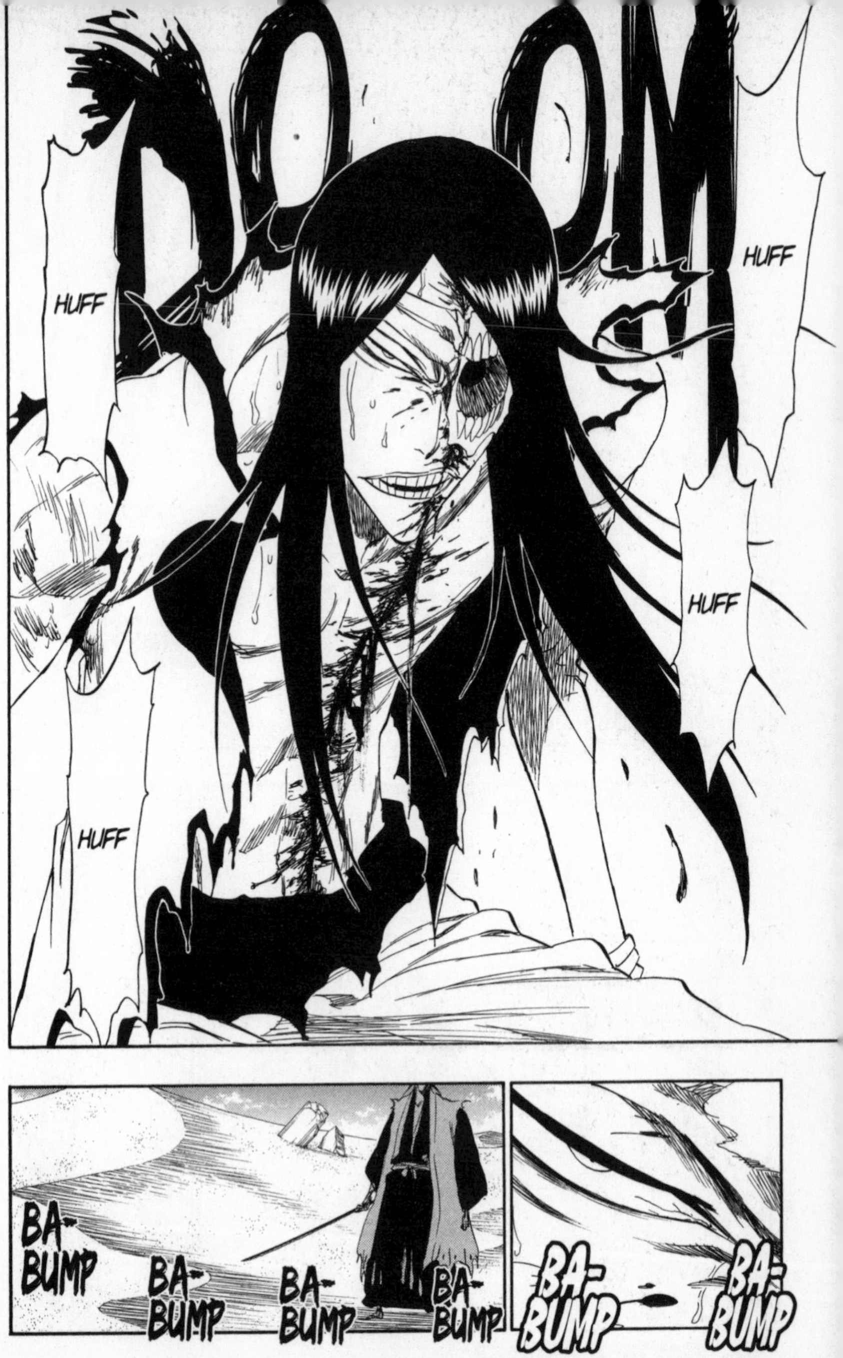
DOOOM
HUFF
HUFF
HUFF
HUFF
BA-BUMP
BA-BUMP
BA-BUMP
BA-BUMP
BA-BUMP
BA-BUMP

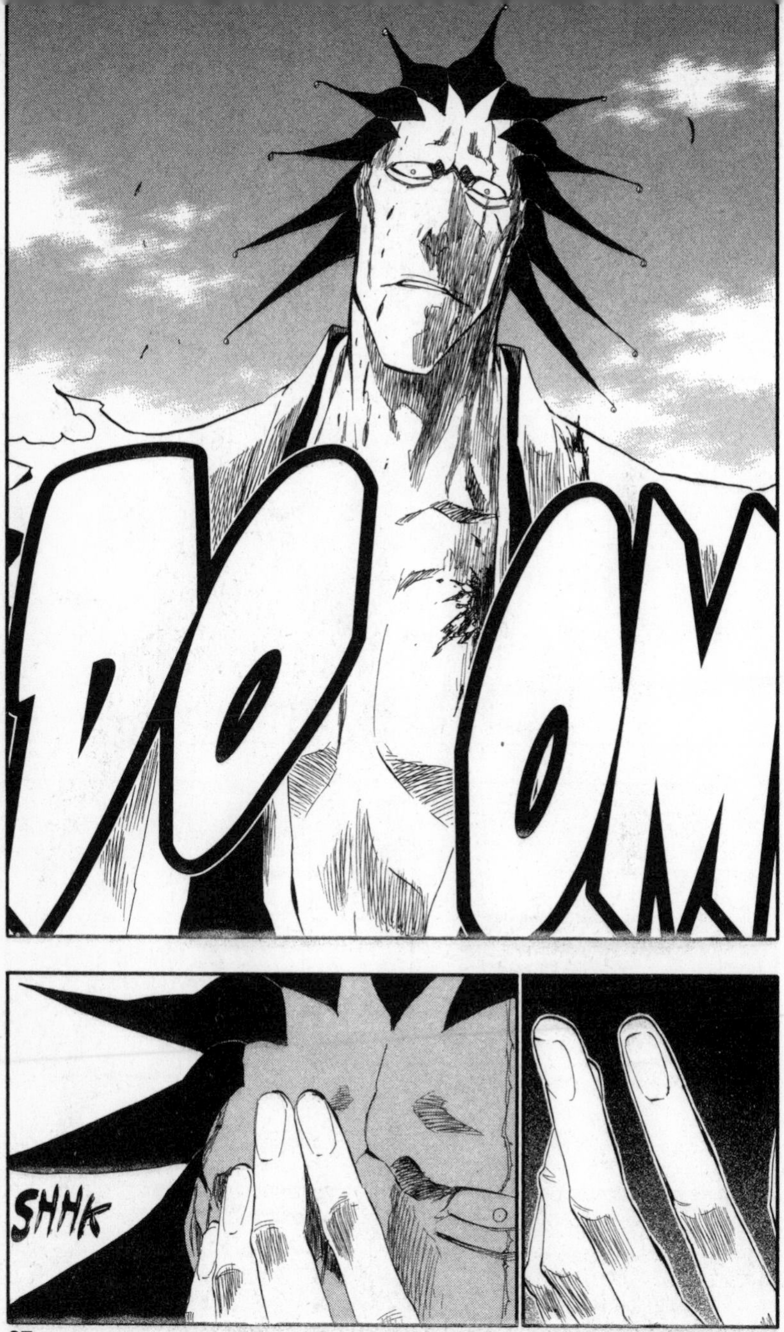
DOOM
SHHK

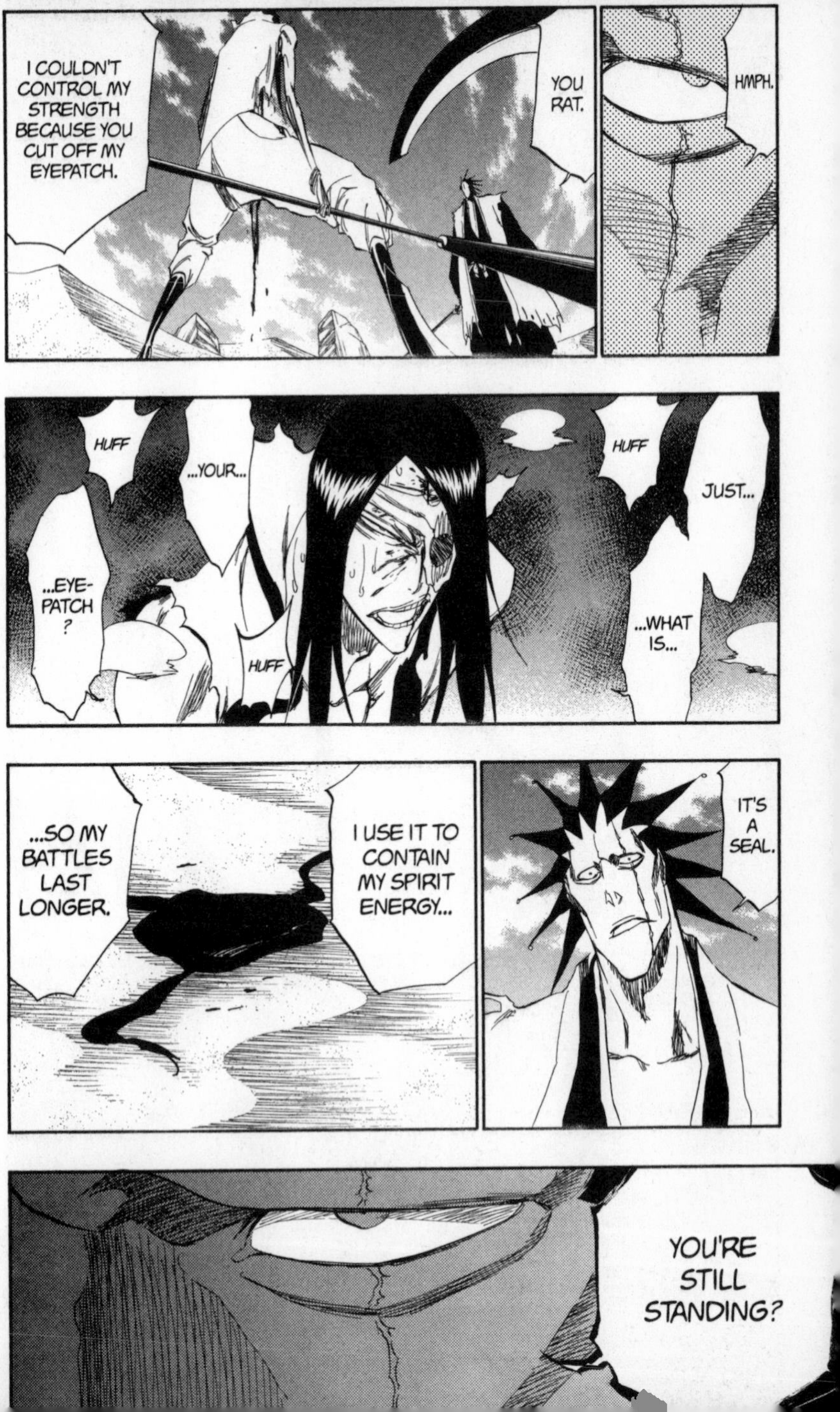
HMPH.
YOU RAT.
I COULDN'T CONTROL MY STRENGTH BECAUSE YOU CUT OFF MY EYEPATCH.
HUFF
JUST...
...WHAT IS...
HUFF
...YOUR...
...EYE-PATCH?
HUFF
IT'S A SEAL.
I USE IT TO CONTAIN MY SPIRIT ENERGY...
...SO MY BATTLES LAST LONGER.
YOU'RE STILL STANDING?

OR ARE YOU JUST ON YOUR LAST BREATH?

YOU'RE ALIVE?

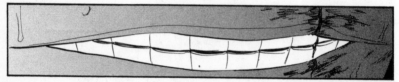

...THAT WOULD KILL ME.

AS IF...

YOU FOOL.

I...

I...

...CAN'T KILL ME.

YOUR

...BLADE...

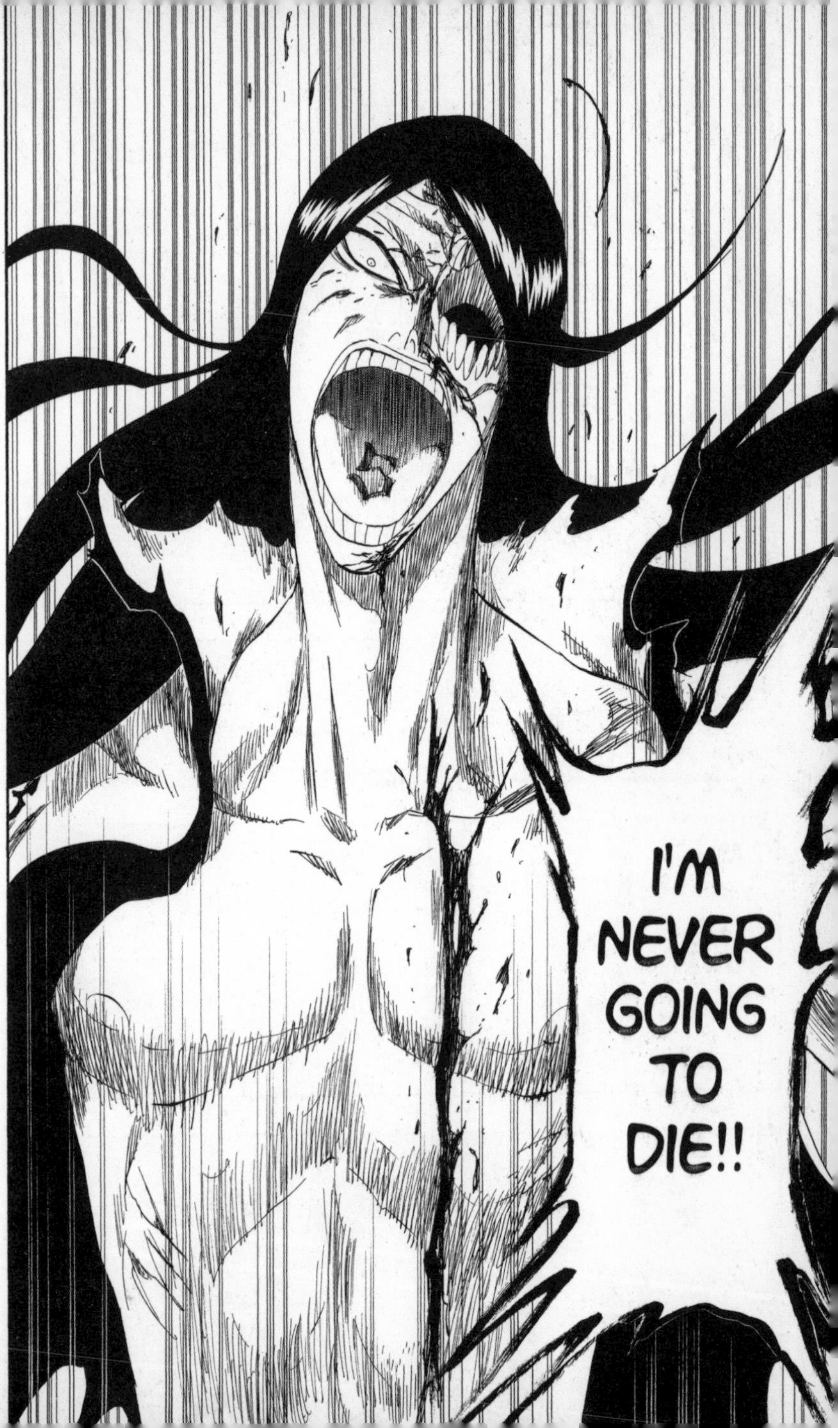
I'M NEVER GOING TO DIE!!

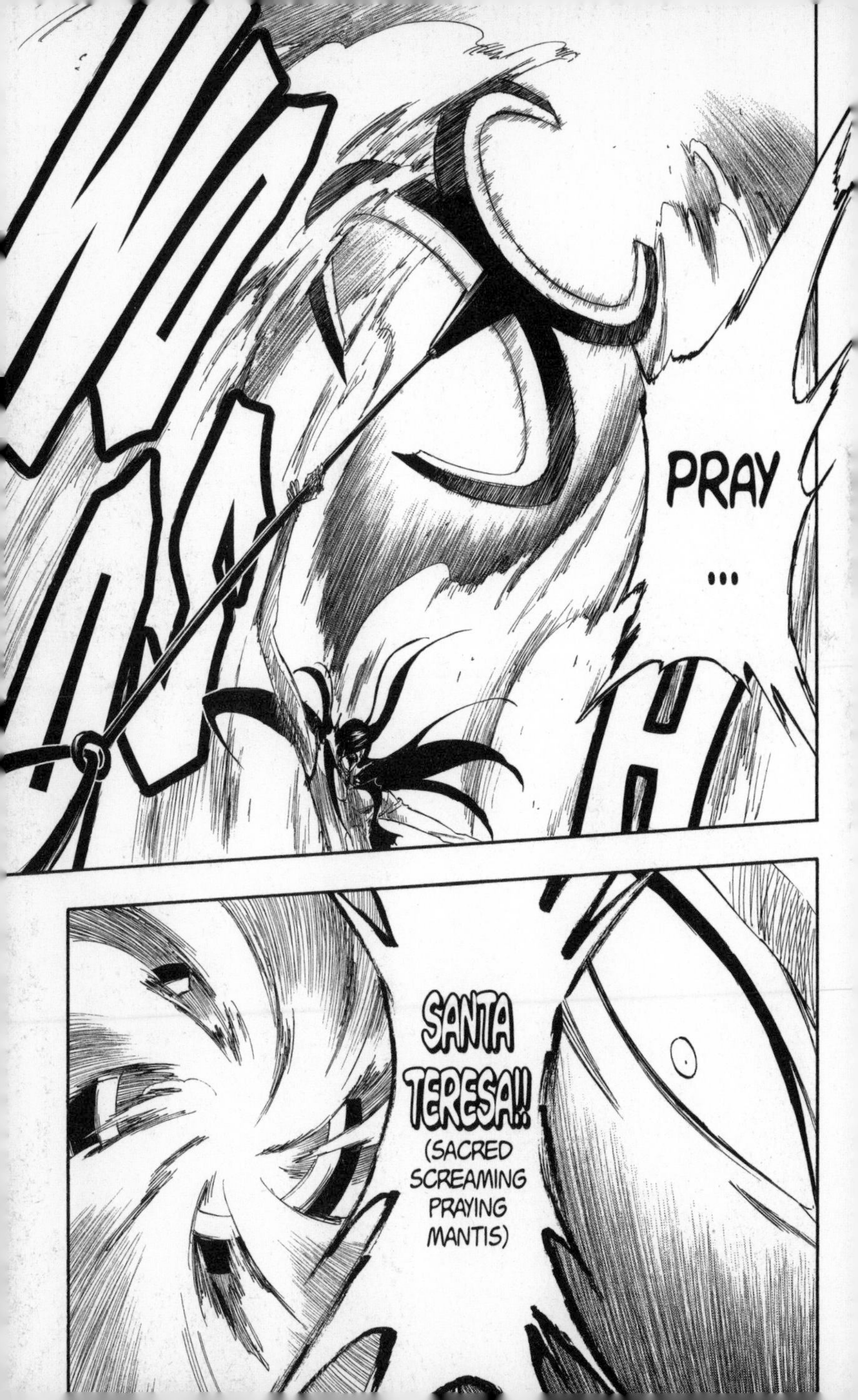
PRAY
...
SANTA TERESA!!
(SACRED SCREAMING PRAYING MANTIS)

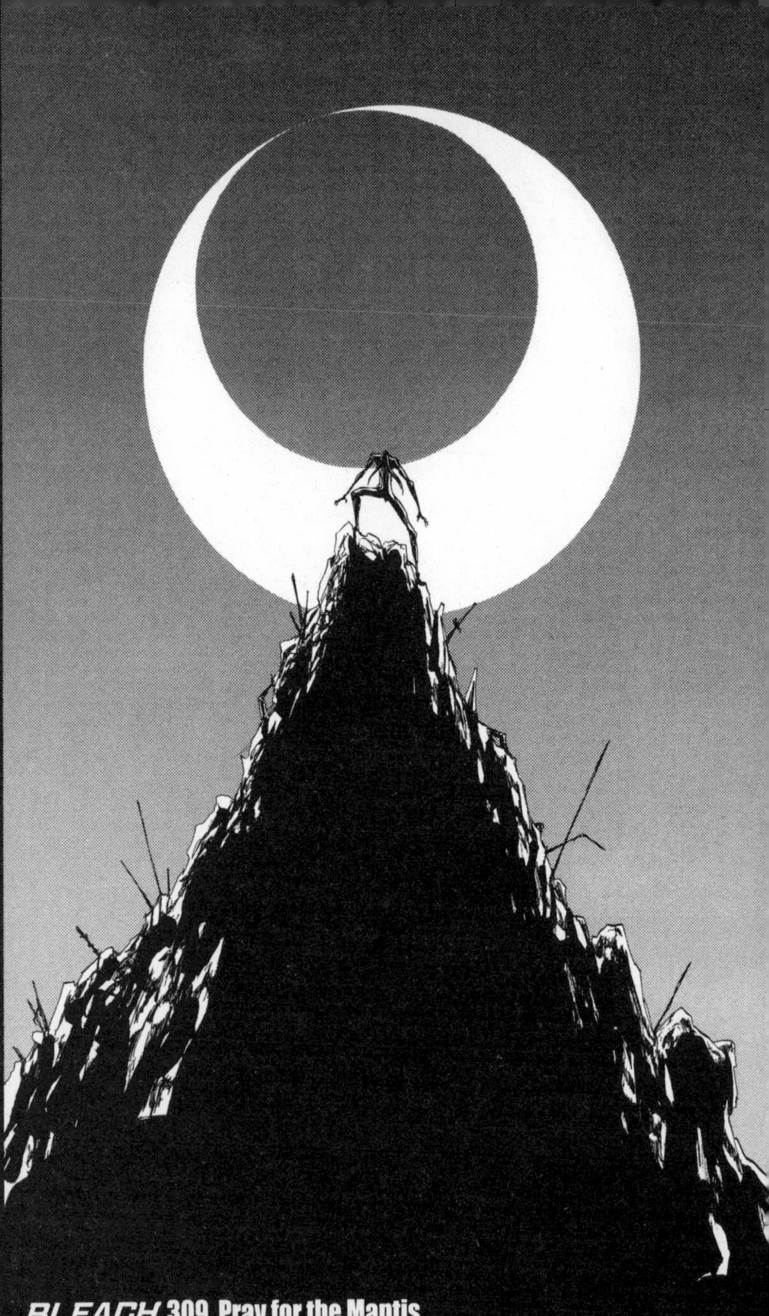

BLEACH 309. Pray for the Mantis

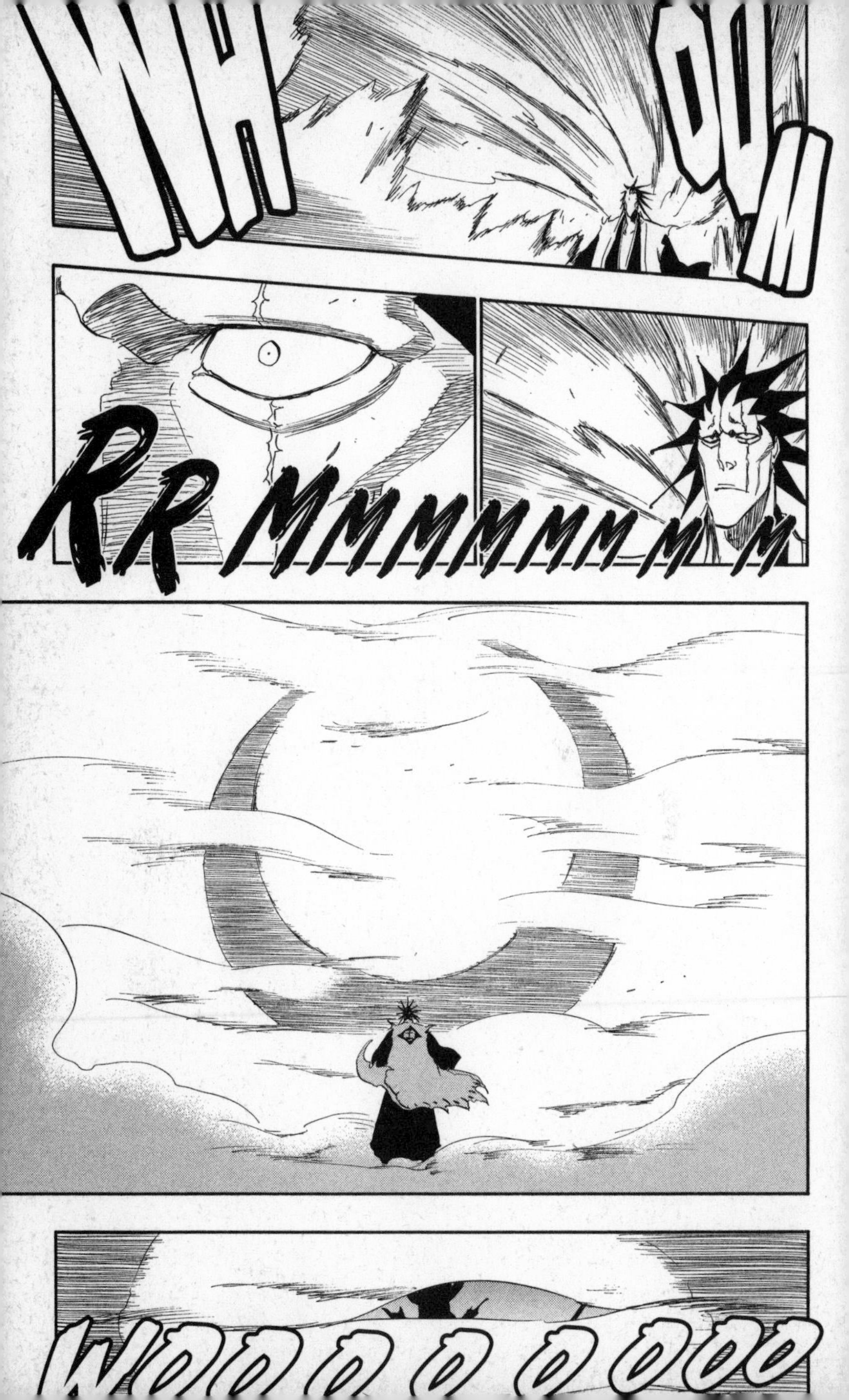
WHAOOM
RRMMMMMMMMM
WOOOOOOOOO

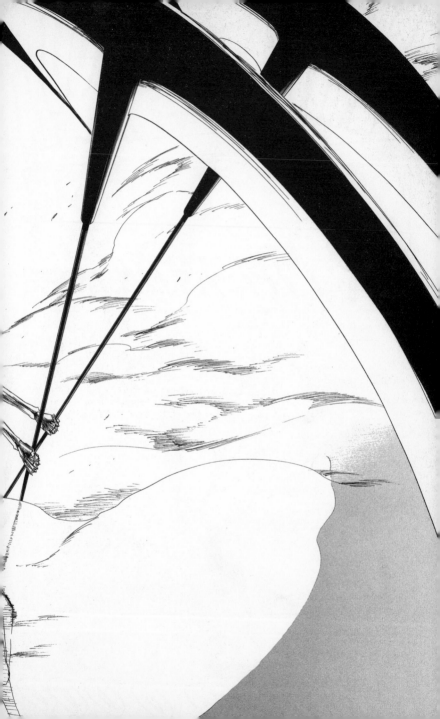

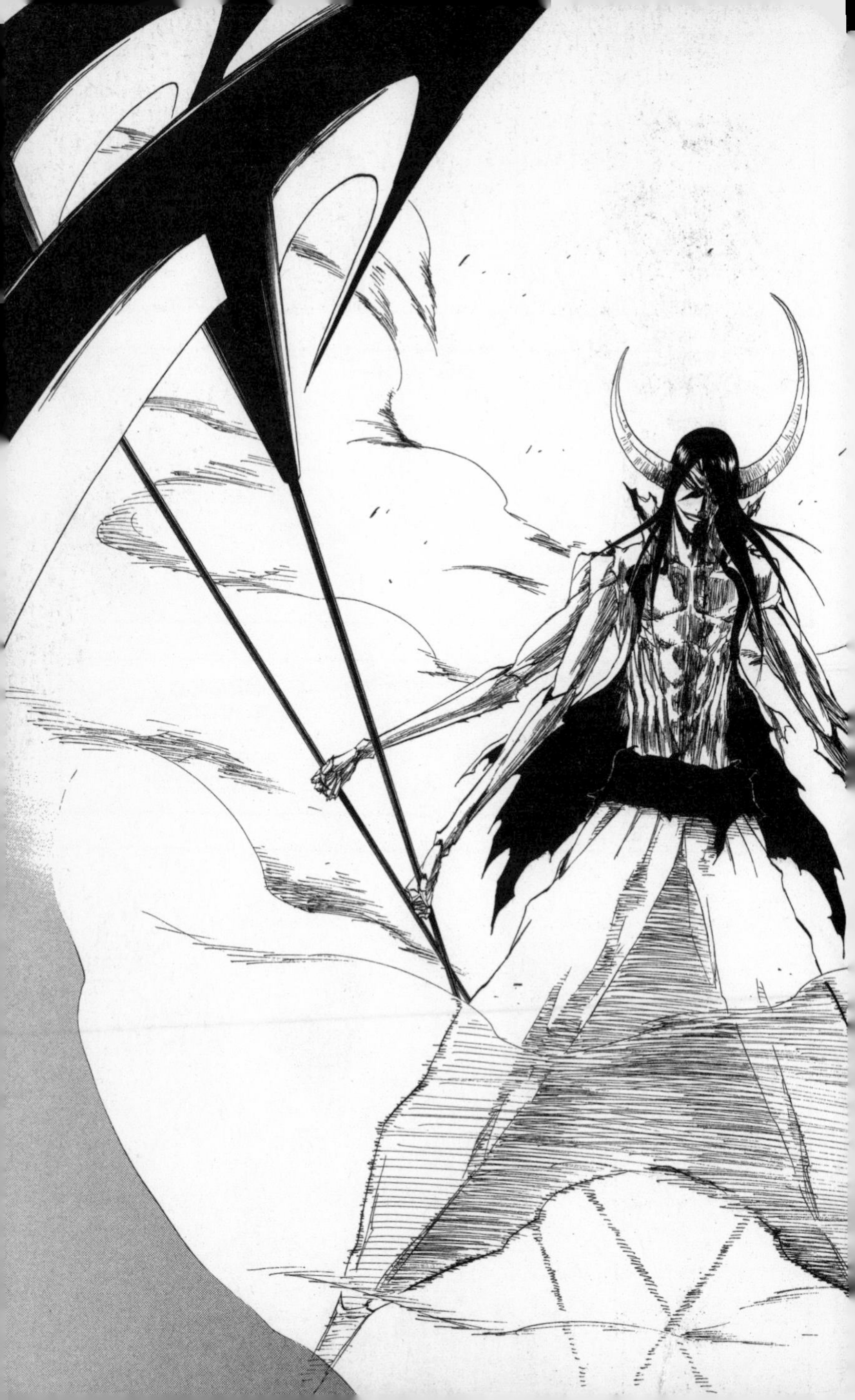

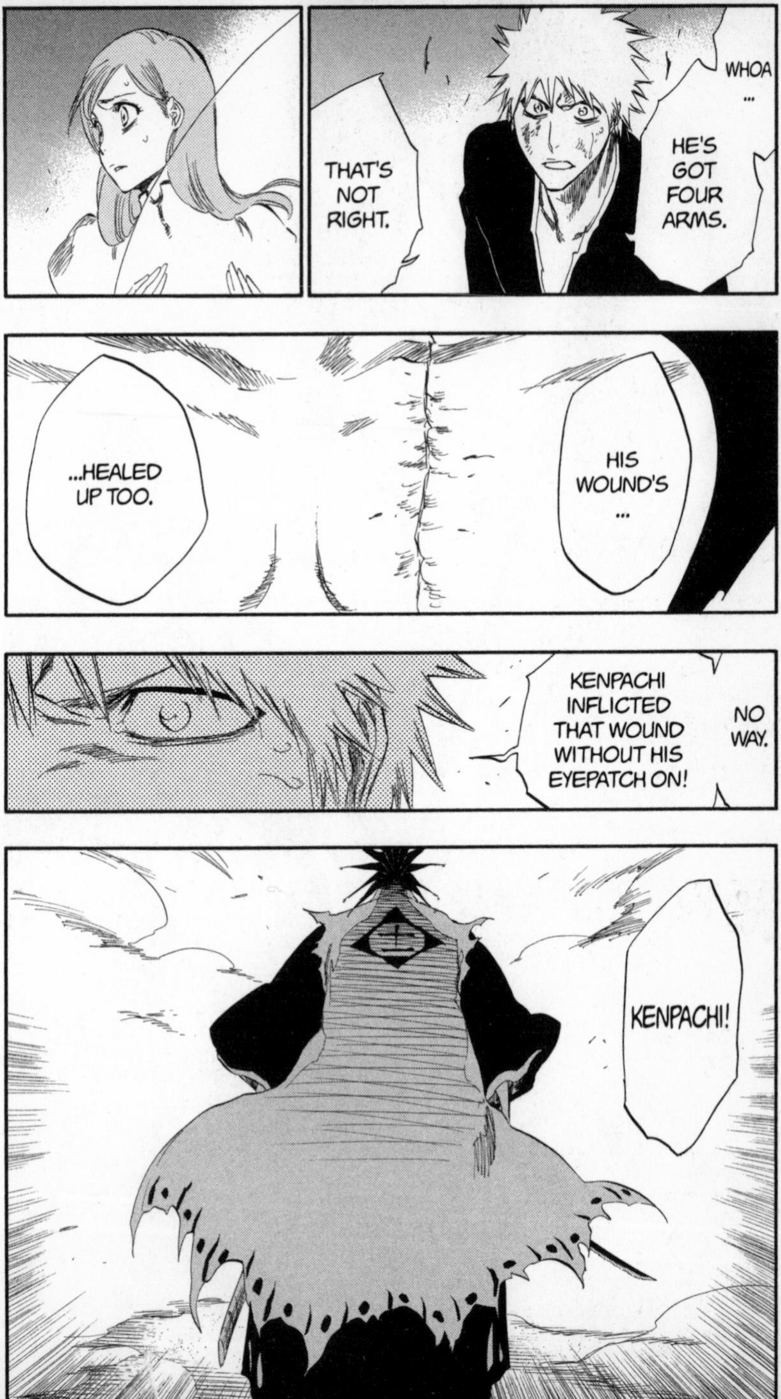
WHOA ...
HE'S GOT FOUR ARMS.
THAT'S NOT RIGHT.
HIS WOUND'S ...
...HEALED UP TOO.
NO WAY.
KENPACHI INFLICTED THAT WOUND WITHOUT HIS EYEPATCH ON!
KENPACHI!

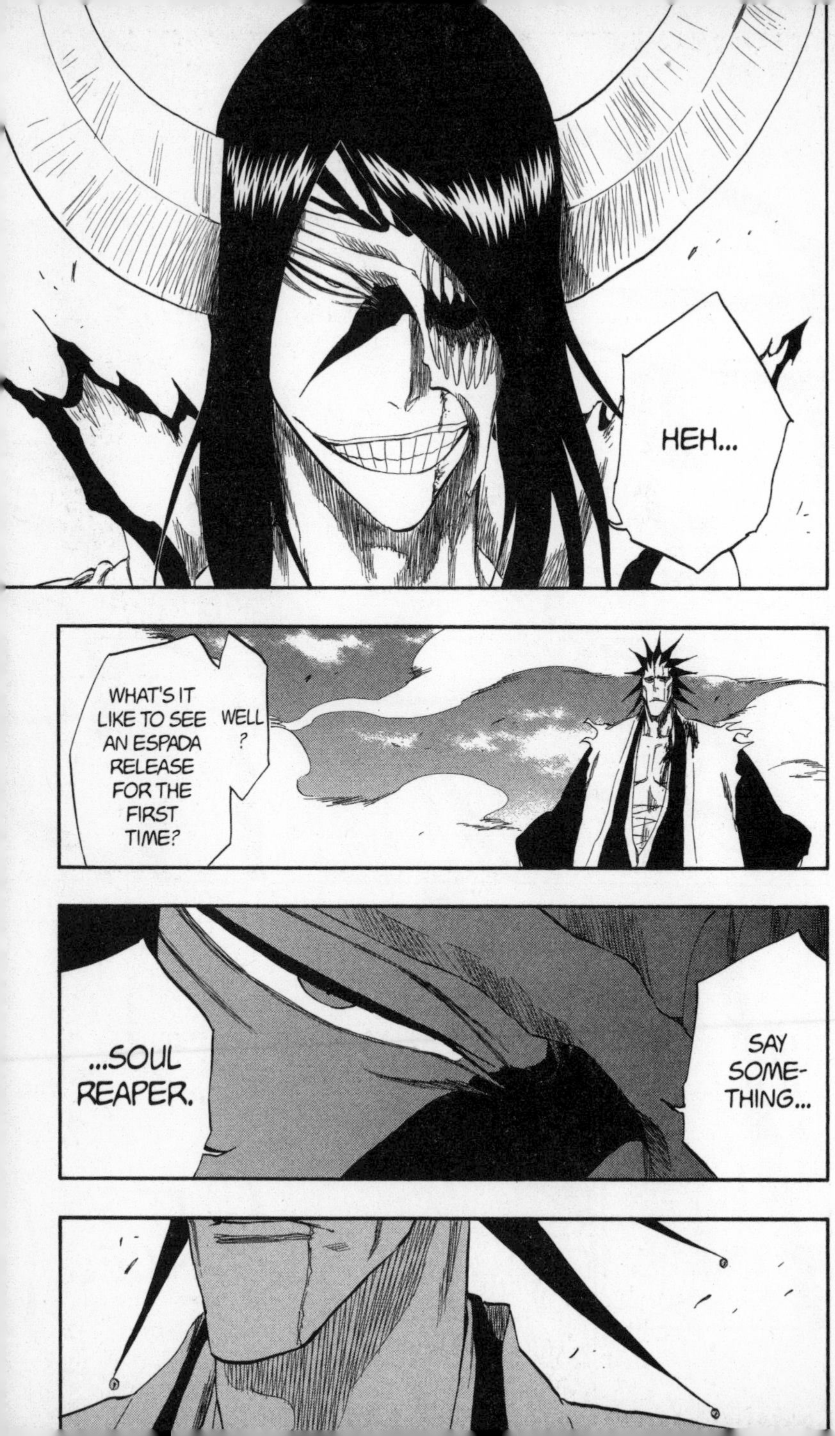
HEH...
WELL?
WHAT'S IT LIKE TO SEE AN ESPADA RELEASE FOR THE FIRST TIME?
SAY SOME-THING...
...SOUL REAPER.

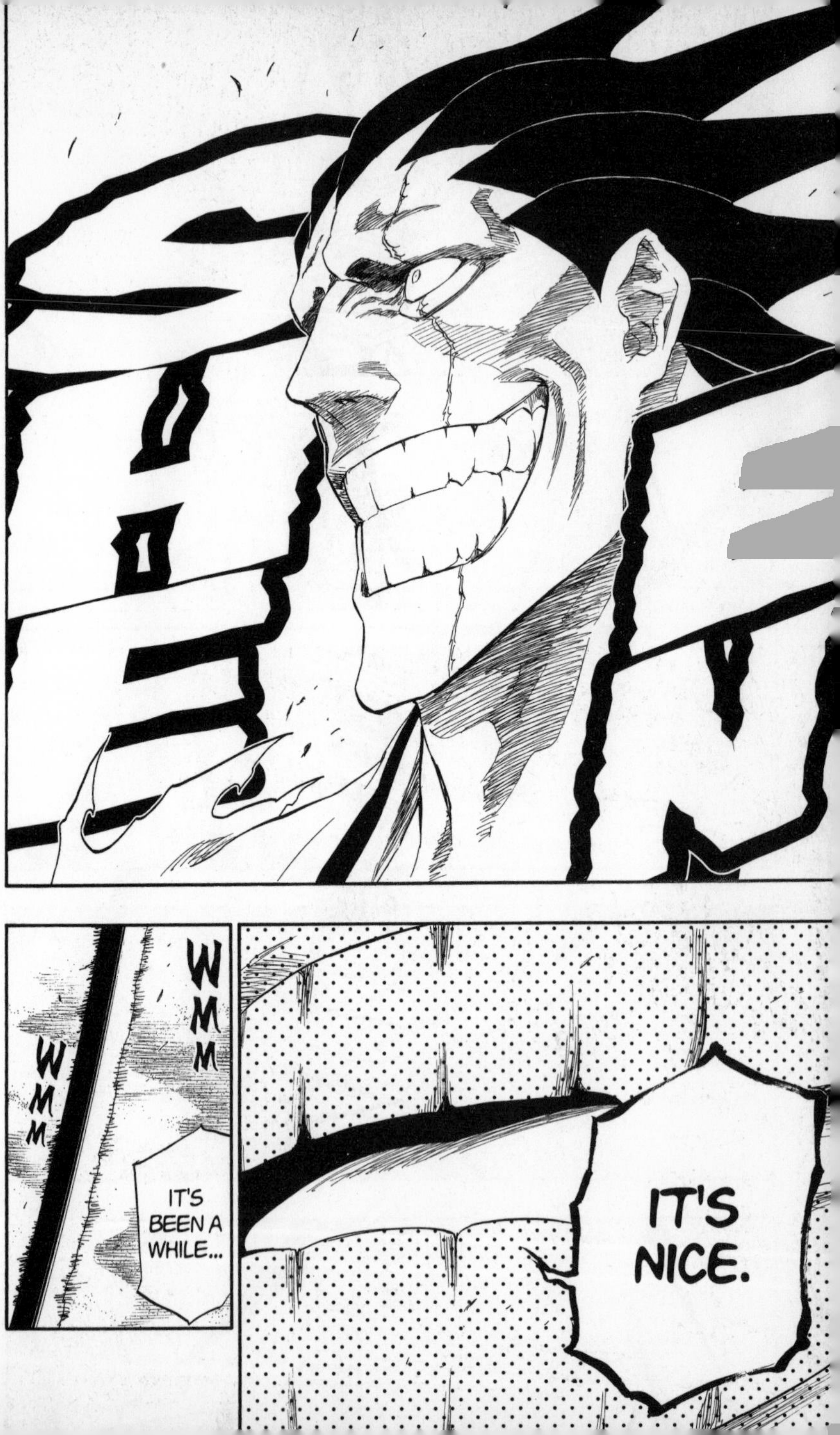
IT'S NICE.
WMM
WMM
IT'S BEEN A WHILE...

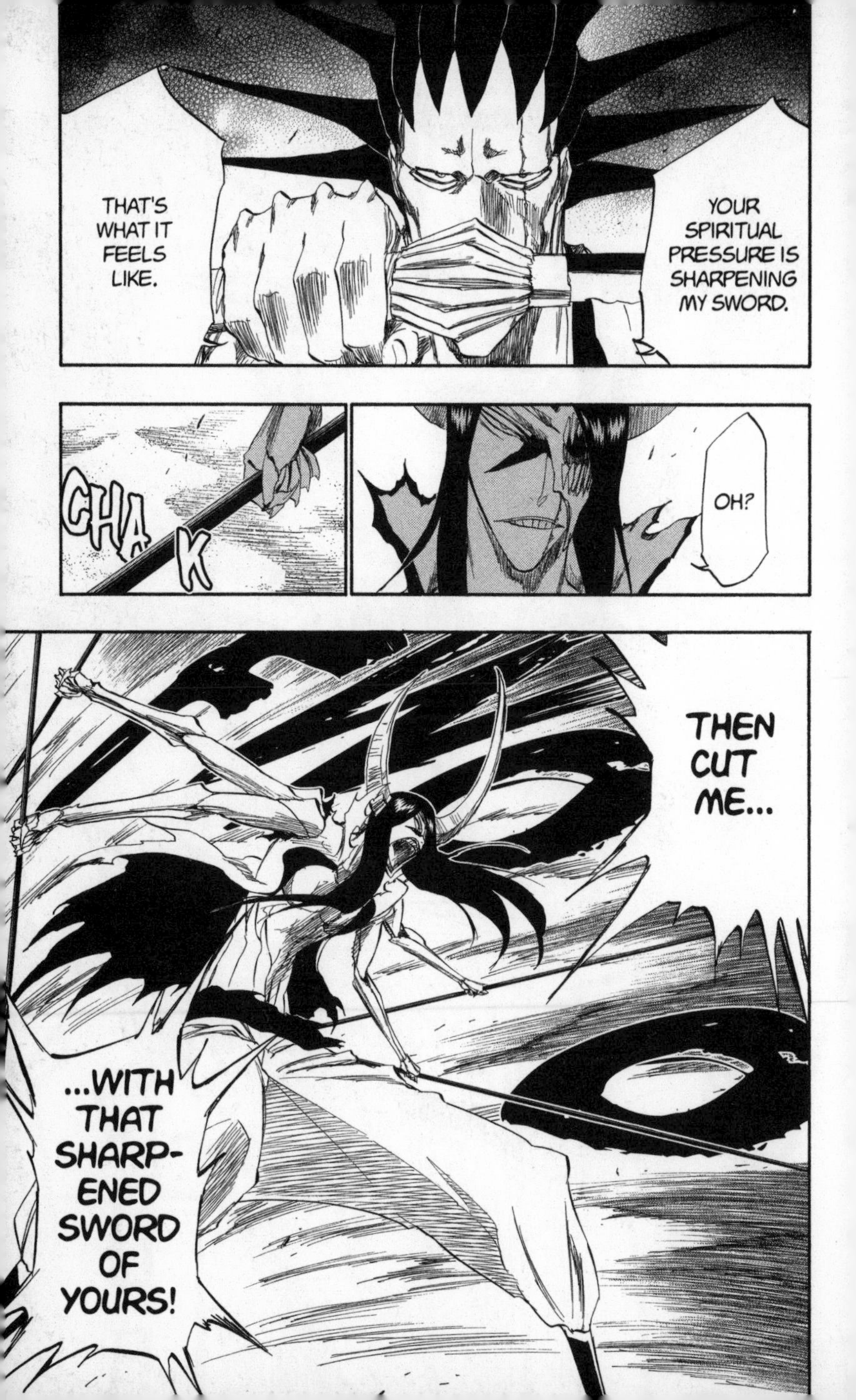
YOUR SPIRITUAL PRESSURE IS SHARPENING MY SWORD.
THAT'S WHAT IT FEELS LIKE.
OH?
CHAK
THEN CUT ME...
...WITH THAT SHARP-ENED SWORD OF YOURS!

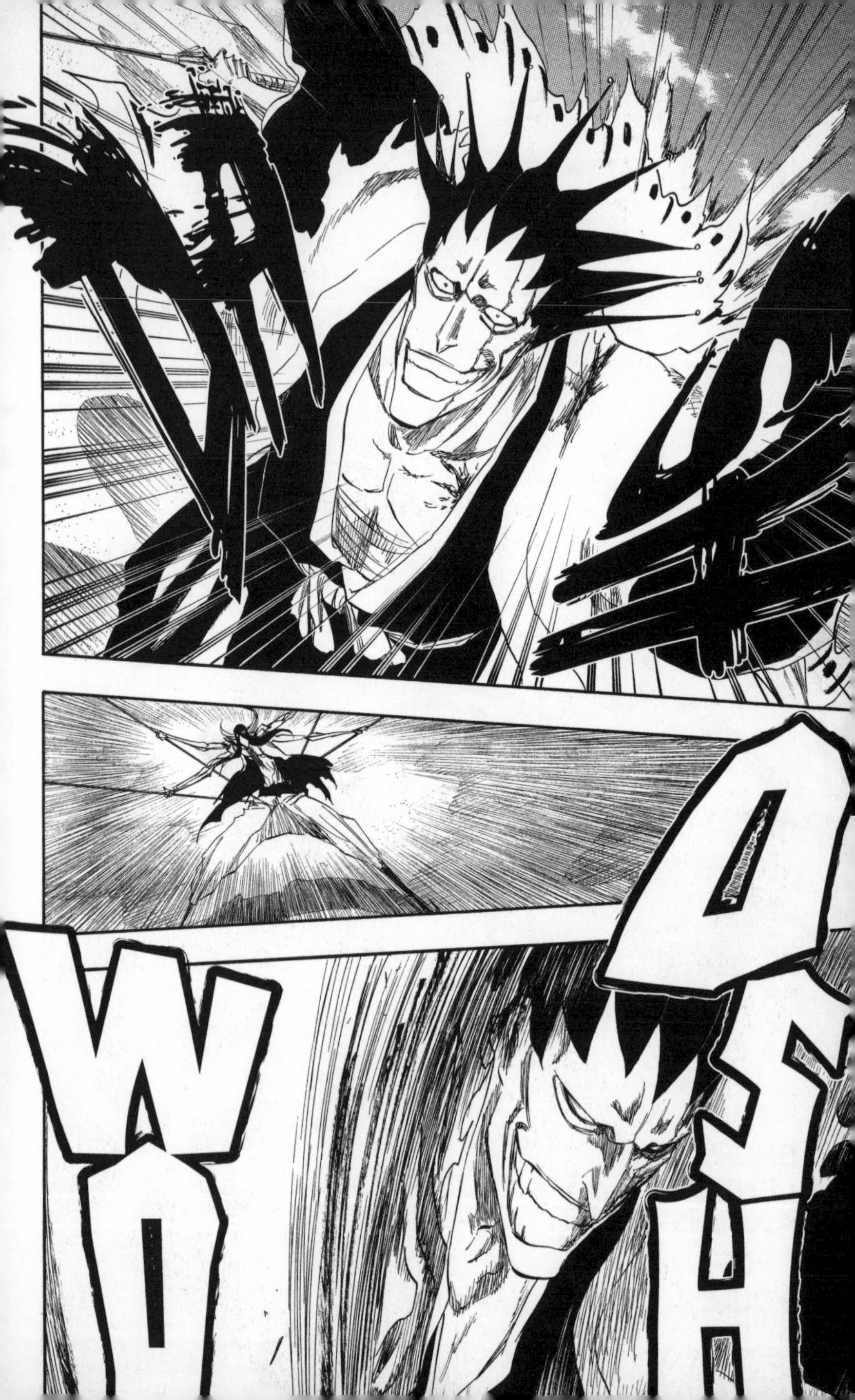

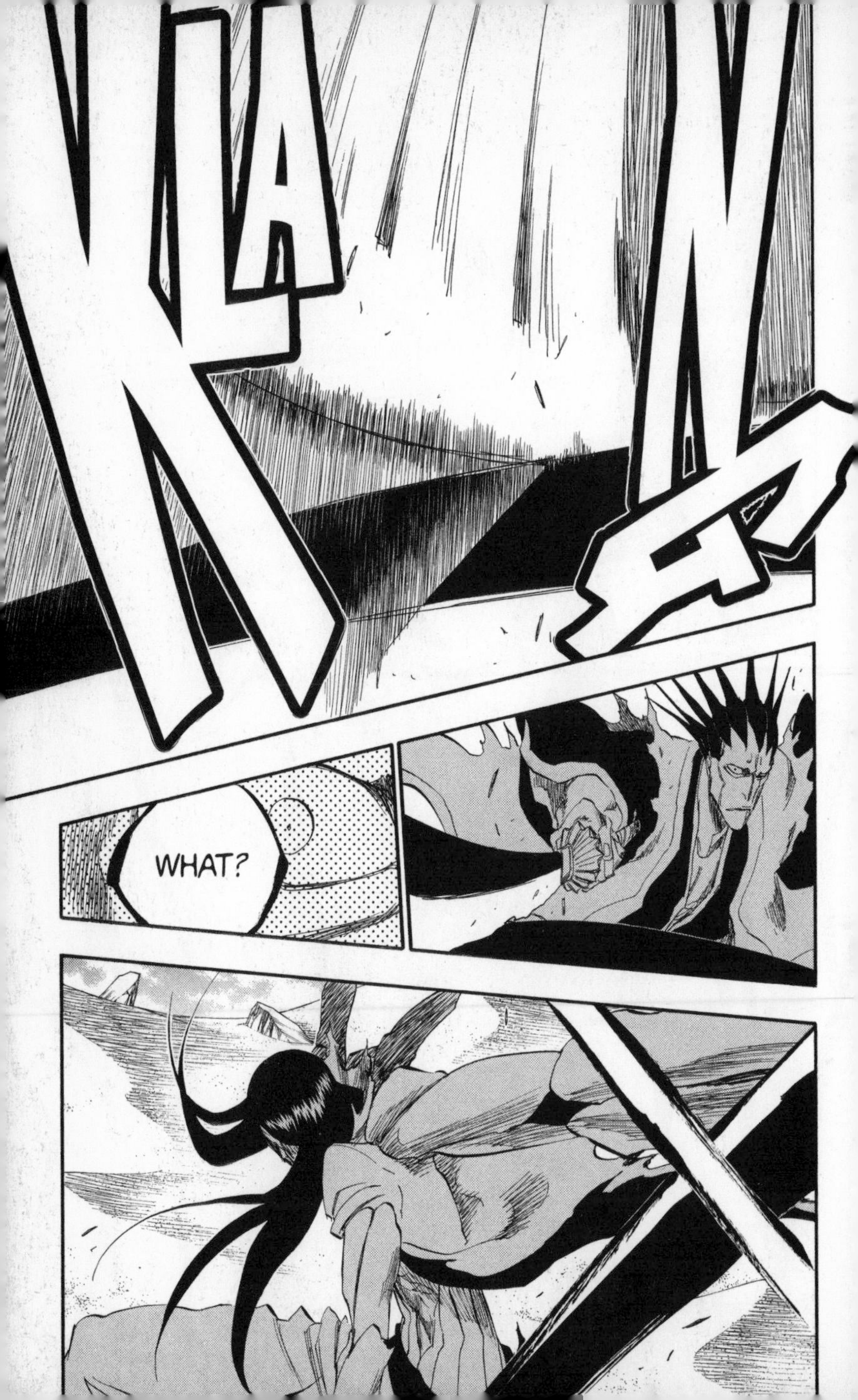
WHAT?

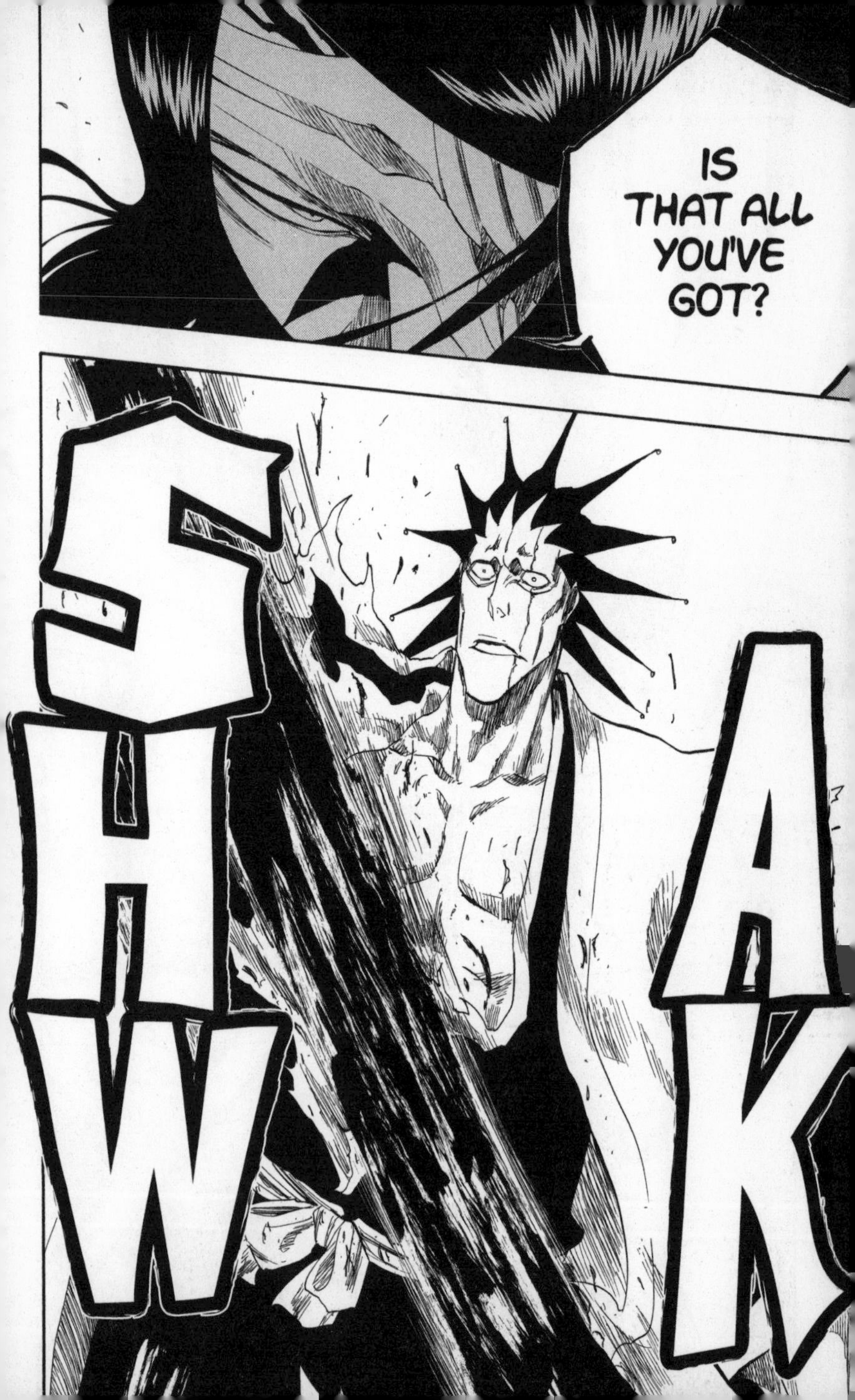
IS THAT ALL YOU'VE GOT?
SHWAK

READ THIS WAY

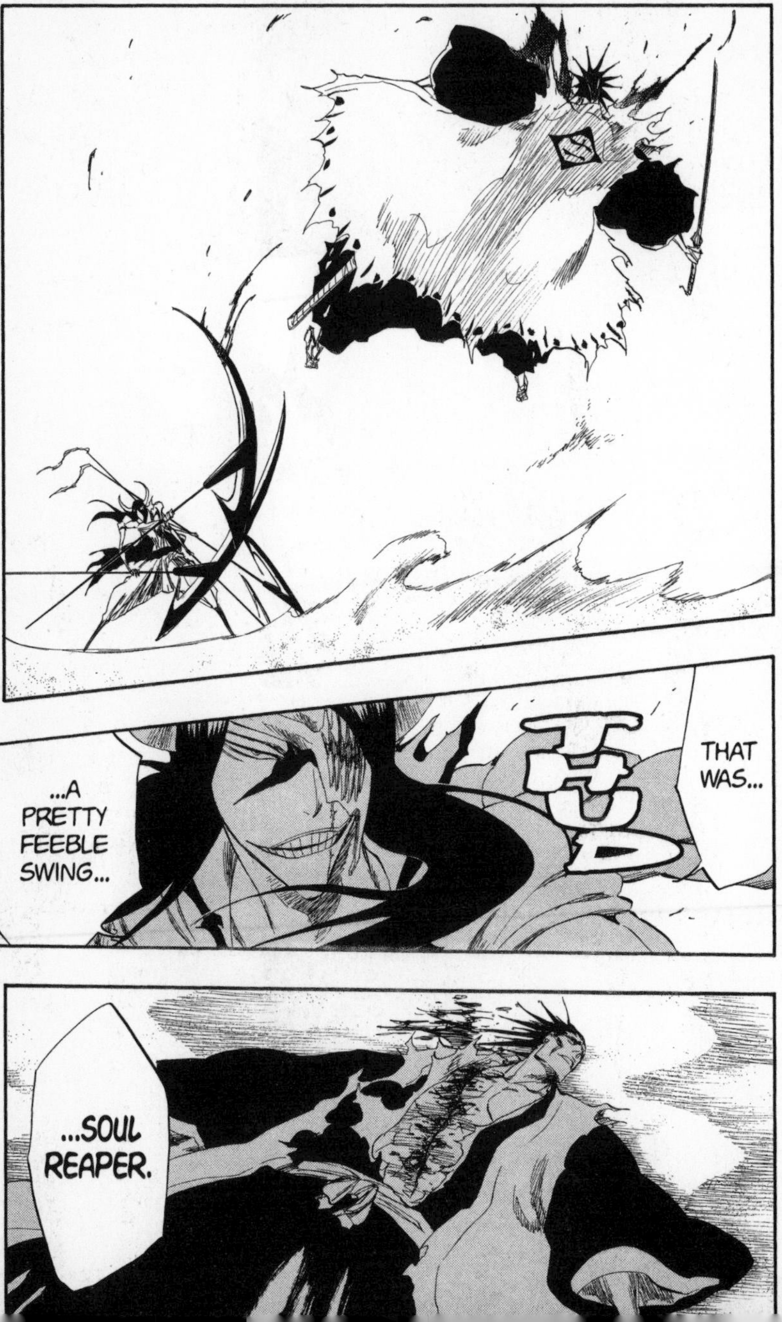
THAT WAS...
THUD
...A PRETTY FEEBLE SWING...
...SOUL REAPER.

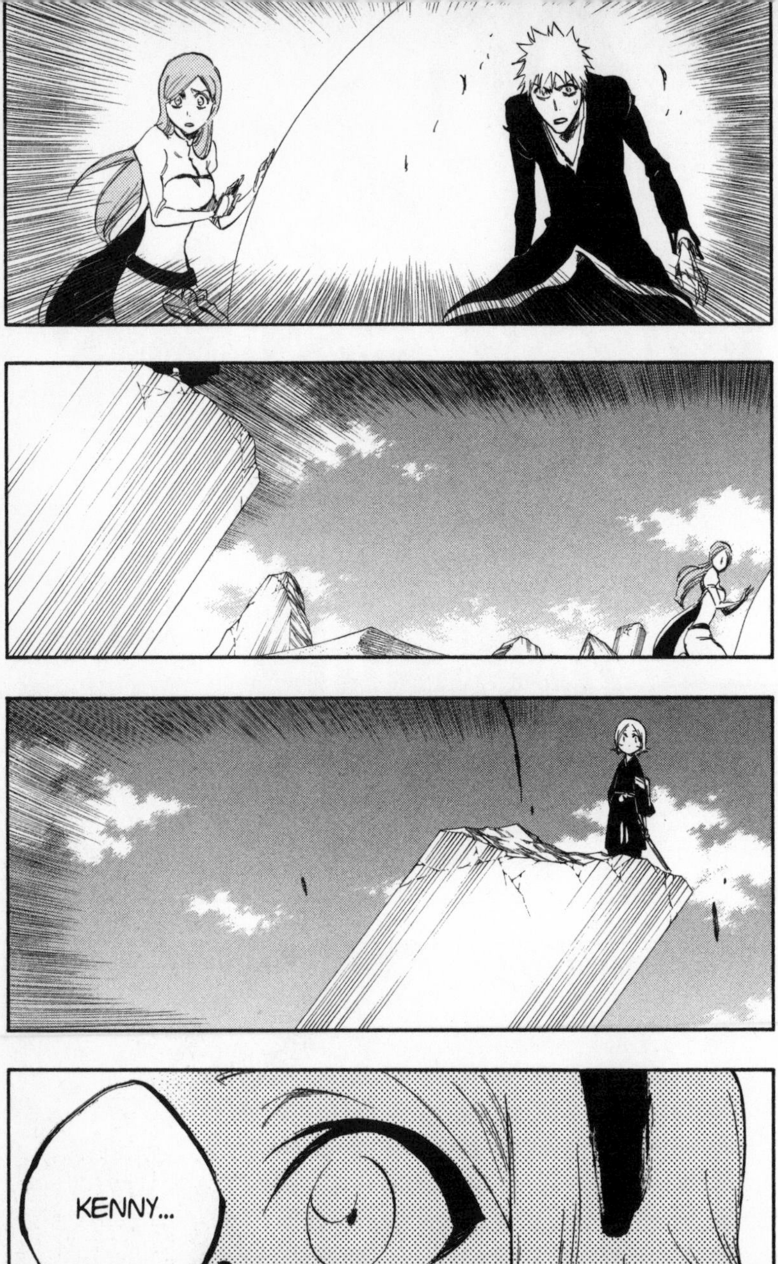
KENNY...

310. FOUR ARMS TO KILLING YOU

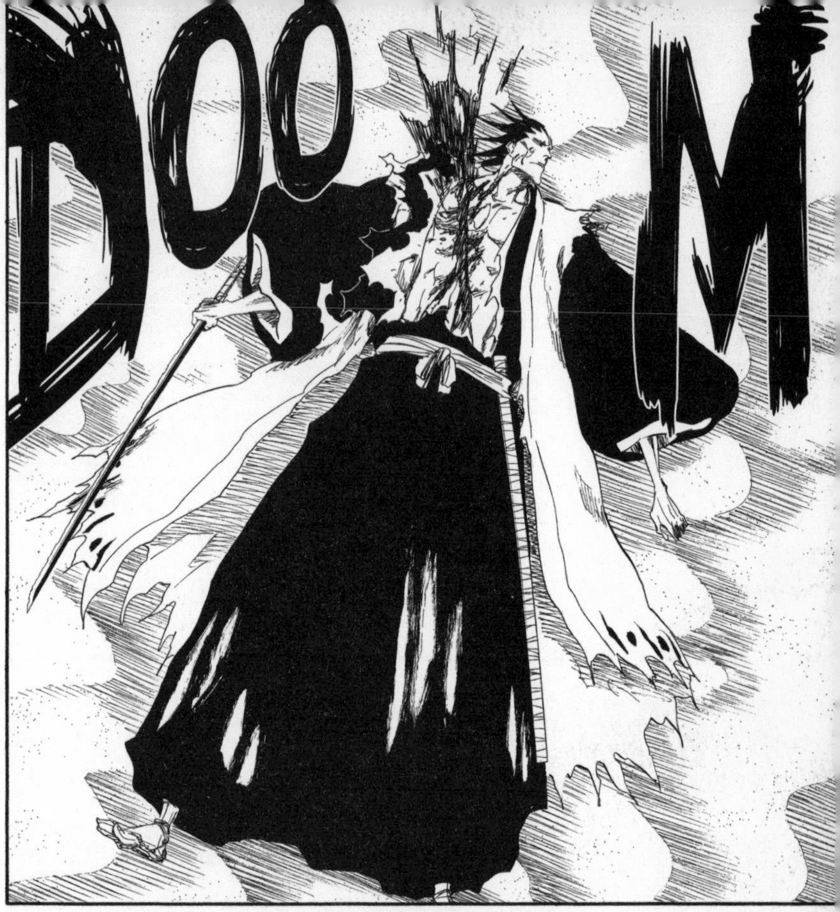
DOOM

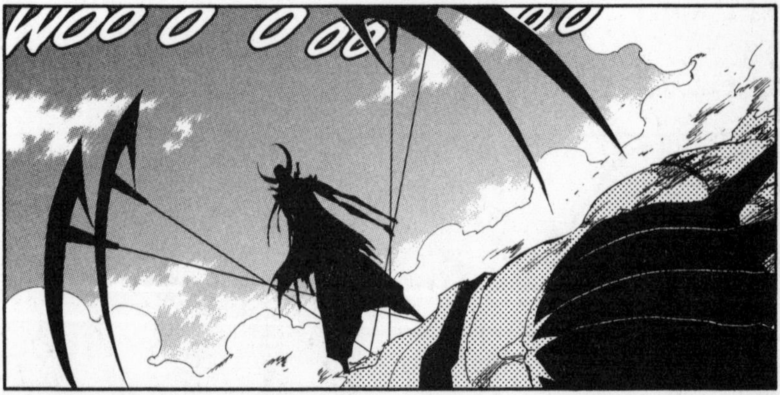
WOO O O OO

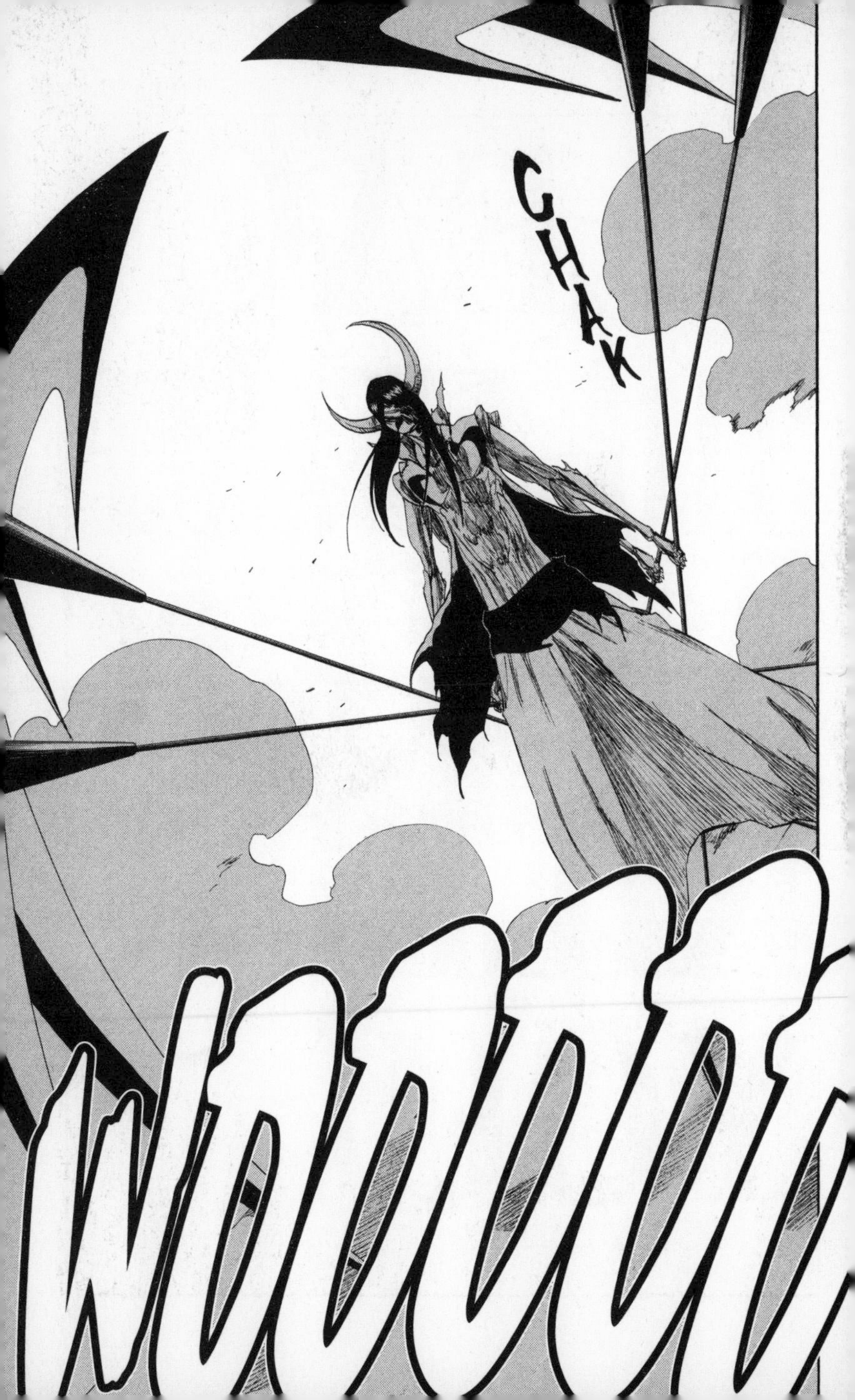
CHAK

BLEACH 310. FOUR ARMS TO KILLING YOU,

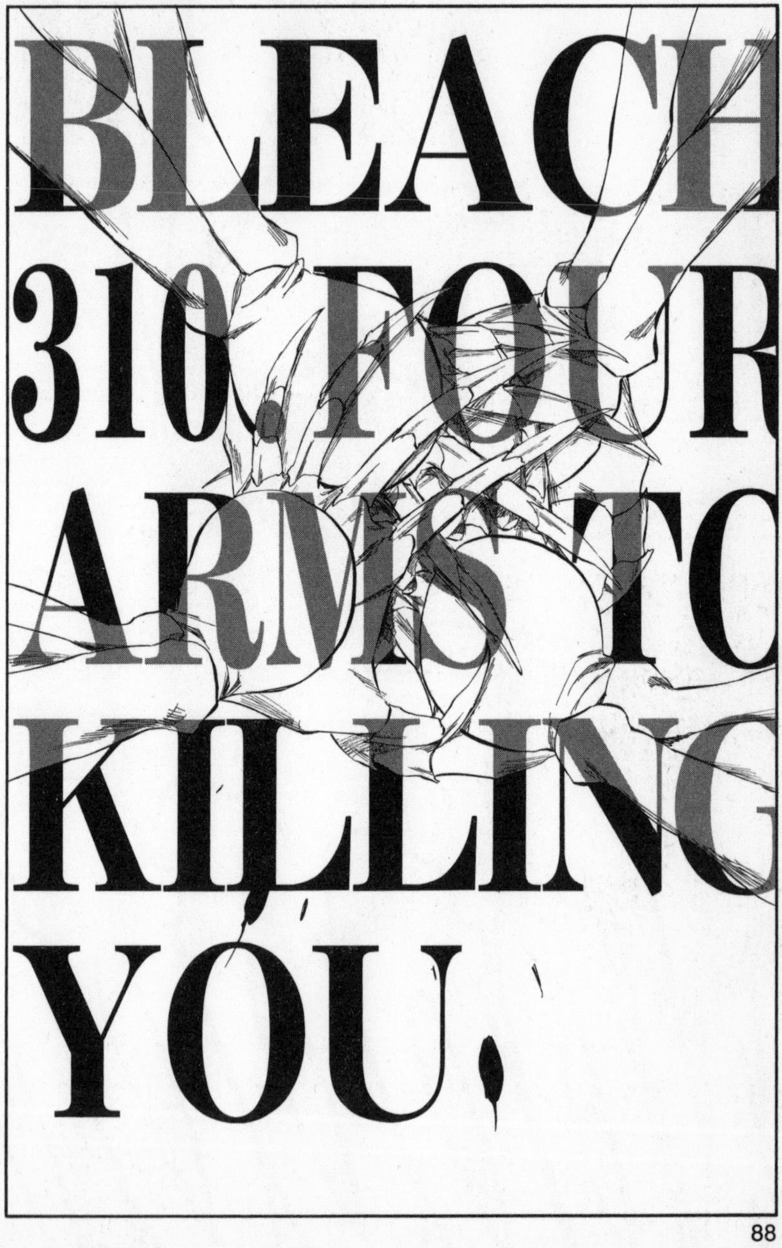

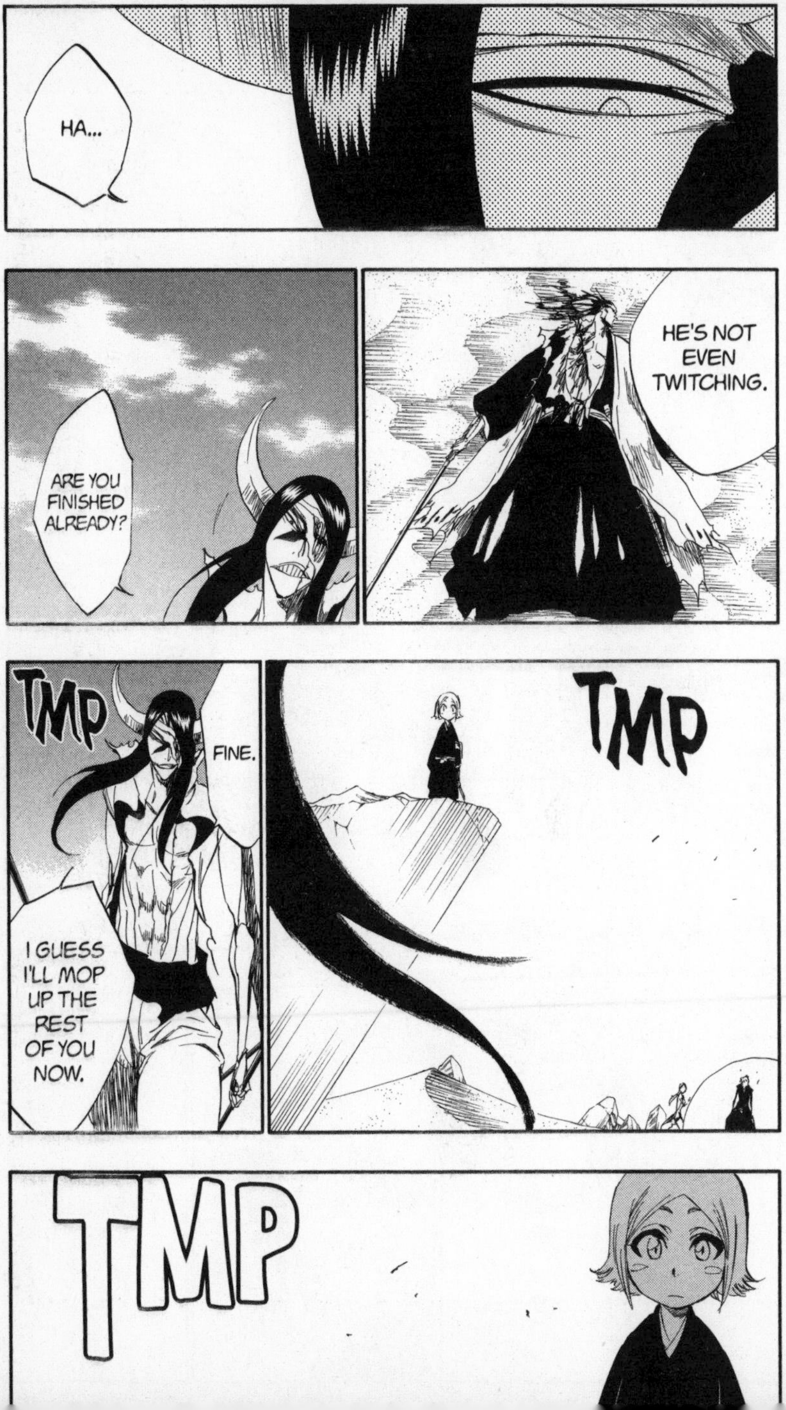
HA...
HE'S NOT EVEN TWITCHING.
ARE YOU FINISHED ALREADY?
TMP
TMP
FINE.
I GUESS I'LL MOP UP THE REST OF YOU NOW.
TMP

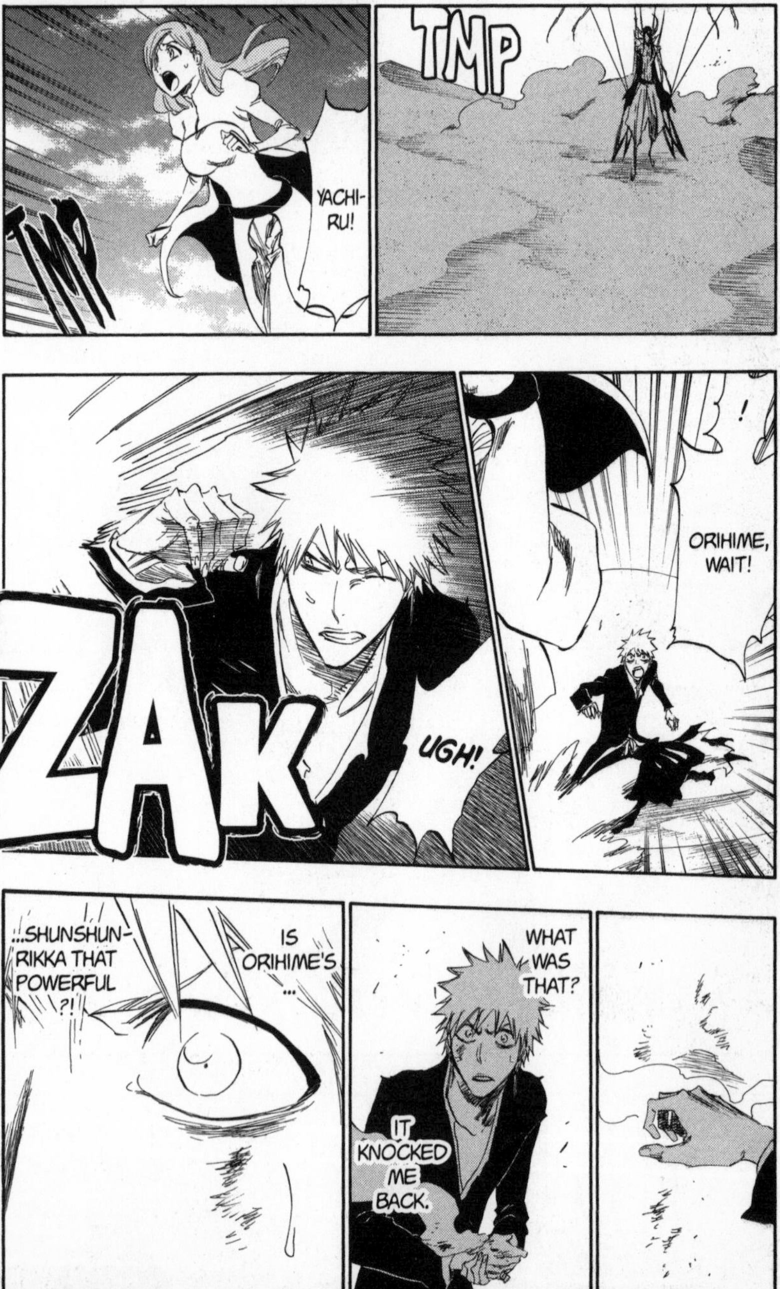
TMP
YACHI-RU!
TMP
!
ORIHIME, WAIT!
UGH!
ZAK
WHAT WAS THAT?
IT KNOCKED ME BACK.
IS ORIHIME'S...
...SHUNSHUN-RIKKA THAT POWERFUL?!

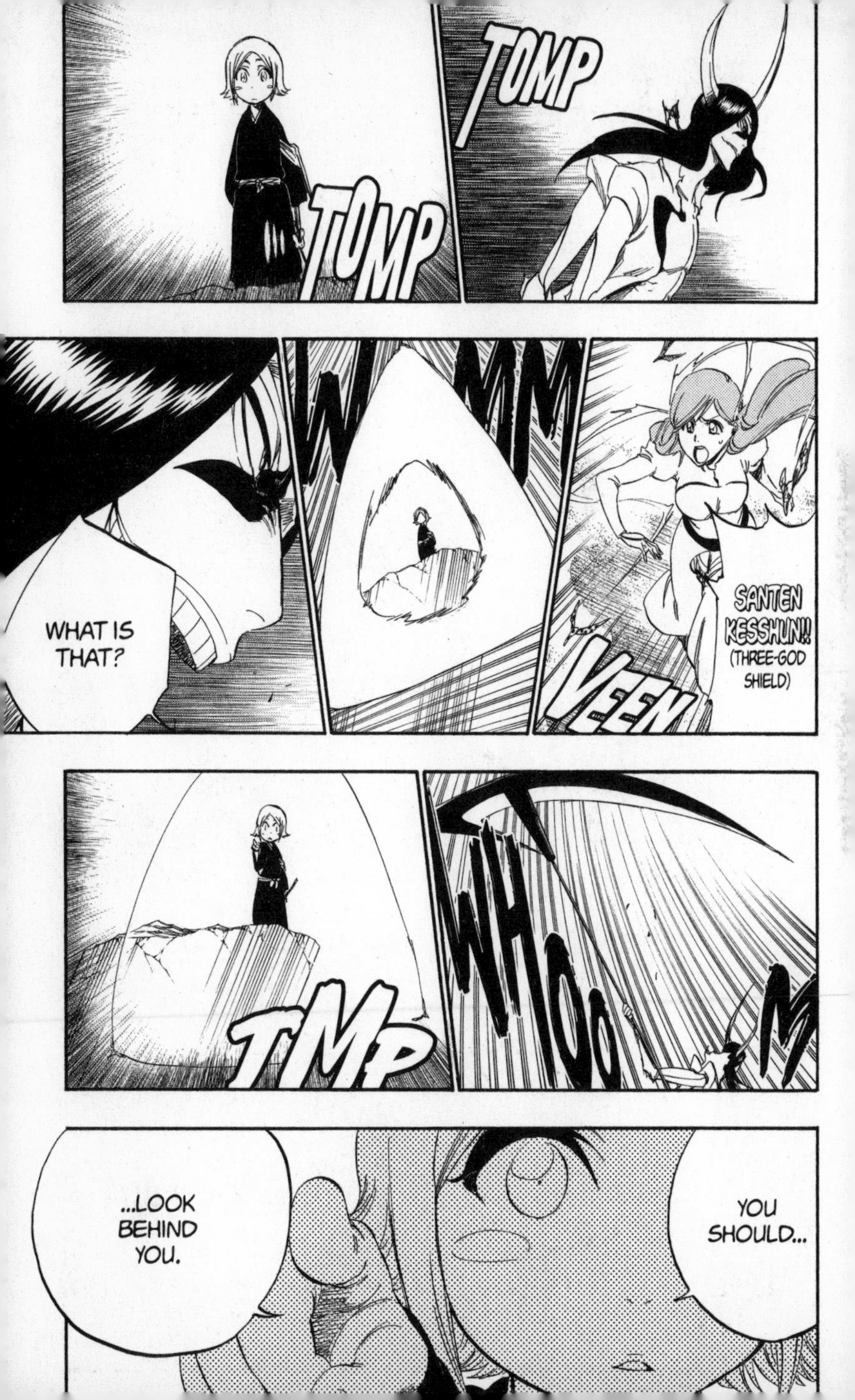
TOMP
TOMP
SANTEN KESSHUN!! (THREE-GOD SHIELD)
VEEN
WMM
WHAT IS THAT?
WHOOM
TMP
YOU SHOULD...
...LOOK BEHIND YOU.

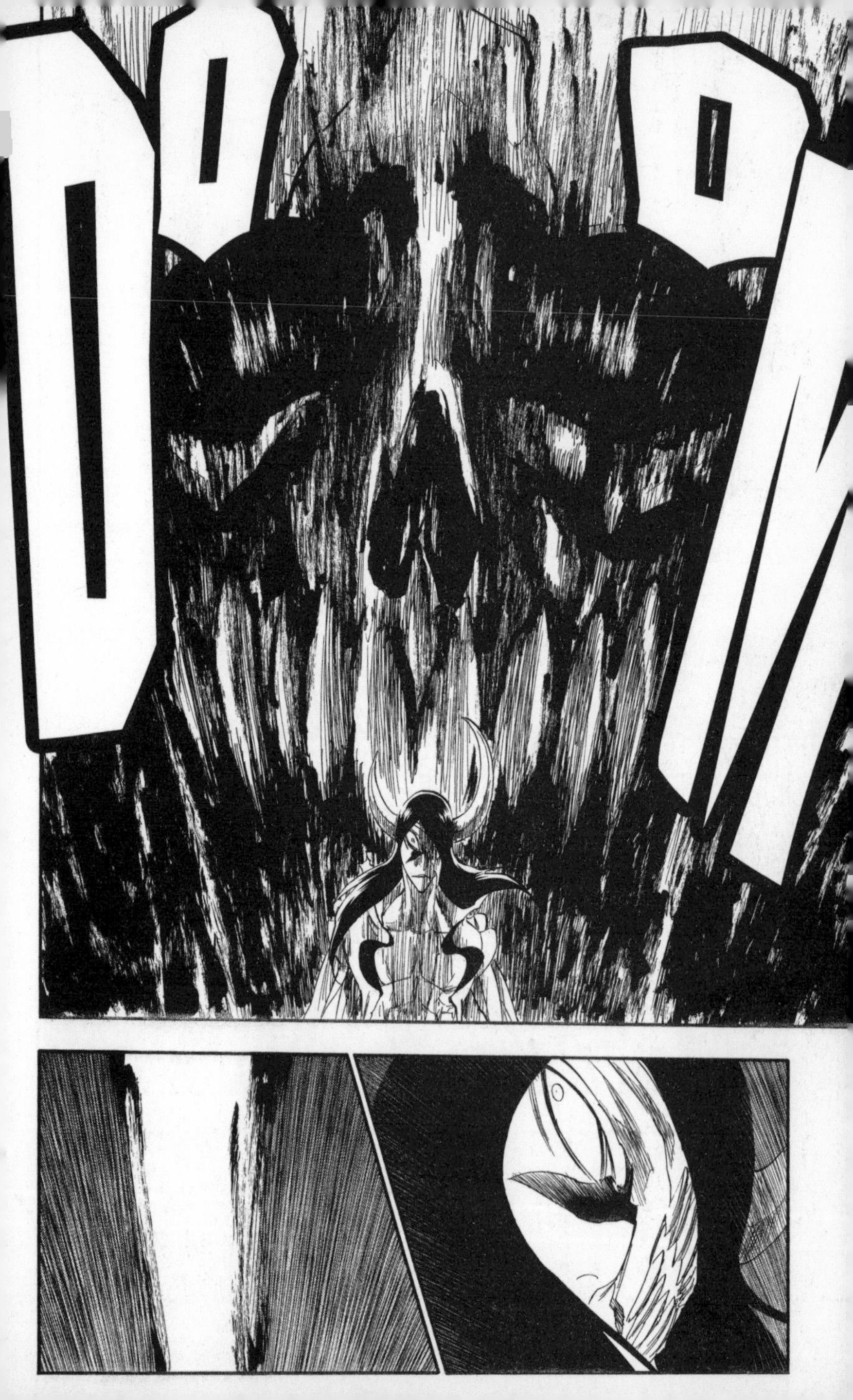

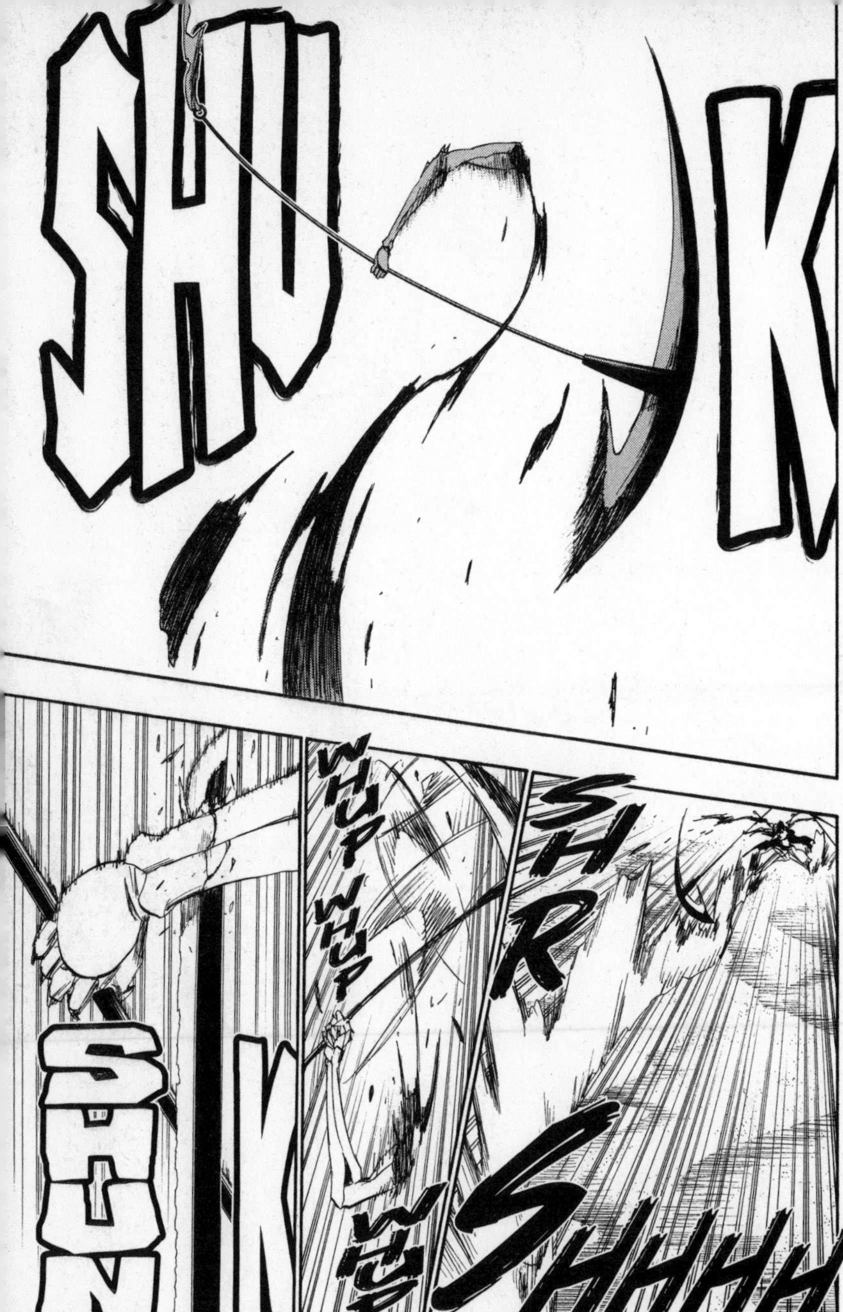
SHUNK
SHR
SHHHH
WHUP WHUP
WHUP
SCHNK

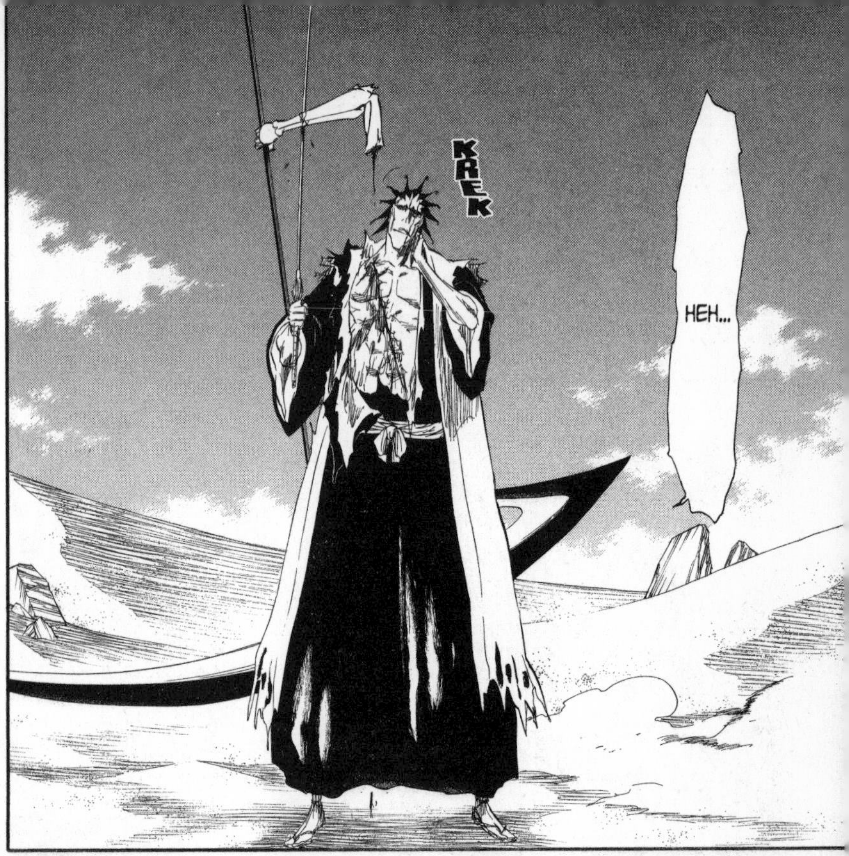
KREK
HEH...
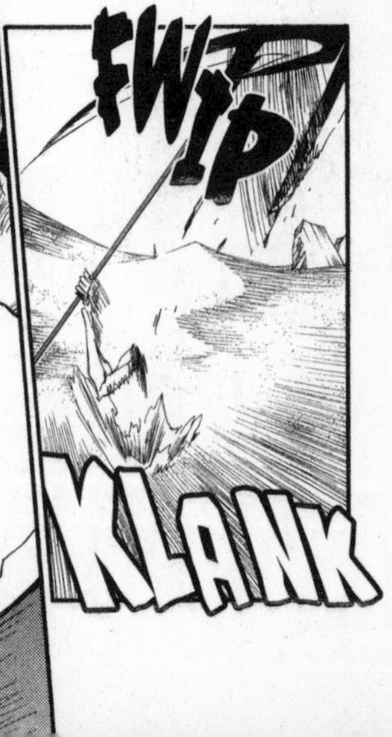
FWIP
KLANK
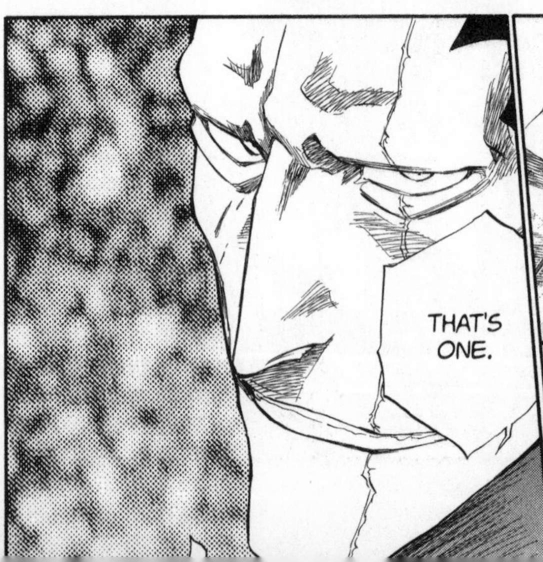
THAT'S ONE.

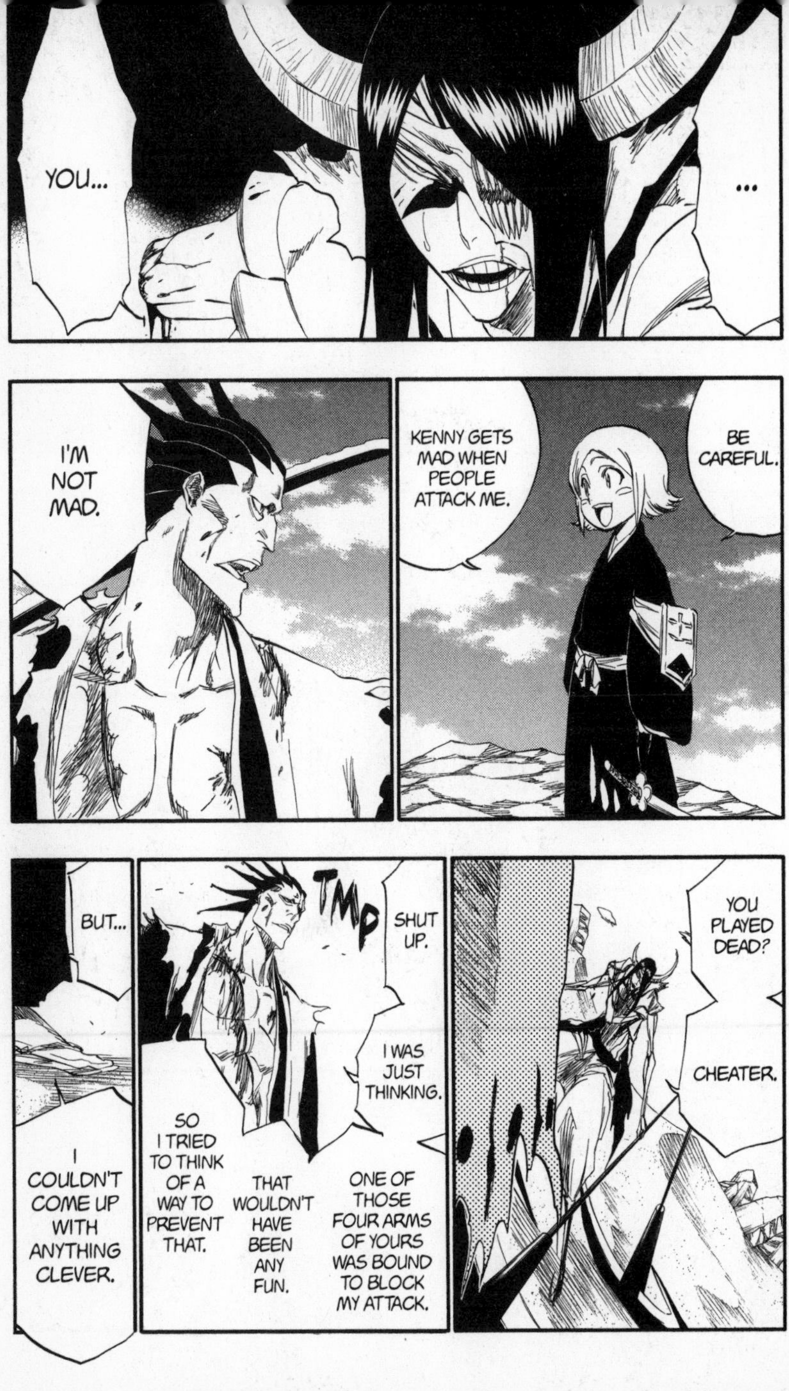
...
YOU...
BE CAREFUL.
KENNY GETS MAD WHEN PEOPLE ATTACK ME.
I'M NOT MAD.
YOU PLAYED DEAD?
CHEATER.
TMP
SHUT UP.
I WAS JUST THINKING.
ONE OF THOSE FOUR ARMS OF YOURS WAS BOUND TO BLOCK MY ATTACK.
THAT WOULDN'T HAVE BEEN ANY FUN.
SO I TRIED TO THINK OF A WAY TO PREVENT THAT.
BUT...
I COULDN'T COME UP WITH ANYTHING CLEVER.

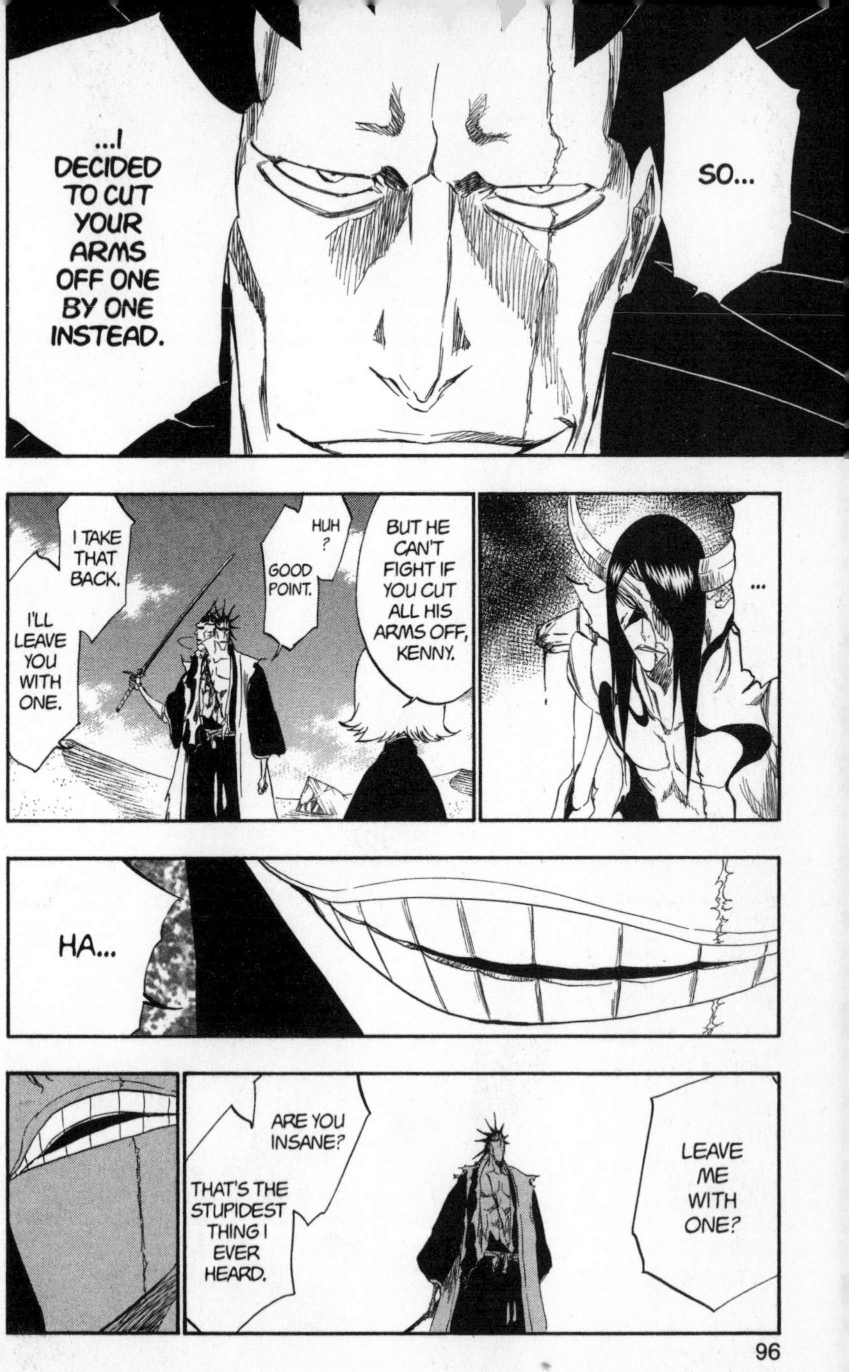
SO...
...I DECIDED TO CUT YOUR ARMS OFF ONE BY ONE INSTEAD.
...
BUT HE CAN'T FIGHT IF YOU CUT ALL HIS ARMS OFF, KENNY.
HUH?
GOOD POINT.
I TAKE THAT BACK.
I'LL LEAVE YOU WITH ONE.
HA...
LEAVE ME WITH ONE?
ARE YOU INSANE?
THAT'S THE STUPIDEST THING I EVER HEARD.

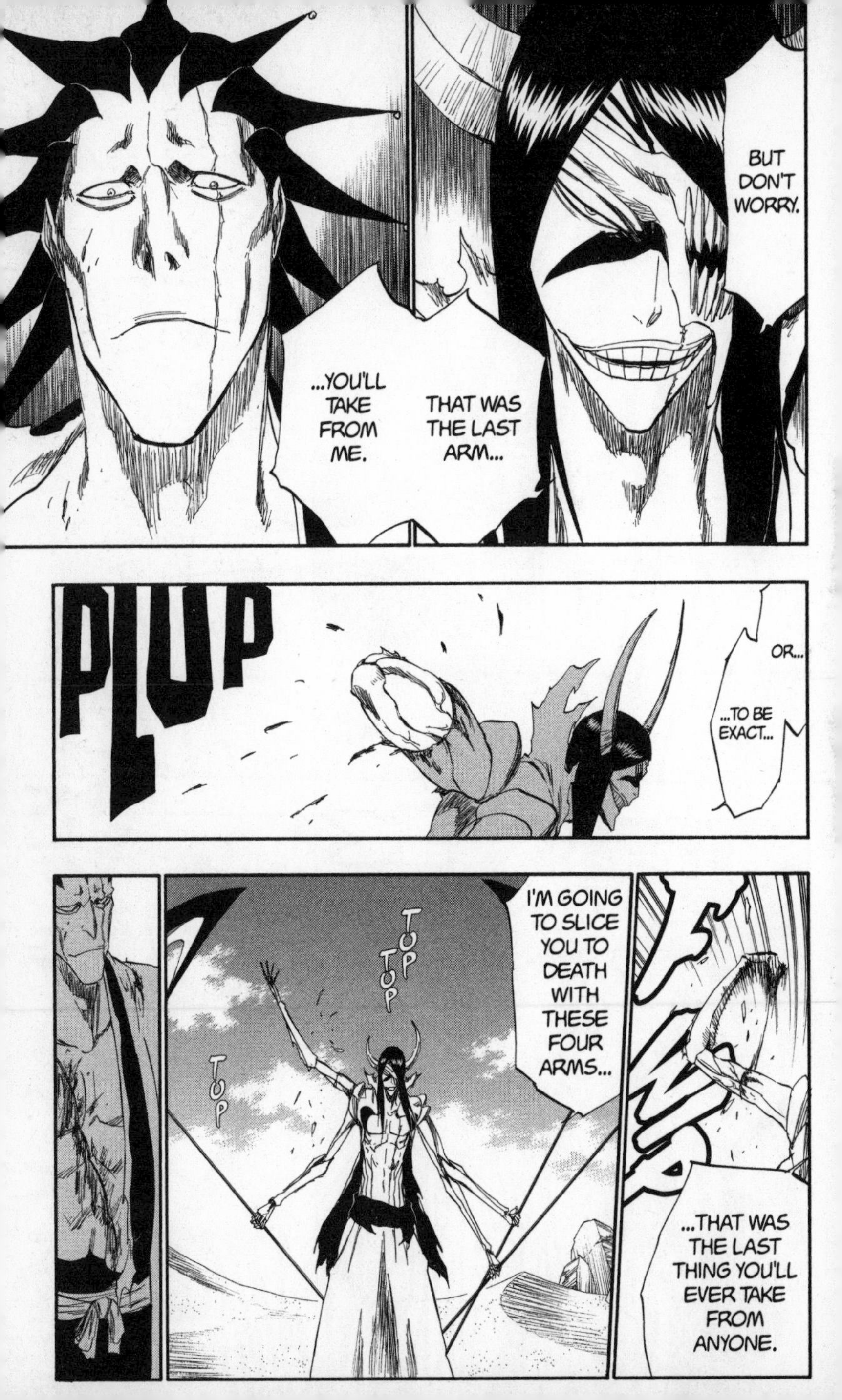
BUT DON'T WORRY.
THAT WAS THE LAST ARM...
...YOU'LL TAKE FROM ME.
OR...
...TO BE EXACT...
PLUP
...THAT WAS THE LAST THING YOU'LL EVER TAKE FROM ANYONE.
I'M GOING TO SLICE YOU TO DEATH WITH THESE FOUR ARMS...
TOP
TOP
TOP
TOP

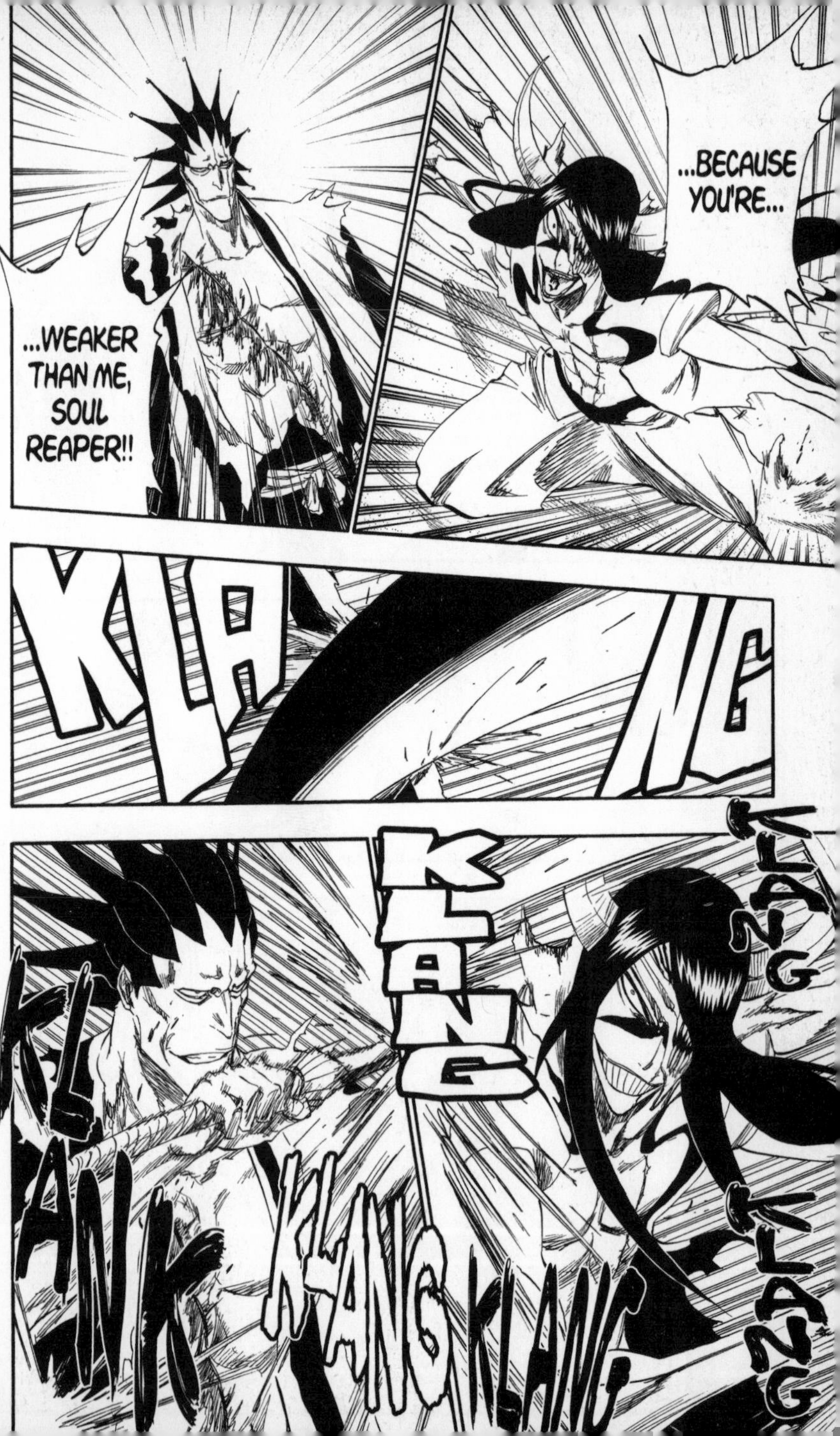
...BECAUSE YOU'RE...
...WEAKER THAN ME, SOUL REAPER!!
KLANG
KLANG
KLANG
KLANG
KLANG KLANG
KLANK

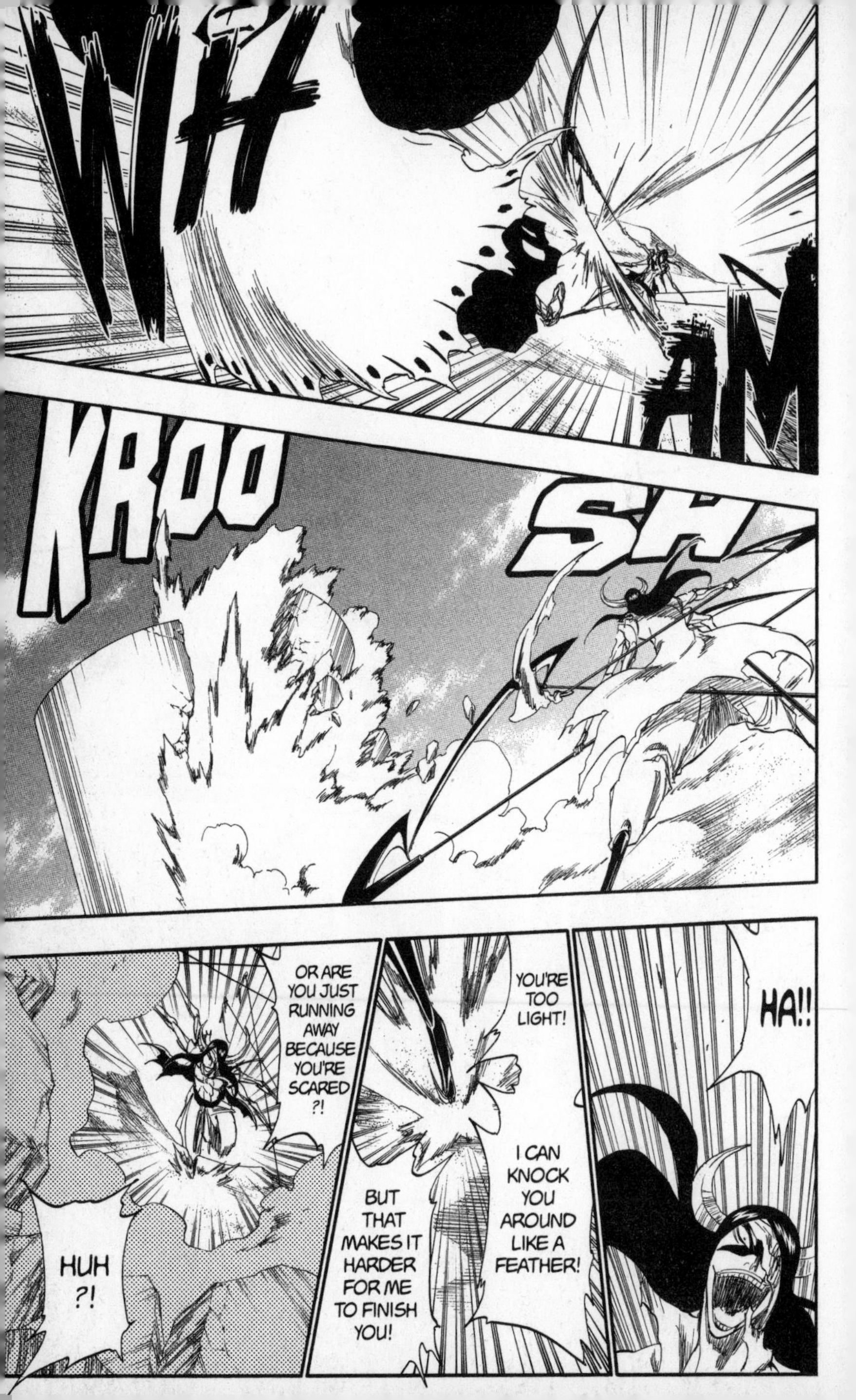

WH
AM
KROO
SH
HA!!
YOU'RE TOO LIGHT!
I CAN KNOCK YOU AROUND LIKE A FEATHER!
BUT THAT MAKES IT HARDER FOR ME TO FINISH YOU!
OR ARE YOU JUST RUNNING AWAY BECAUSE YOU'RE SCARED?!
HUH?!

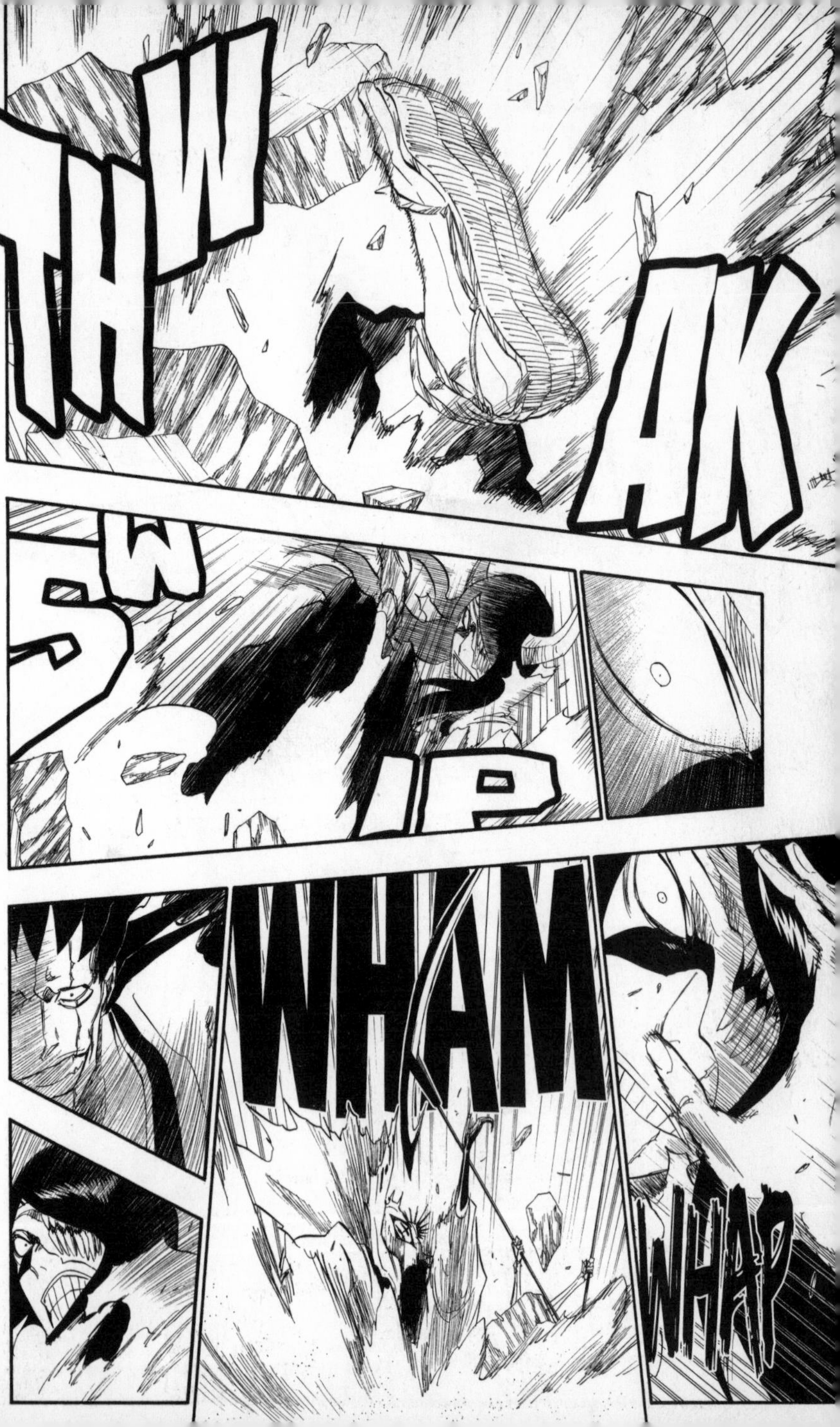
THWAK
SWIP
WHAP
WHAM

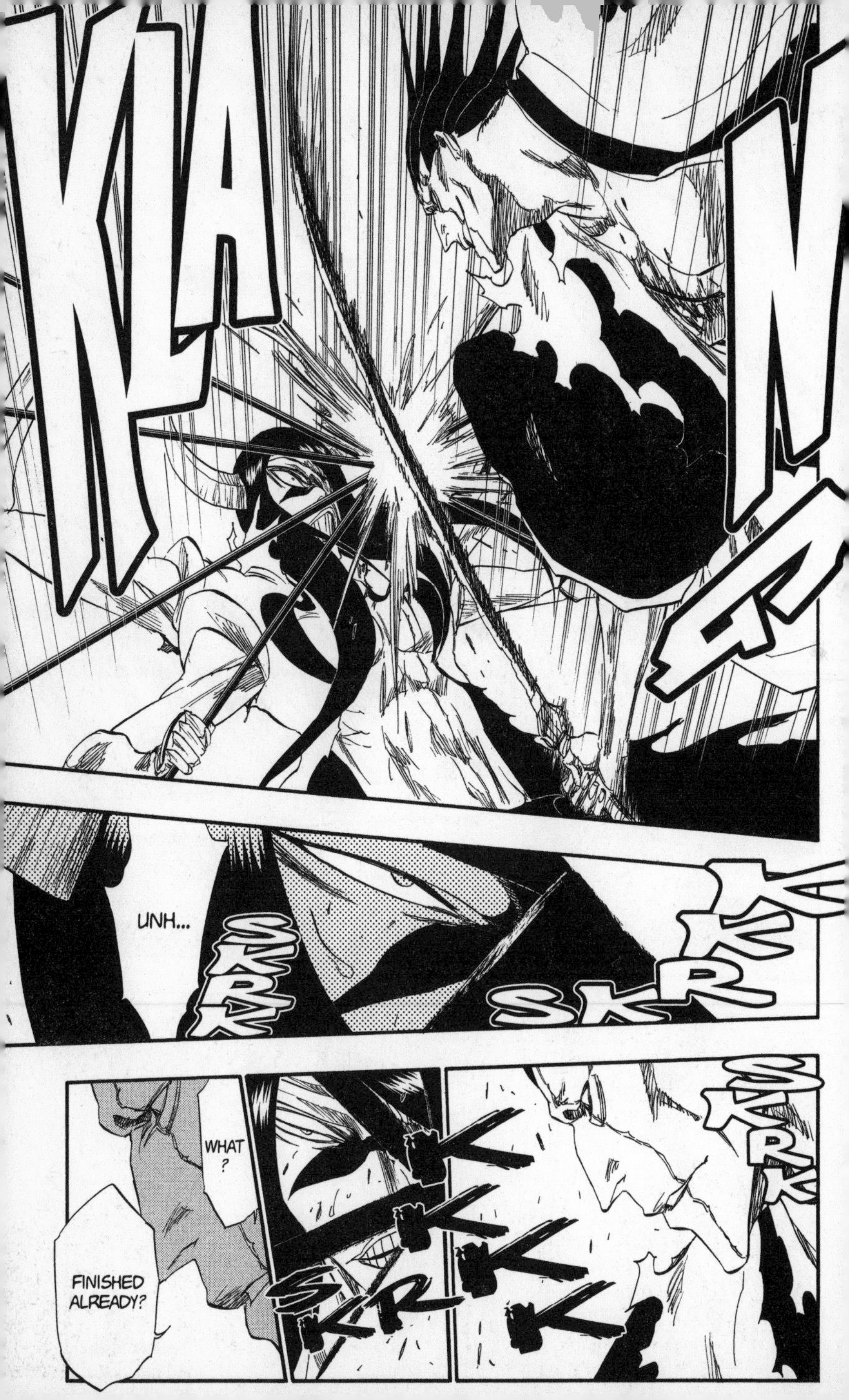
KLANG
SKRK
UNH...
SKRK
SKRK
SKRK
WHAT?
FINISHED ALREADY?

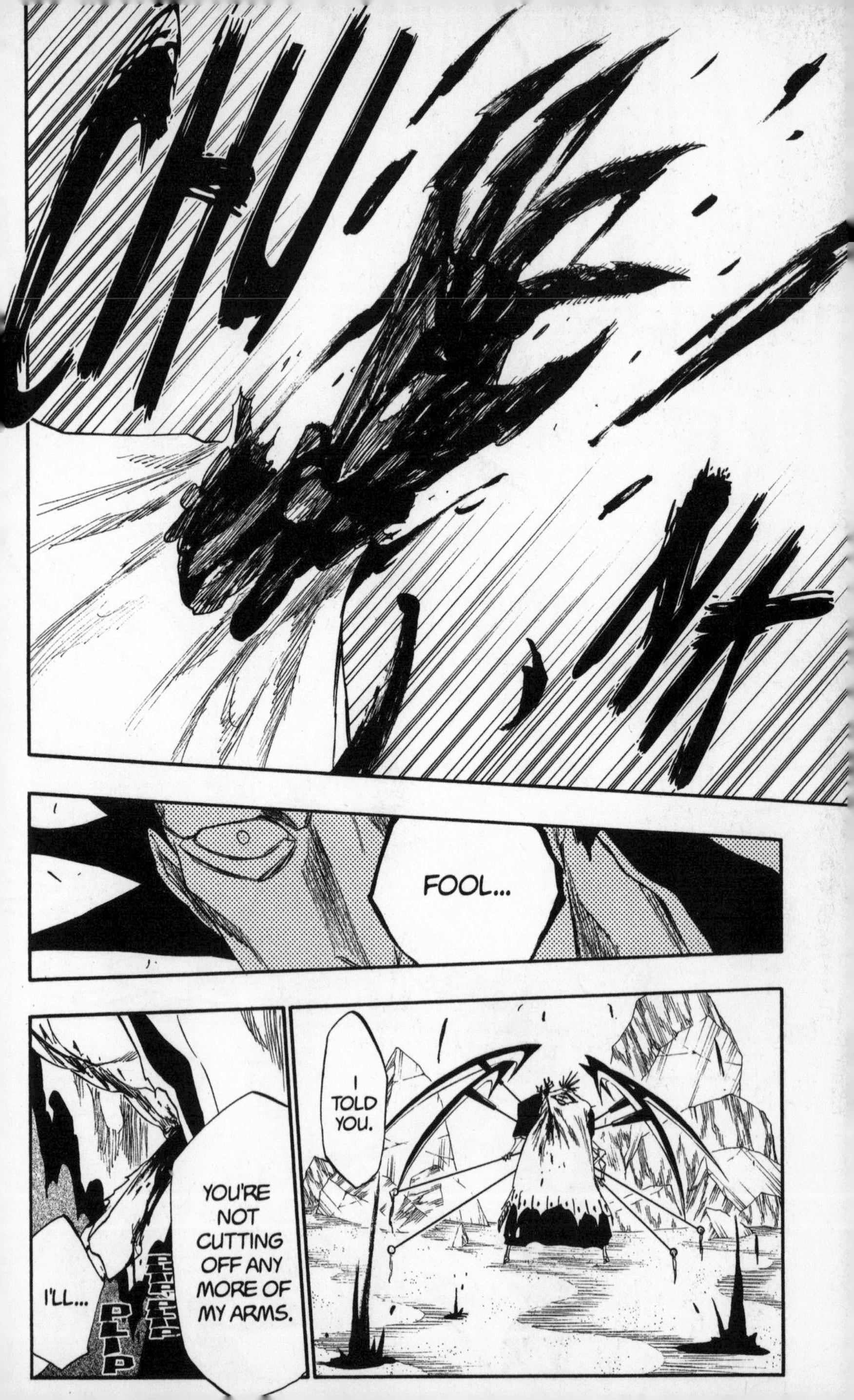
FOOL...
I TOLD YOU.
YOU'RE NOT CUTTING OFF ANY MORE OF MY ARMS.
PLIP
I'LL...

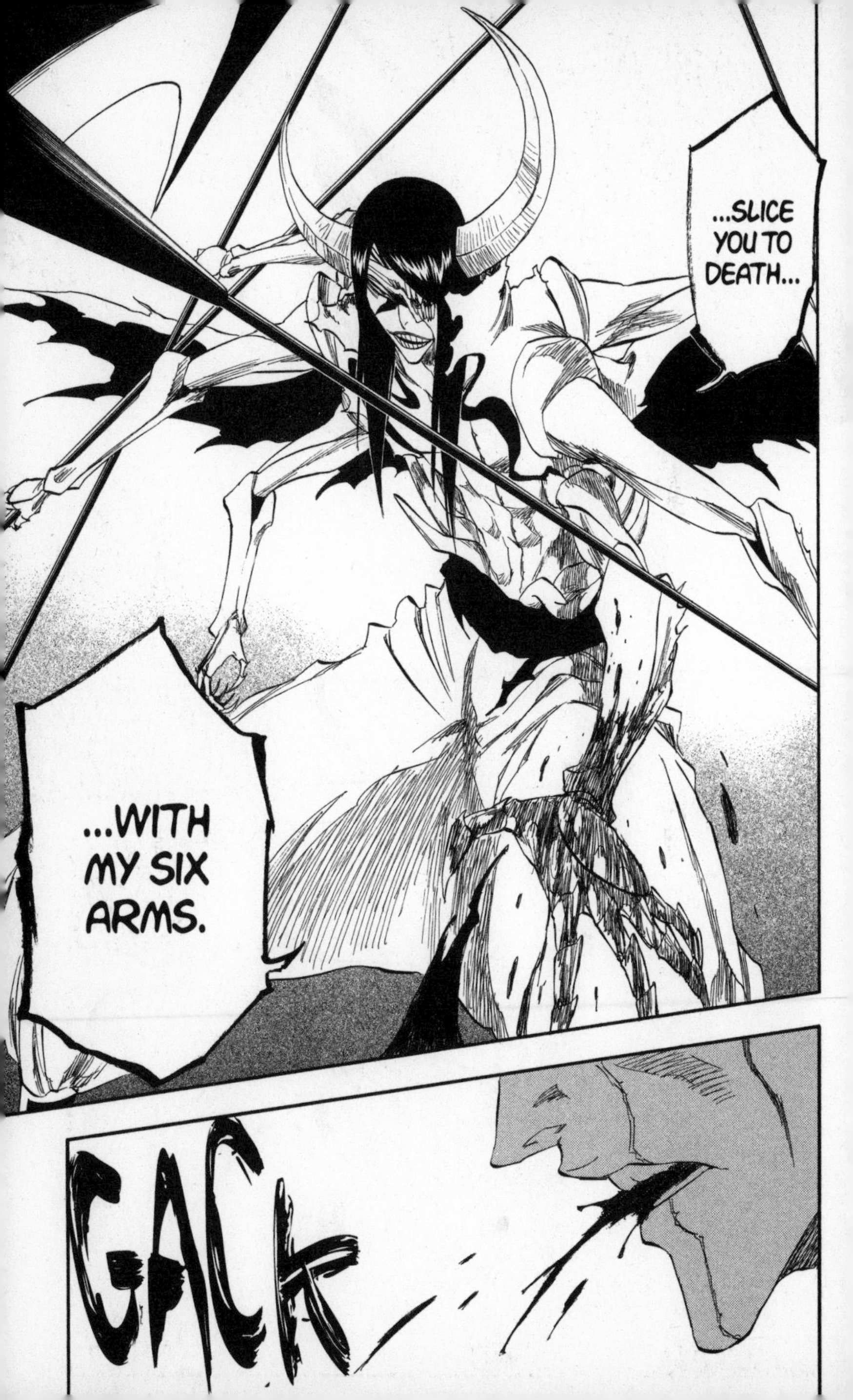
...SLICE YOU TO DEATH...
...WITH MY SIX ARMS.
GACK

311. The Undead 4

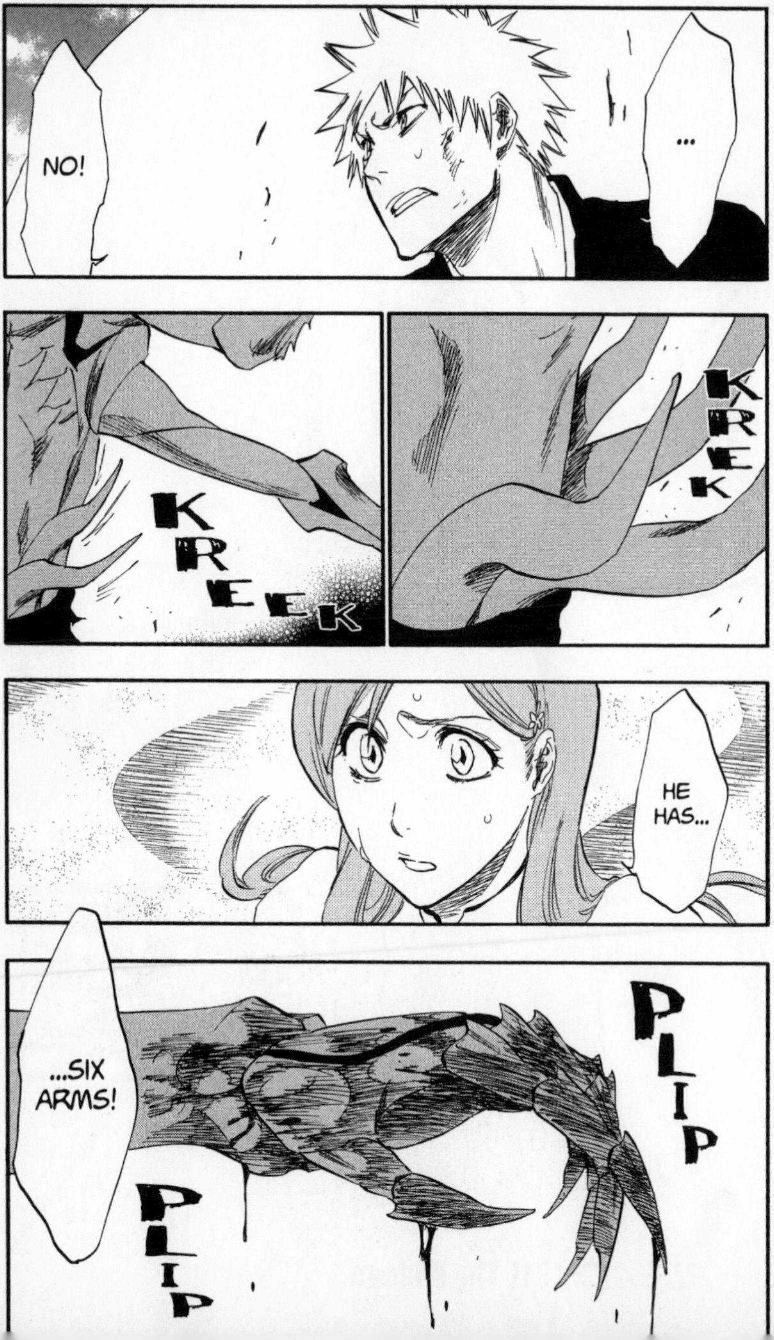
...
NO!
KREK
KREEK
HE HAS...
...SIX ARMS!
PLIP
PLIP

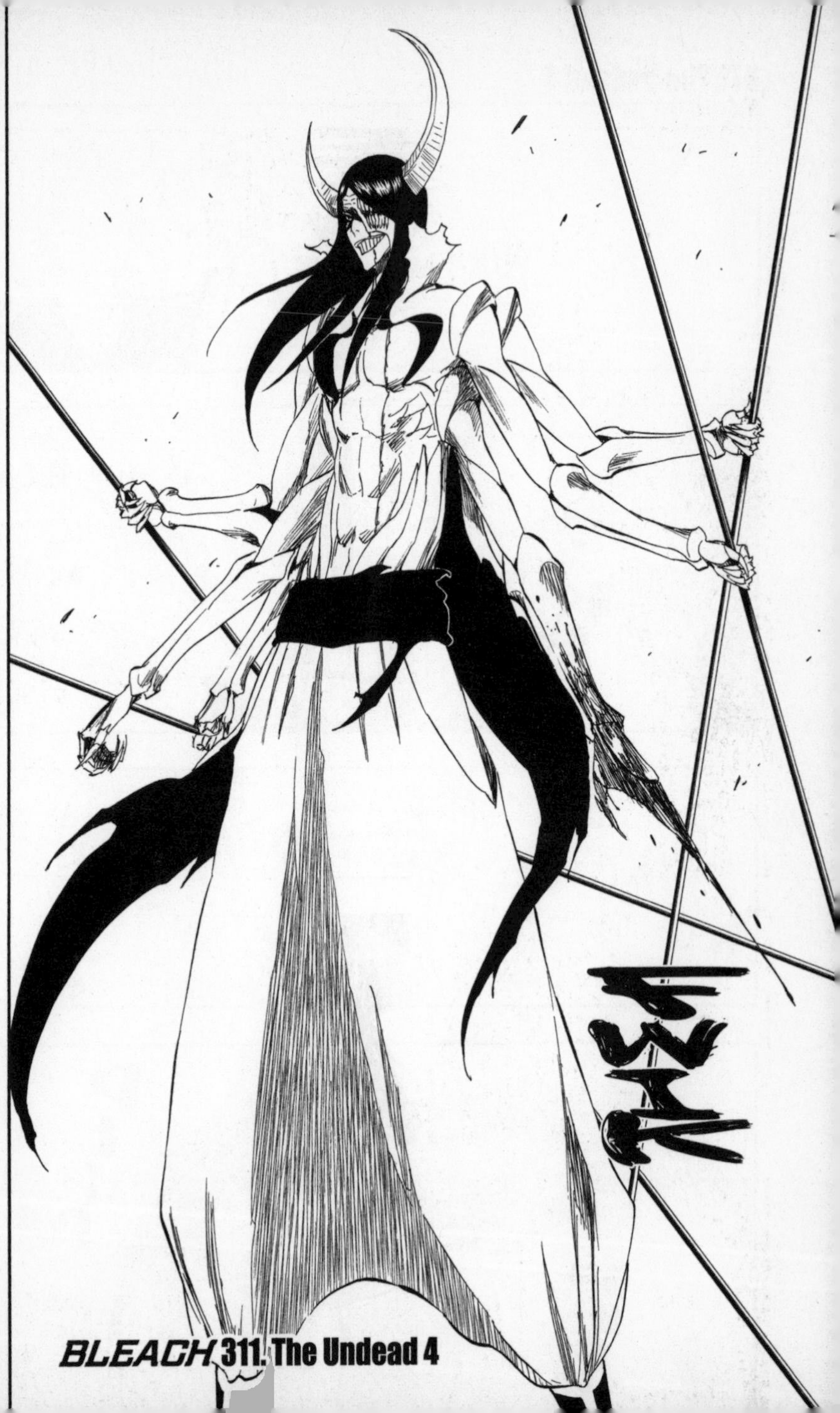

BLEACH 311. The Undead 4

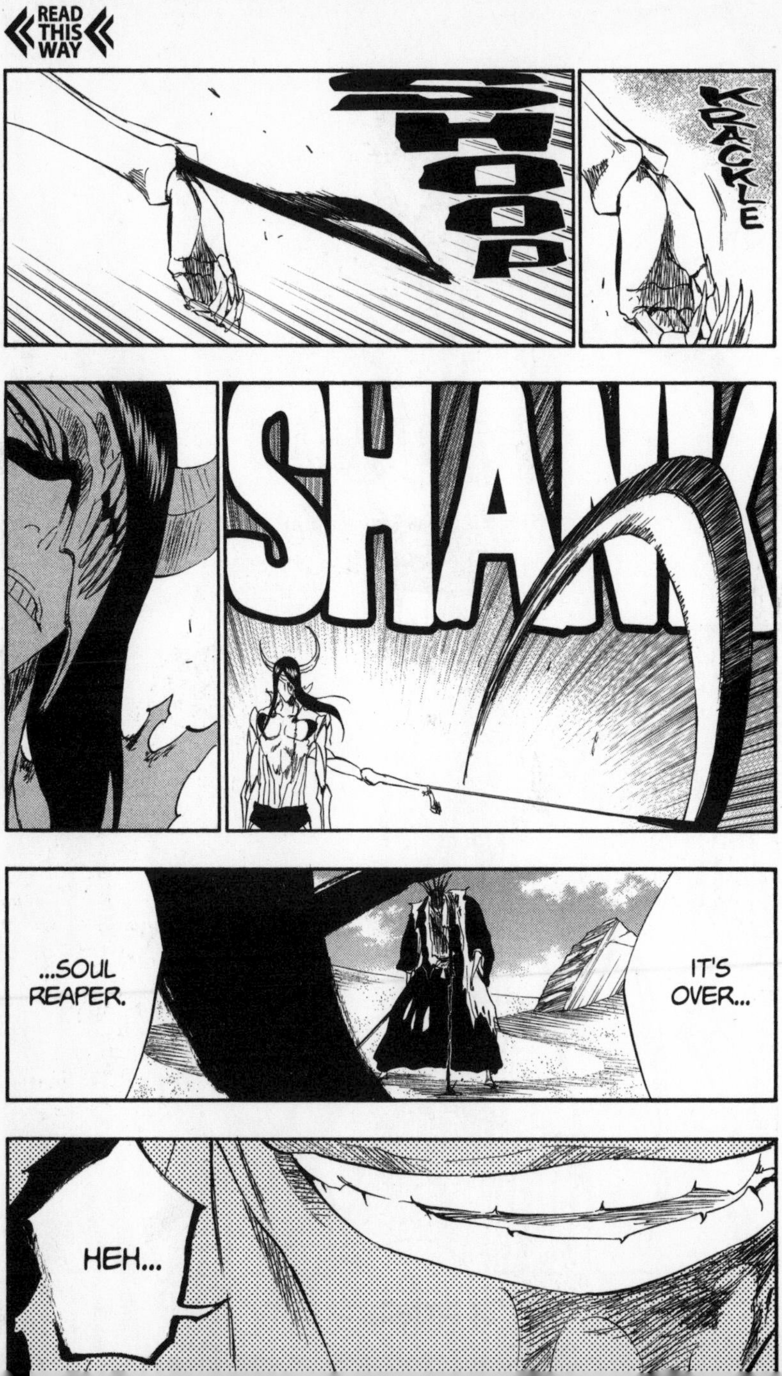
READ THIS WAY
KRACKLE
SHOOP
SHANK
IT'S OVER...
...SOUL REAPER.
HEH...

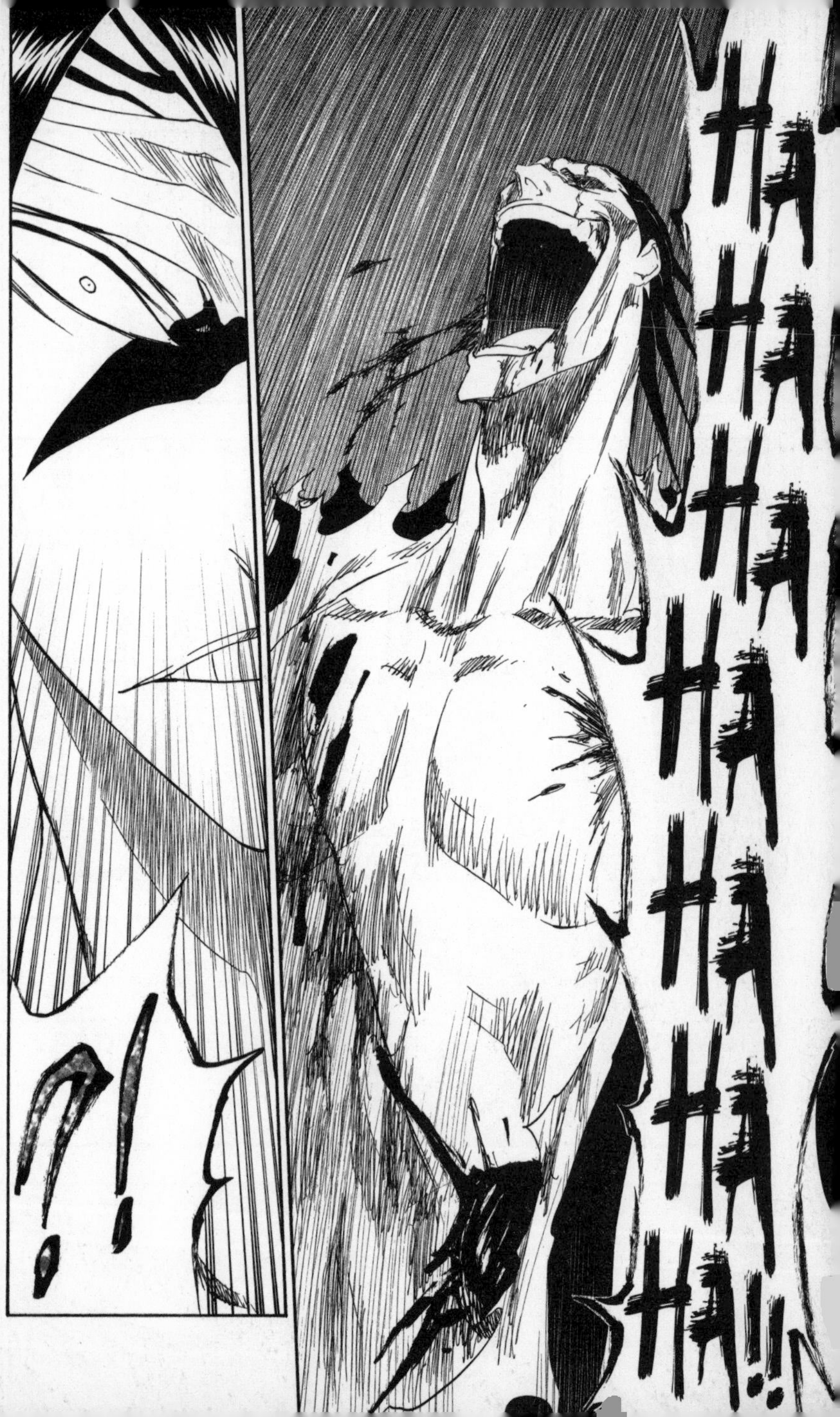
HA HA HA HA HA HA HA HA HA!!
?!

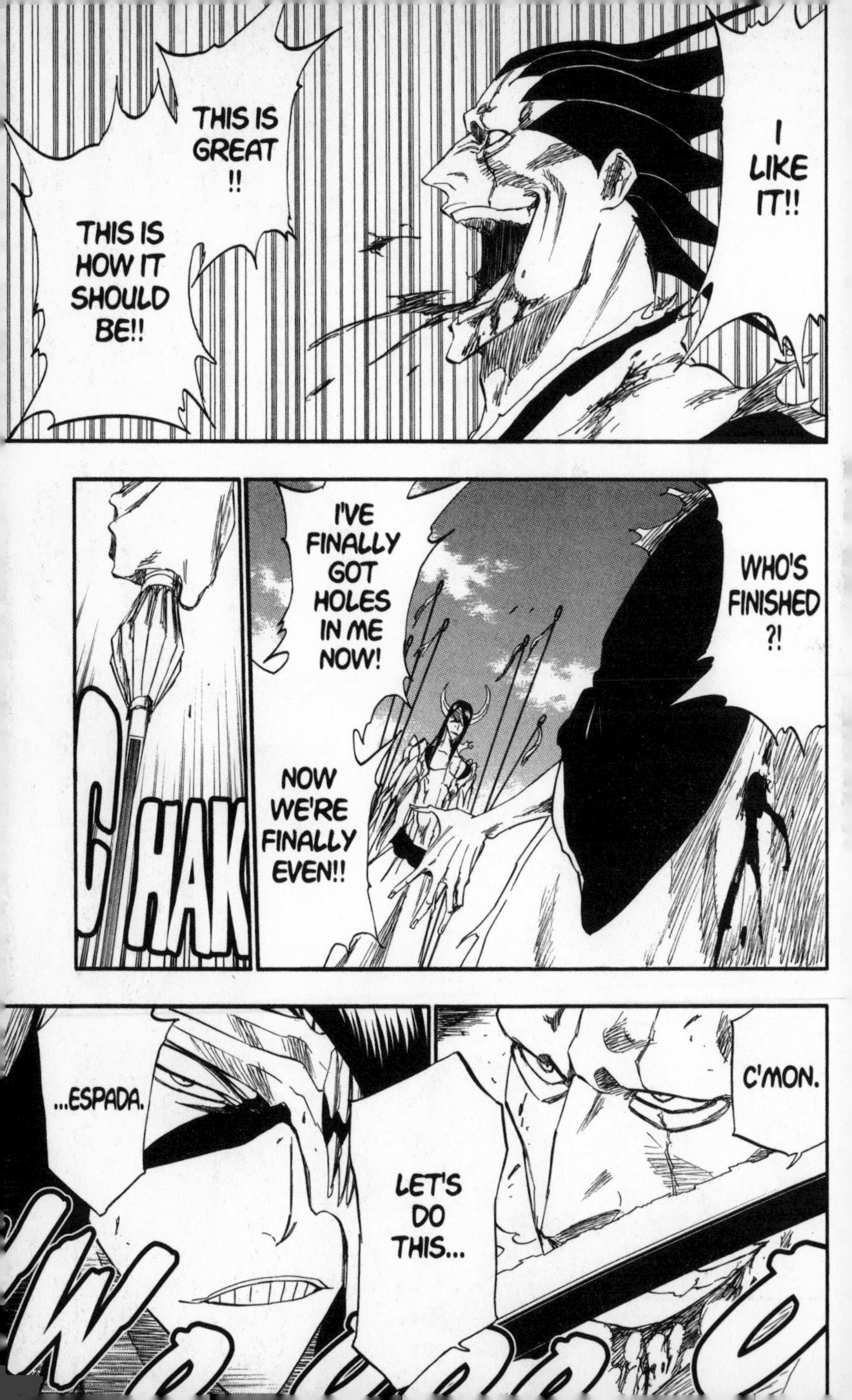
I LIKE IT!!
THIS IS GREAT!!
THIS IS HOW IT SHOULD BE!!
WHO'S FINISHED?!
I'VE FINALLY GOT HOLES IN ME NOW!
NOW WE'RE FINALLY EVEN!!
CHAK
C'MON.
LET'S DO THIS...
...ESPADA.

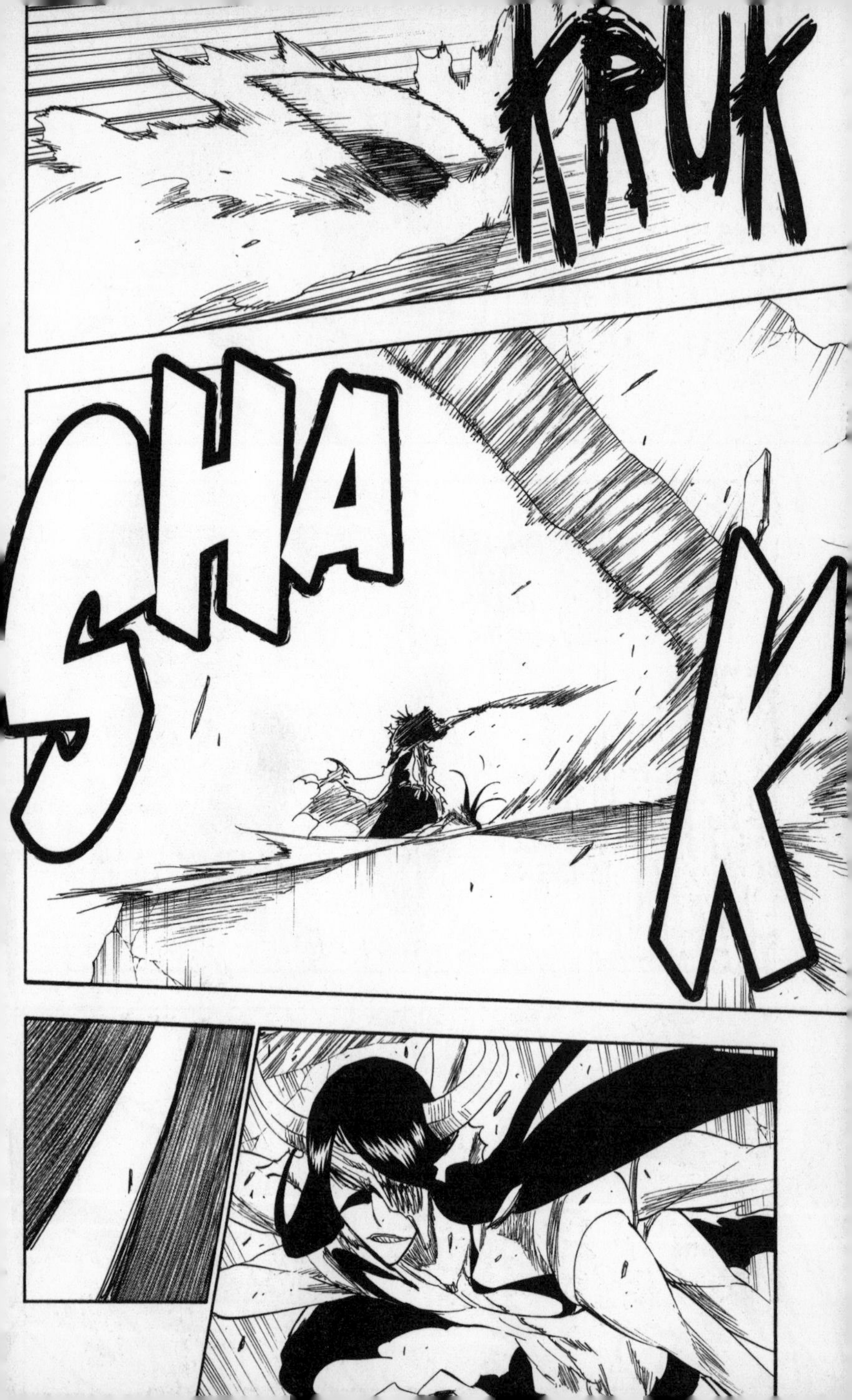
KRUK
SHAKK

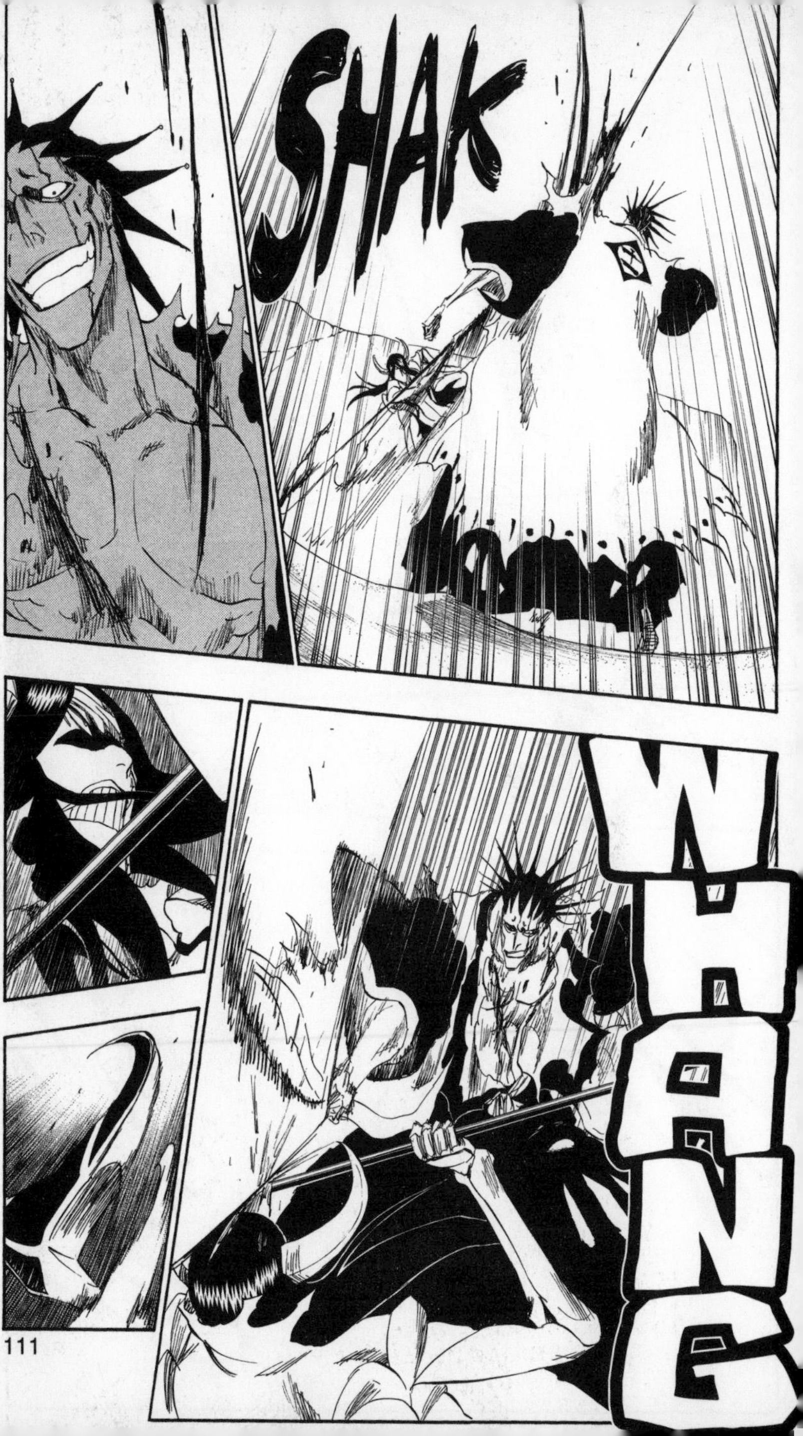
SHAK
WHANG

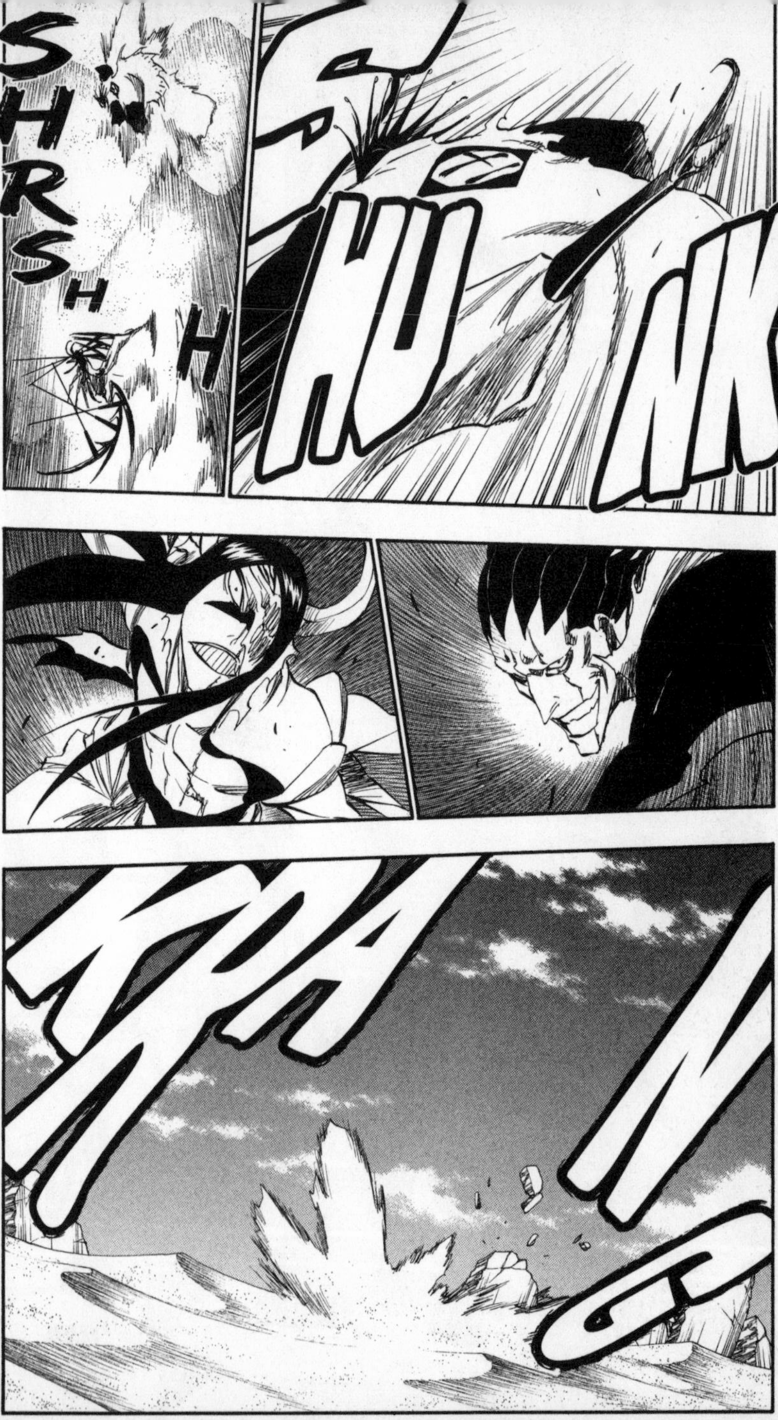
SHRSHH

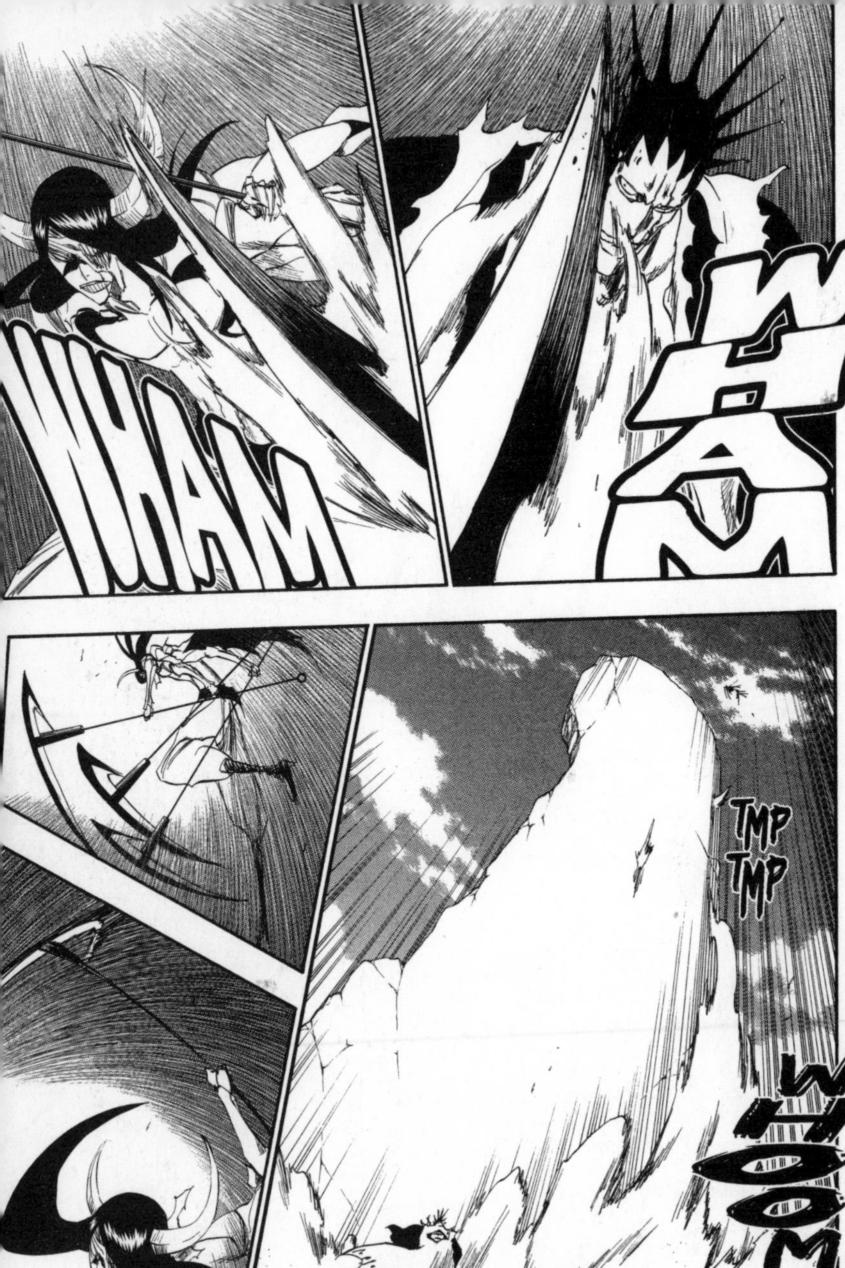
WHAM
WHAM
TMP TMP
WHOOM

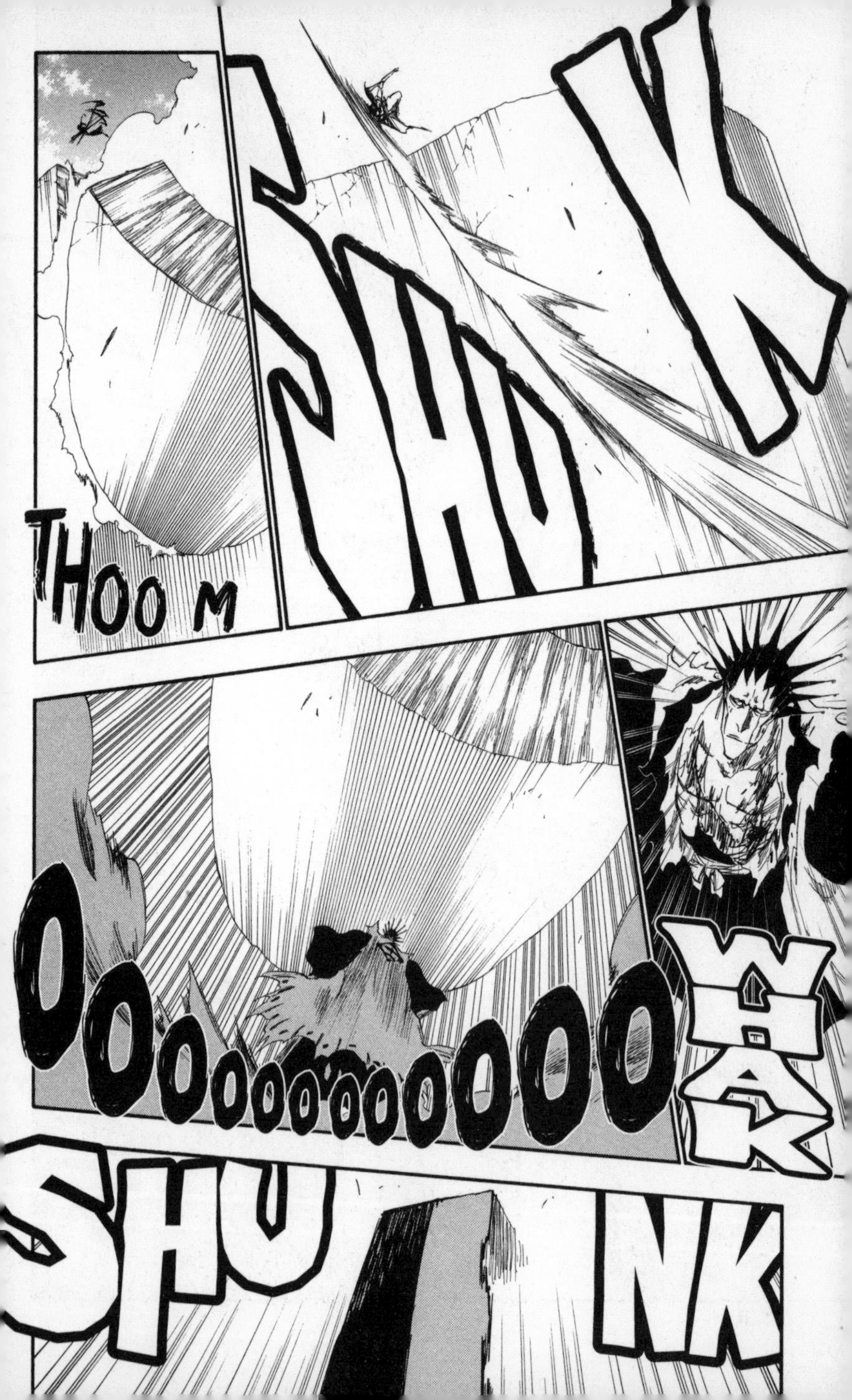
SHUNK
THOOM
WHAR
OOOOOOOOOOOOOOOO
SHU NK

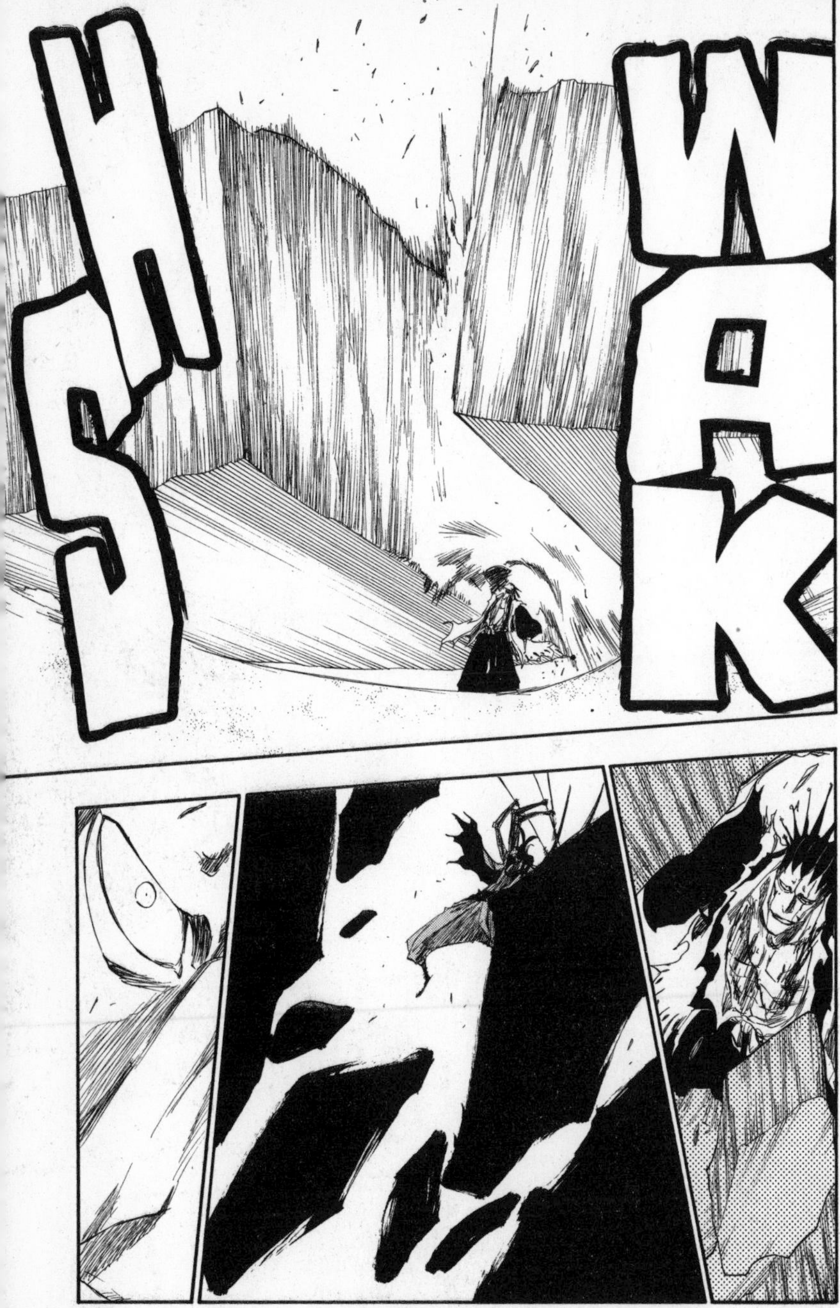
SHWAK

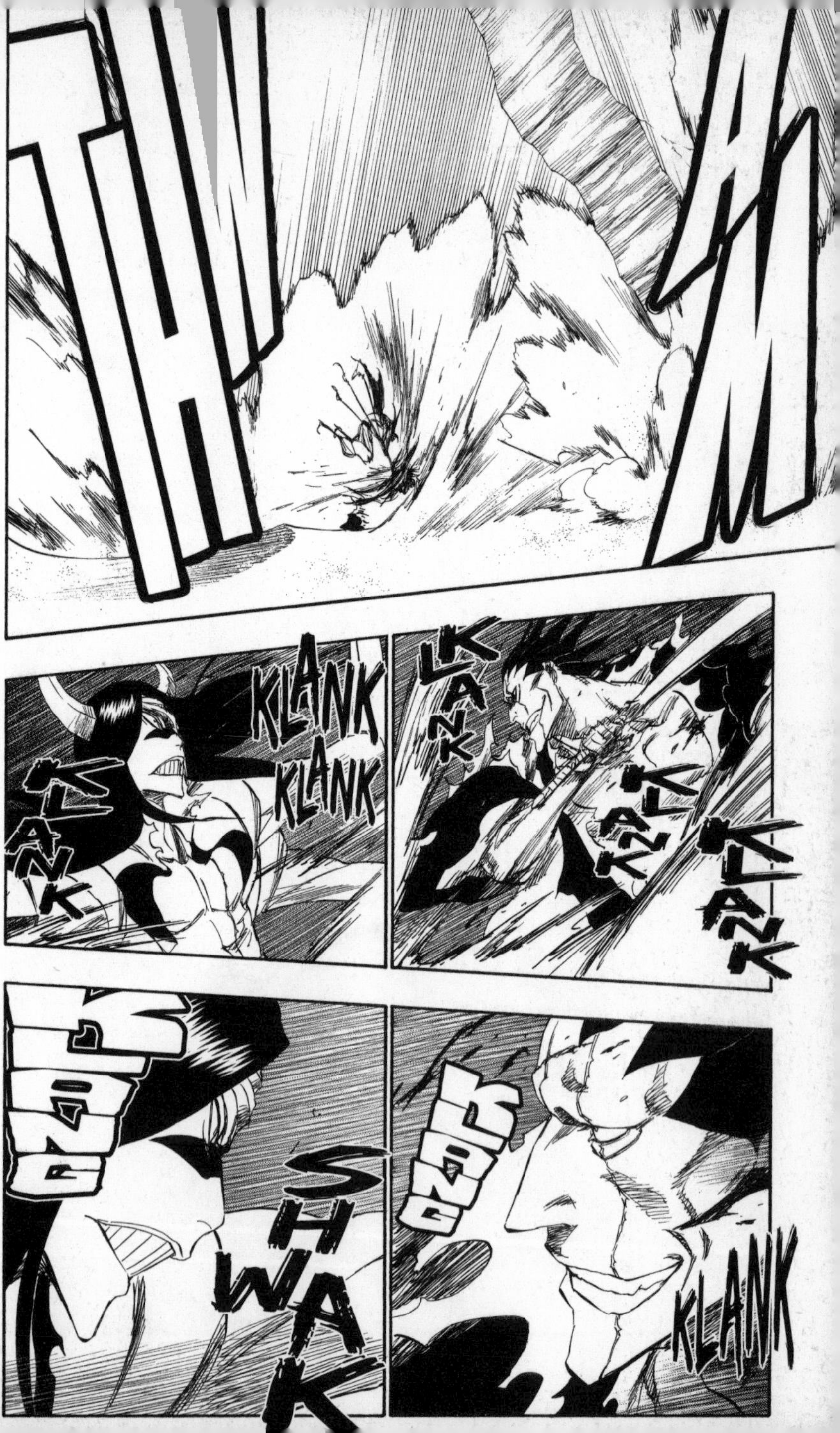

THWAM
KLANK
KLANK
KLANK
KLANK
KLANK
KLANK
KLANG
KLANK
SHWAK

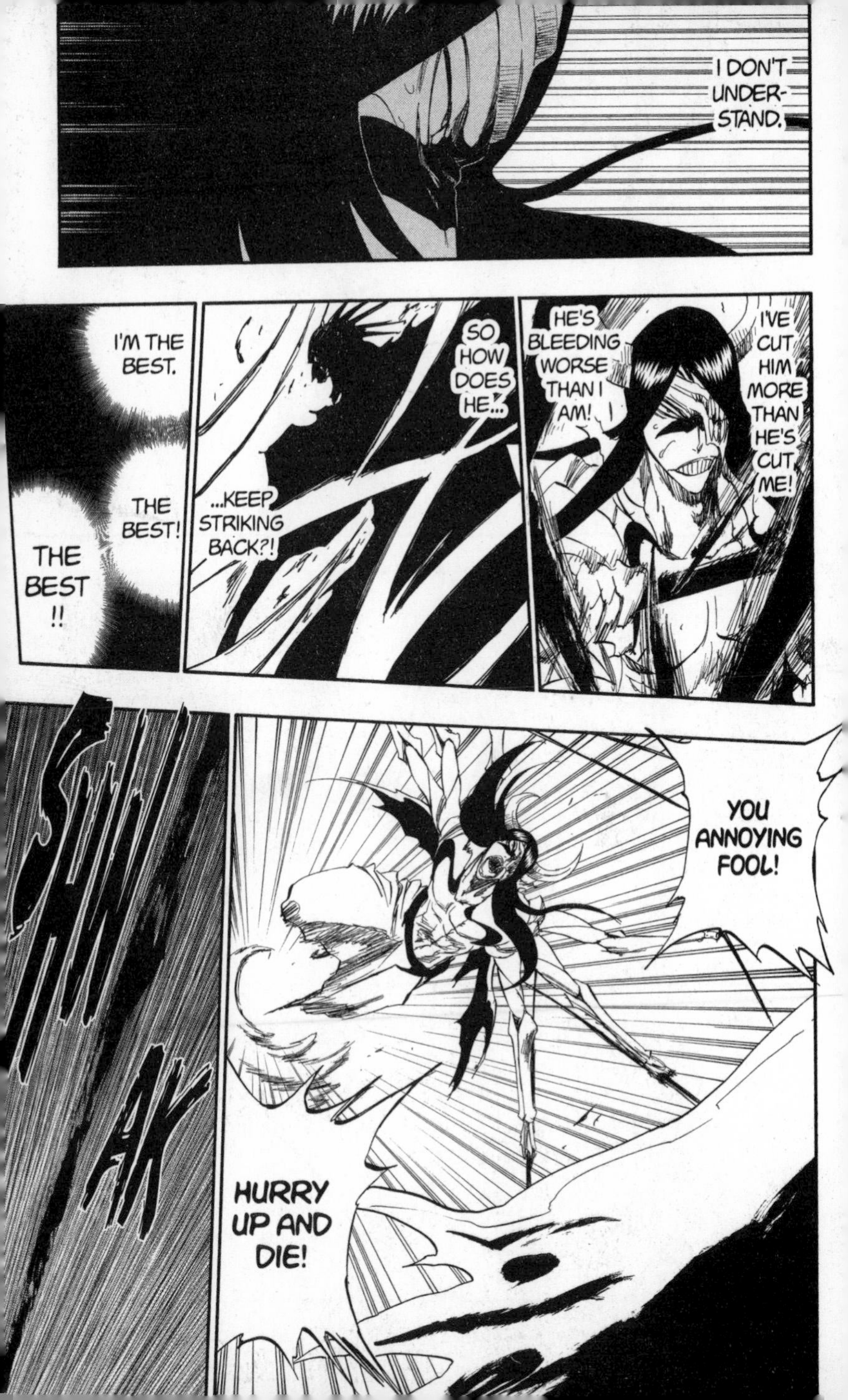
I DON'T UNDER-STAND.
I'VE CUT HIM MORE THAN HE'S CUT ME!
HE'S BLEEDING WORSE THAN I AM!
SO HOW DOES HE...
...KEEP STRIKING BACK?!
I'M THE BEST.
THE BEST!
THE BEST !!
YOU ANNOYING FOOL!
HURRY UP AND DIE!

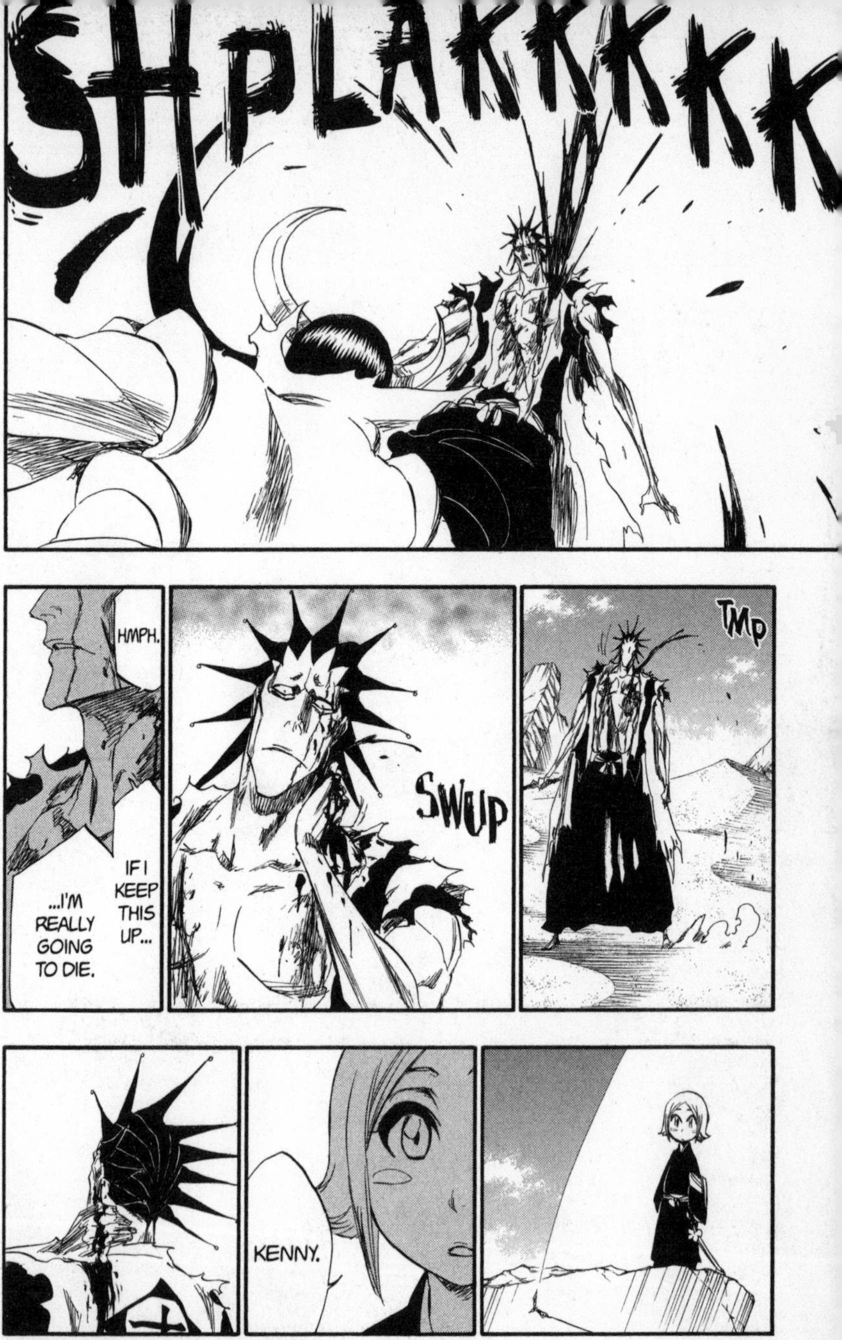
SHPLAKKKKK
TMP
SWUP
HMPH.
IF I KEEP THIS UP...
...I'M REALLY GOING TO DIE.
KENNY.

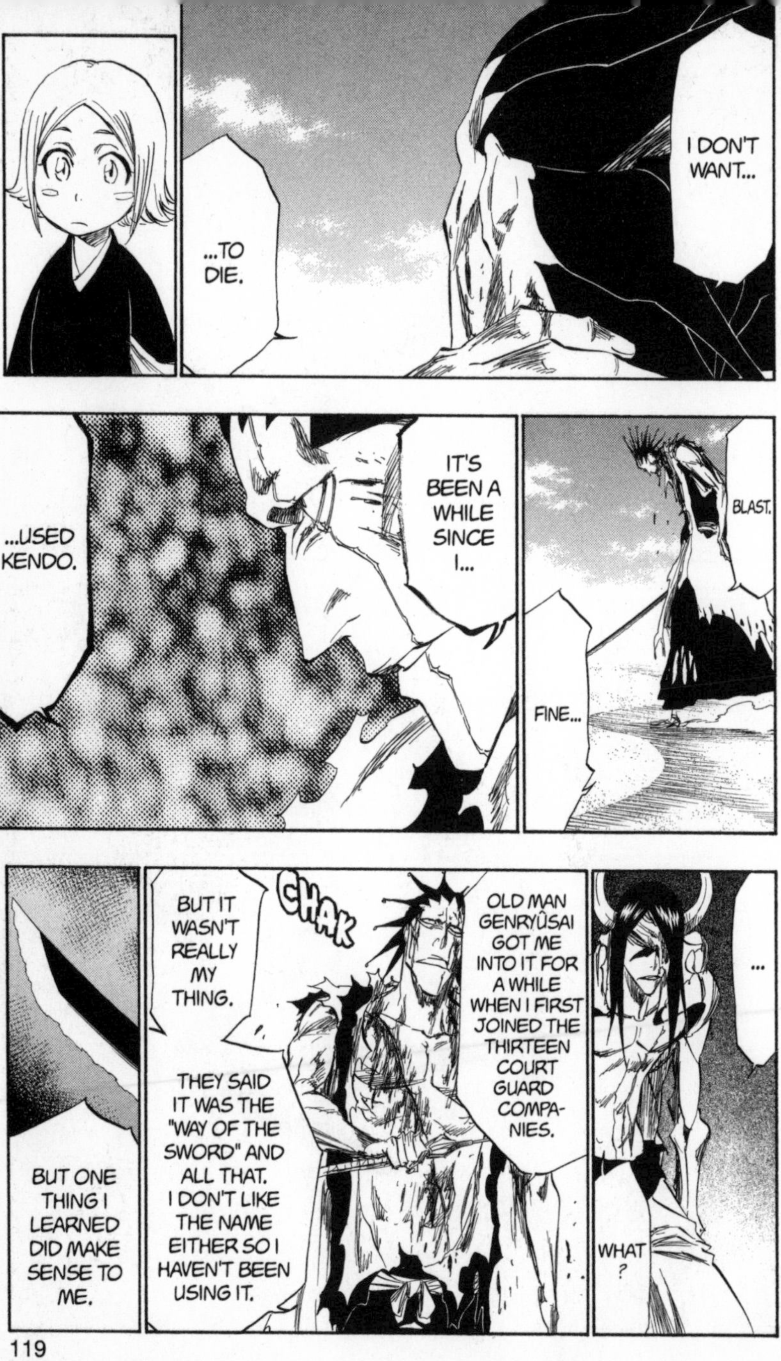
I DON'T WANT...
...TO DIE.
BLAST.
FINE...
IT'S BEEN A WHILE SINCE I...
...USED KENDO.
...
WHAT?
OLD MAN GENRYÛSAI GOT ME INTO IT FOR A WHILE WHEN I FIRST JOINED THE THIRTEEN COURT GUARD COMPA-NIES.
CHAK
BUT IT WASN'T REALLY MY THING.
THEY SAID IT WAS THE "WAY OF THE SWORD" AND ALL THAT. I DON'T LIKE THE NAME EITHER SO I HAVEN'T BEEN USING IT.
BUT ONE THING I LEARNED DID MAKE SENSE TO ME.

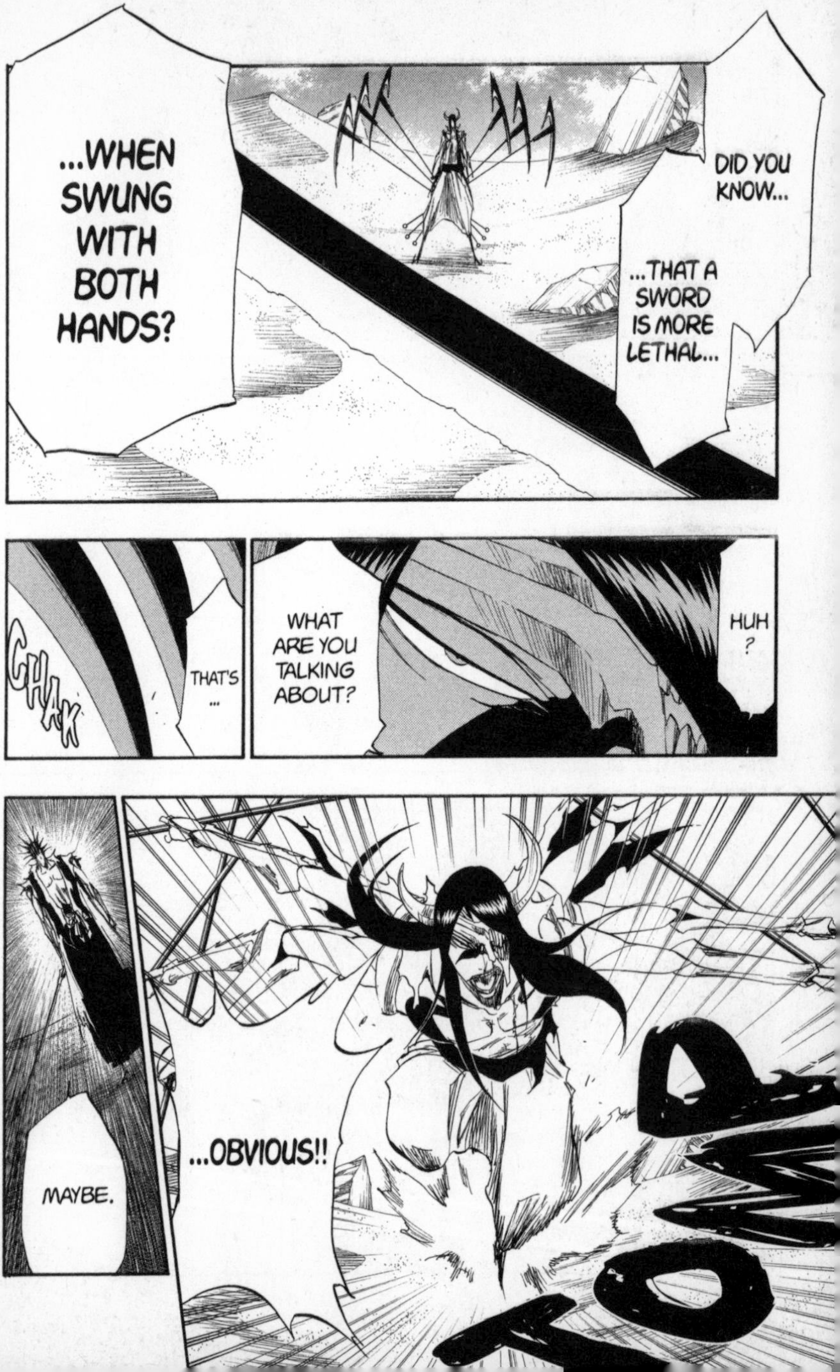
DID YOU KNOW...
...THAT A SWORD IS MORE LETHAL...
...WHEN SWUNG WITH BOTH HANDS?
HUH?
WHAT ARE YOU TALKING ABOUT?
THAT'S ...
CHAK
...OBVIOUS!!
MAYBE.

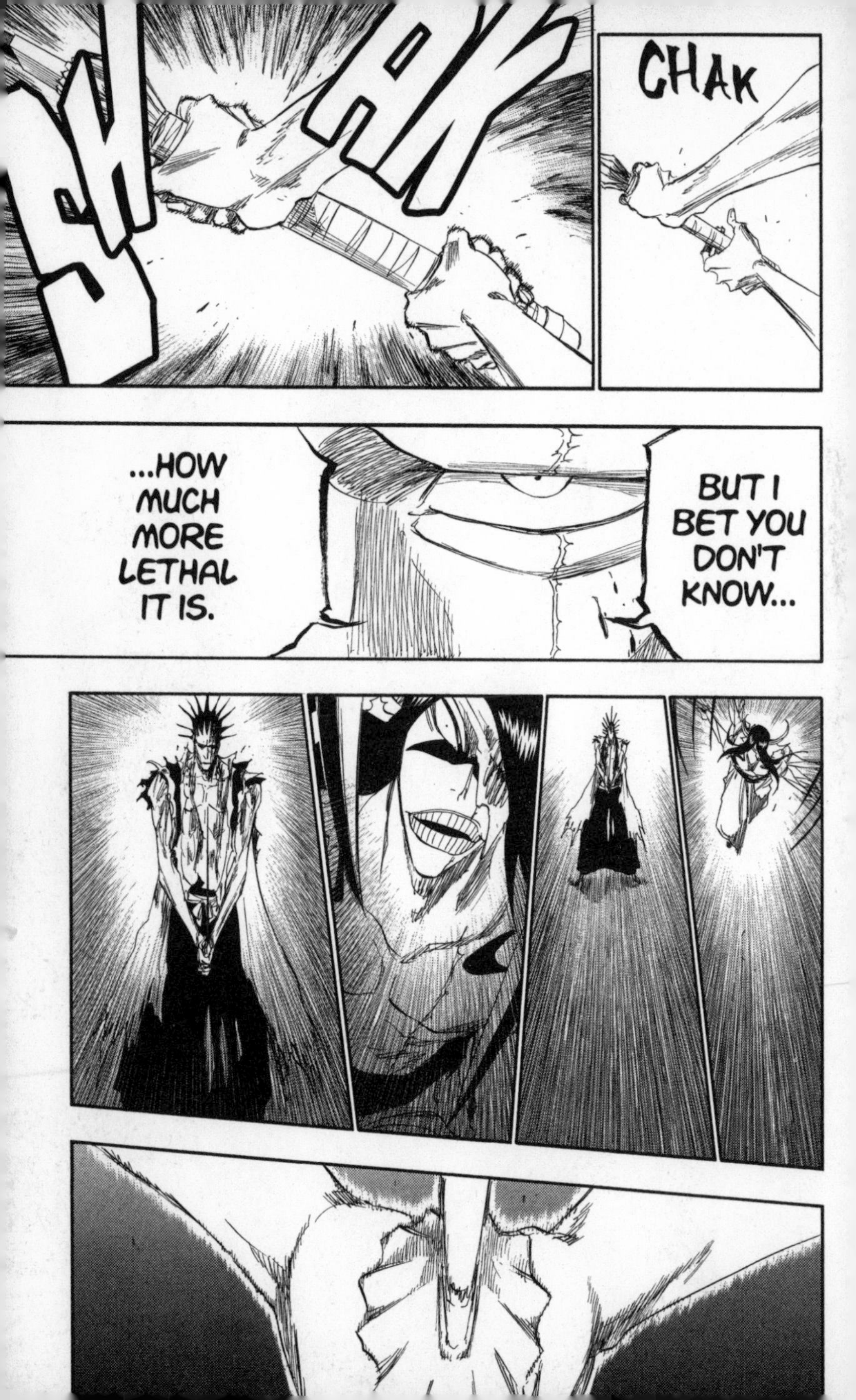
CHAK
BUT I BET YOU DON'T KNOW...
...HOW MUCH MORE LETHAL IT IS.

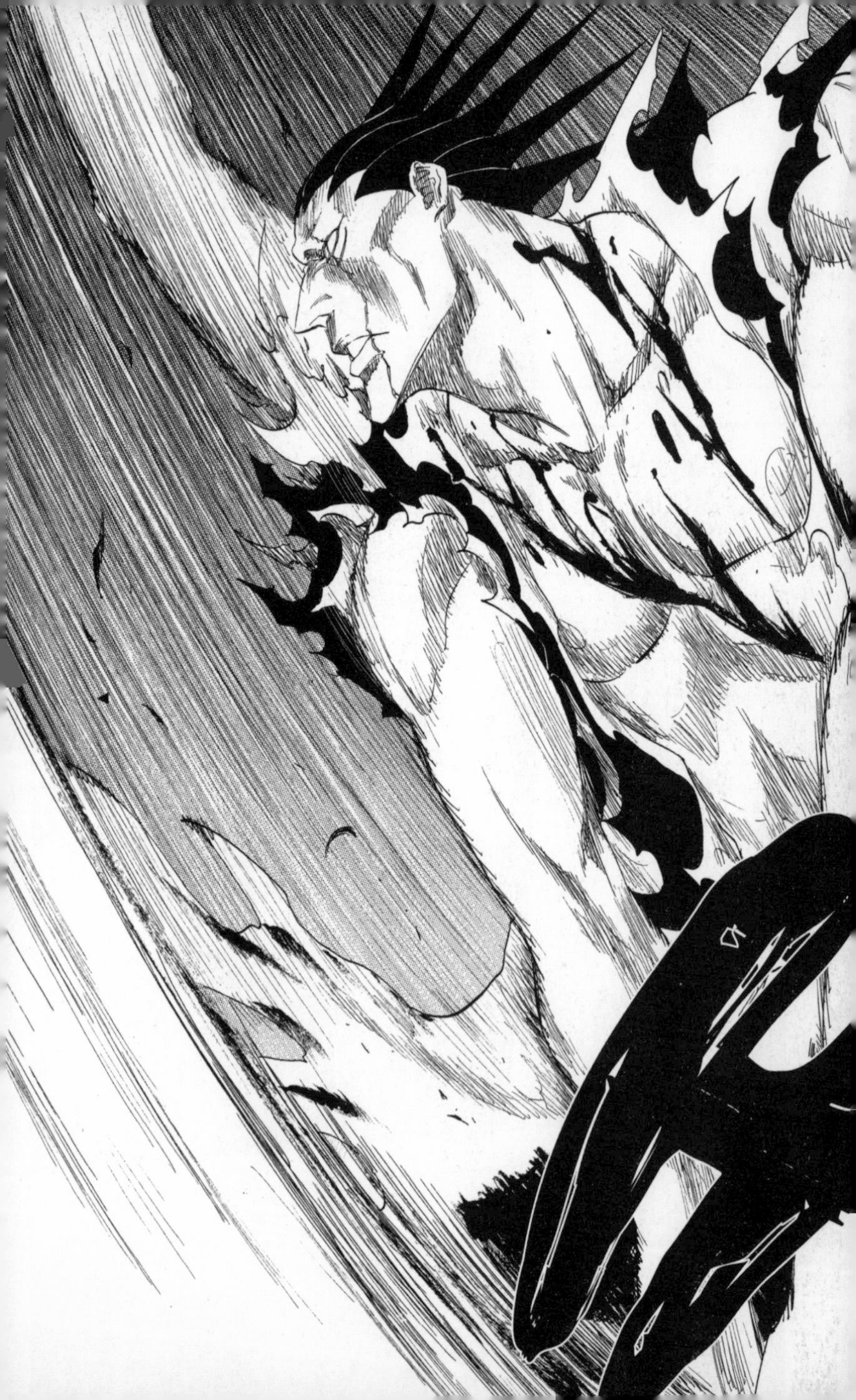

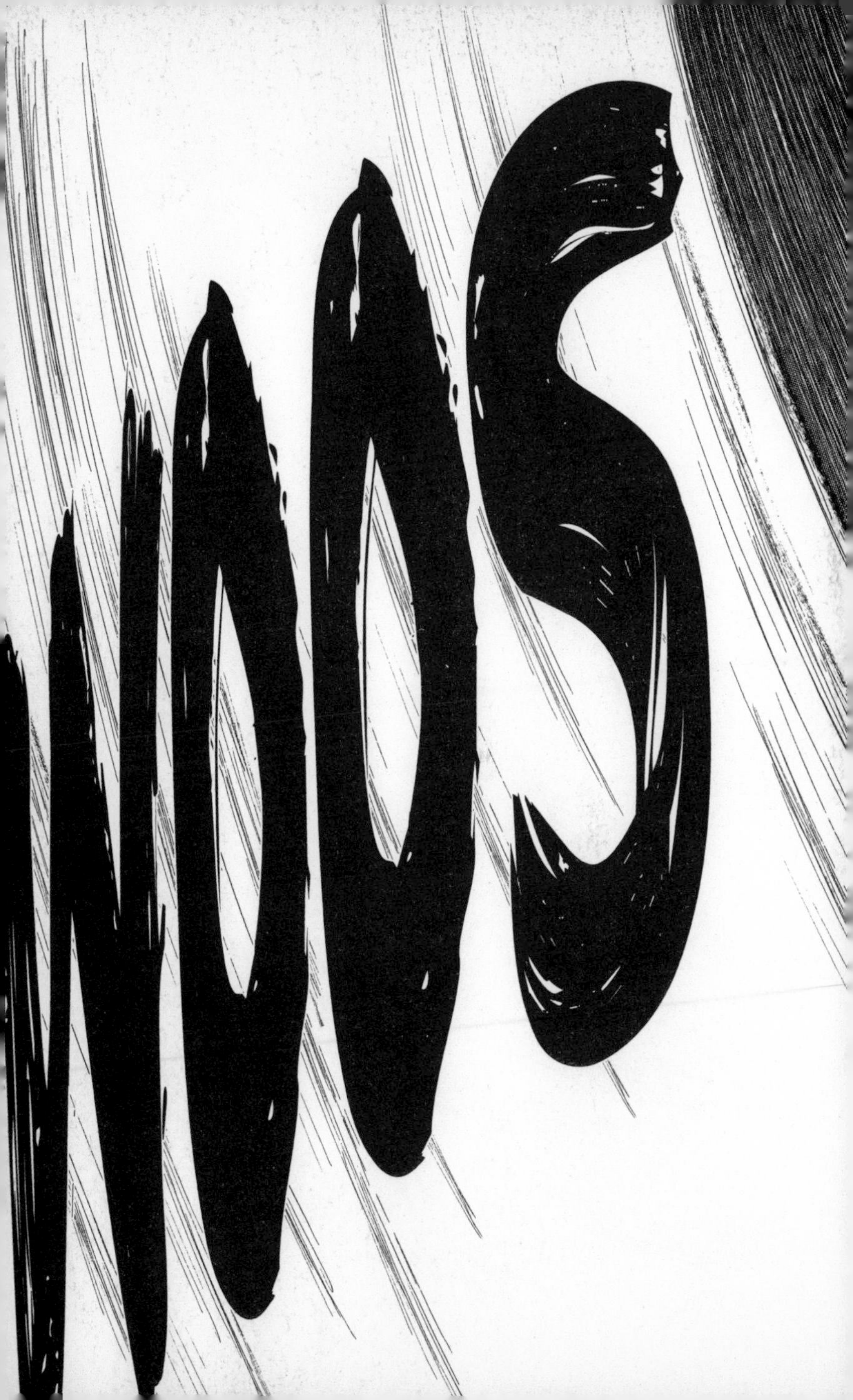
WOOS

312. Higher Than The Moon

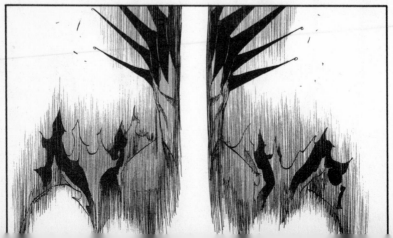

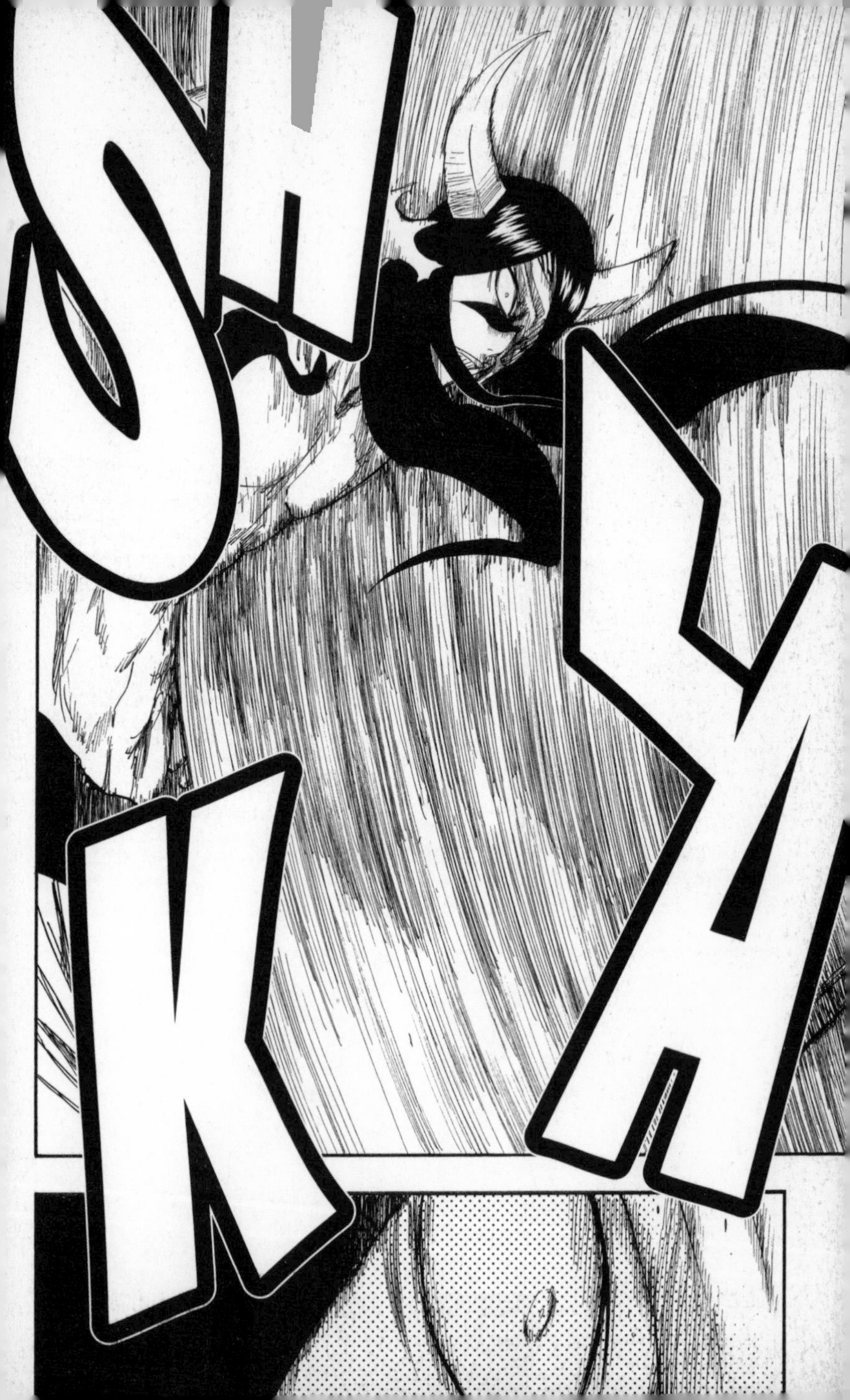

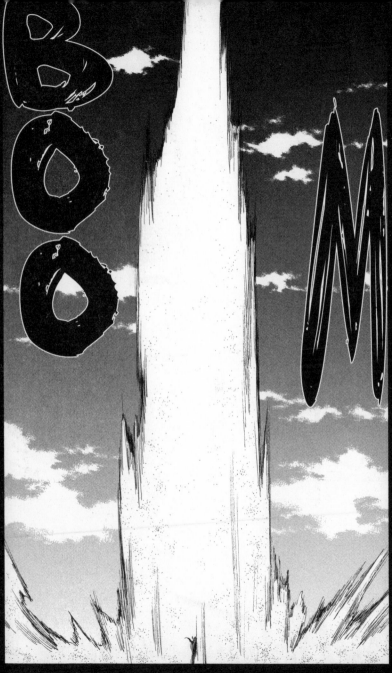

BLEACH 312. Higher Than The Moon

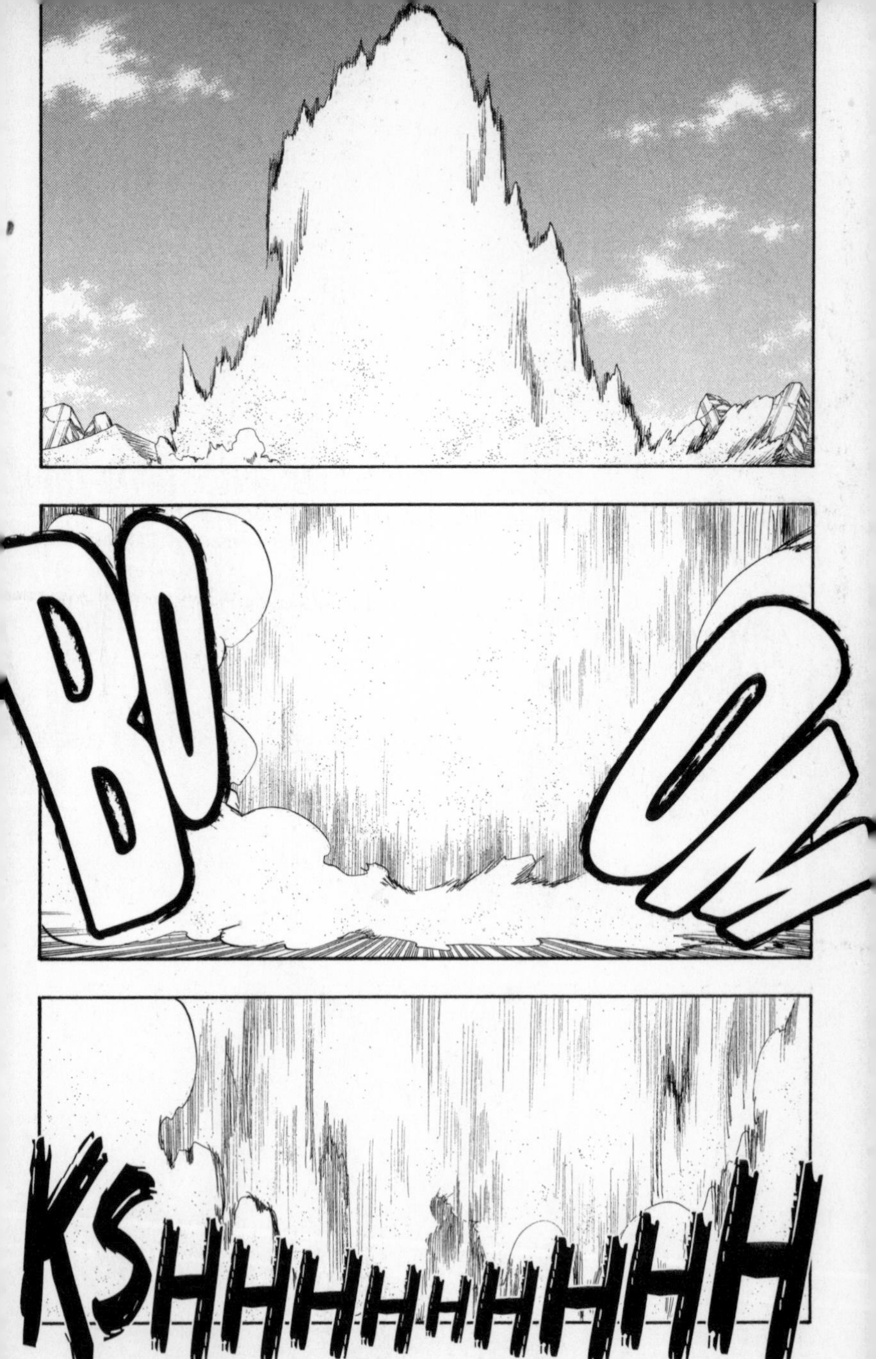
BOOM
KSHHHHHHHHH

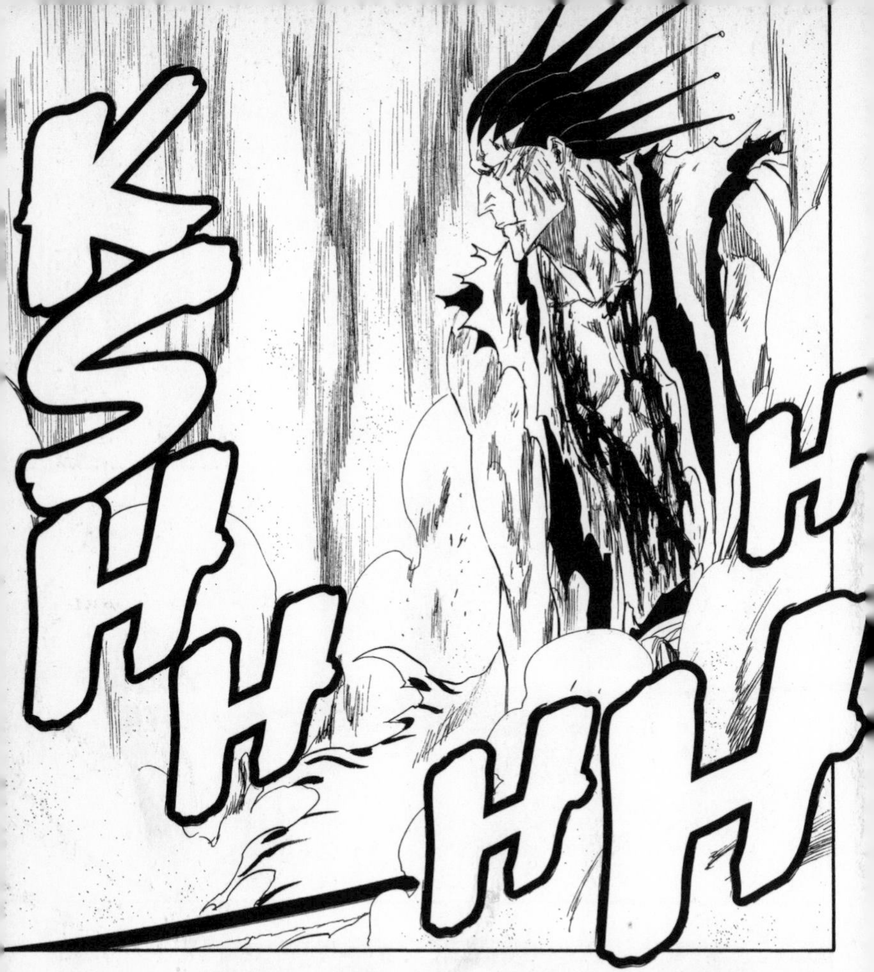
KSHHHHHH

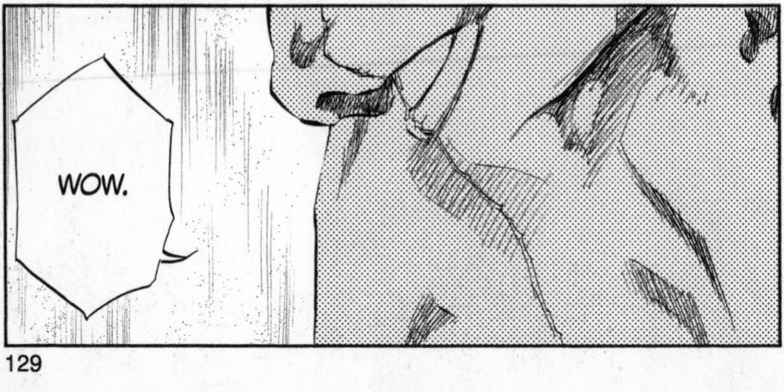
WOW.

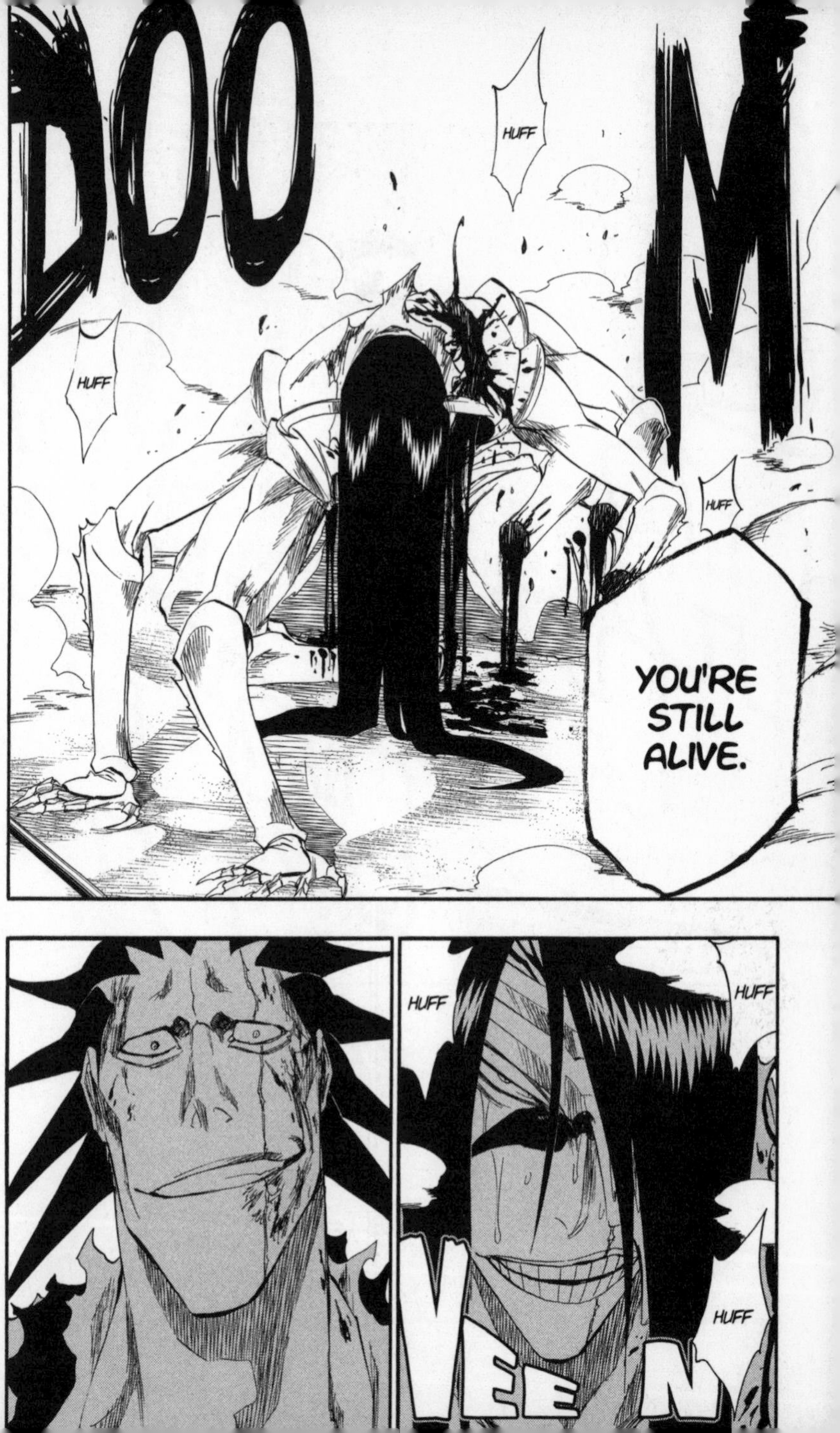
DOOM
HUFF
HUFF
YOU'RE STILL ALIVE.
HUFF
HUFF
HUFF
HUFF
VEEN

READ THIS WAY

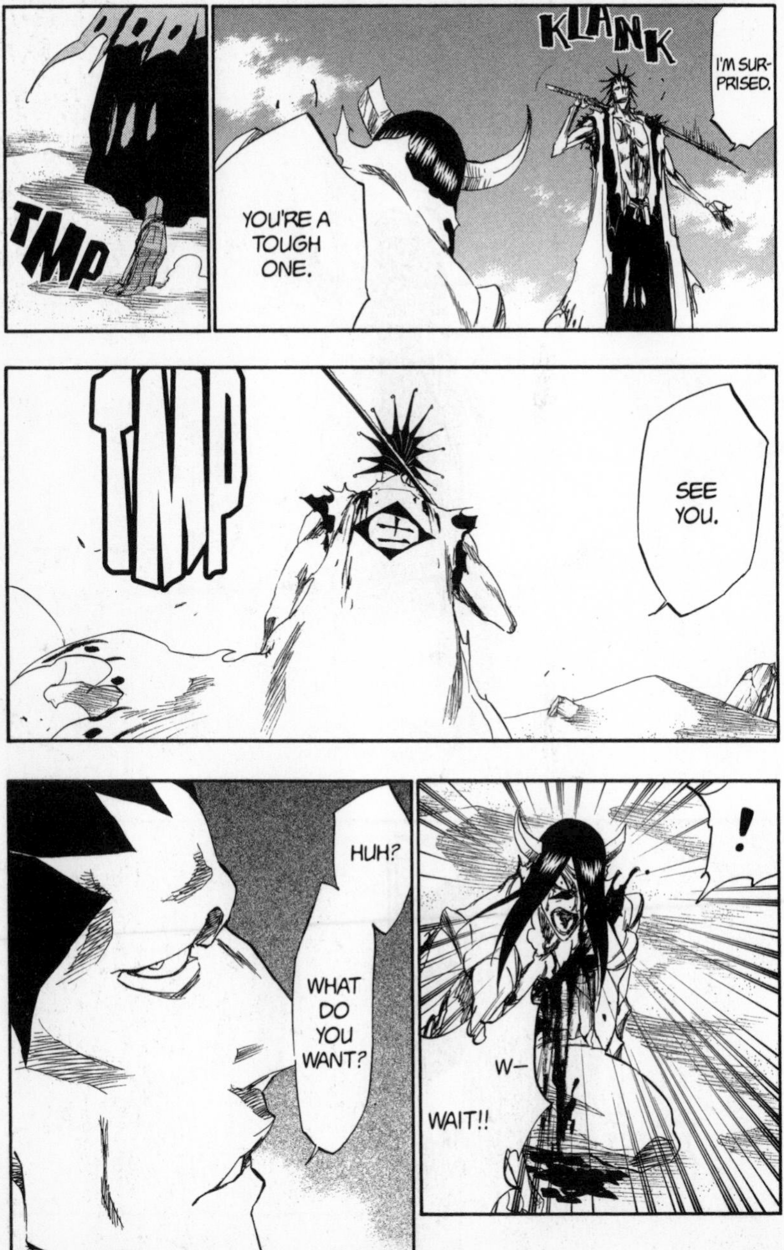
KLANK
I'M SURPRISED.
YOU'RE A TOUGH ONE.
TMP
SEE YOU.
TMP
!
W—
WAIT!!
HUH?
WHAT DO YOU WANT?

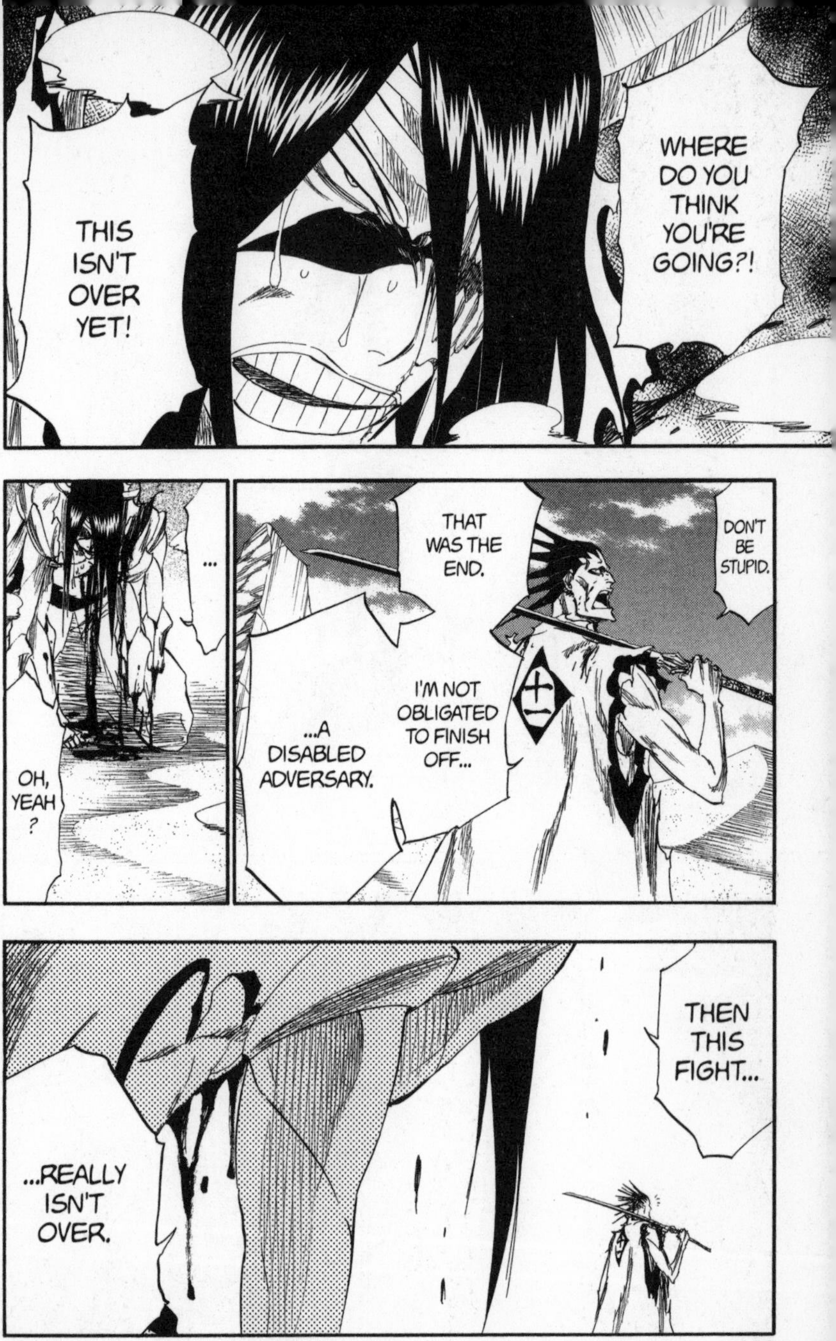
WHERE DO YOU THINK YOU'RE GOING?!
THIS ISN'T OVER YET!
DON'T BE STUPID.
THAT WAS THE END.
I'M NOT OBLIGATED TO FINISH OFF...
...A DISABLED ADVERSARY.
...
OH, YEAH?
THEN THIS FIGHT...
...REALLY ISN'T OVER.

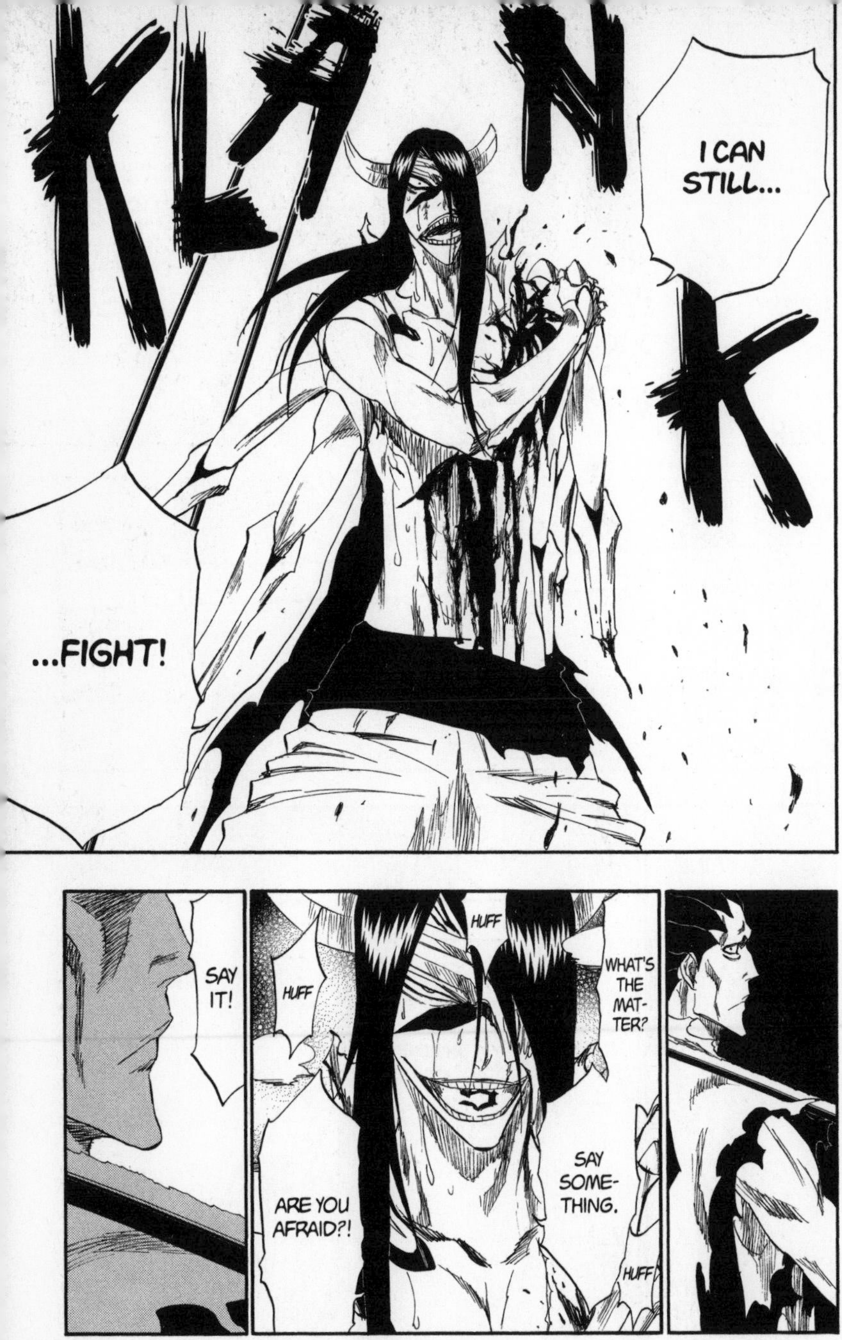
KLANK
I CAN STILL...
...FIGHT!
HUFF
WHAT'S THE MAT-TER?
HUFF
SAY SOME-THING.
ARE YOU AFRAID?!
HUFF
SAY IT!

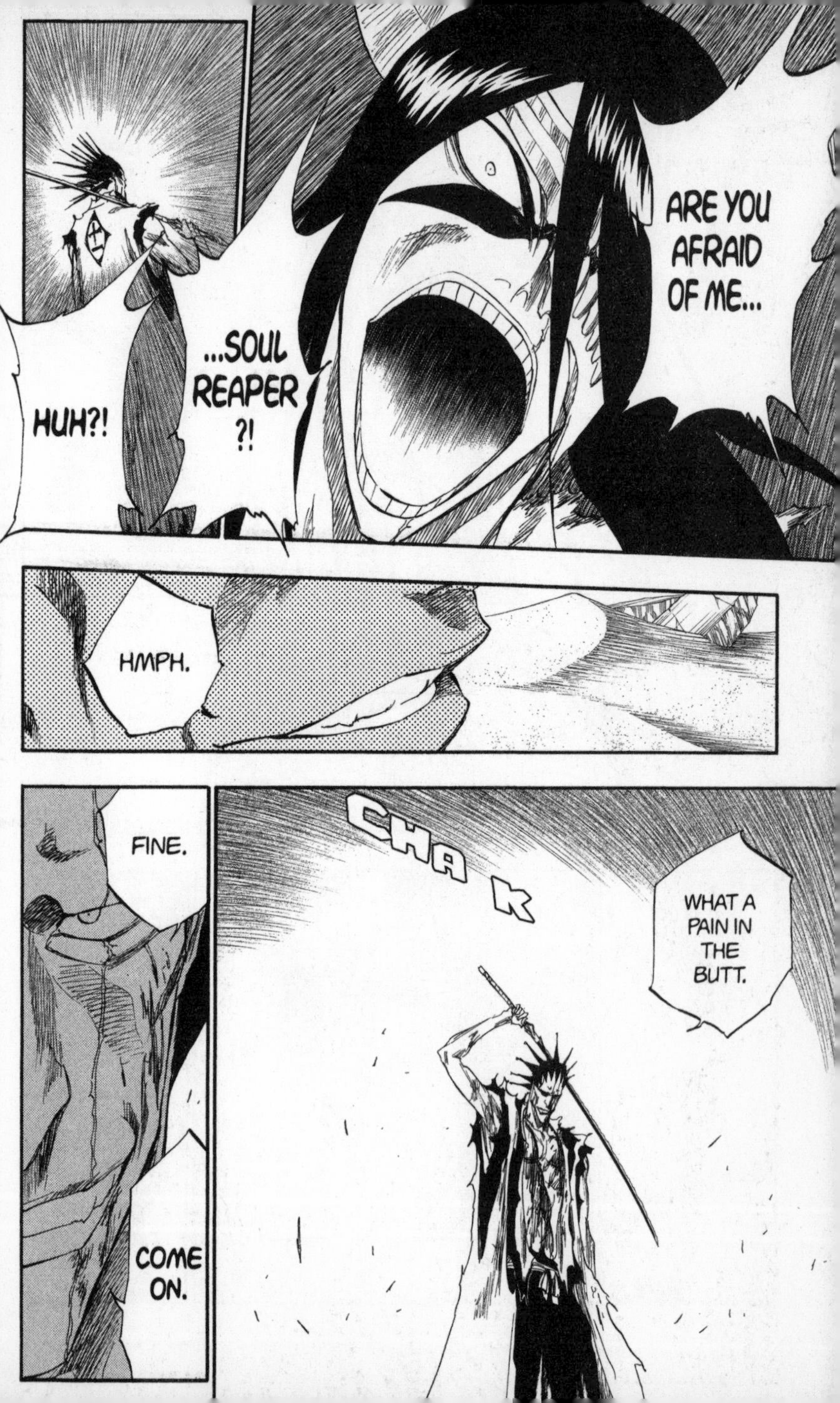
ARE YOU AFRAID OF ME...
...SOUL REAPER ?!
HUH?!
HMPH.
CHAK
WHAT A PAIN IN THE BUTT.
FINE.
COME ON.

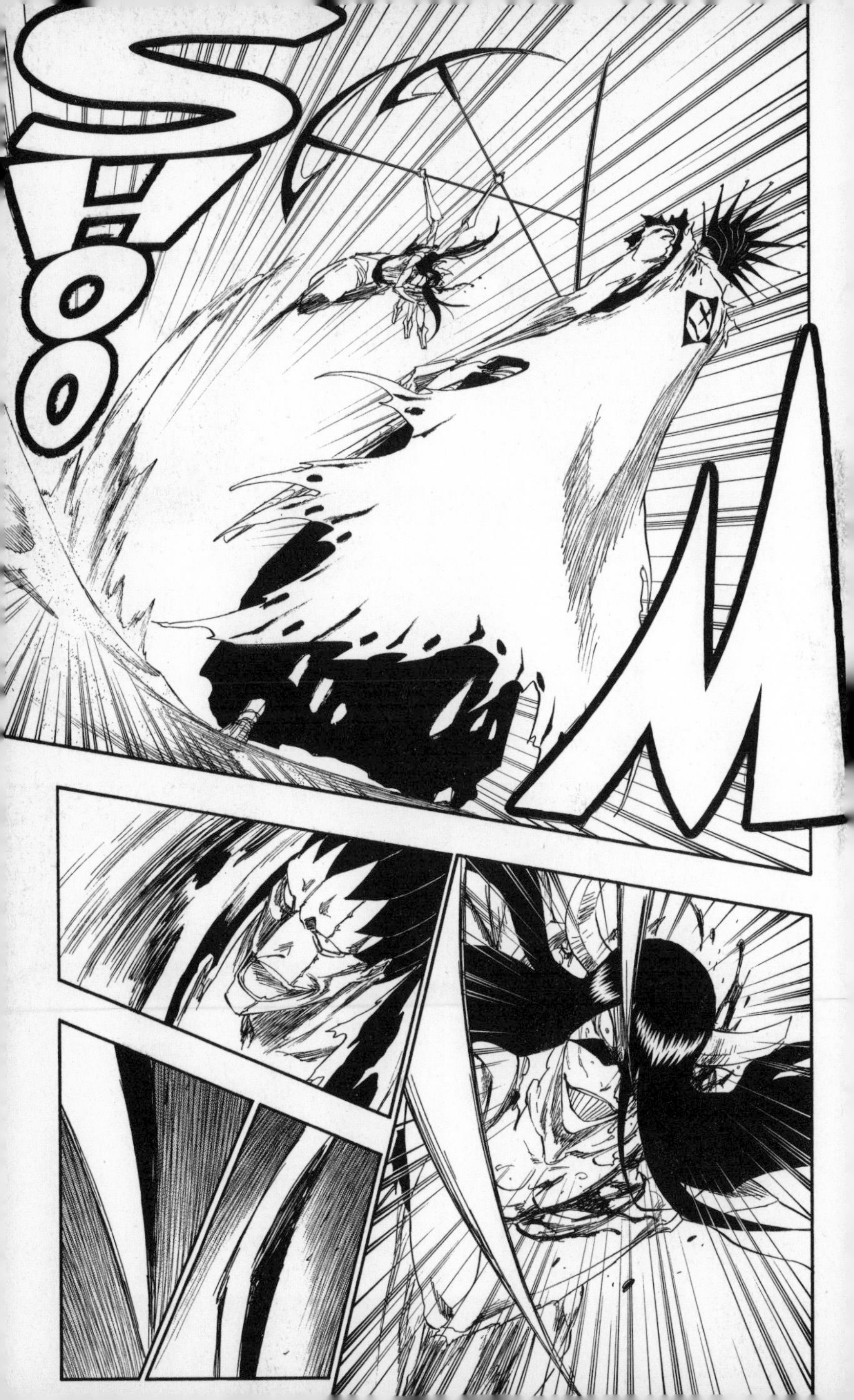
SHOOOM

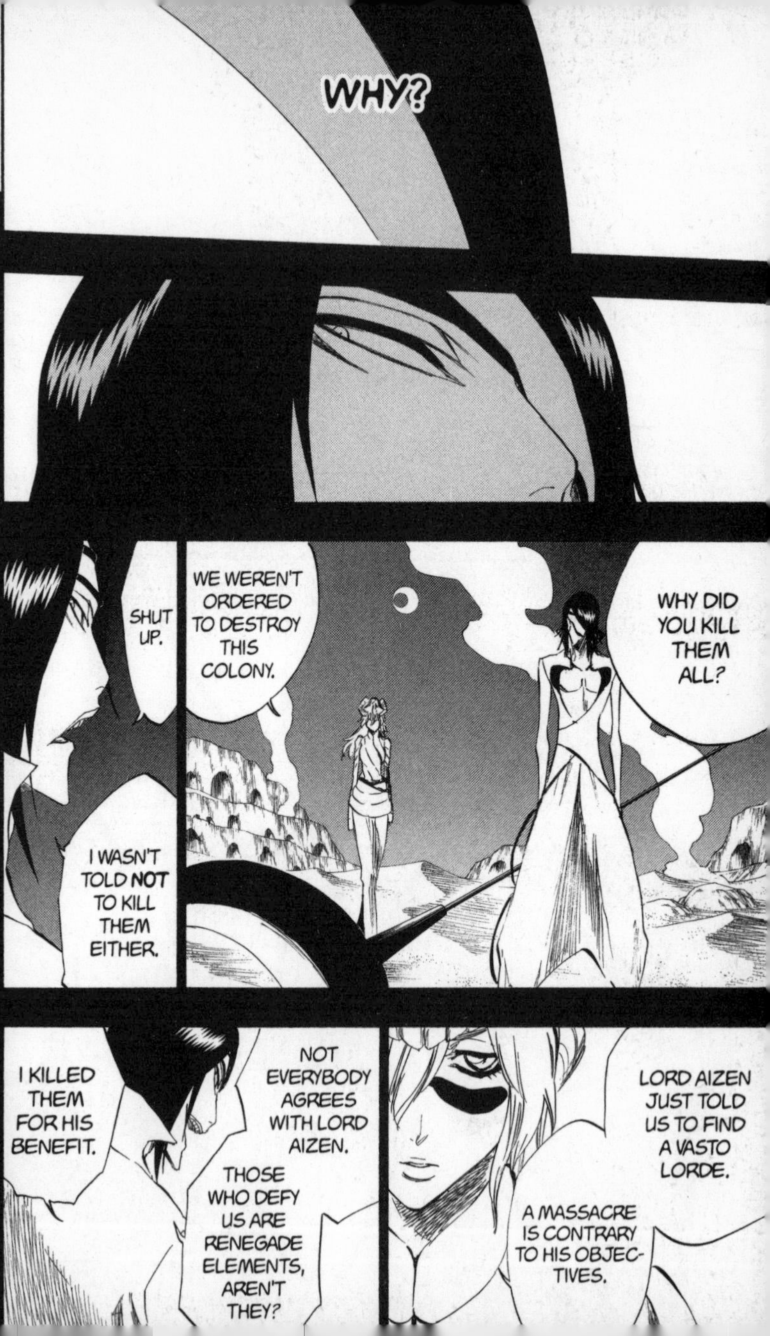
WHY?
WHY DID YOU KILL THEM ALL?
WE WEREN'T ORDERED TO DESTROY THIS COLONY.
SHUT UP.
I WASN'T TOLD **NOT** TO KILL THEM EITHER.
LORD AIZEN JUST TOLD US TO FIND A VASTO LORDE.
A MASSACRE IS CONTRARY TO HIS OBJEC-TIVES.
NOT EVERYBODY AGREES WITH LORD AIZEN.
THOSE WHO DEFY US ARE RENEGADE ELEMENTS, AREN'T THEY?
I KILLED THEM FOR HIS BENEFIT.

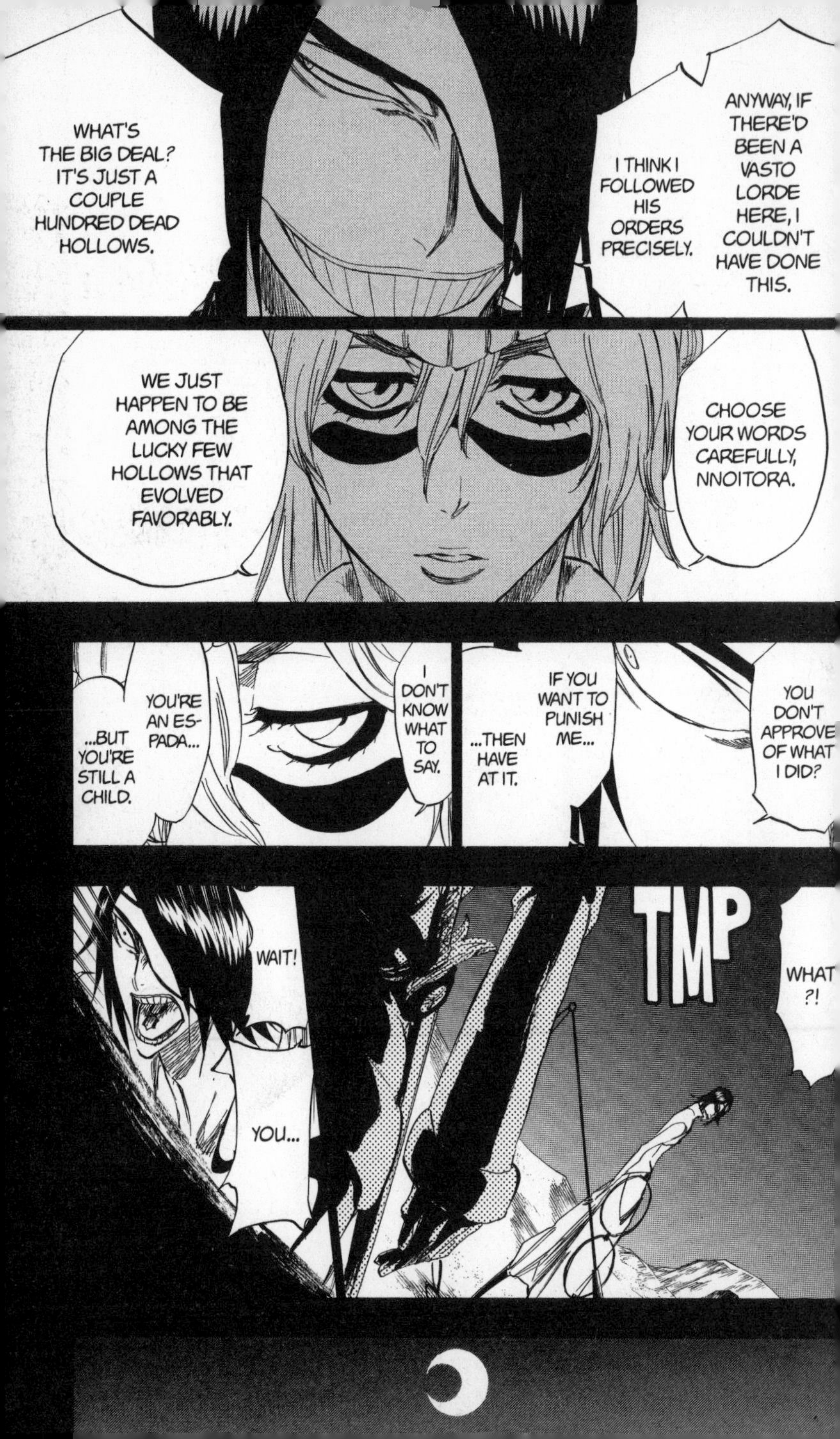
ANYWAY, IF THERE'D BEEN A VASTO LORDE HERE, I COULDN'T HAVE DONE THIS.
I THINK I FOLLOWED HIS ORDERS PRECISELY.
WHAT'S THE BIG DEAL? IT'S JUST A COUPLE HUNDRED DEAD HOLLOWS.
CHOOSE YOUR WORDS CAREFULLY, NNOITORA.
WE JUST HAPPEN TO BE AMONG THE LUCKY FEW HOLLOWS THAT EVOLVED FAVORABLY.
YOU DON'T APPROVE OF WHAT I DID?
IF YOU WANT TO PUNISH ME...
...THEN HAVE AT IT.
I DON'T KNOW WHAT TO SAY.
YOU'RE AN ES-PADA...
...BUT YOU'RE STILL A CHILD.
TMP
WHAT?!
WAIT!
YOU...

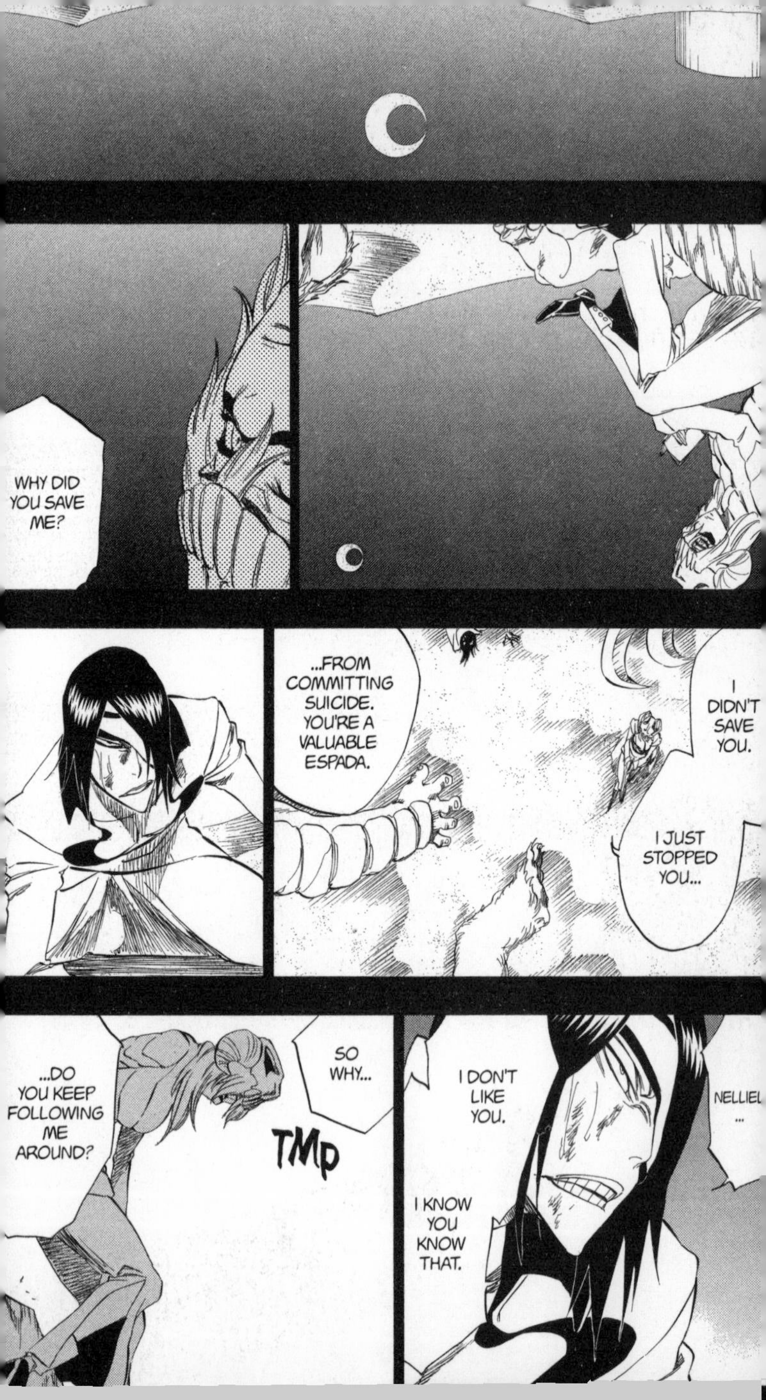
WHY DID YOU SAVE ME?
I DIDN'T SAVE YOU.
I JUST STOPPED YOU...
...FROM COMMITTING SUICIDE. YOU'RE A VALUABLE ESPADA.
NELLIEL...
I DON'T LIKE YOU.
I KNOW YOU KNOW THAT.
SO WHY...
TMP
...DO YOU KEEP FOLLOWING ME AROUND?

READ THIS WAY

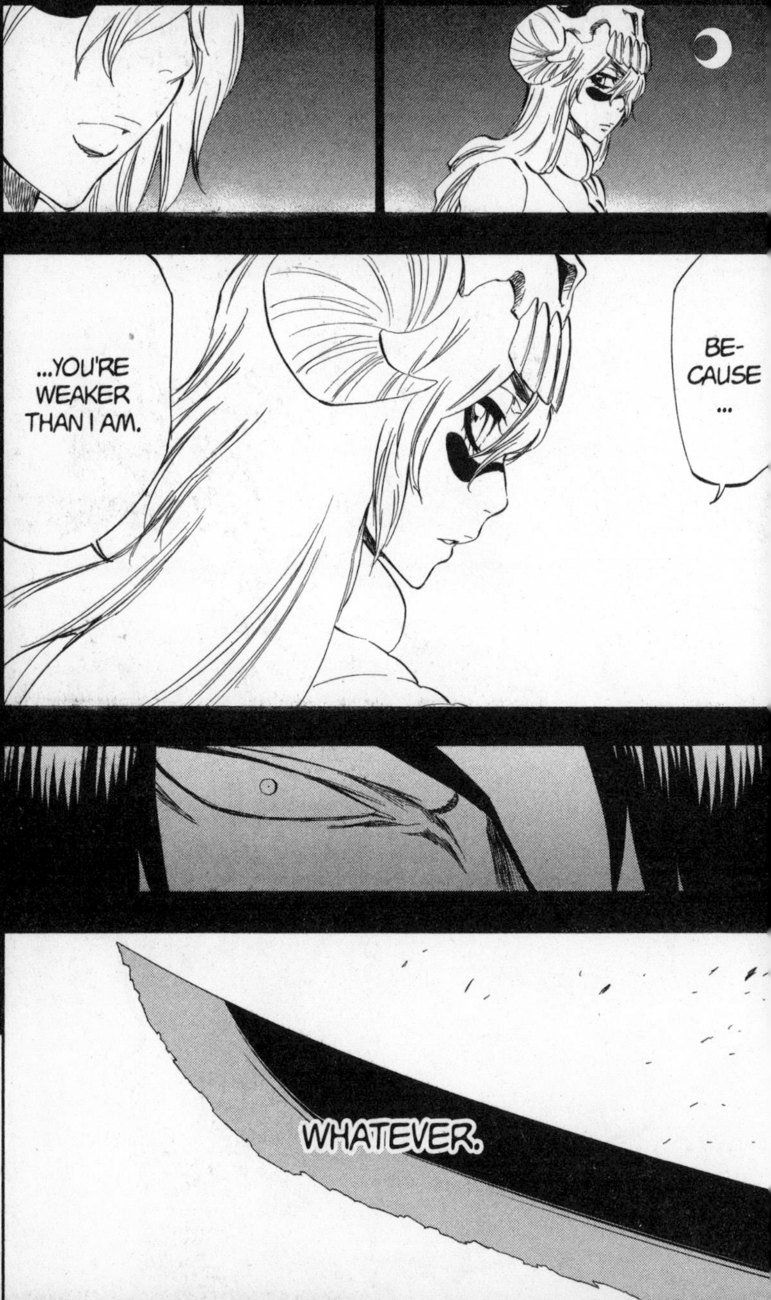
BE-CAUSE ...
...YOU'RE WEAKER THAN I AM.
WHATEVER.

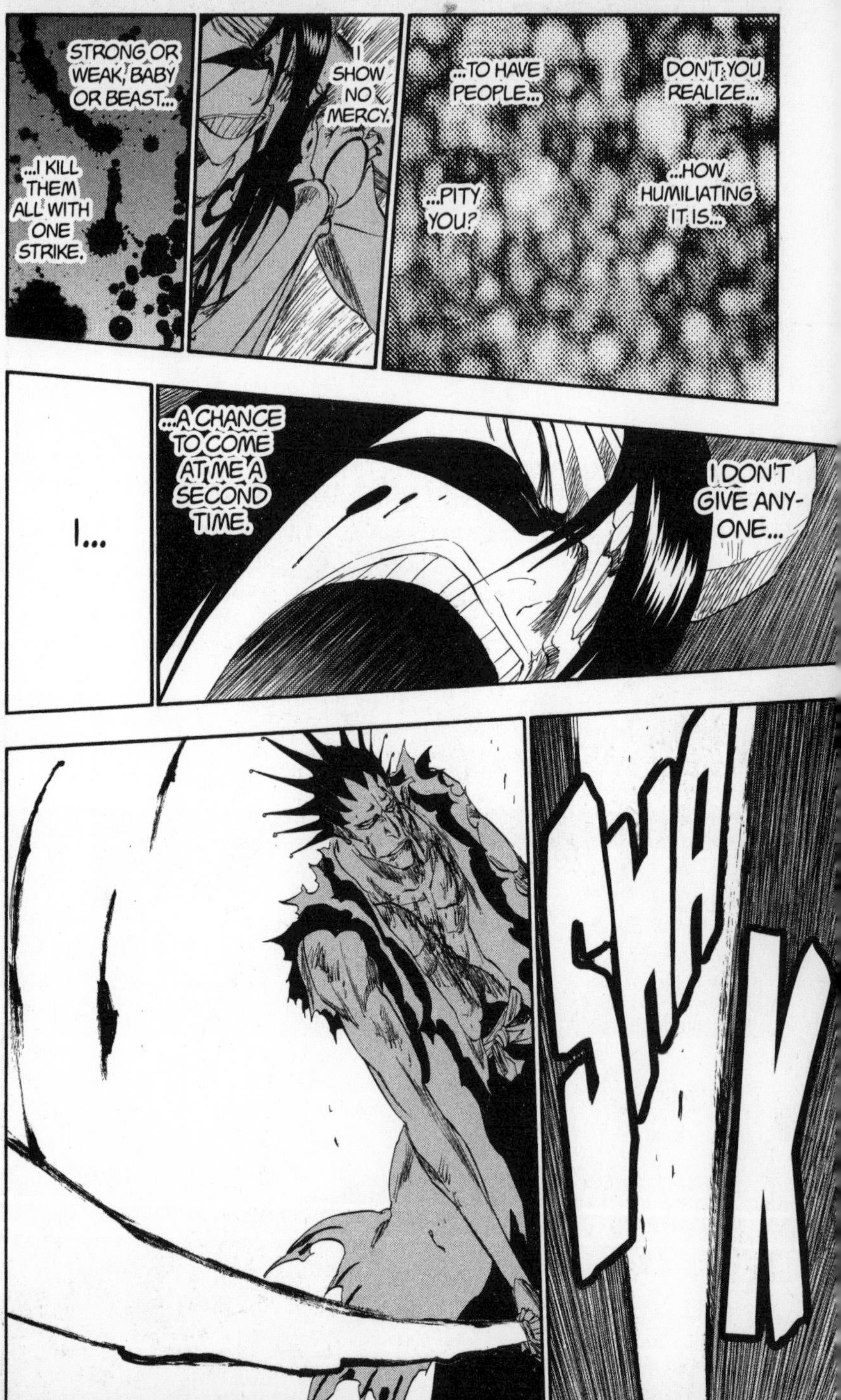
DON'T YOU REALIZE...
...HOW HUMILIATING IT IS...
...TO HAVE PEOPLE...
...PITY YOU?
I SHOW NO MERCY.
STRONG OR WEAK, BABY OR BEAST...
...I KILL THEM ALL WITH ONE STRIKE.
I DON'T GIVE ANY-ONE...
...A CHANCE TO COME AT ME A SECOND TIME.
I...
SHAK

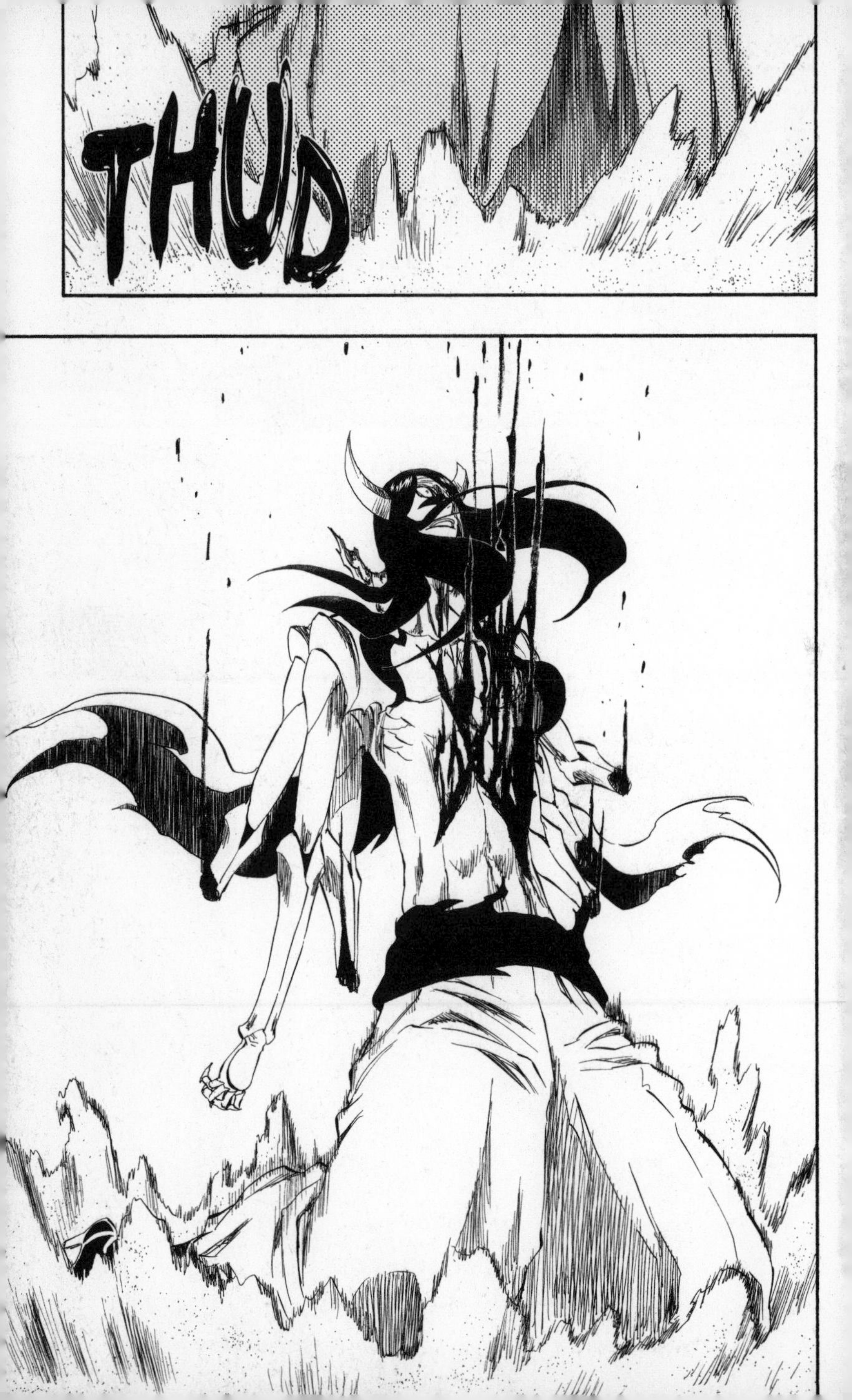
THUD

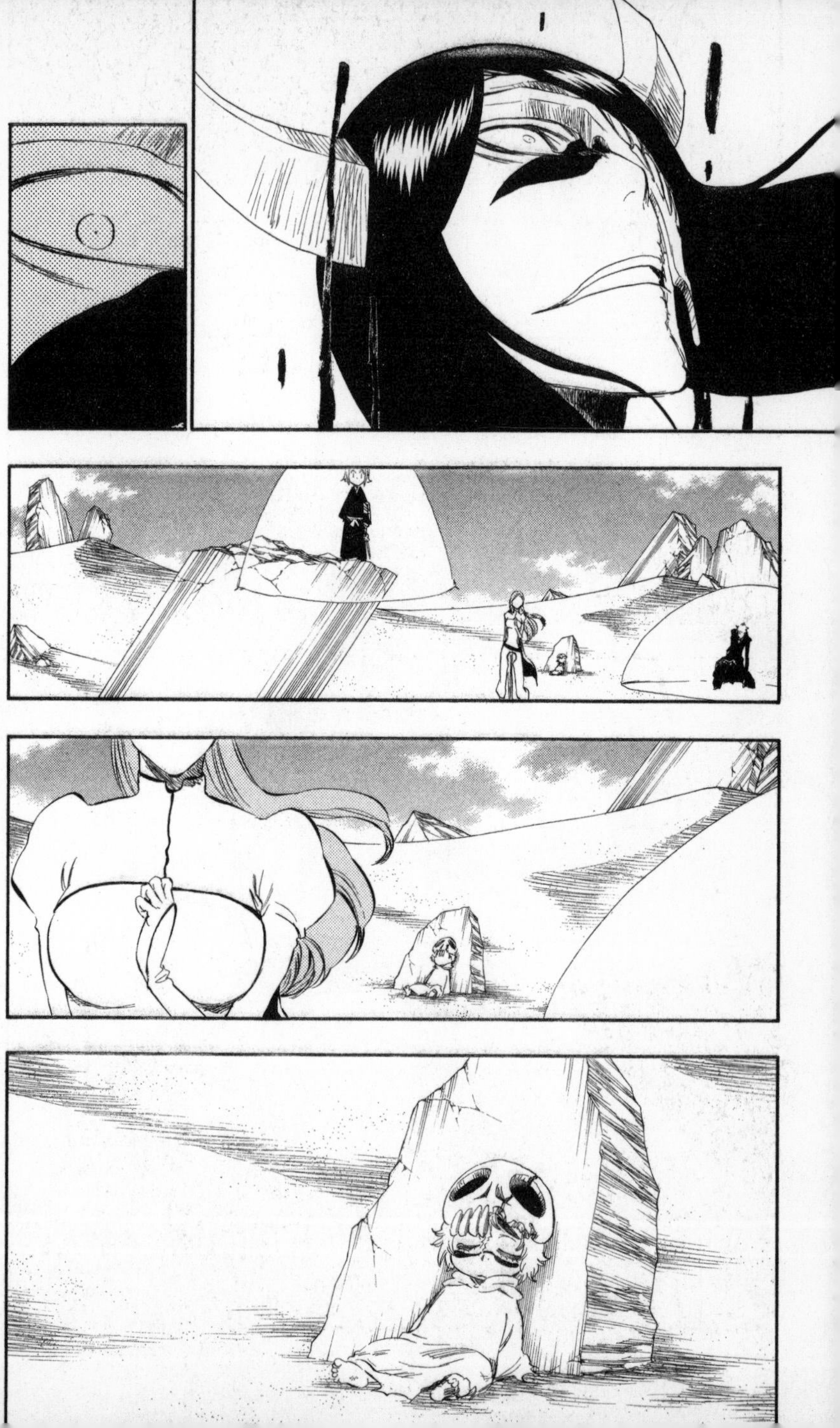

...TORA?

NNOI...

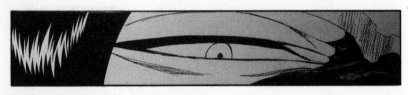

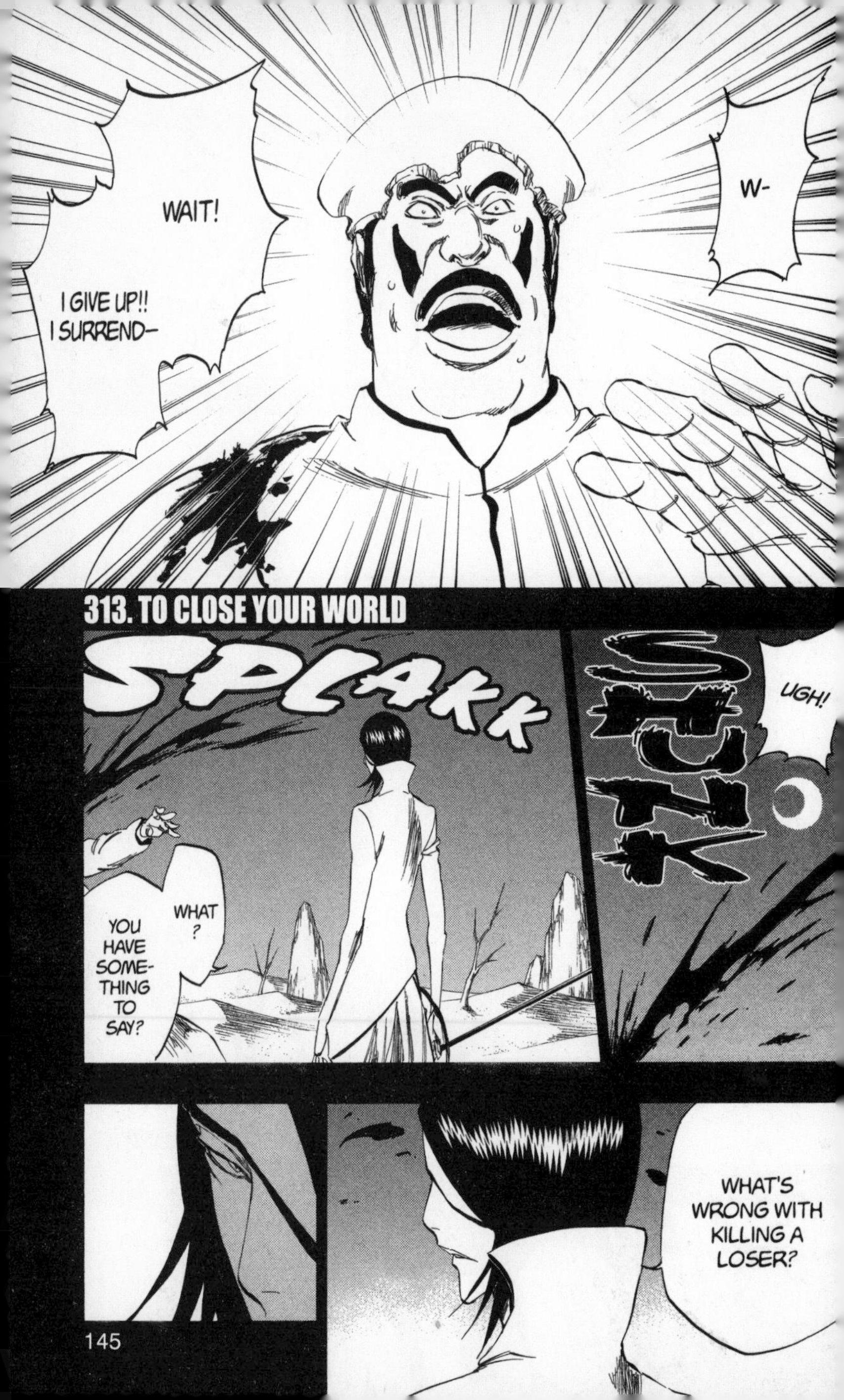
W-
WAIT!
I GIVE UP!! I SURRENDER-
313. TO CLOSE YOUR WORLD
SHTK
UGH!
SPLAKK
WHAT?
YOU HAVE SOMETHING TO SAY?
WHAT'S WRONG WITH KILLING A LOSER?

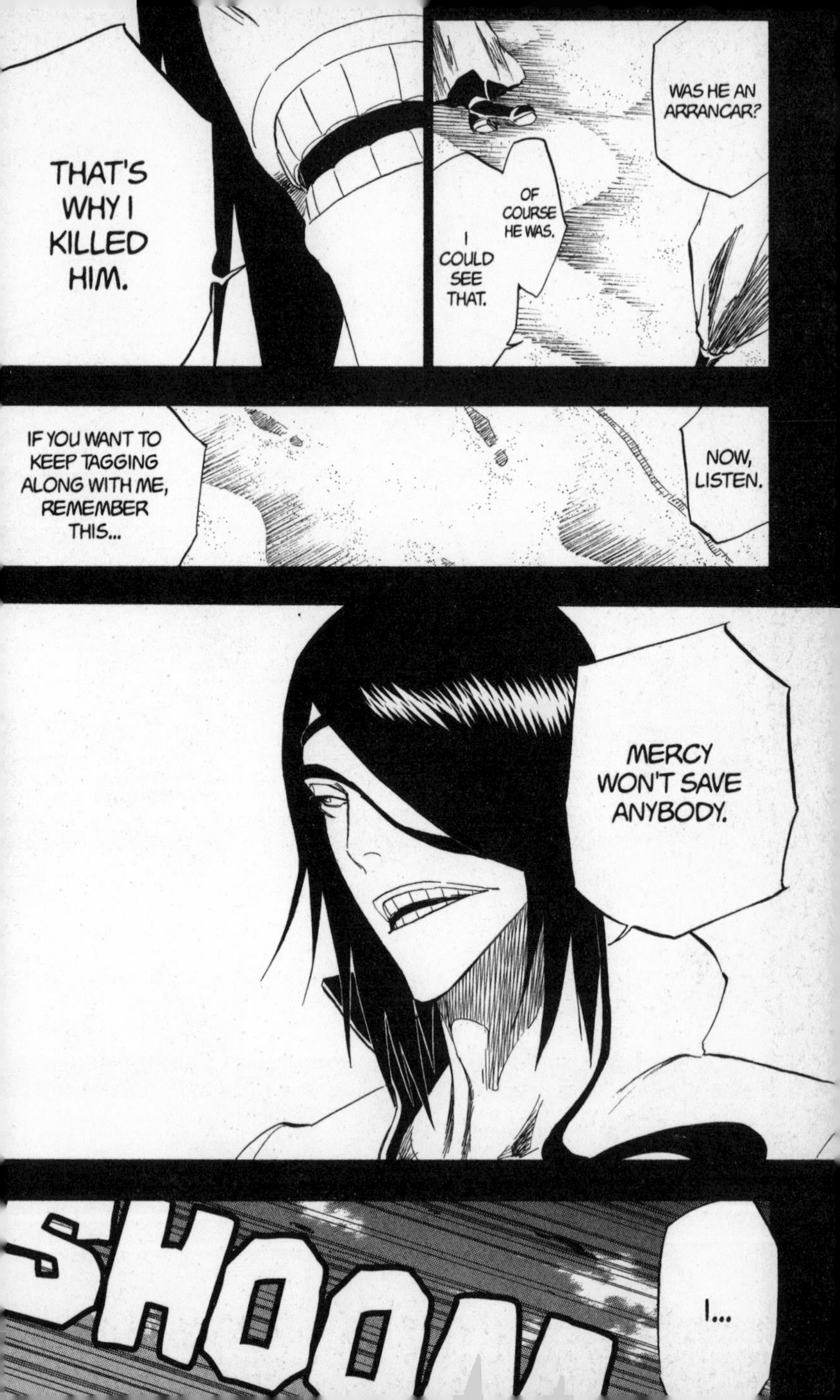
WAS HE AN ARRANCAR?
OF COURSE HE WAS.
I COULD SEE THAT.
THAT'S WHY I KILLED HIM.
NOW, LISTEN.
IF YOU WANT TO KEEP TAGGING ALONG WITH ME, REMEMBER THIS...
MERCY WON'T SAVE ANYBODY.
I...
SHOO

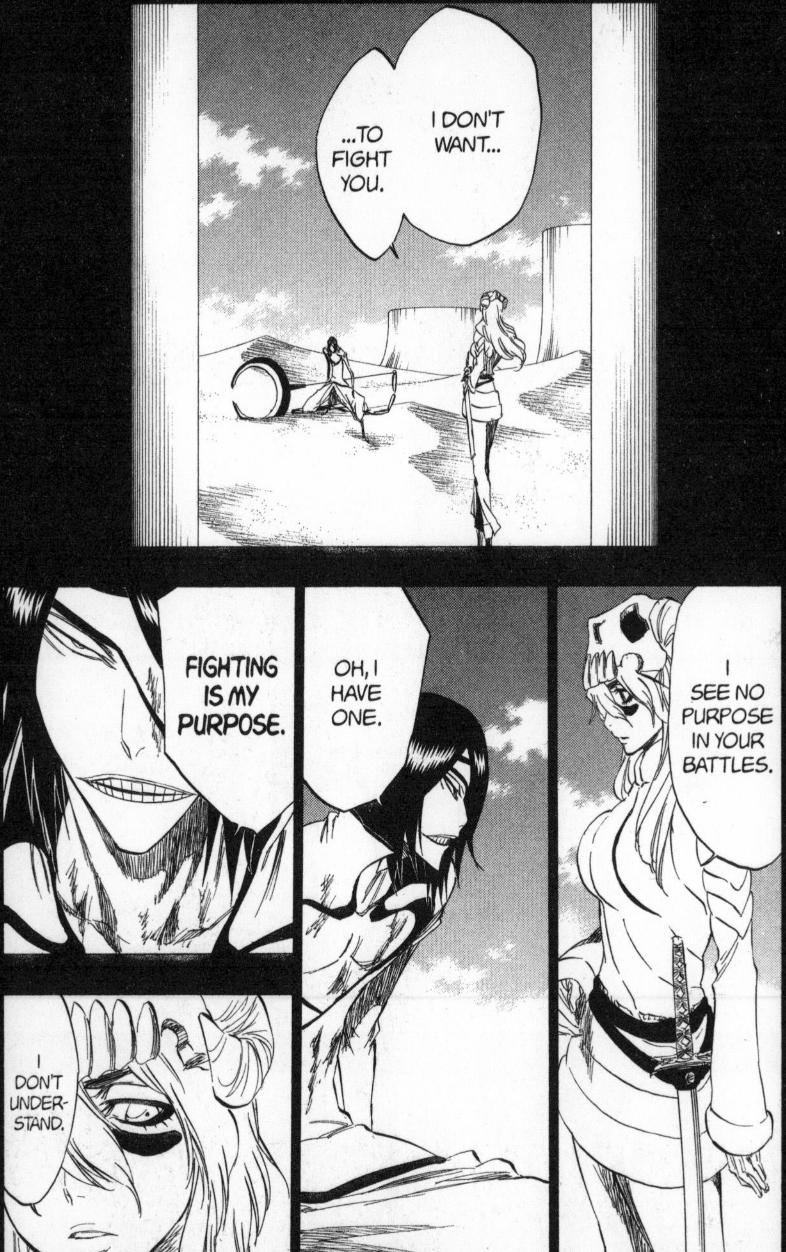
I DON'T WANT...
...TO FIGHT YOU.
I SEE NO PURPOSE IN YOUR BATTLES.
OH, I HAVE ONE.
FIGHTING IS MY PURPOSE.
I DON'T UNDER-STAND.

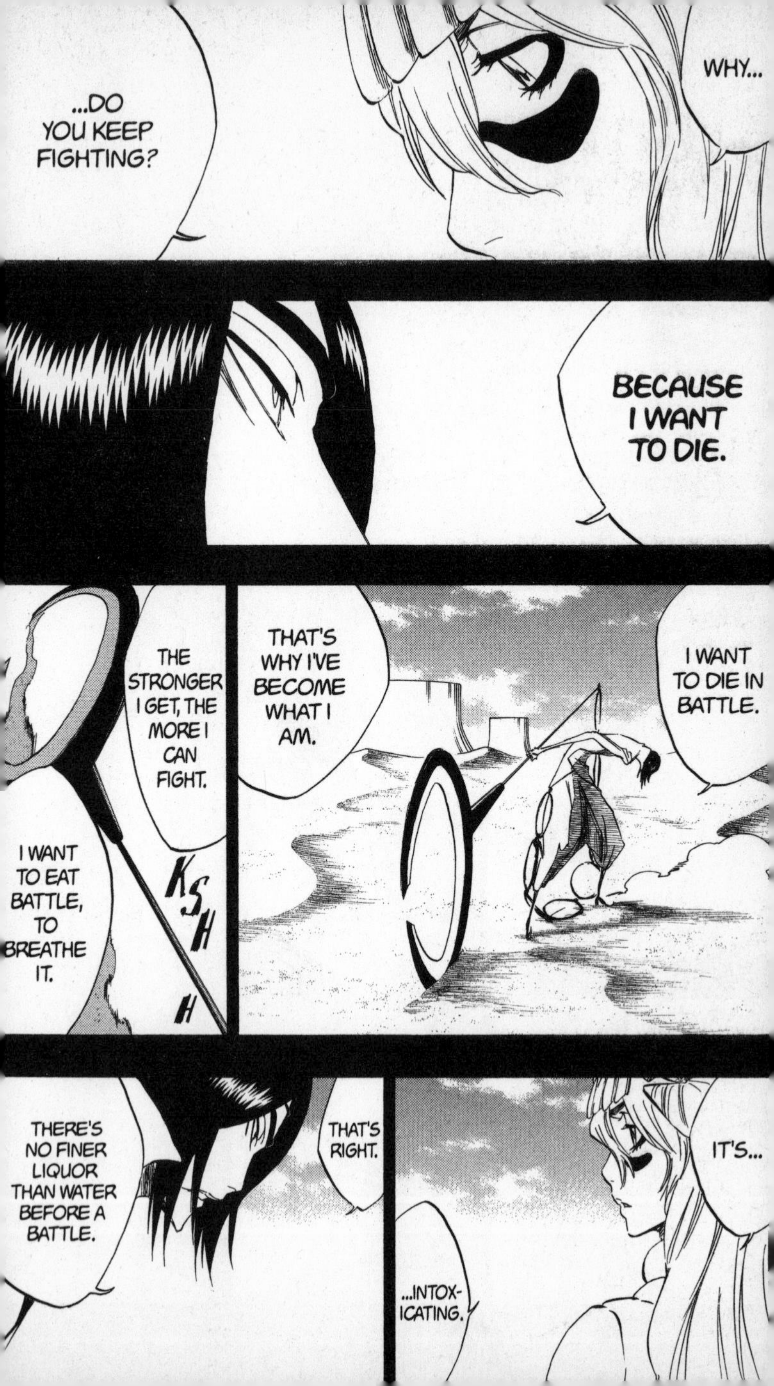
WHY...
...DO YOU KEEP FIGHTING?
BECAUSE I WANT TO DIE.
I WANT TO DIE IN BATTLE.
THAT'S WHY I'VE BECOME WHAT I AM.
THE STRONGER I GET, THE MORE I CAN FIGHT.
I WANT TO EAT BATTLE, TO BREATHE IT.
KSHH
IT'S...
...INTOX-ICATING.
THAT'S RIGHT.
THERE'S NO FINER LIQUOR THAN WATER BEFORE A BATTLE.

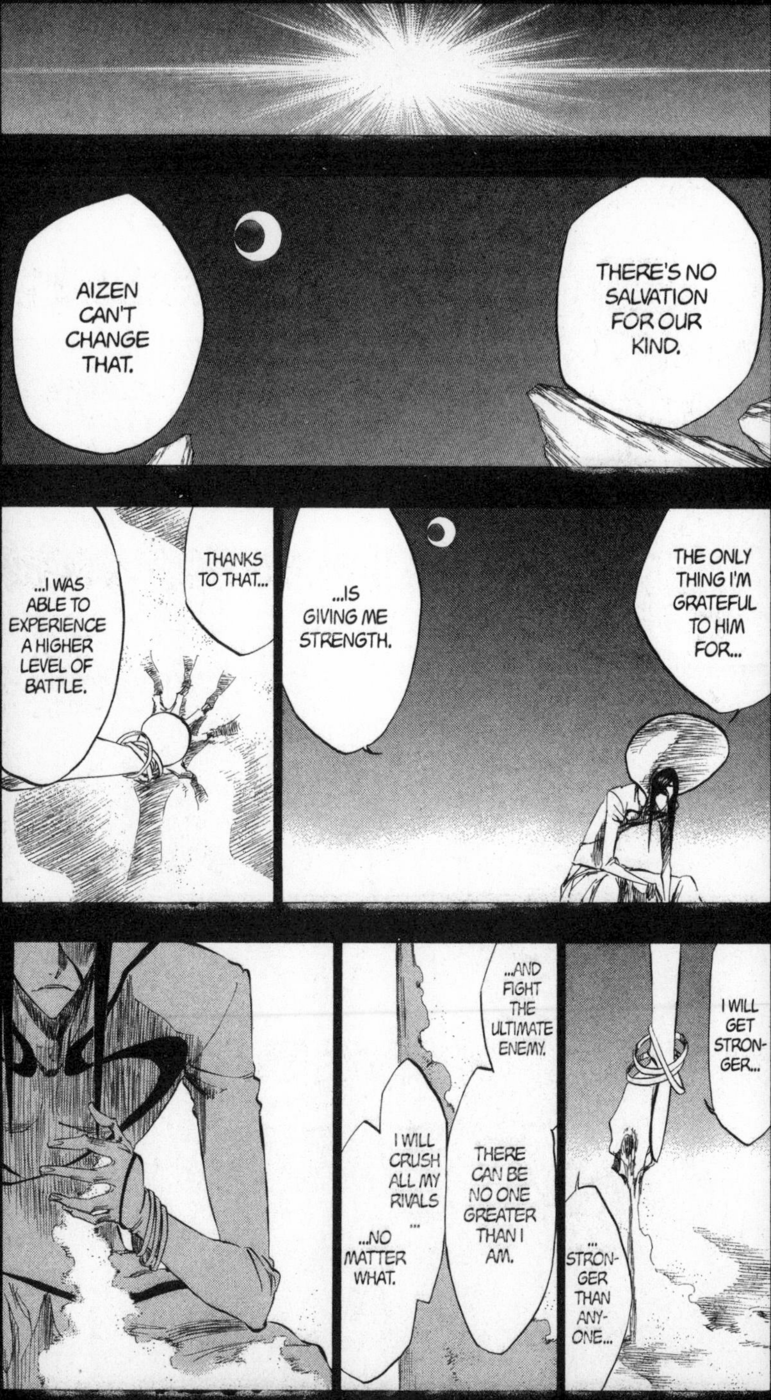
THERE'S NO SALVATION FOR OUR KIND.
AIZEN CAN'T CHANGE THAT.
THE ONLY THING I'M GRATEFUL TO HIM FOR...
...IS GIVING ME STRENGTH.
THANKS TO THAT...
...I WAS ABLE TO EXPERIENCE A HIGHER LEVEL OF BATTLE.
I WILL GET STRON-GER...
...STRON-GER THAN ANY-ONE...
...AND FIGHT THE ULTIMATE ENEMY.
THERE CAN BE NO ONE GREATER THAN I AM.
I WILL CRUSH ALL MY RIVALS...
...NO MATTER WHAT.

I WANT LIFE TO HAVE FLED MY BODY...
...BEFORE IT HITS THE GROUND.
THAT'S HOW I WANT TO DIE.

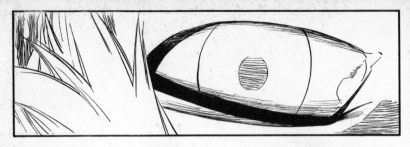

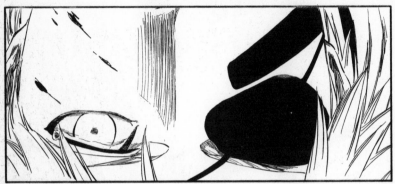

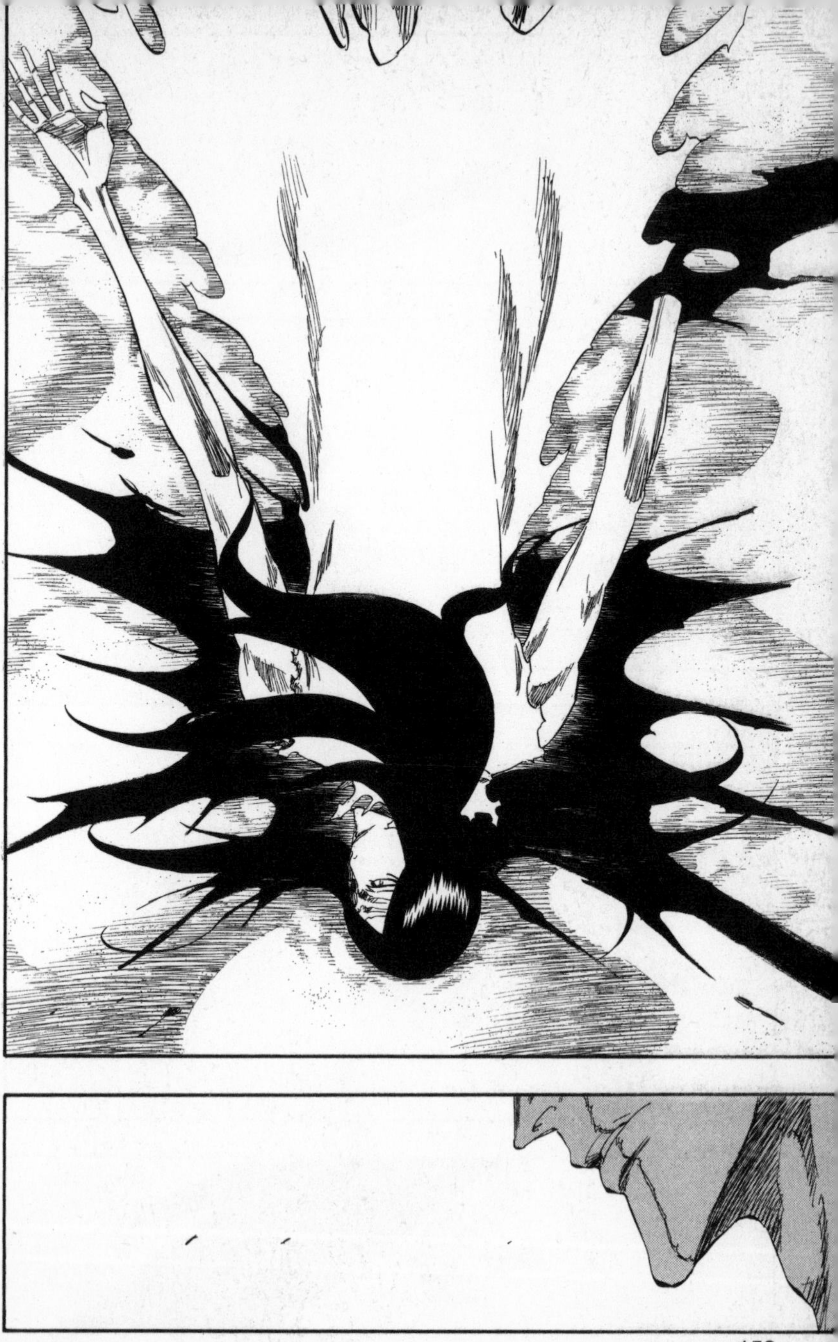

WELL, IT'S BEEN FUN...

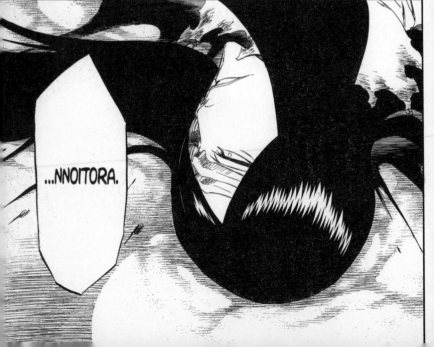

...NNOITORA.

REACH
OUT

TO
CLOSE
YOUR
WORLD

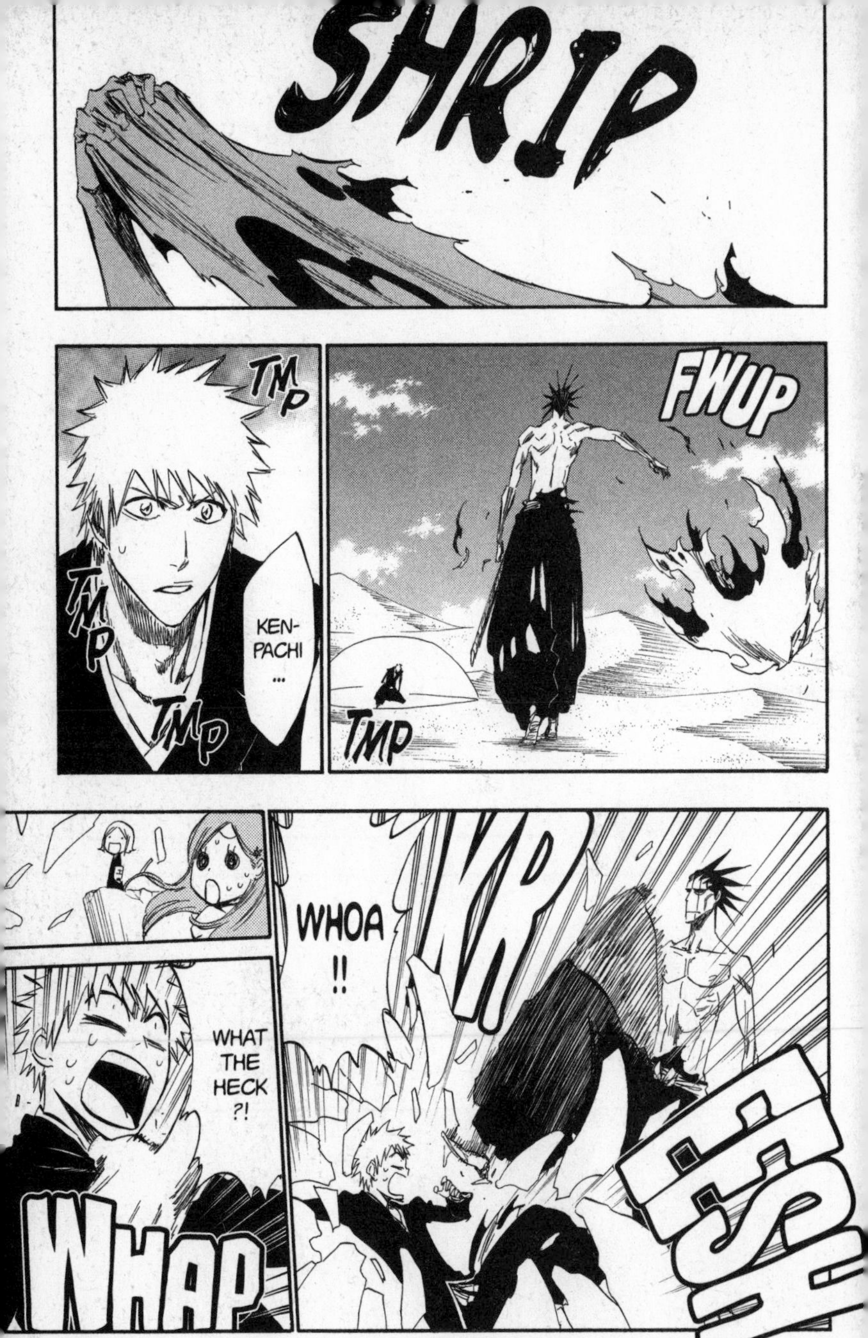
SHRIP
FWUP
TMP
TMP
KEN-PACHI ...
TMP
TMP
WHOA !!
WHAT THE HECK ?!
WHAP

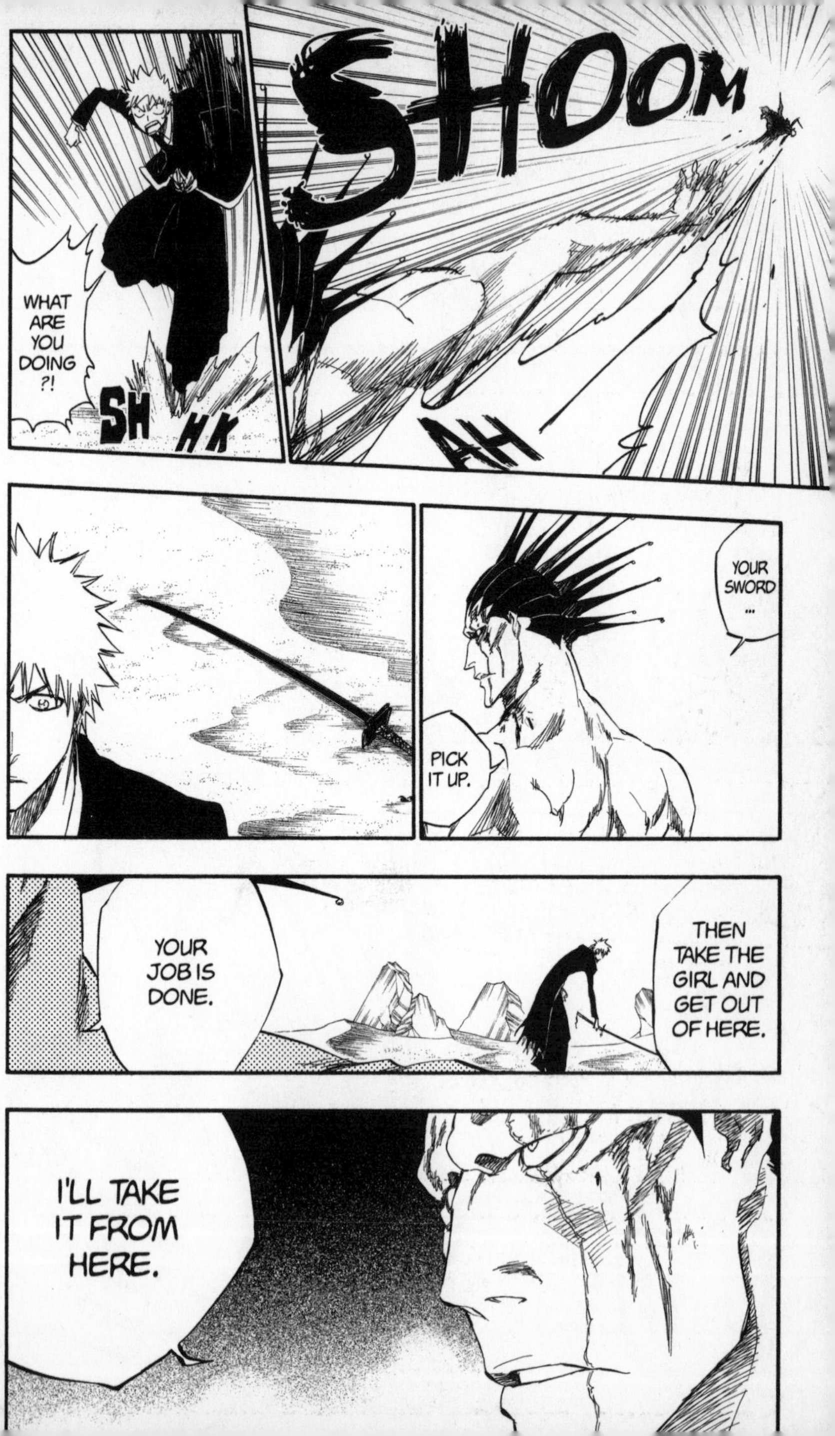

SHOOM
AH
WHAT ARE YOU DOING ?!
SHHK
YOUR SWORD ...
PICK IT UP.
THEN TAKE THE GIRL AND GET OUT OF HERE.
YOUR JOB IS DONE.
I'LL TAKE IT FROM HERE.

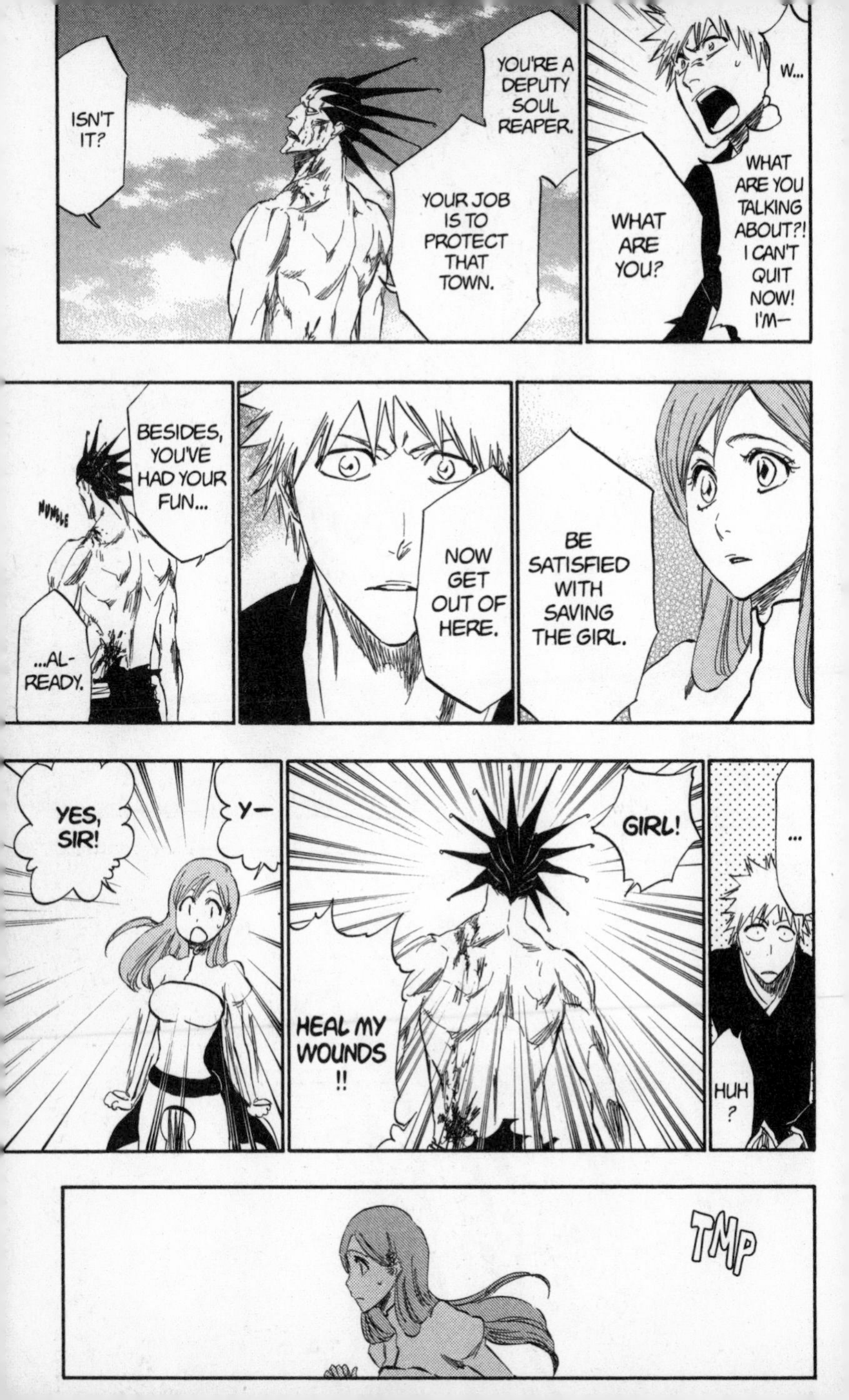
W...
WHAT ARE YOU TALKING ABOUT?! I CAN'T QUIT NOW! I'M—
WHAT ARE YOU?
YOU'RE A DEPUTY SOUL REAPER.
YOUR JOB IS TO PROTECT THAT TOWN.
ISN'T IT?
BE SATISFIED WITH SAVING THE GIRL.
NOW GET OUT OF HERE.
BESIDES, YOU'VE HAD YOUR FUN...
MUMBLE
...AL-READY.
...
HUH?
GIRL!
HEAL MY WOUNDS !!
Y—
YES, SIR!
TMP

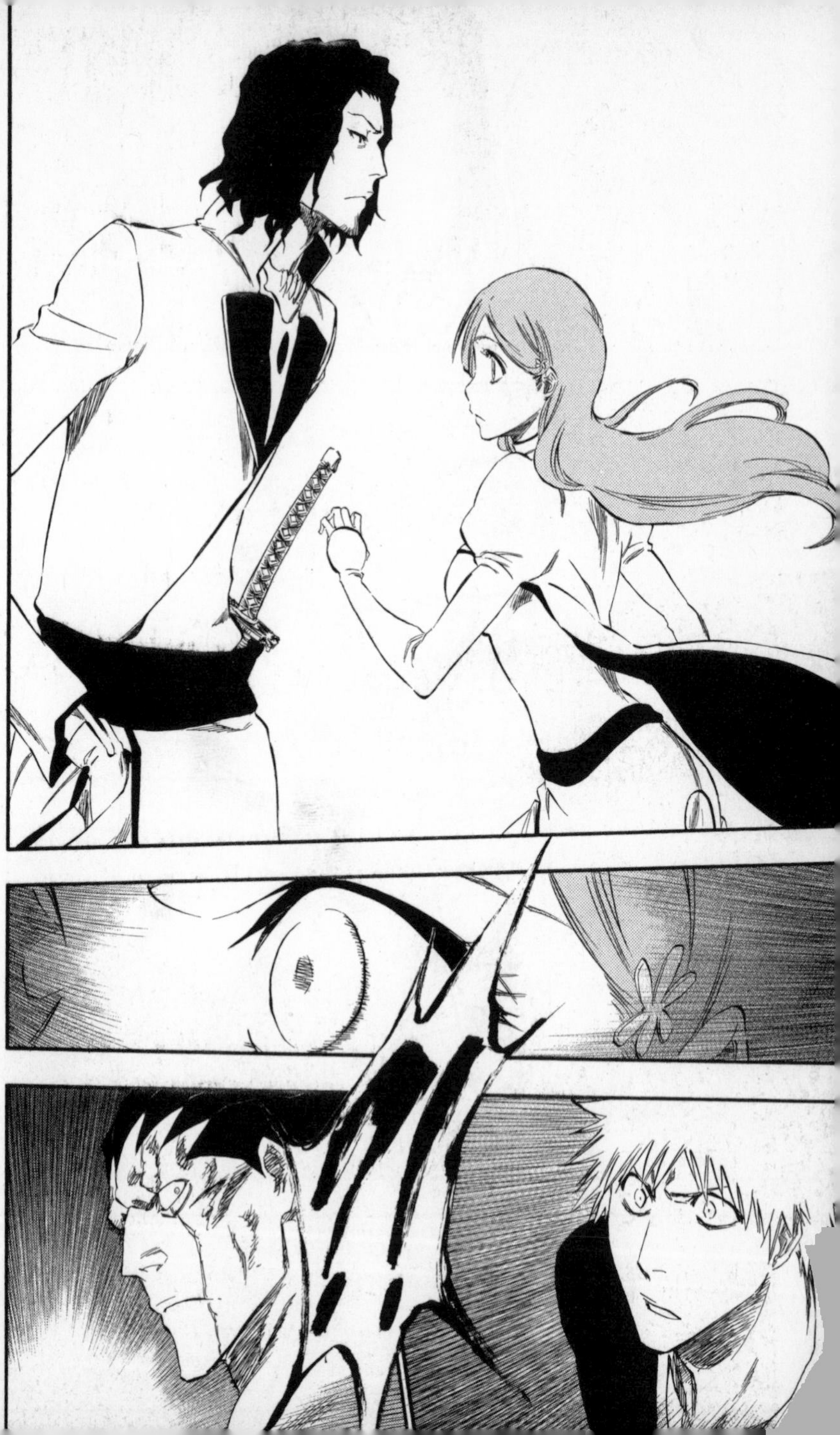

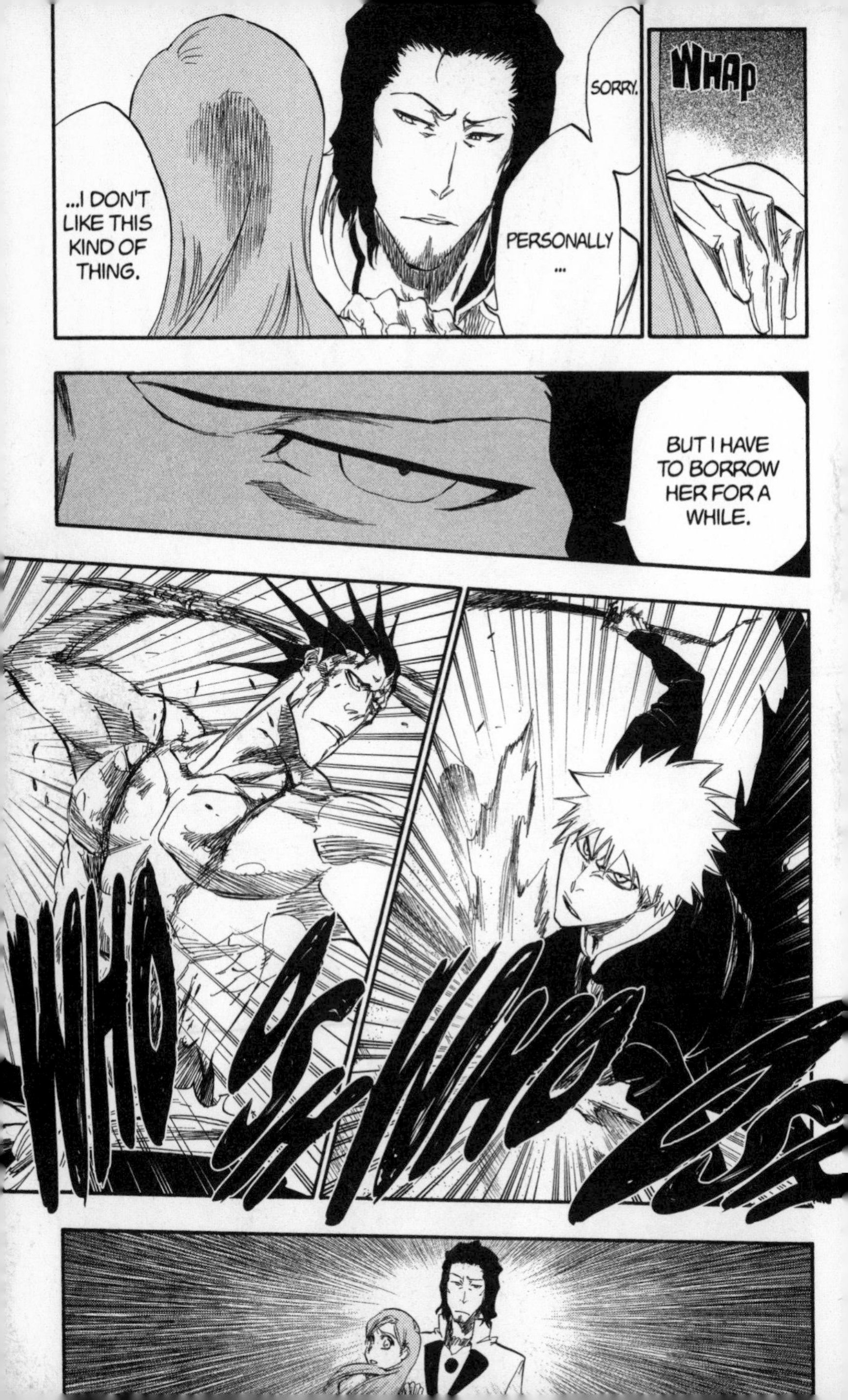
WHAP
SORRY.
PERSONALLY ...
...I DON'T LIKE THIS KIND OF THING.
BUT I HAVE TO BORROW HER FOR A WHILE.
WHOOSH
WHOOSH

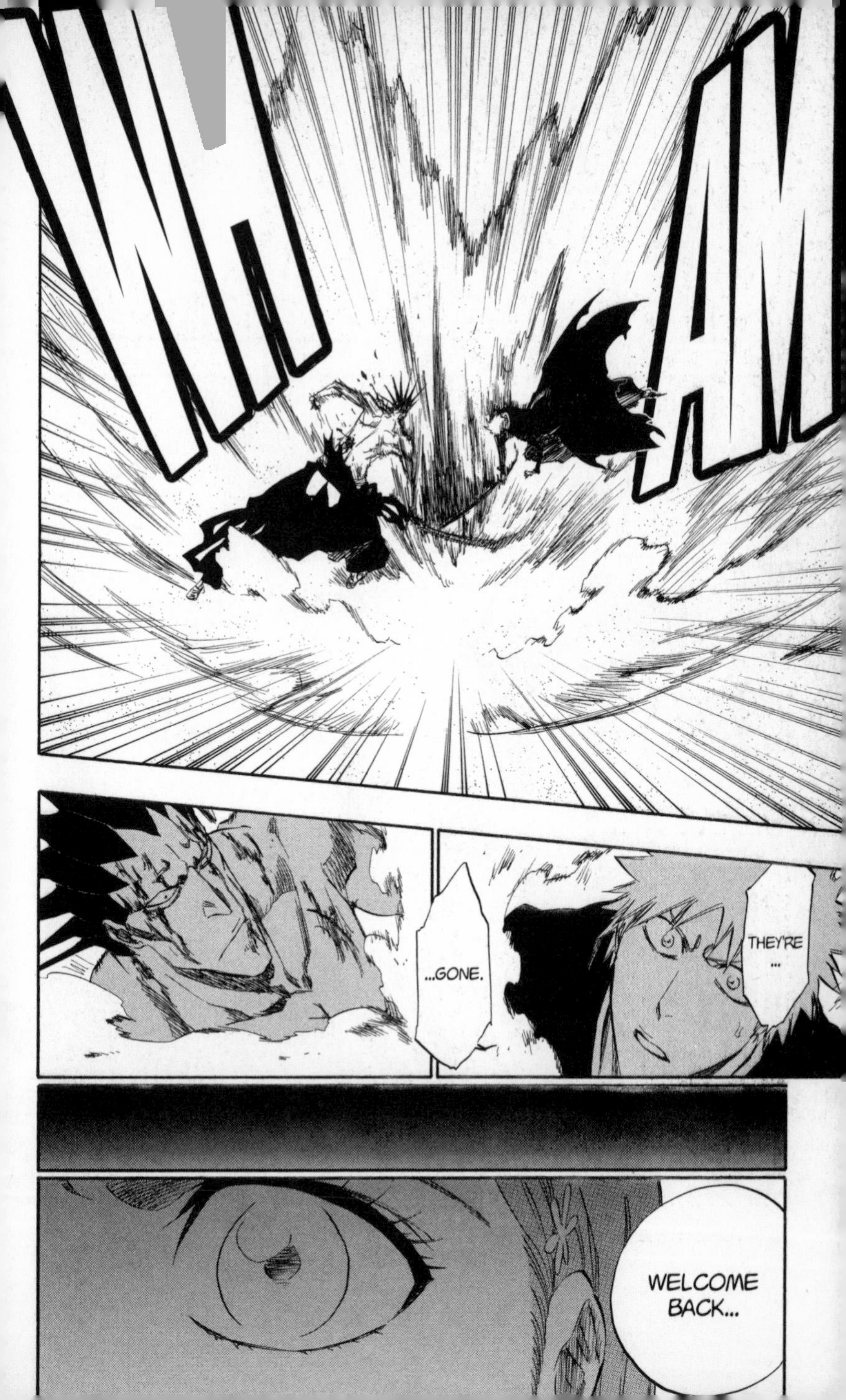
WHAM
THEY'RE ...
...GONE.
WELCOME BACK...

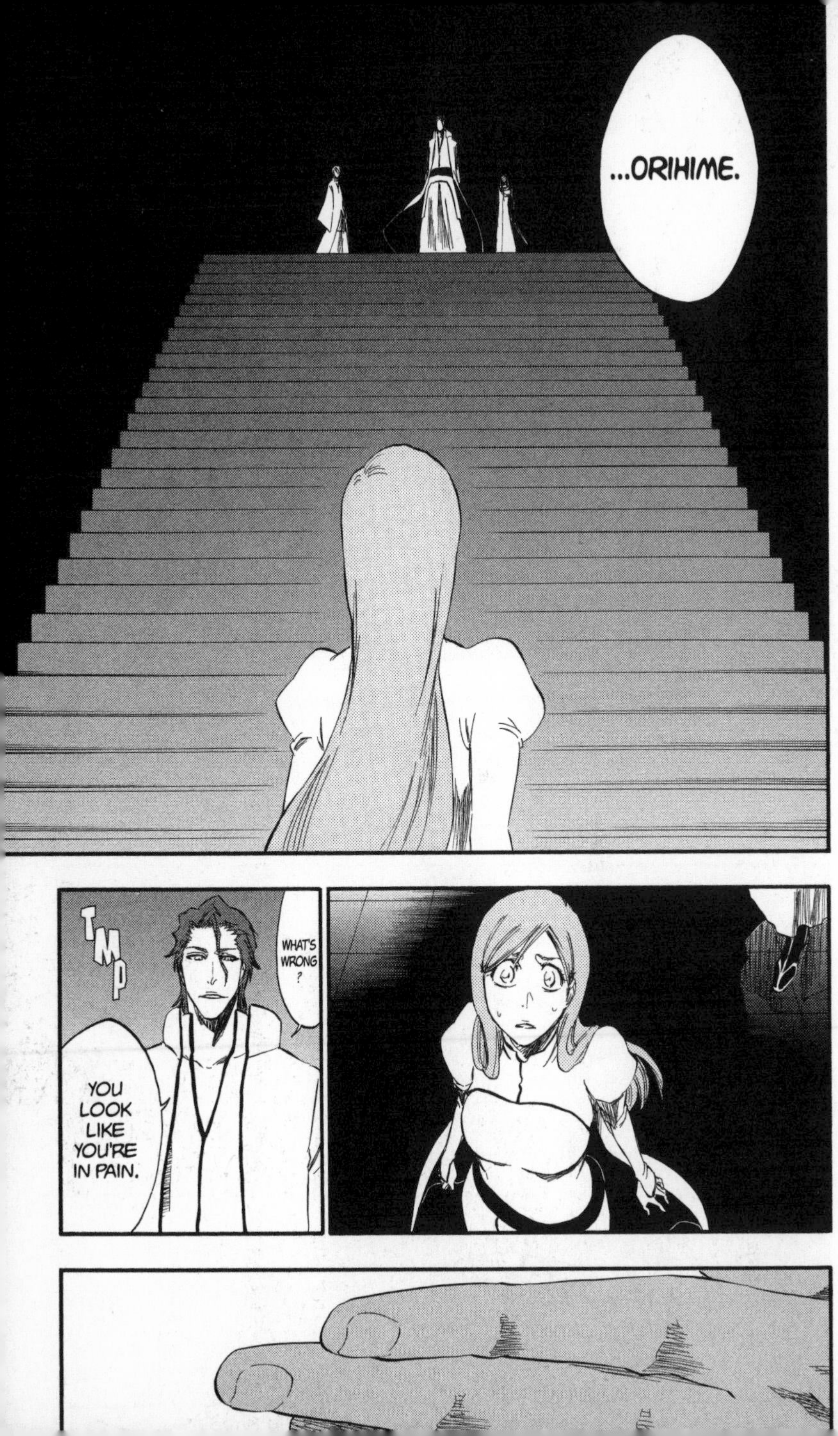
...ORIHIME.
WHAT'S WRONG?
TMP
YOU LOOK LIKE YOU'RE IN PAIN.

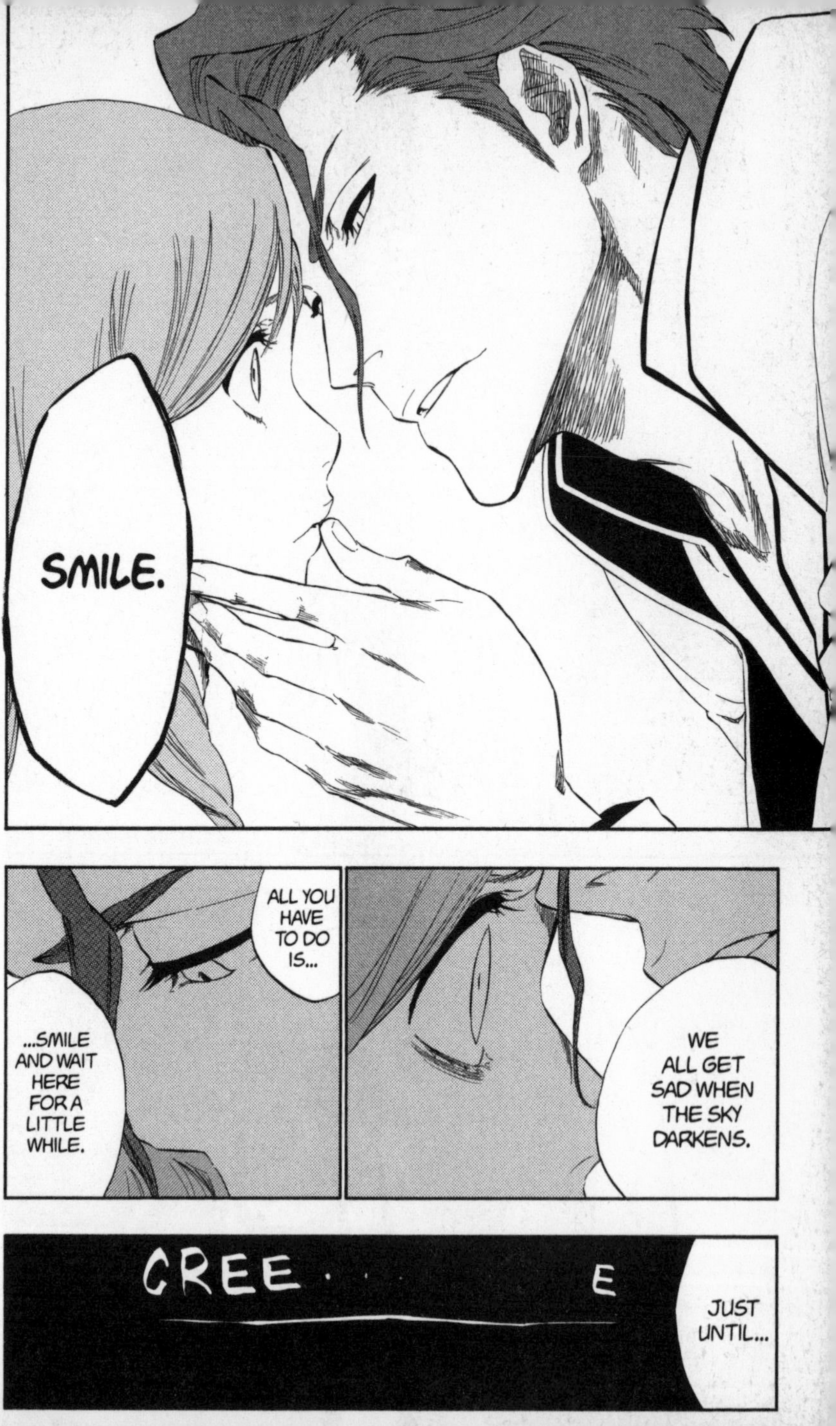
SMILE.
WE ALL GET SAD WHEN THE SKY DARKENS.
ALL YOU HAVE TO DO IS...
...SMILE AND WAIT HERE FOR A LITTLE WHILE.
JUST UNTIL...
CREE... E

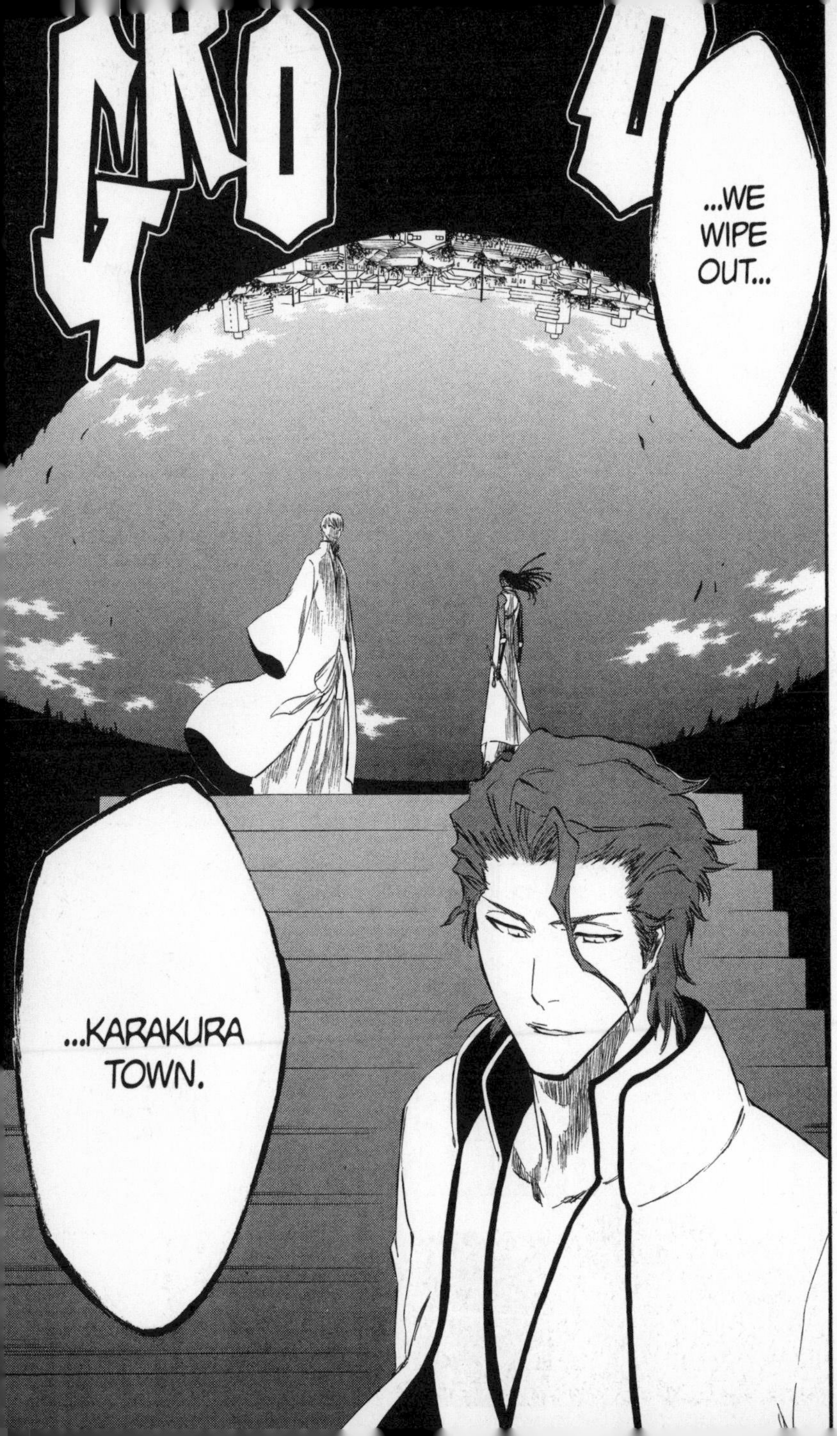
...WE WIPE OUT...
...KARAKURA TOWN.

the end is near.

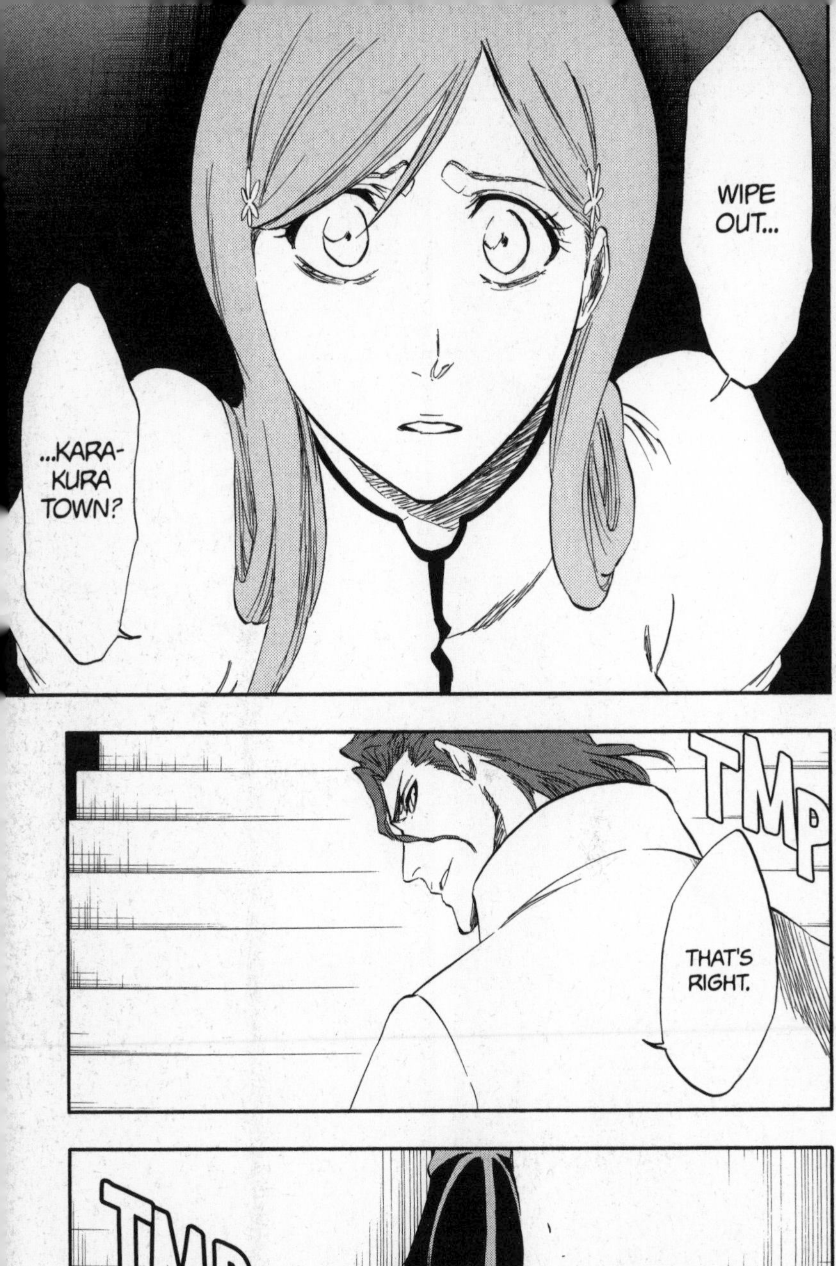
WIPE OUT...
...KARA-KURA TOWN?
TMP
THAT'S RIGHT.
TMP

314. Night Side of Abduction

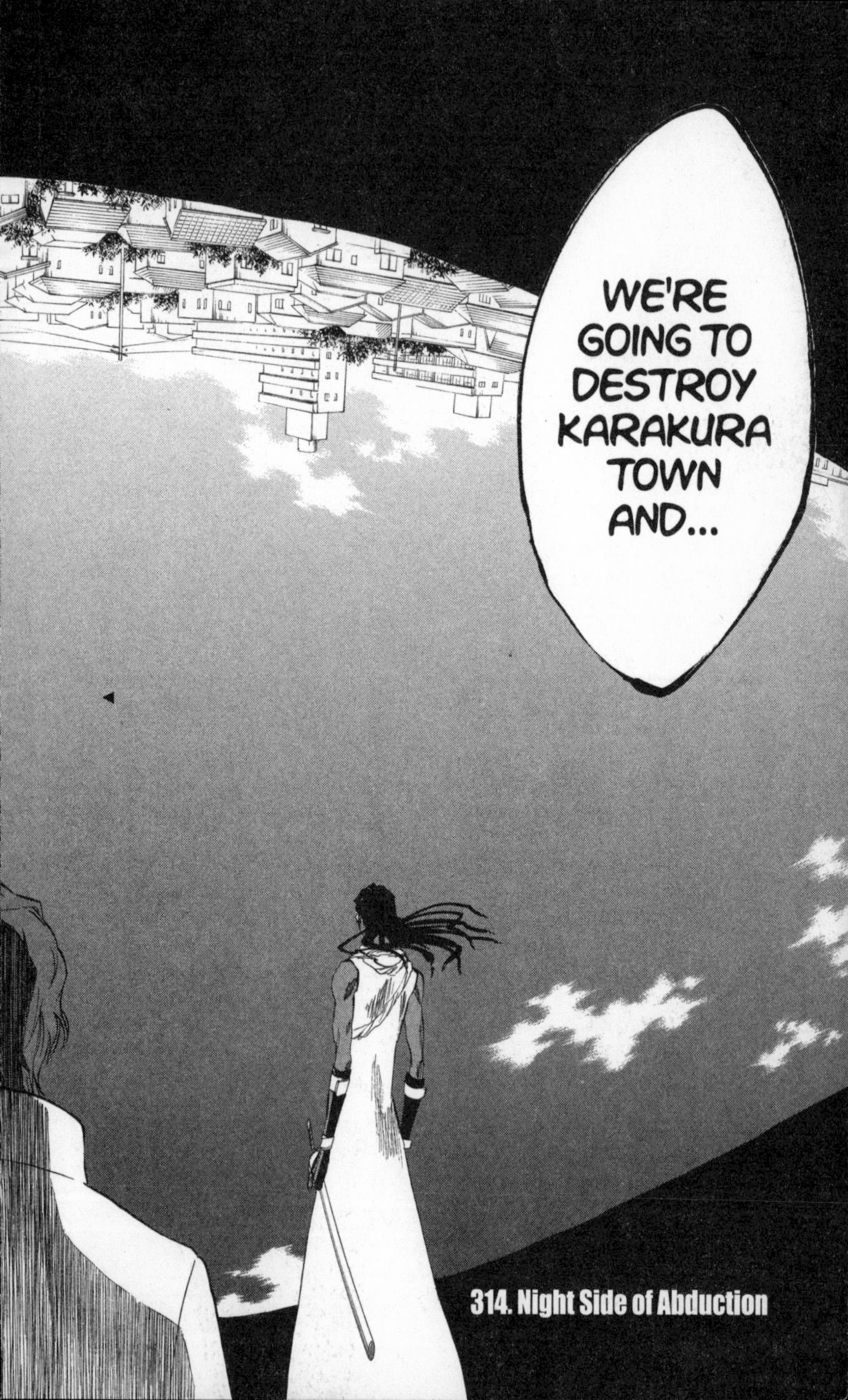
WE'RE GOING TO DESTROY KARAKURA TOWN AND...

314. Night Side of Abduction

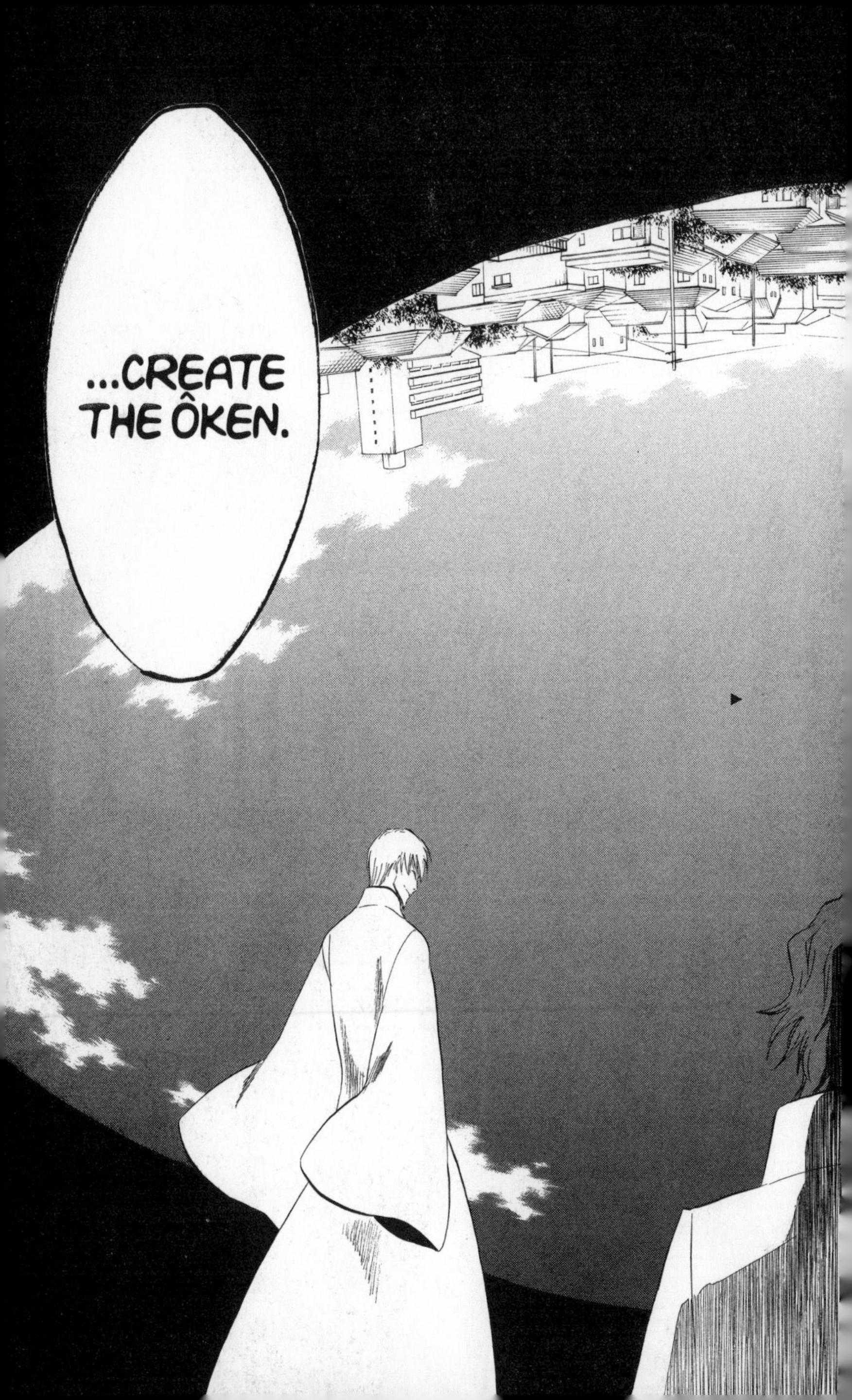
...CREATE THE ÔKEN.

THE TENTEI KÛRA. (HEAVENLY CHARGED SKY NET)

KANAME...

YES, SIR.

KLIK

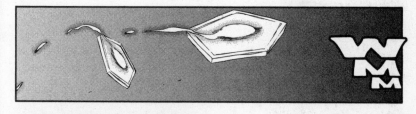

SKREEK

SKREEK

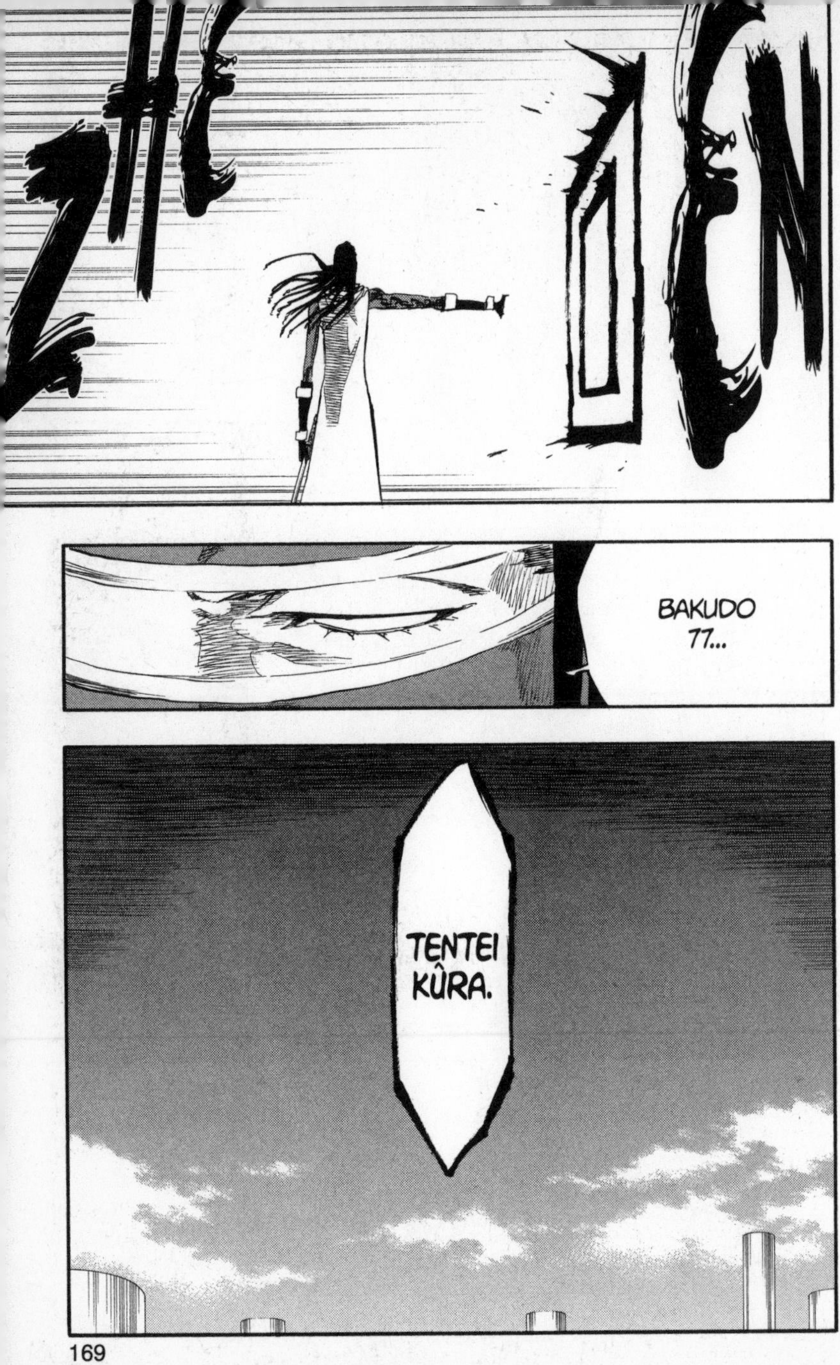
BAKUDO 77...
TENTEI KÛRA.

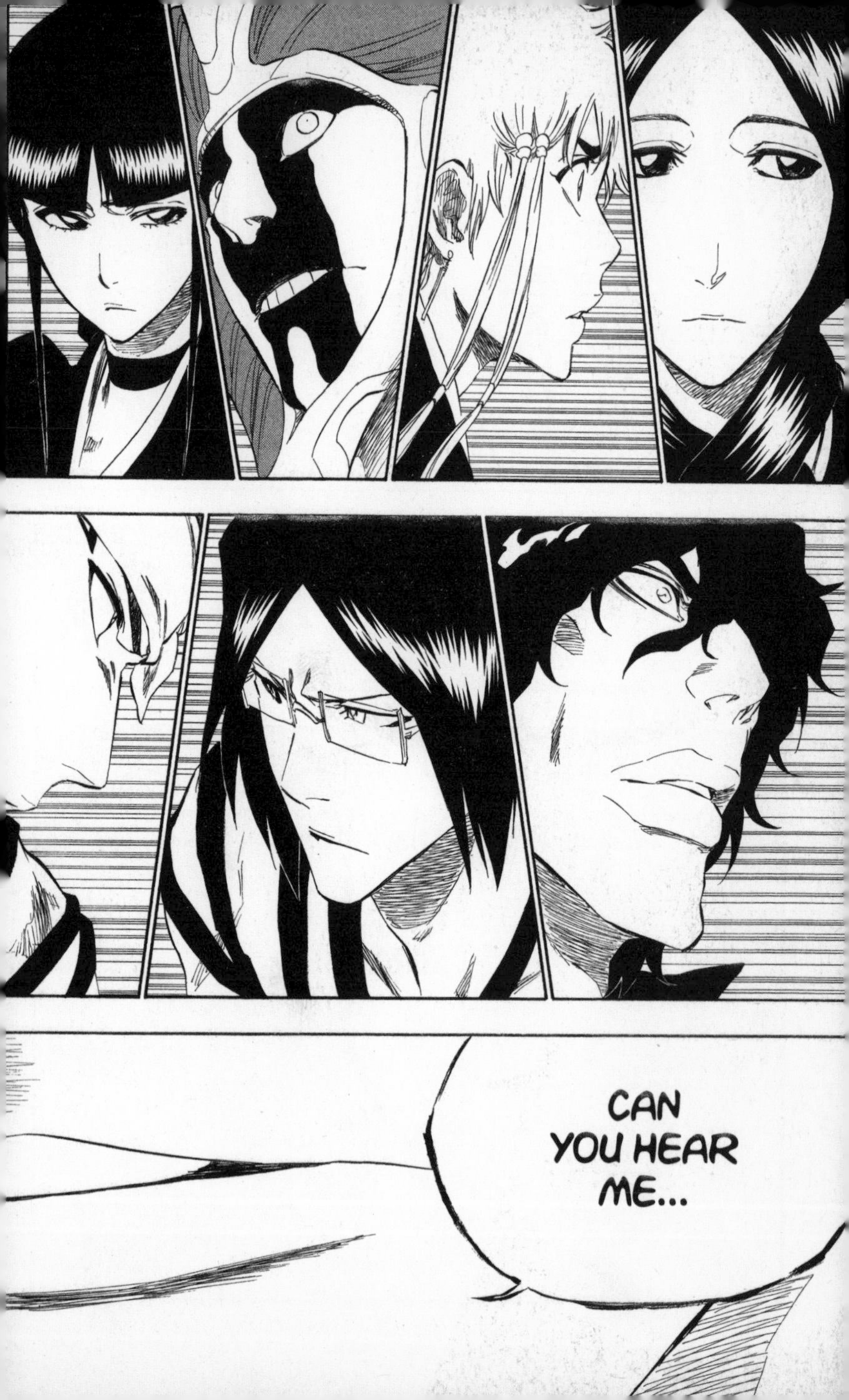
CAN
YOU HEAR
ME...

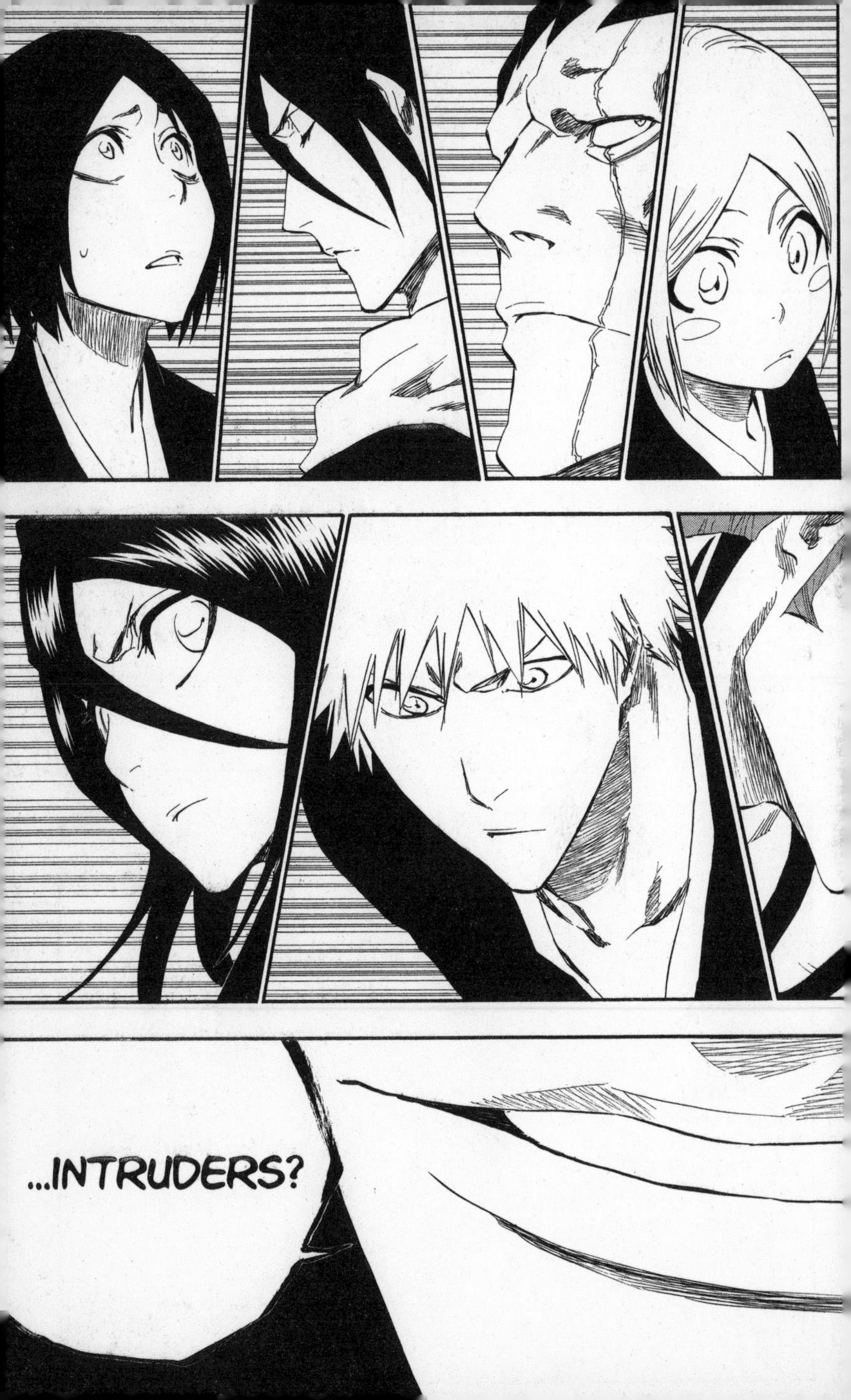
...INTRUDERS?

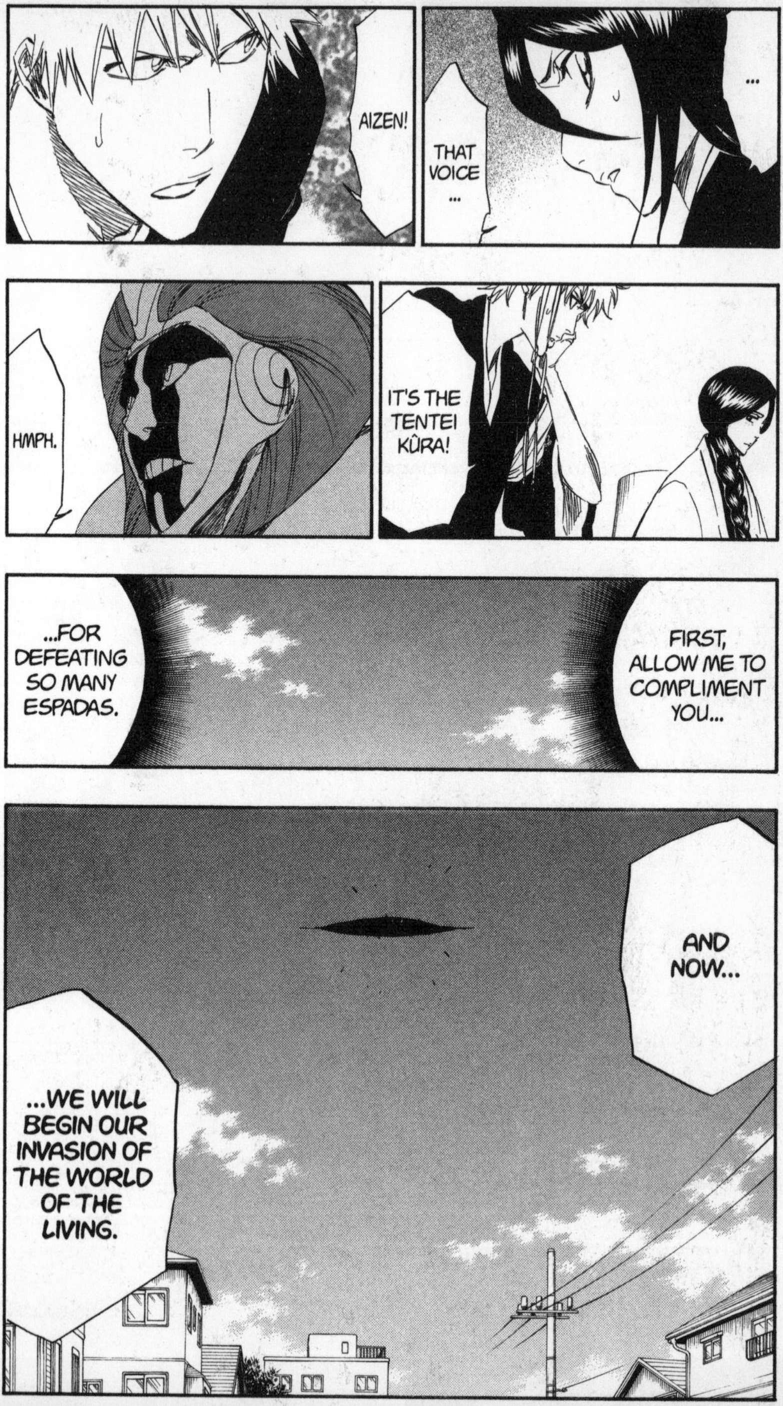
...
THAT VOICE ...
AIZEN!
IT'S THE TENTEI KÛRA!
HMPH.
FIRST, ALLOW ME TO COMPLIMENT YOU...
...FOR DEFEATING SO MANY ESPADAS.
AND NOW...
...WE WILL BEGIN OUR INVASION OF THE WORLD OF THE LIVING.

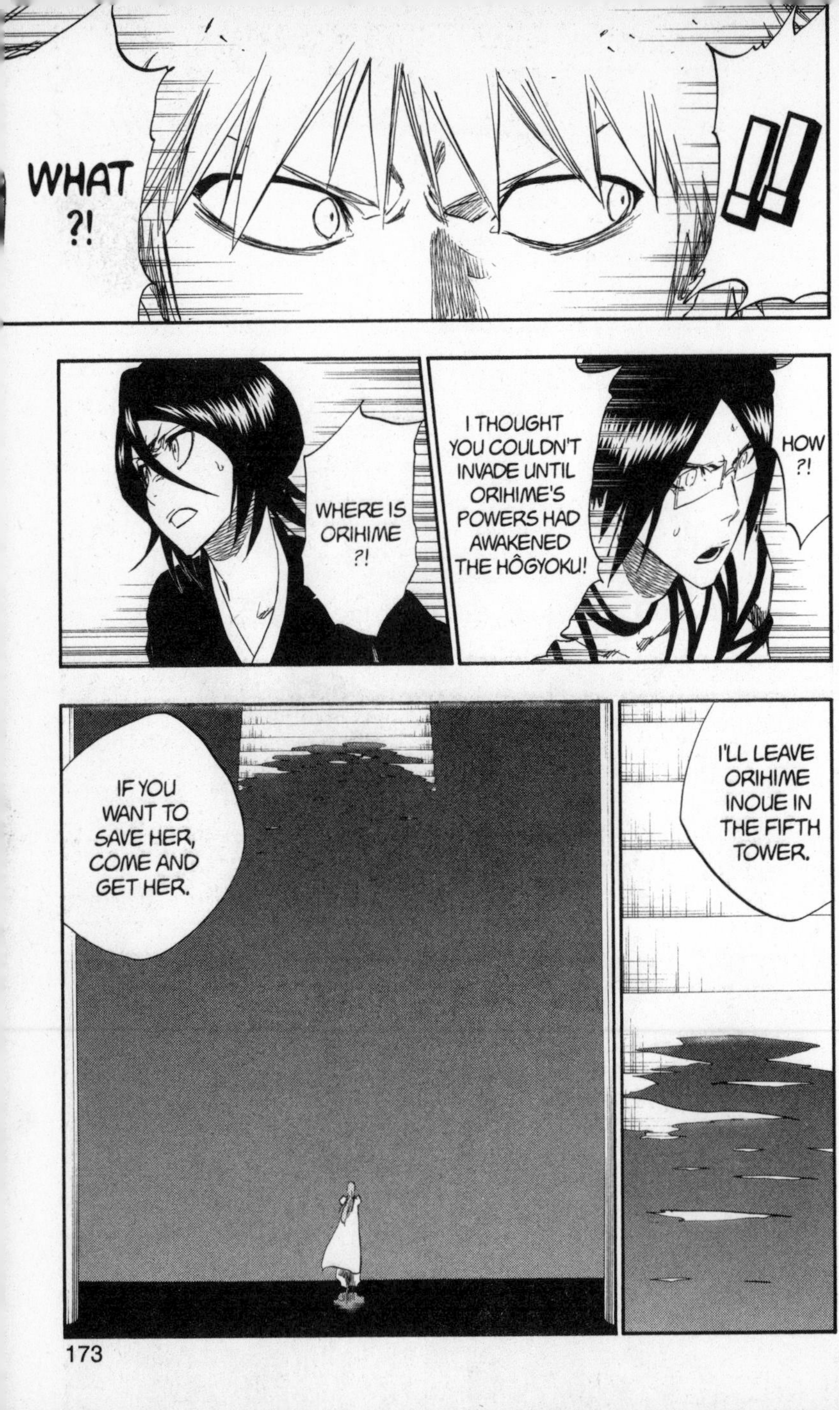
!!
WHAT ?!
HOW ?!
I THOUGHT YOU COULDN'T INVADE UNTIL ORIHIME'S POWERS HAD AWAKENED THE HÔGYOKU!
WHERE IS ORIHIME ?!
I'LL LEAVE ORIHIME INOUE IN THE FIFTH TOWER.
IF YOU WANT TO SAVE HER, COME AND GET HER.

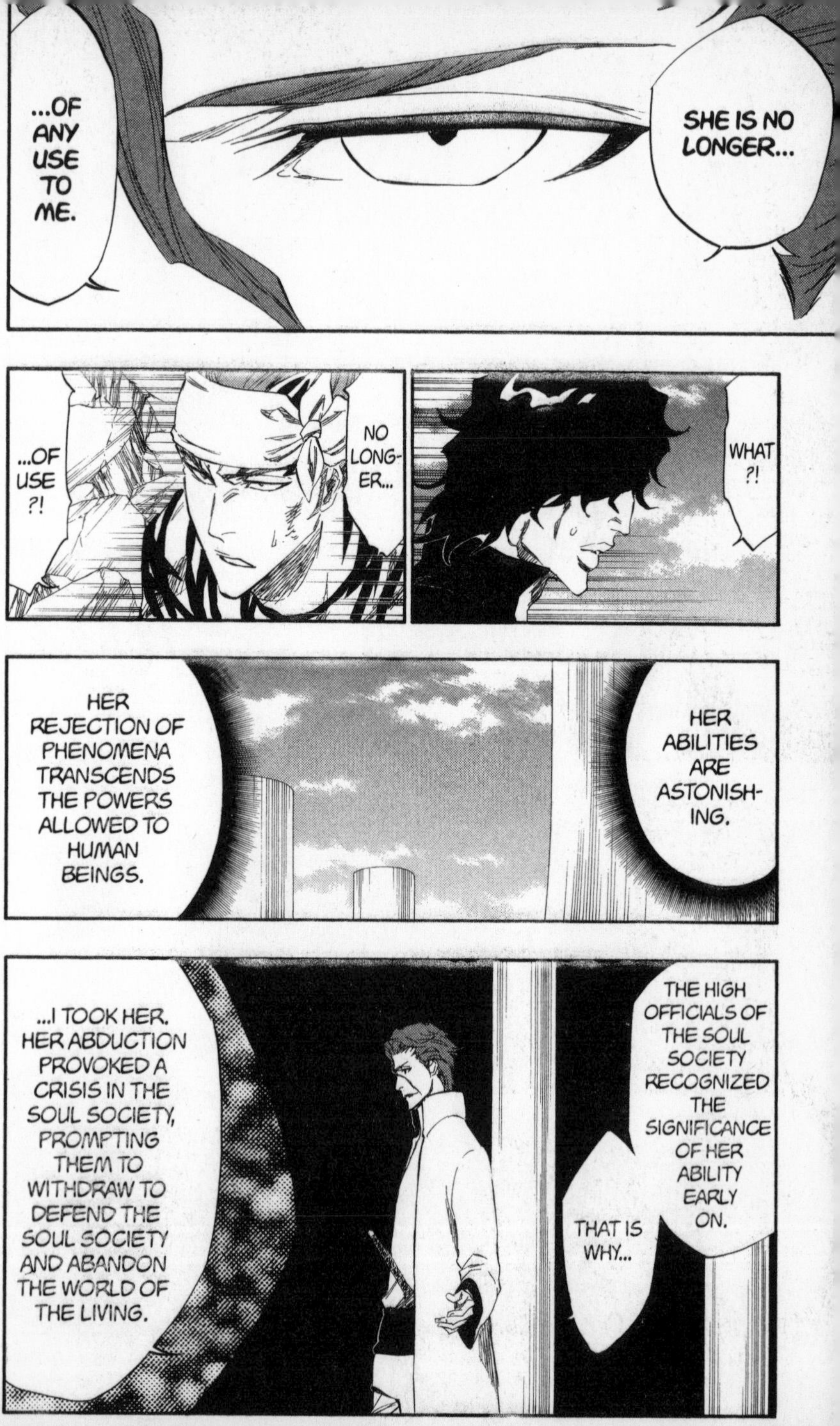
SHE IS NO LONGER...
...OF ANY USE TO ME.
WHAT?!
NO LONGER...
...OF USE?!
HER HIGH ABILITIES ARE ASTONISHING.
HER REJECTION OF PHENOMENA TRANSCENDS THE POWERS ALLOWED TO HUMAN BEINGS.
THE HIGH OFFICIALS OF THE SOUL SOCIETY RECOGNIZED THE SIGNIFICANCE OF HER ABILITY EARLY ON.
THAT IS WHY...
...I TOOK HER. HER ABDUCTION PROVOKED A CRISIS IN THE SOUL SOCIETY, PROMPTING THEM TO WITHDRAW TO DEFEND THE SOUL SOCIETY AND ABANDON THE WORLD OF THE LIVING.

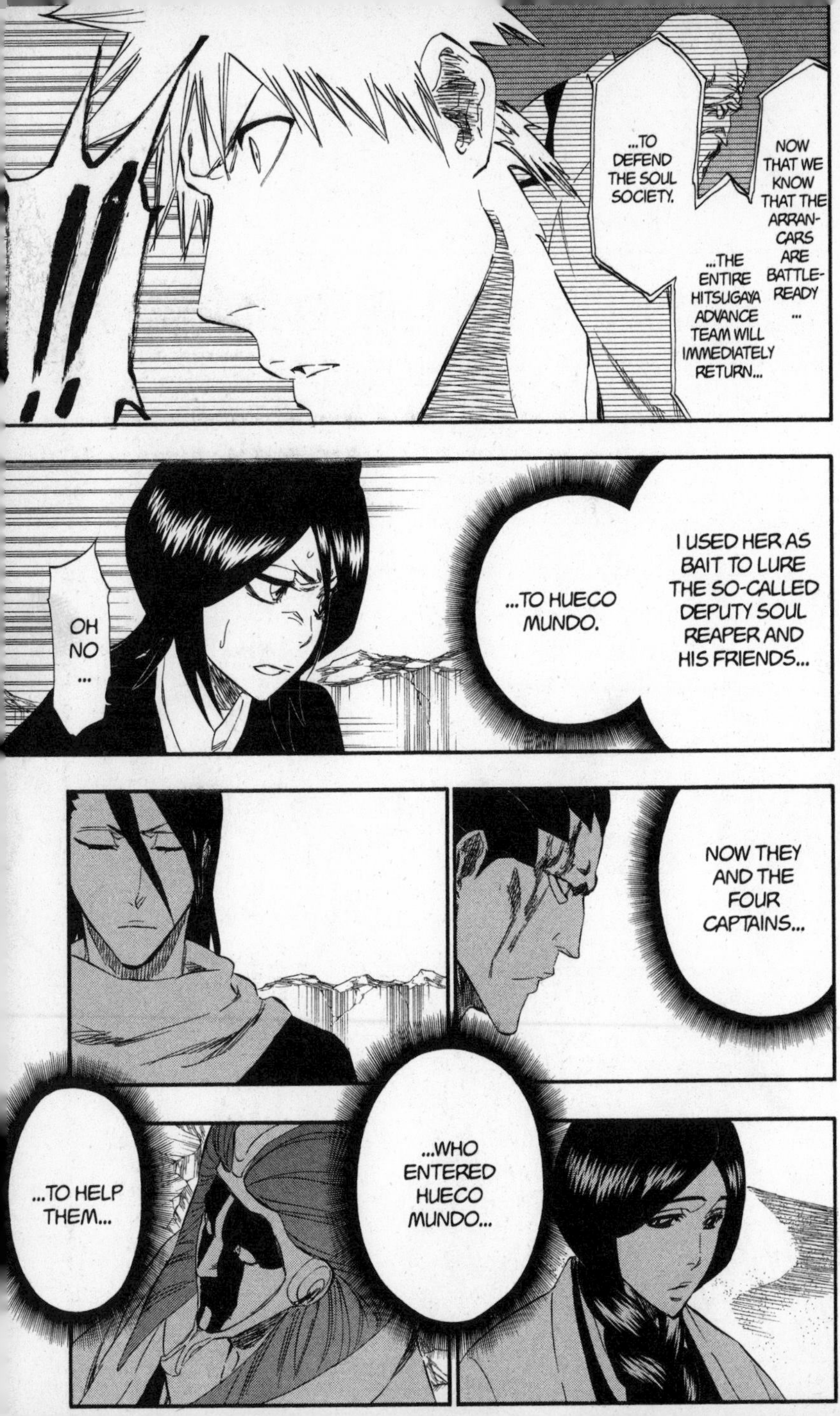
NOW THAT WE KNOW THAT THE ARRAN-CARS ARE BATTLE-READY ...
...THE ENTIRE HITSUGAYA ADVANCE TEAM WILL IMMEDIATELY RETURN...
...TO DEFEND THE SOUL SOCIETY.
I USED HER AS BAIT TO LURE THE SO-CALLED DEPUTY SOUL REAPER AND HIS FRIENDS...
...TO HUECO MUNDO.
OH NO ...
NOW THEY AND THE FOUR CAPTAINS...
...WHO ENTERED HUECO MUNDO...
...TO HELP THEM...

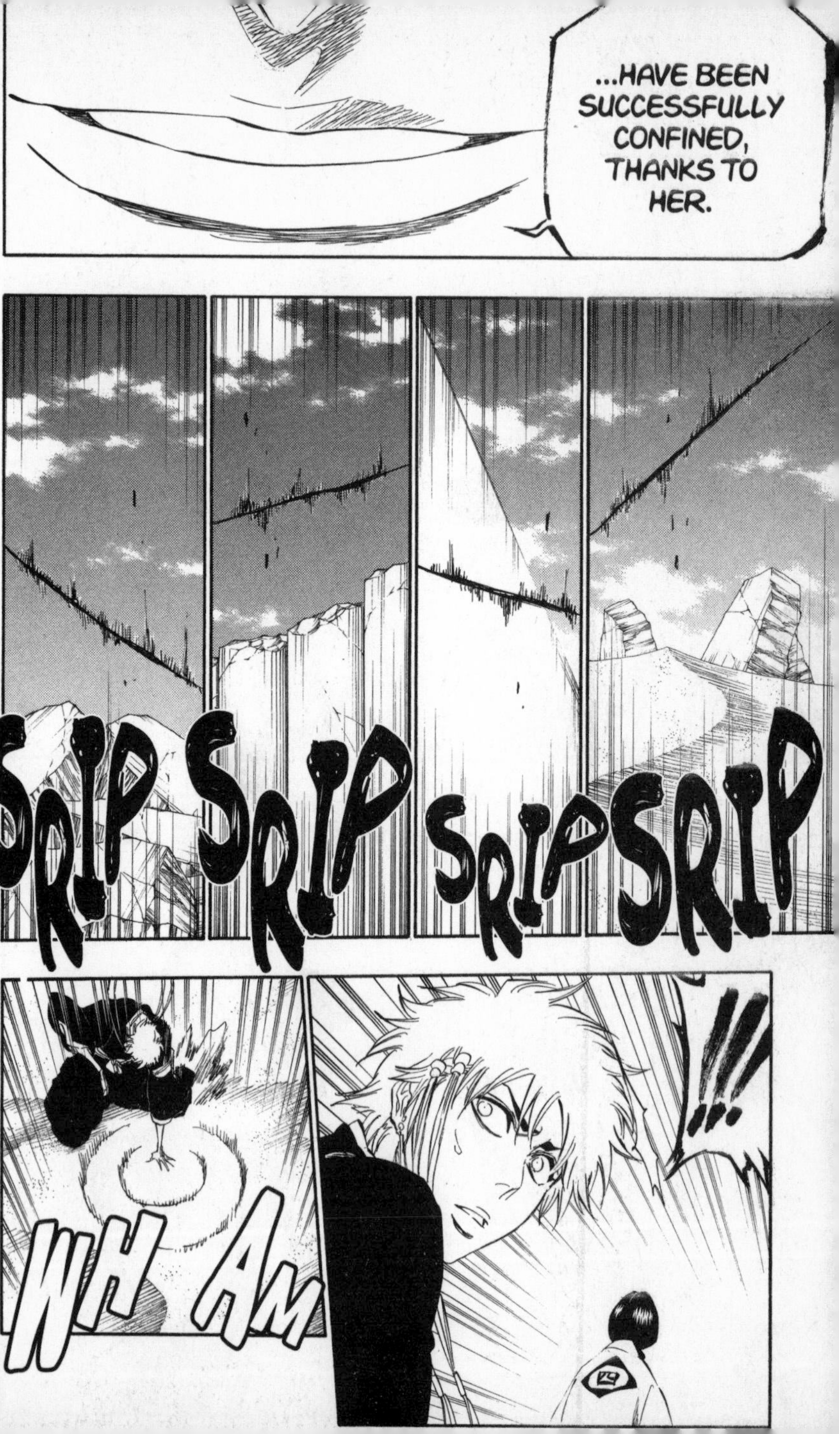
...HAVE BEEN SUCCESSFULLY CONFINED, THANKS TO HER.
SRIP
SRIP
SRIP
SRIP
!!
WHAM

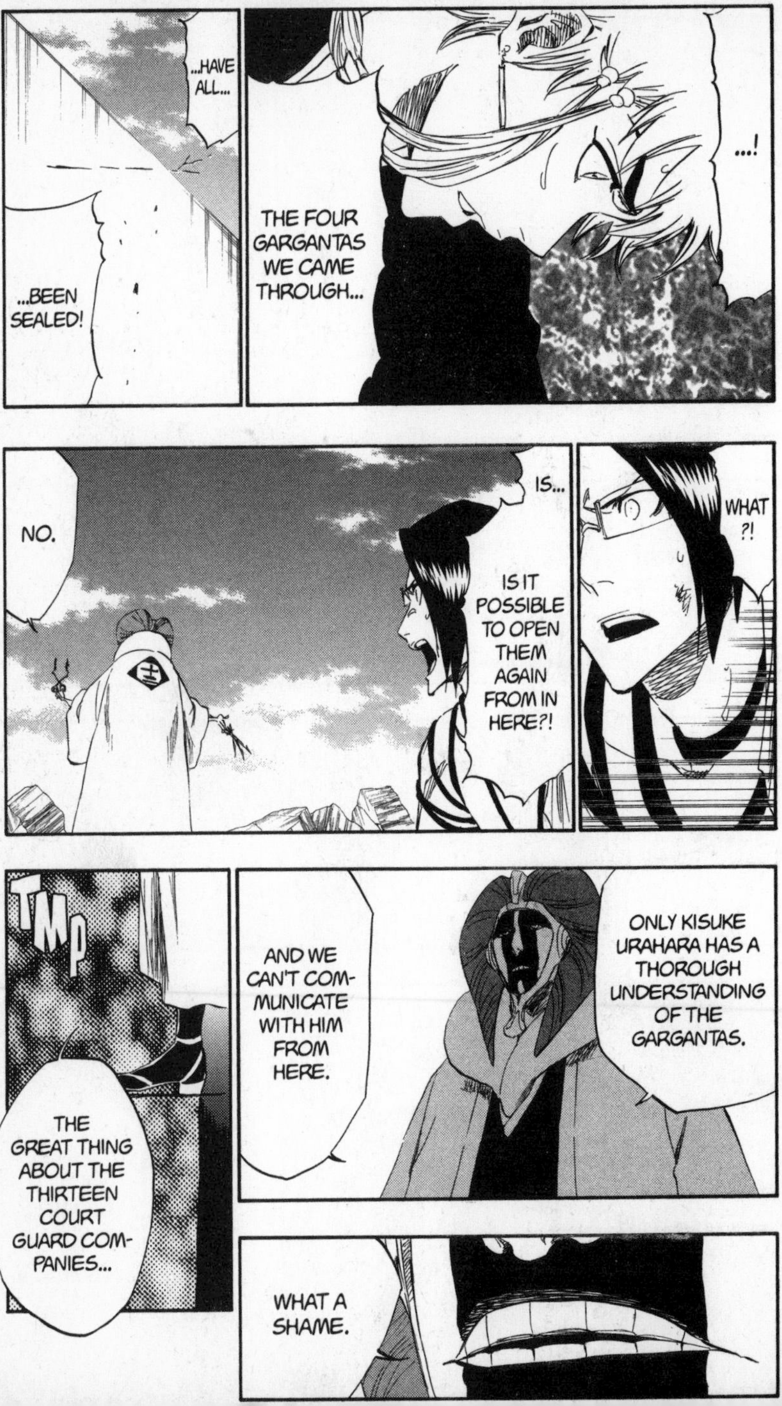
...!
THE FOUR GARGANTAS WE CAME THROUGH...
...HAVE ALL...
...BEEN SEALED!
WHAT ?!
IS...
IS IT POSSIBLE TO OPEN THEM AGAIN FROM IN HERE?!
NO.
ONLY KISUKE URAHARA HAS A THOROUGH UNDERSTANDING OF THE GARGANTAS.
AND WE CAN'T COMMUNICATE WITH HIM FROM HERE.
WHAT A SHAME.
TMP
THE GREAT THING ABOUT THE THIRTEEN COURT GUARD COMPANIES...

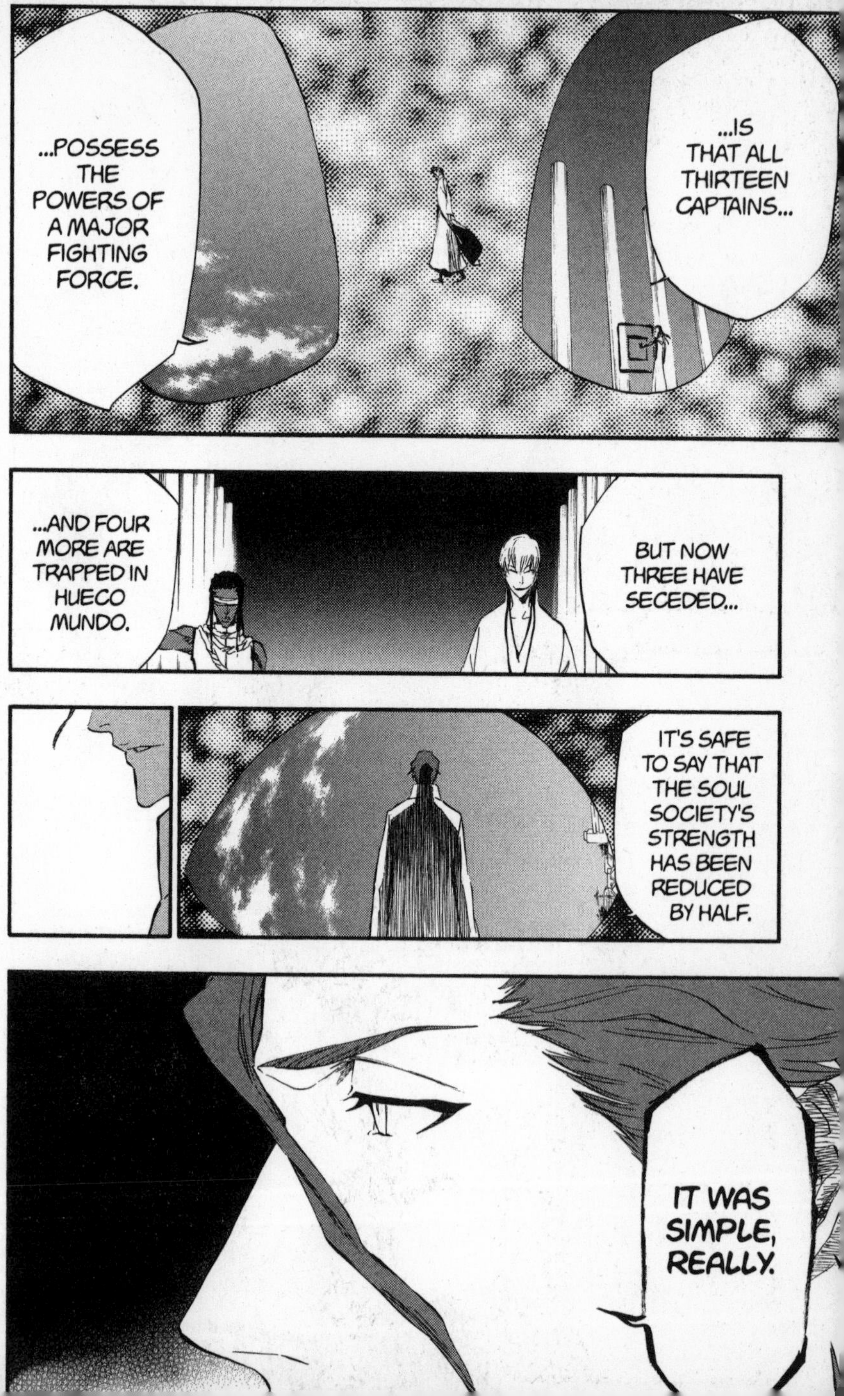
...IS THAT ALL THIRTEEN CAPTAINS...
...POSSESS THE POWERS OF A MAJOR FIGHTING FORCE.
BUT NOW THREE HAVE SECEDED...
...AND FOUR MORE ARE TRAPPED IN HUECO MUNDO.
IT'S SAFE TO SAY THAT THE SOUL SOCIETY'S STRENGTH HAS BEEN REDUCED BY HALF.
IT WAS SIMPLE, REALLY.

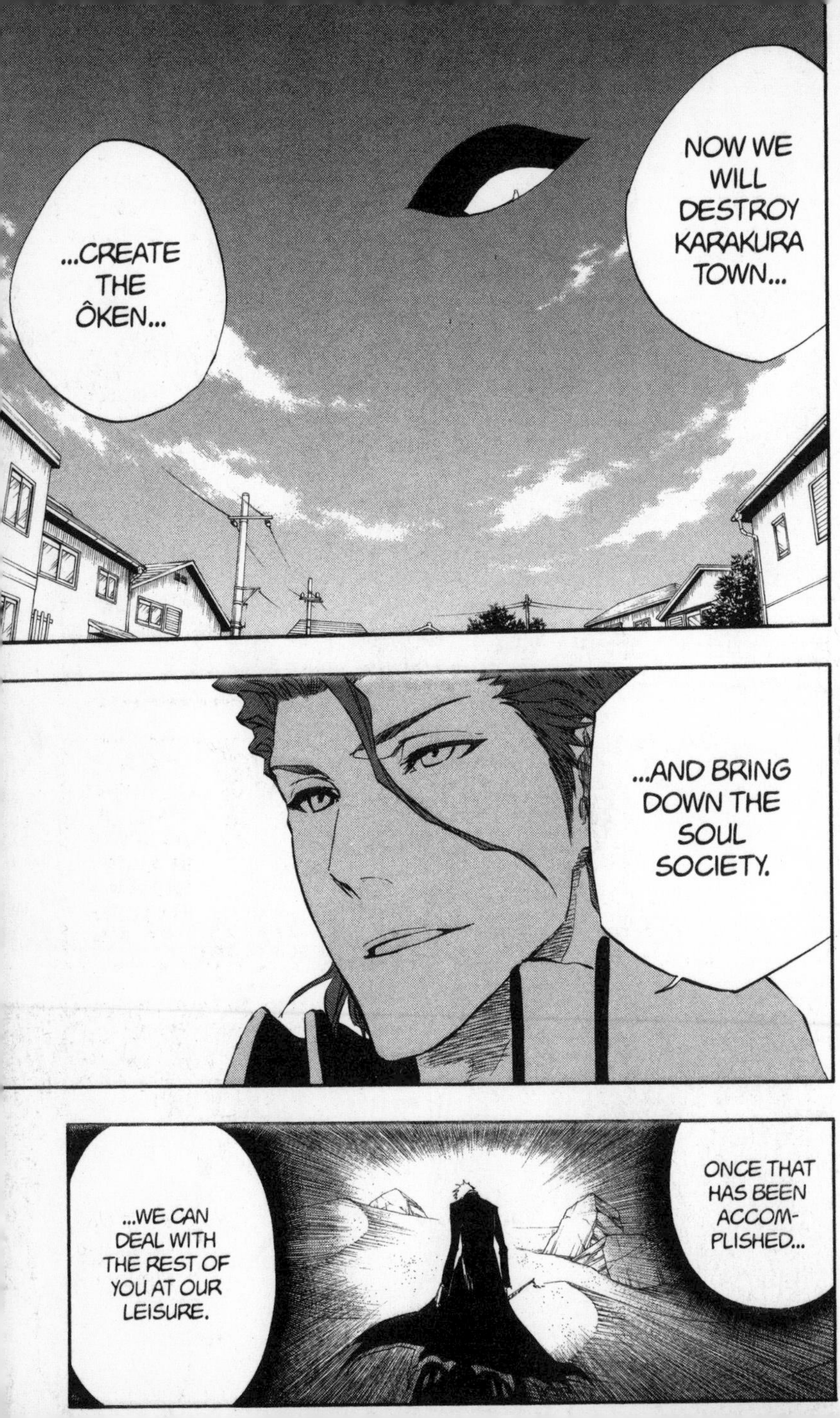
NOW WE WILL DESTROY KARAKURA TOWN...
...CREATE THE ÔKEN...
...AND BRING DOWN THE SOUL SOCIETY.
ONCE THAT HAS BEEN ACCOM-PLISHED...
...WE CAN DEAL WITH THE REST OF YOU AT OUR LEISURE.

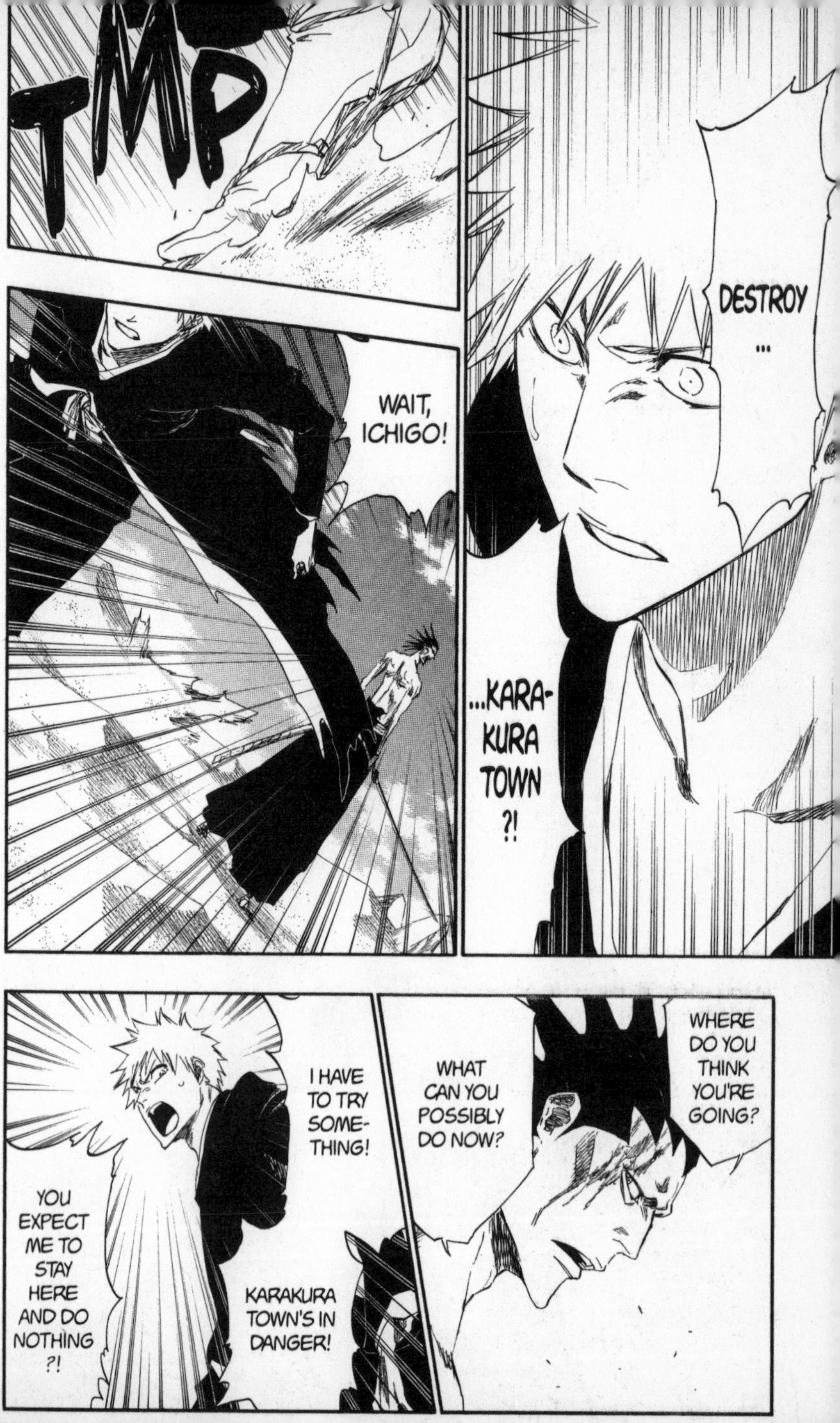
DESTROY ...
...KARA-KURA TOWN ?!
TMP
WAIT, ICHIGO!
WHERE DO YOU THINK YOU'RE GOING?
WHAT CAN YOU POSSIBLY DO NOW?
I HAVE TO TRY SOME-THING!
KARAKURA TOWN'S IN DANGER!
YOU EXPECT ME TO STAY HERE AND DO NOTHING ?!

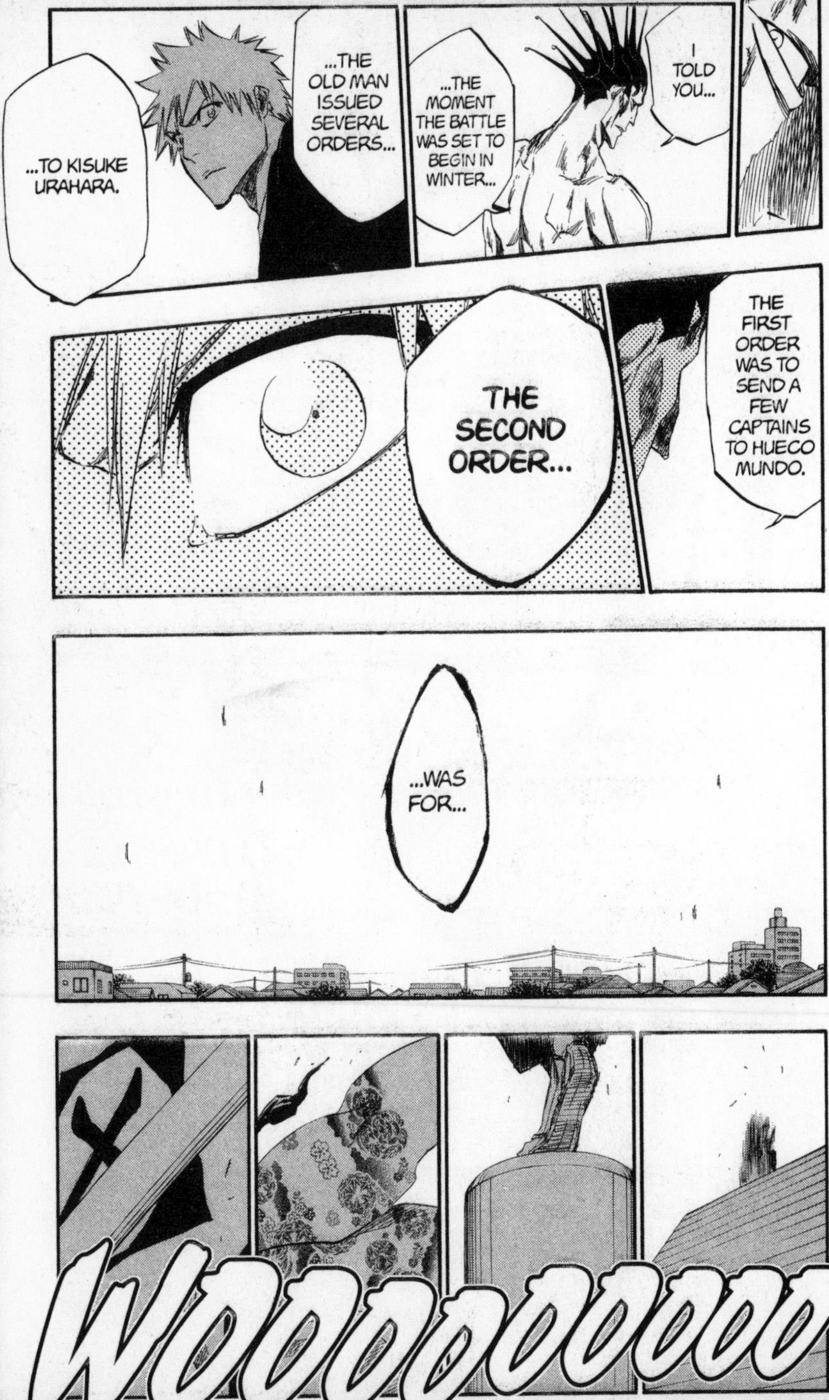
I TOLD YOU...
...THE MOMENT THE BATTLE WAS SET TO BEGIN IN WINTER...
...THE OLD MAN ISSUED SEVERAL ORDERS...
...TO KISUKE URAHARA.
THE FIRST ORDER WAS TO SEND A FEW CAPTAINS TO HUECO MUNDO.
THE SECOND ORDER...
...WAS FOR...
WOOOOOOOOO

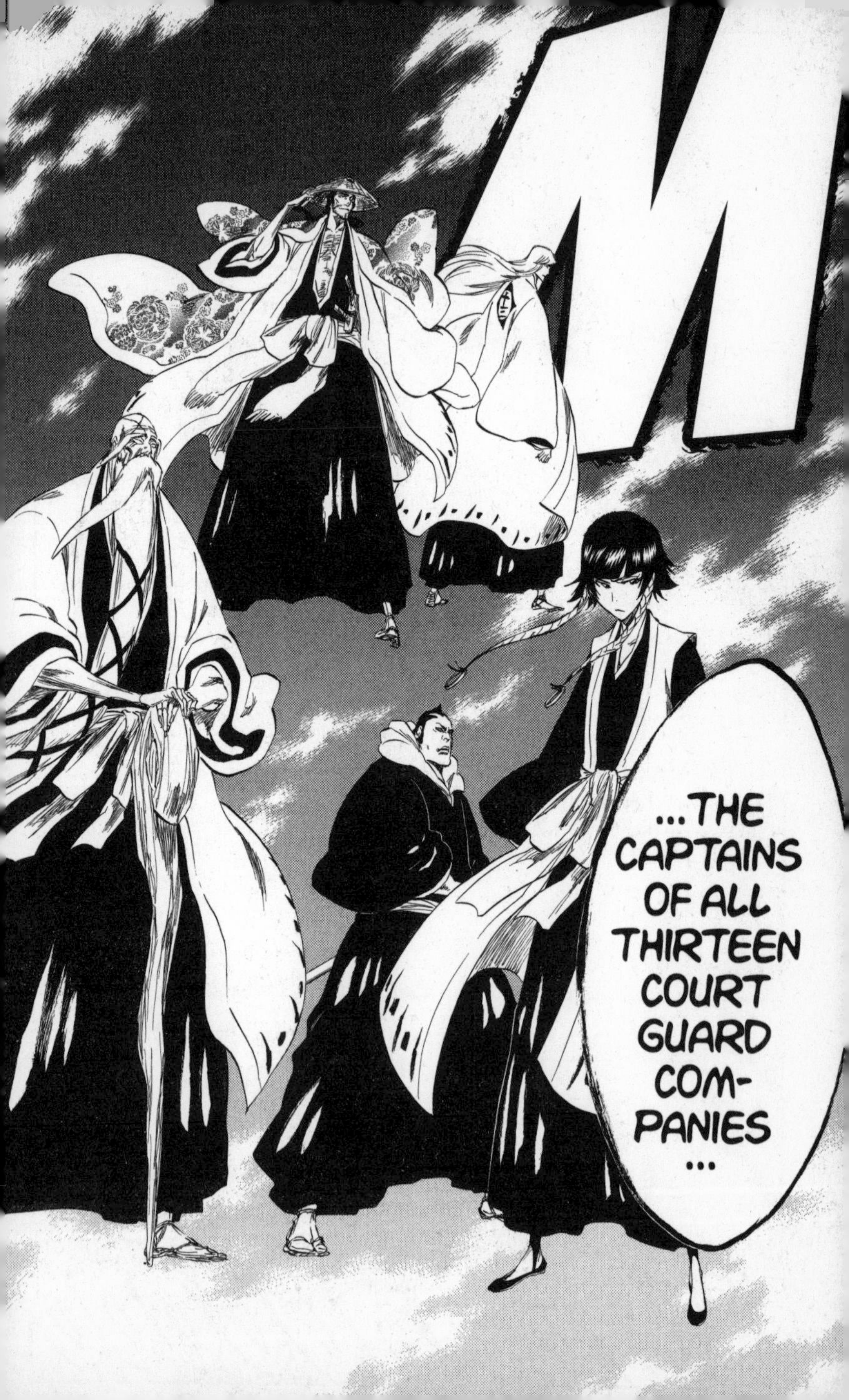
M
...THE CAPTAINS OF ALL THIRTEEN COURT GUARD COM-PANIES...

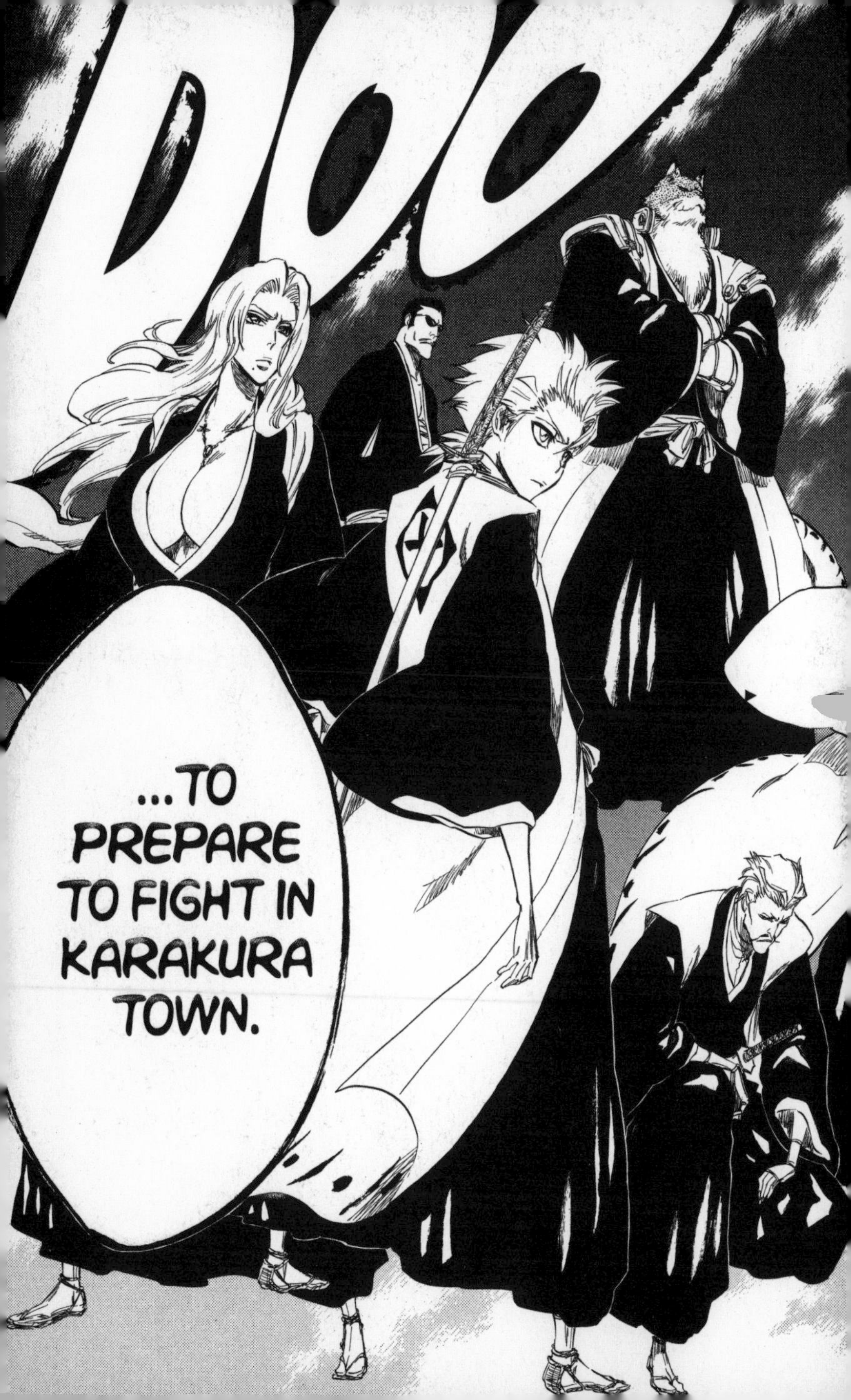
DOO
...TO PREPARE TO FIGHT IN KARAKURA TOWN.

the end is far.

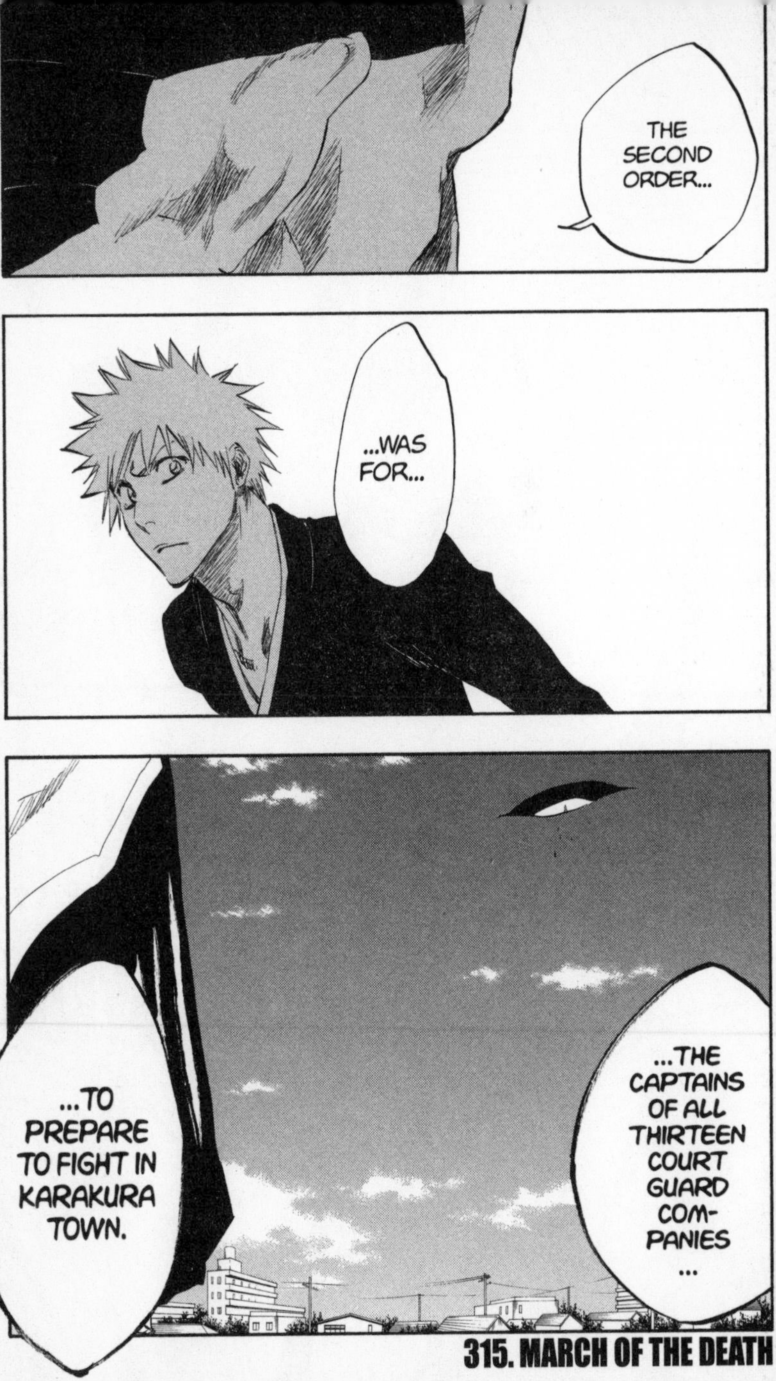
THE SECOND ORDER...
...WAS FOR...
...THE CAPTAINS OF ALL THIRTEEN COURT GUARD COM-PANIES ...
...TO PREPARE TO FIGHT IN KARAKURA TOWN.

315. MARCH OF THE DEATH

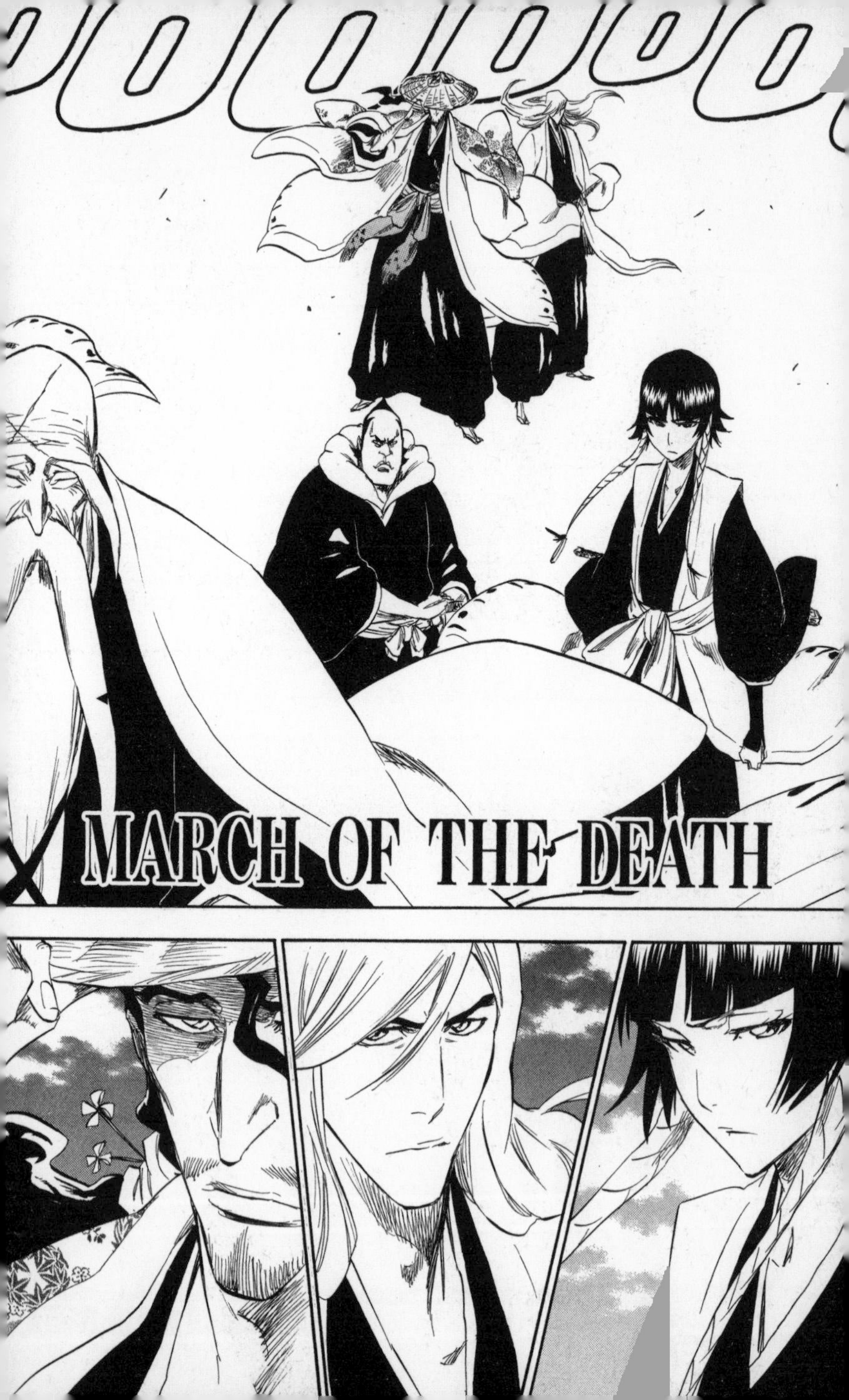

DOOOOOOO
MARCH OF THE DEATH

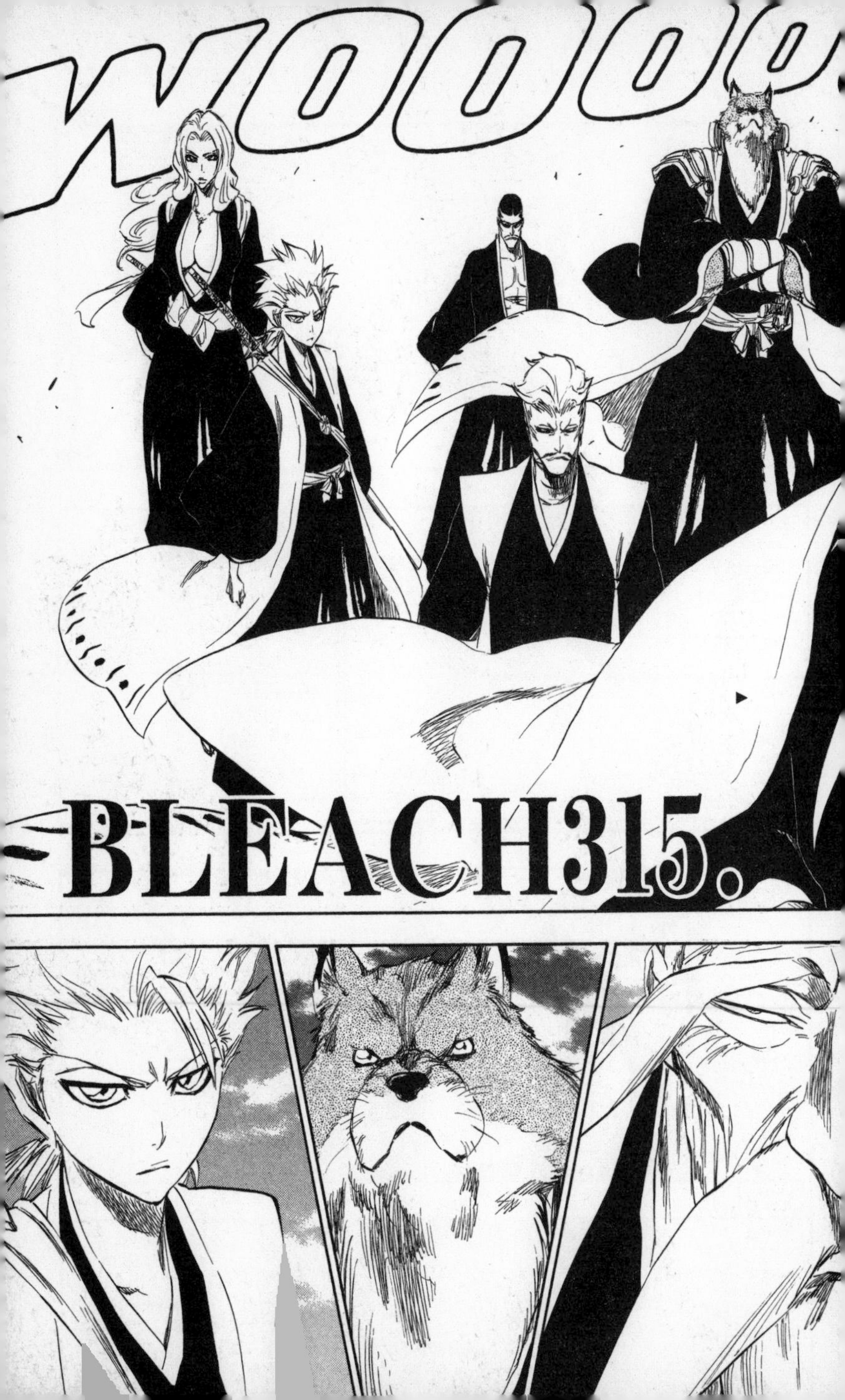
WOOOO
BLEACH315.

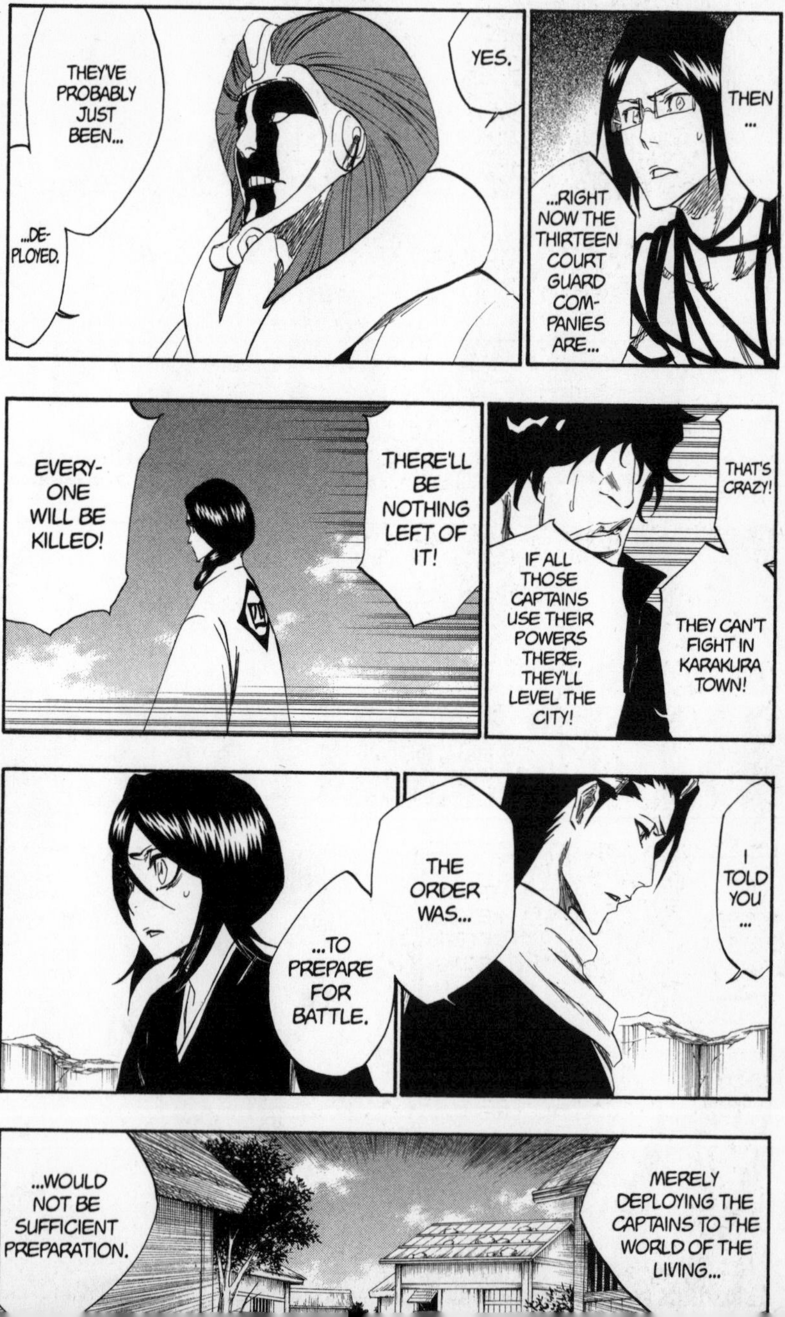
THEN ...
...RIGHT NOW THE THIRTEEN COURT GUARD COMPANIES ARE...
YES.
THEY'VE PROBABLY JUST BEEN...
...DEPLOYED.
THAT'S CRAZY!
THEY CAN'T FIGHT IN KARAKURA TOWN!
IF ALL THOSE CAPTAINS USE THEIR POWERS THERE, THEY'LL LEVEL THE CITY!
THERE'LL BE NOTHING LEFT OF IT!
EVERYONE WILL BE KILLED!
I TOLD YOU ...
THE ORDER WAS...
...TO PREPARE FOR BATTLE.
MERELY DEPLOYING THE CAPTAINS TO THE WORLD OF THE LIVING...
...WOULD NOT BE SUFFICIENT PREPARATION.

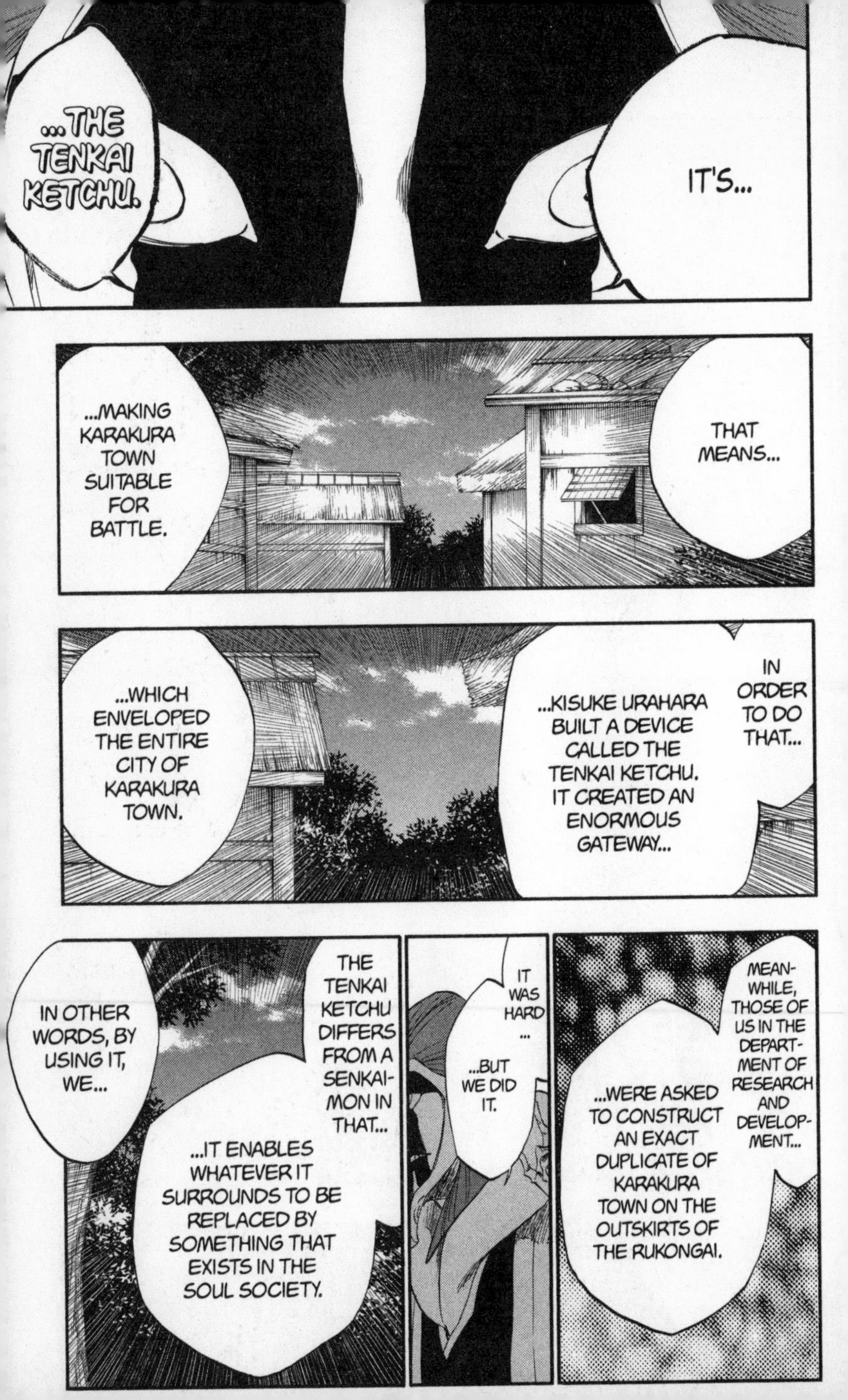
IT'S...
...THE TENKAI KETCHU.
THAT MEANS...
...MAKING KARAKURA TOWN SUITABLE FOR BATTLE.
IN ORDER TO DO THAT...
...KISUKE URAHARA BUILT A DEVICE CALLED THE TENKAI KETCHU. IT CREATED AN ENORMOUS GATEWAY...
...WHICH ENVELOPED THE ENTIRE CITY OF KARAKURA TOWN.
MEAN-WHILE, THOSE OF US IN THE DEPART-MENT OF RESEARCH AND DEVELOP-MENT...
...WERE ASKED TO CONSTRUCT AN EXACT DUPLICATE OF KARAKURA TOWN ON THE OUTSKIRTS OF THE RUKONGAI.
IT WAS HARD...
...BUT WE DID IT.
THE TENKAI KETCHU DIFFERS FROM A SENKAI-MON IN THAT...
...IT ENABLES WHATEVER IT SURROUNDS TO BE REPLACED BY SOMETHING THAT EXISTS IN THE SOUL SOCIETY.
IN OTHER WORDS, BY USING IT, WE...

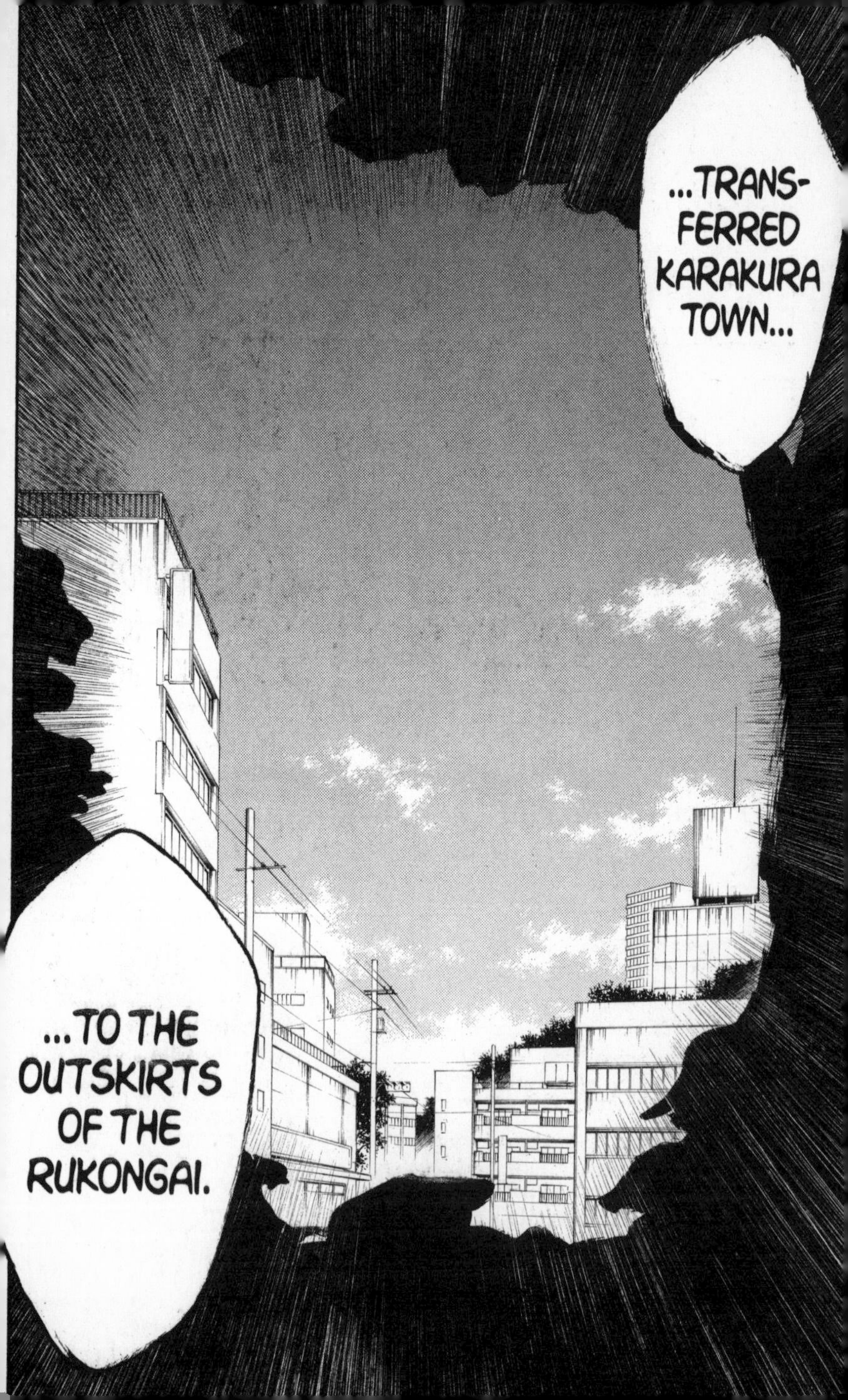
...TRANS-FERRED KARAKURA TOWN...
...TO THE OUTSKIRTS OF THE RUKONGAI.

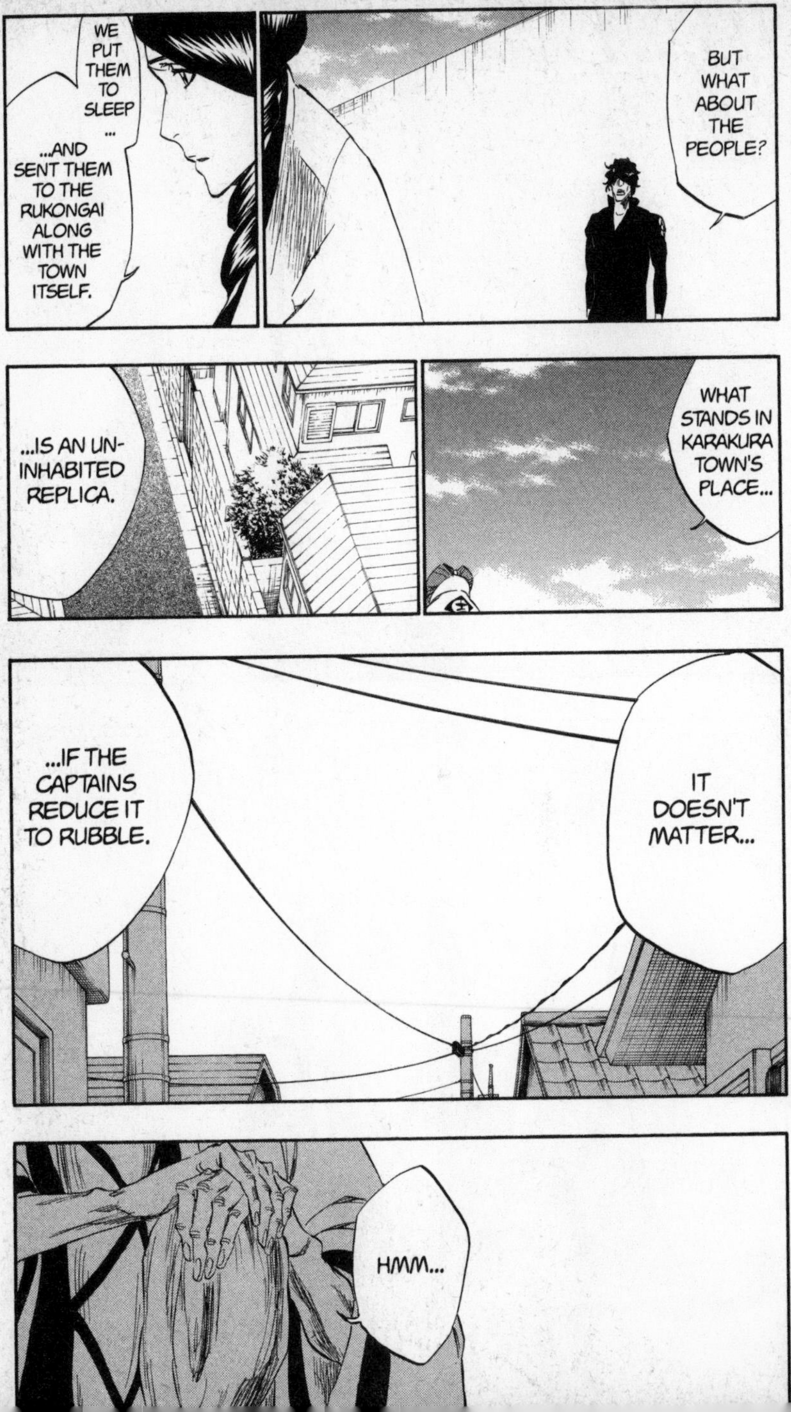
BUT WHAT ABOUT THE PEOPLE?
WE PUT THEM TO SLEEP ...
...AND SENT THEM TO THE RUKONGAI ALONG WITH THE TOWN ITSELF.
WHAT STANDS IN KARAKURA TOWN'S PLACE...
...IS AN UN-INHABITED REPLICA.
IT DOESN'T MATTER...
...IF THE CAPTAINS REDUCE IT TO RUBBLE.
HMM...

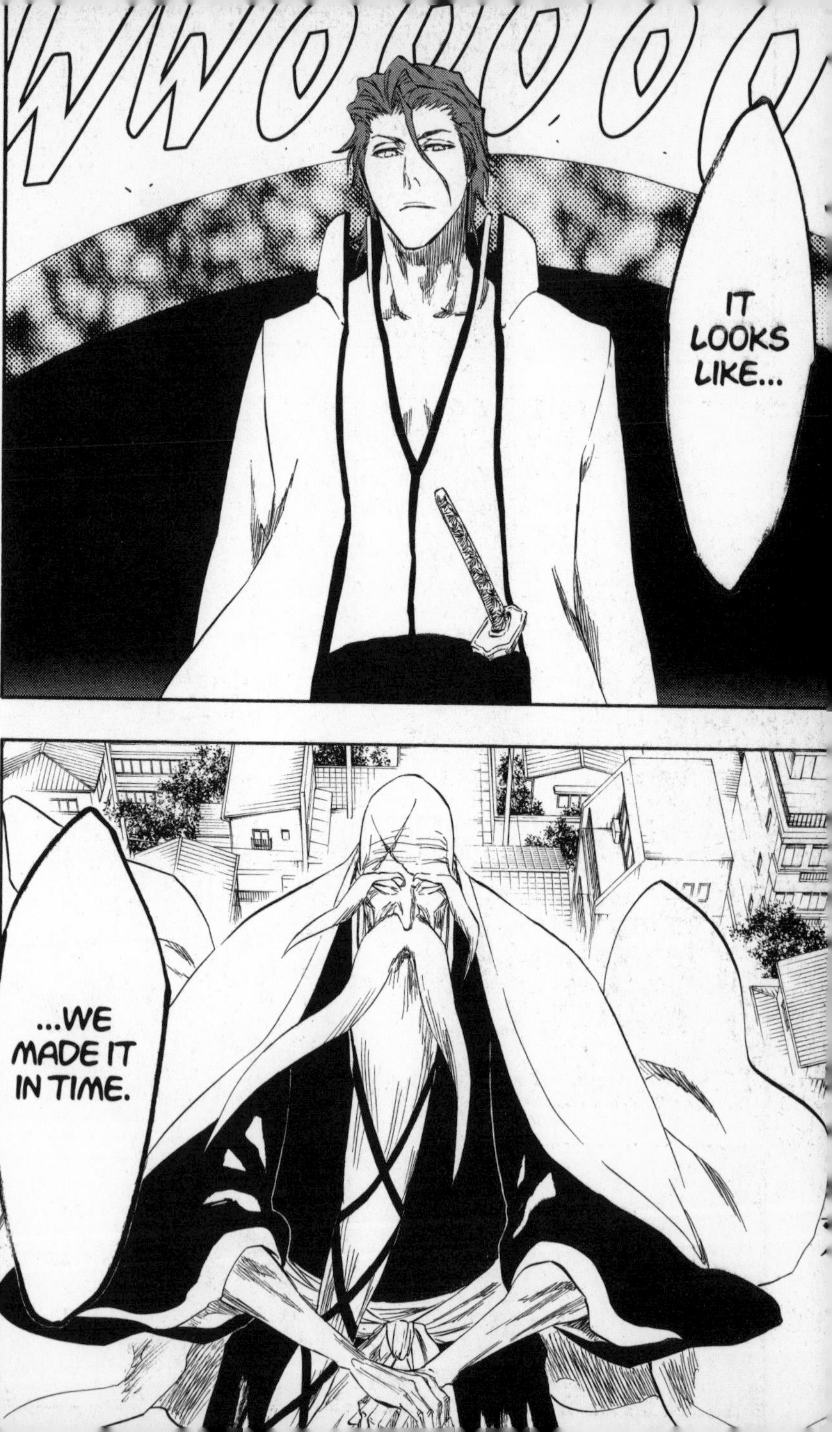
WOOOOOO
IT LOOKS LIKE...
...WE MADE IT IN TIME.

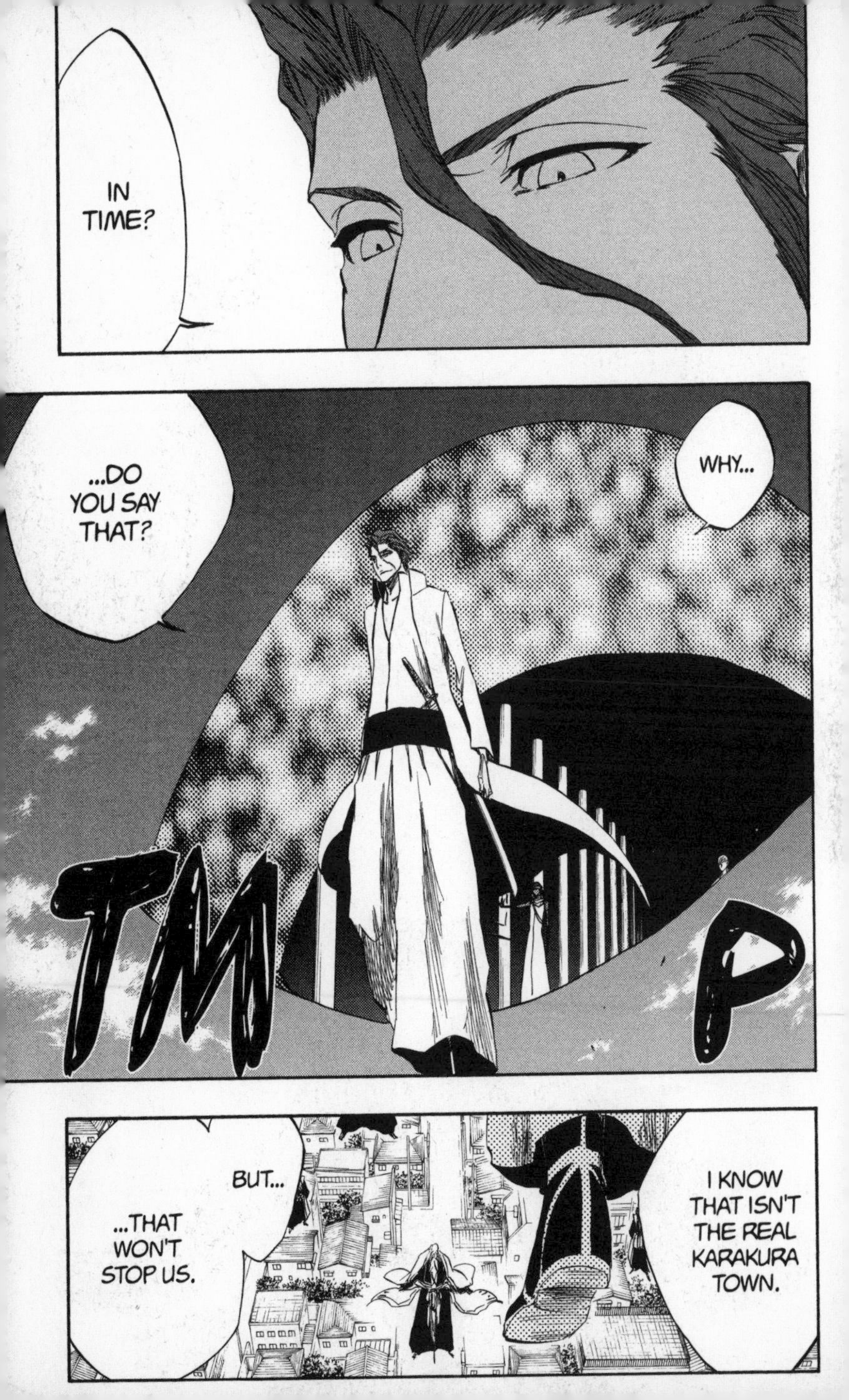
IN TIME?
WHY...
...DO YOU SAY THAT?
TMP
I KNOW THAT ISN'T THE REAL KARAKURA TOWN.
BUT...
...THAT WON'T STOP US.

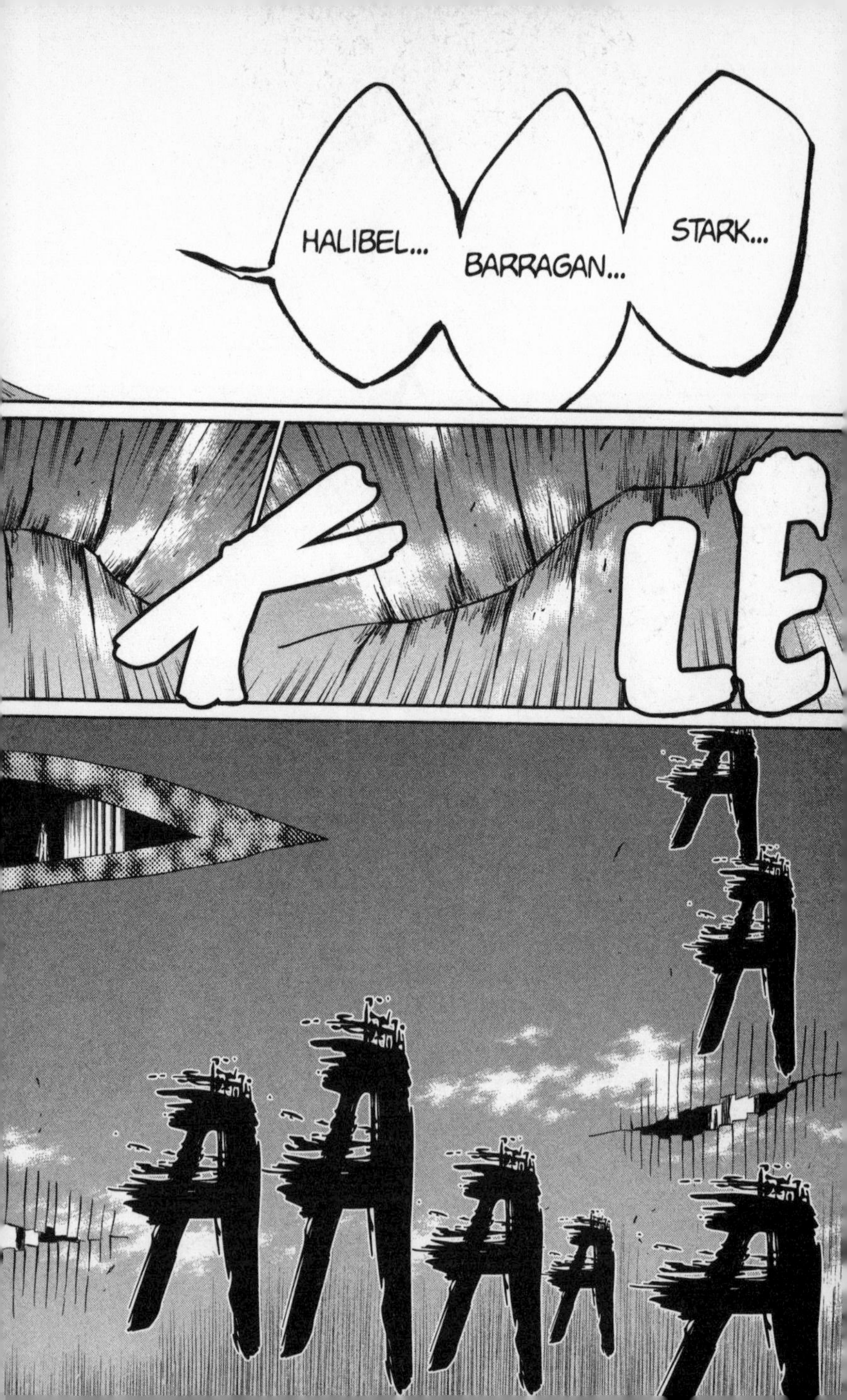
STARK...
BARRAGAN...
HALIBEL...
KLE

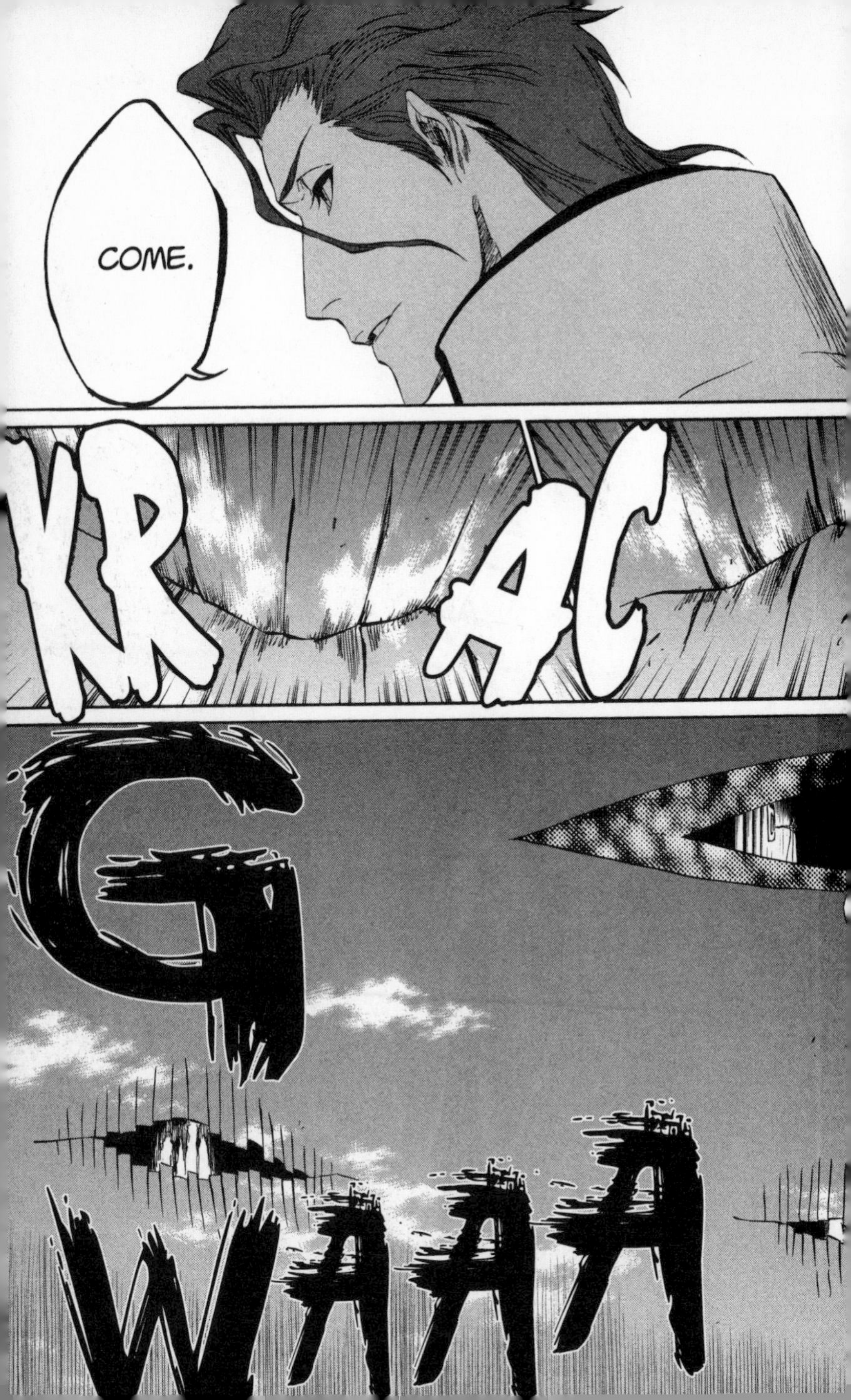
COME.
KRAC
GWAAA

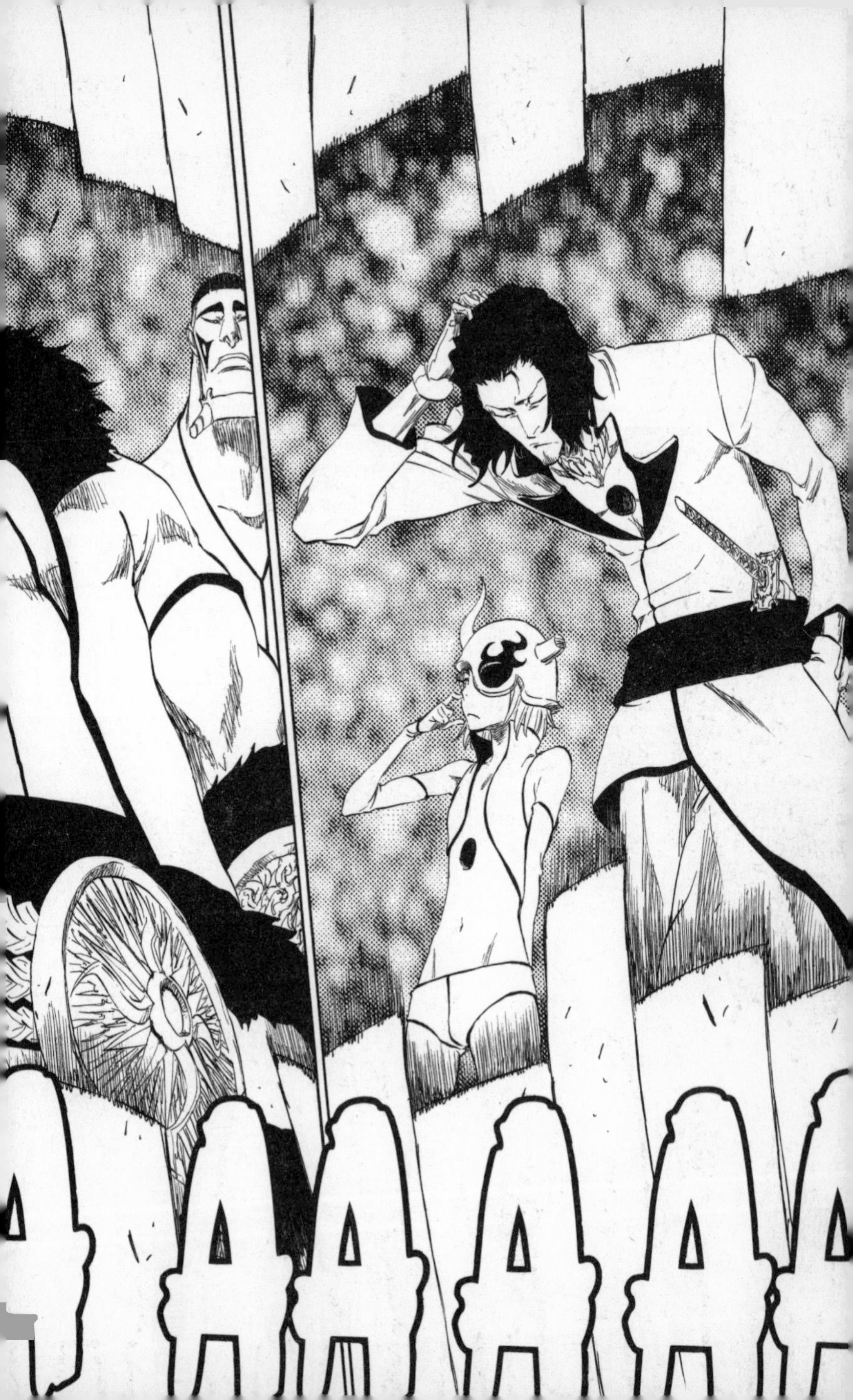
AAAA

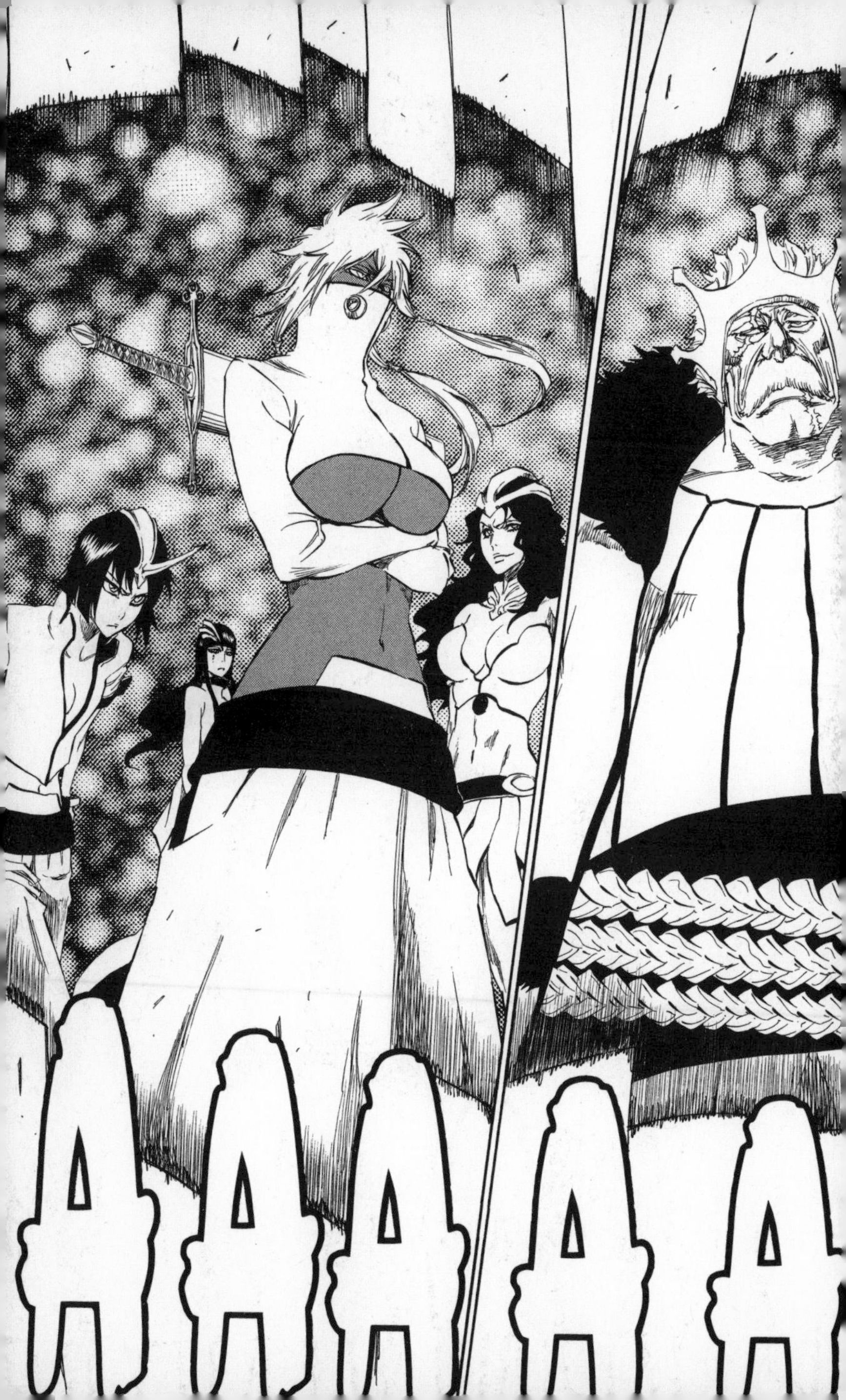
AAAAAA

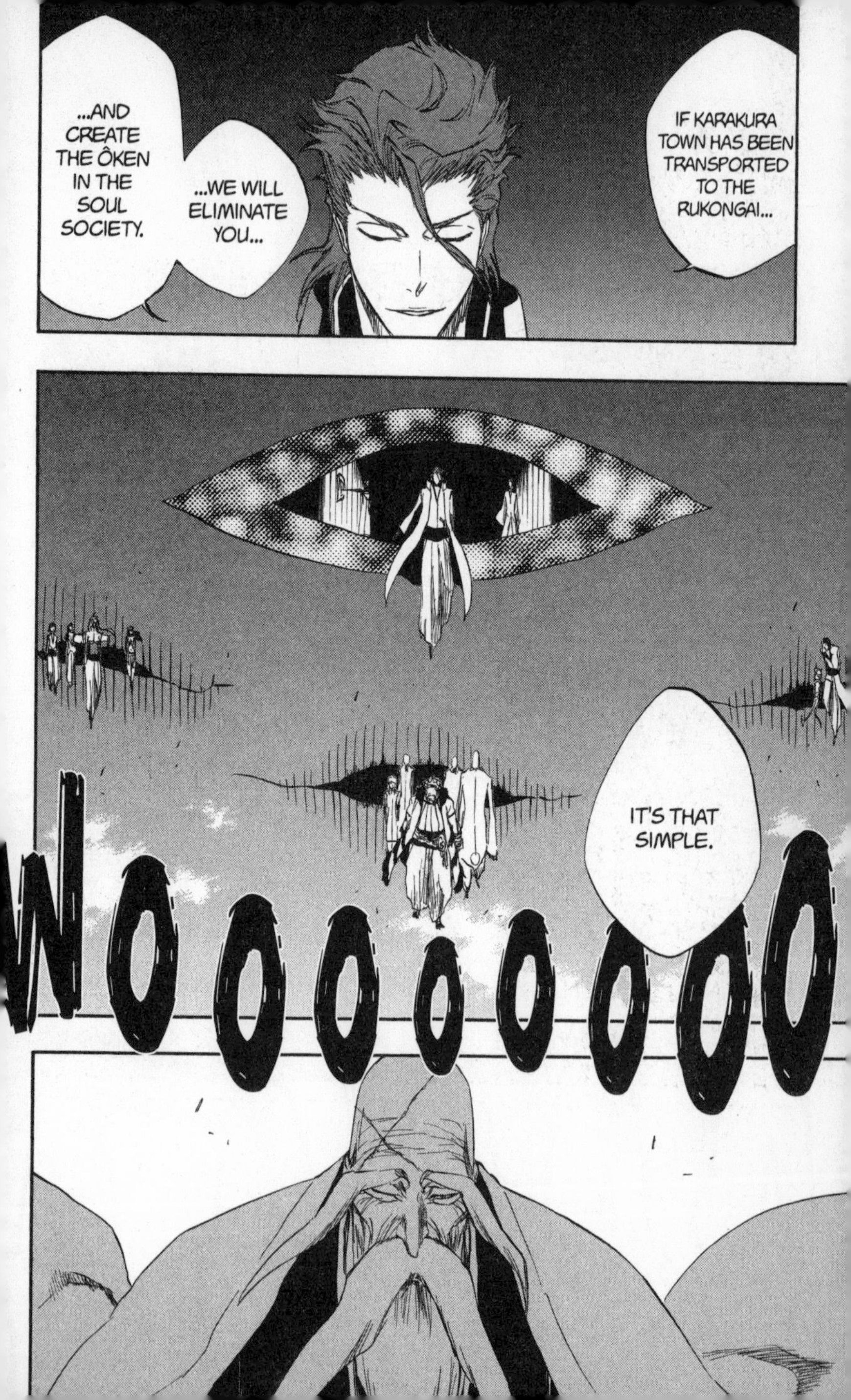
IF KARAKURA TOWN HAS BEEN TRANSPORTED TO THE RUKONGAI...
...WE WILL ELIMINATE YOU...
...AND CREATE THE ÔKEN IN THE SOUL SOCIETY.
IT'S THAT SIMPLE.
WOOOOOOOO

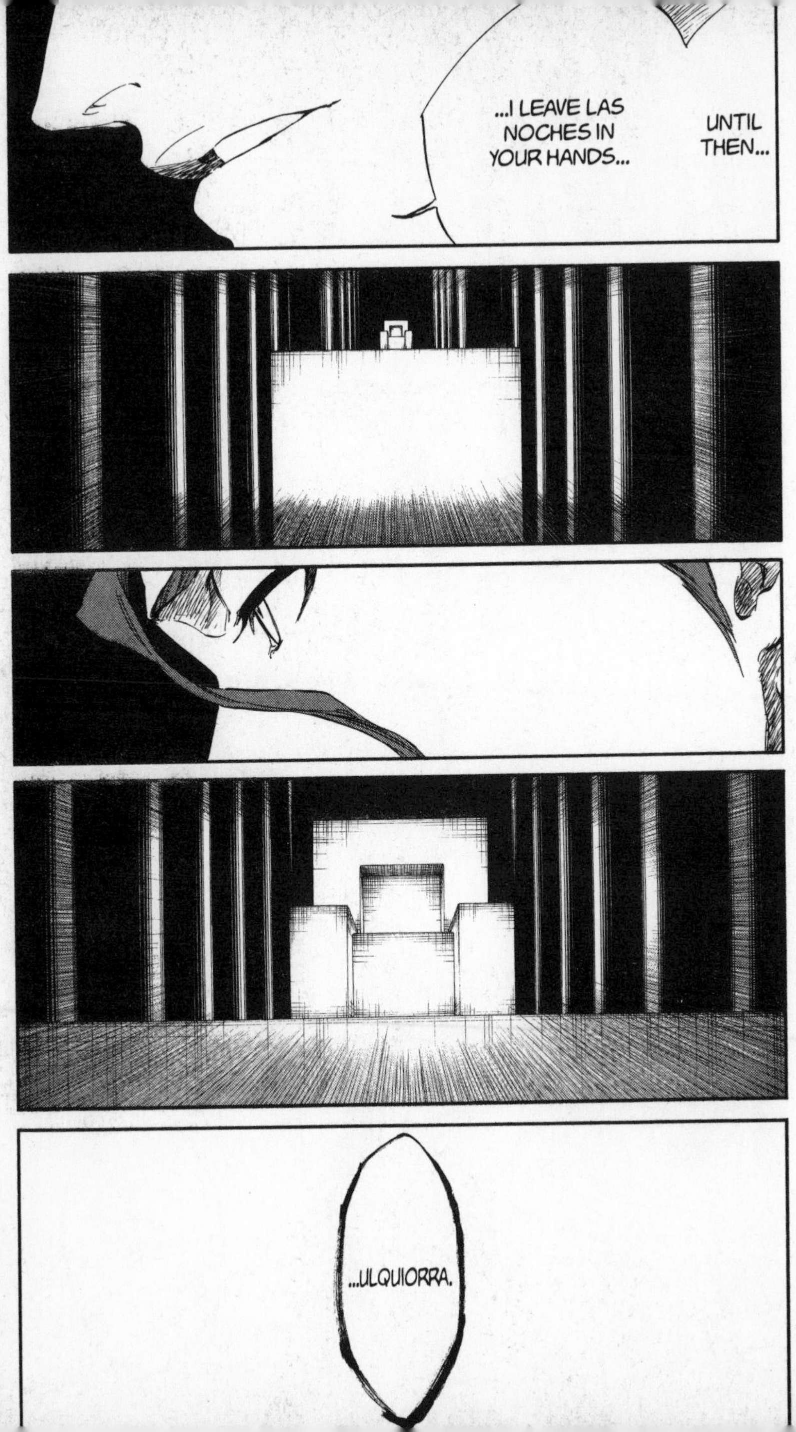
UNTIL THEN...
...I LEAVE LAS NOCHES IN YOUR HANDS...
...ULQUIORRA.

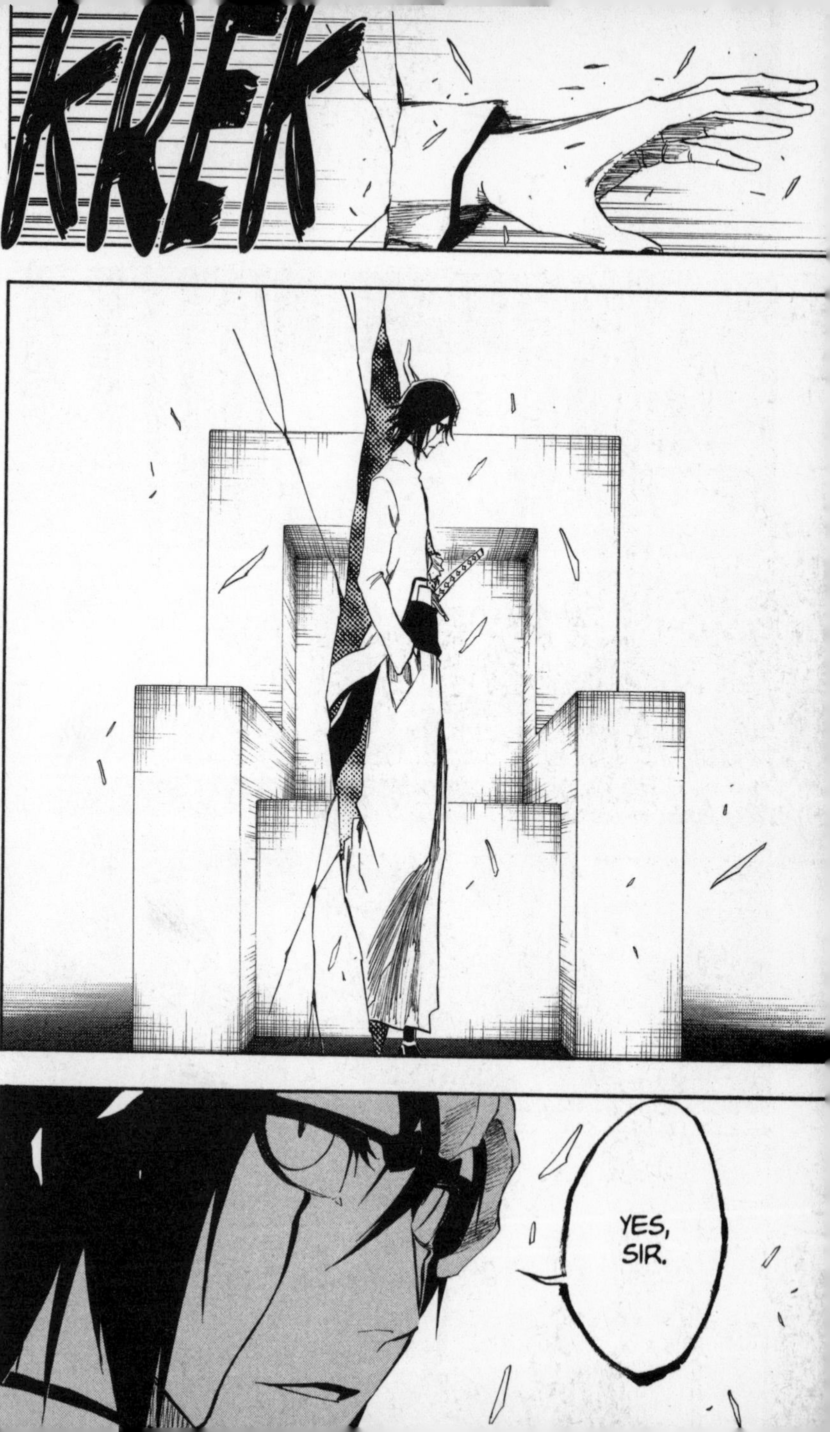
KREK
YES, SIR.

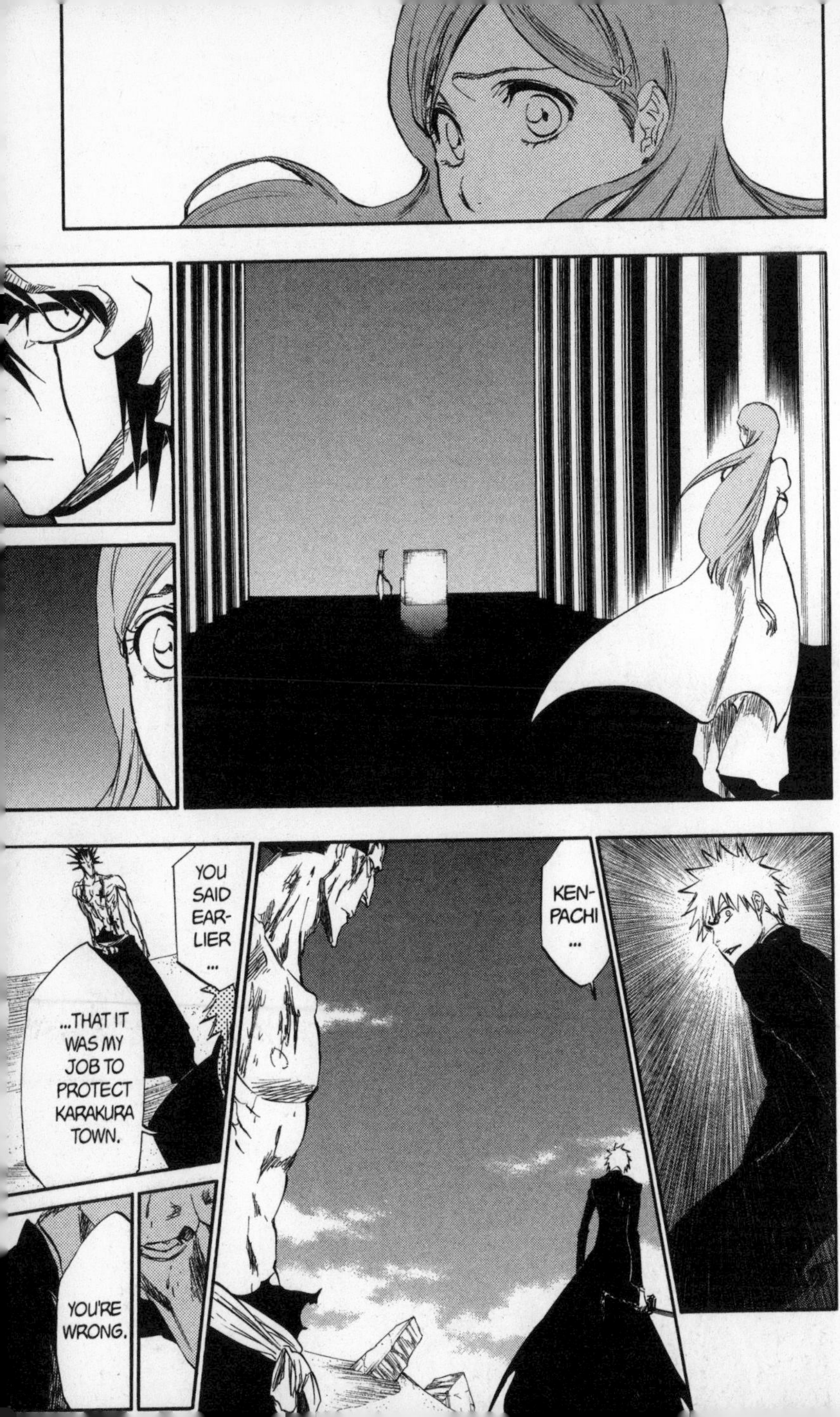
KEN-PACHI...
YOU SAID EARLIER...
...THAT IT WAS MY JOB TO PROTECT KARAKURA TOWN.
YOU'RE WRONG.

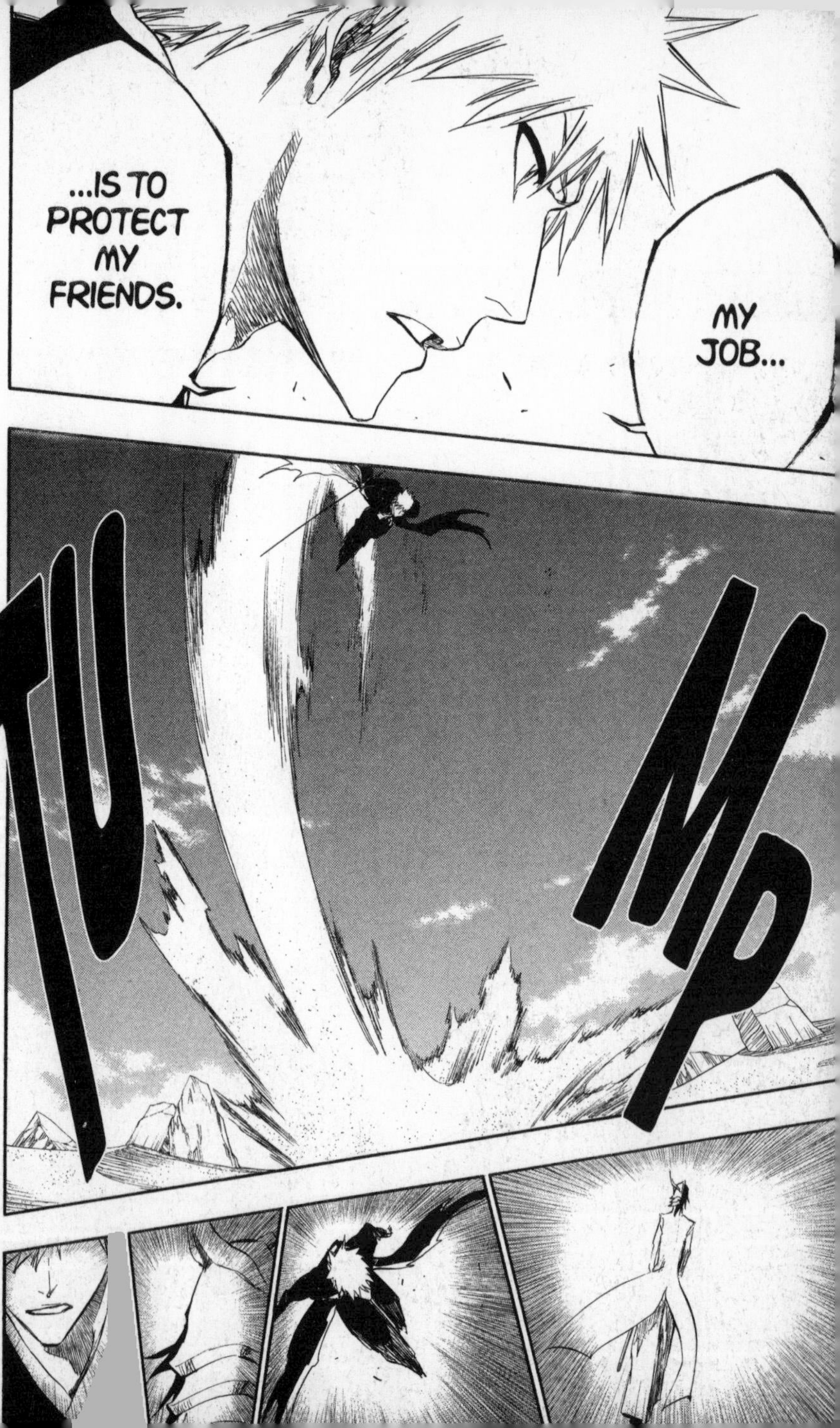
MY JOB...
...IS TO PROTECT MY FRIENDS.
TUMP

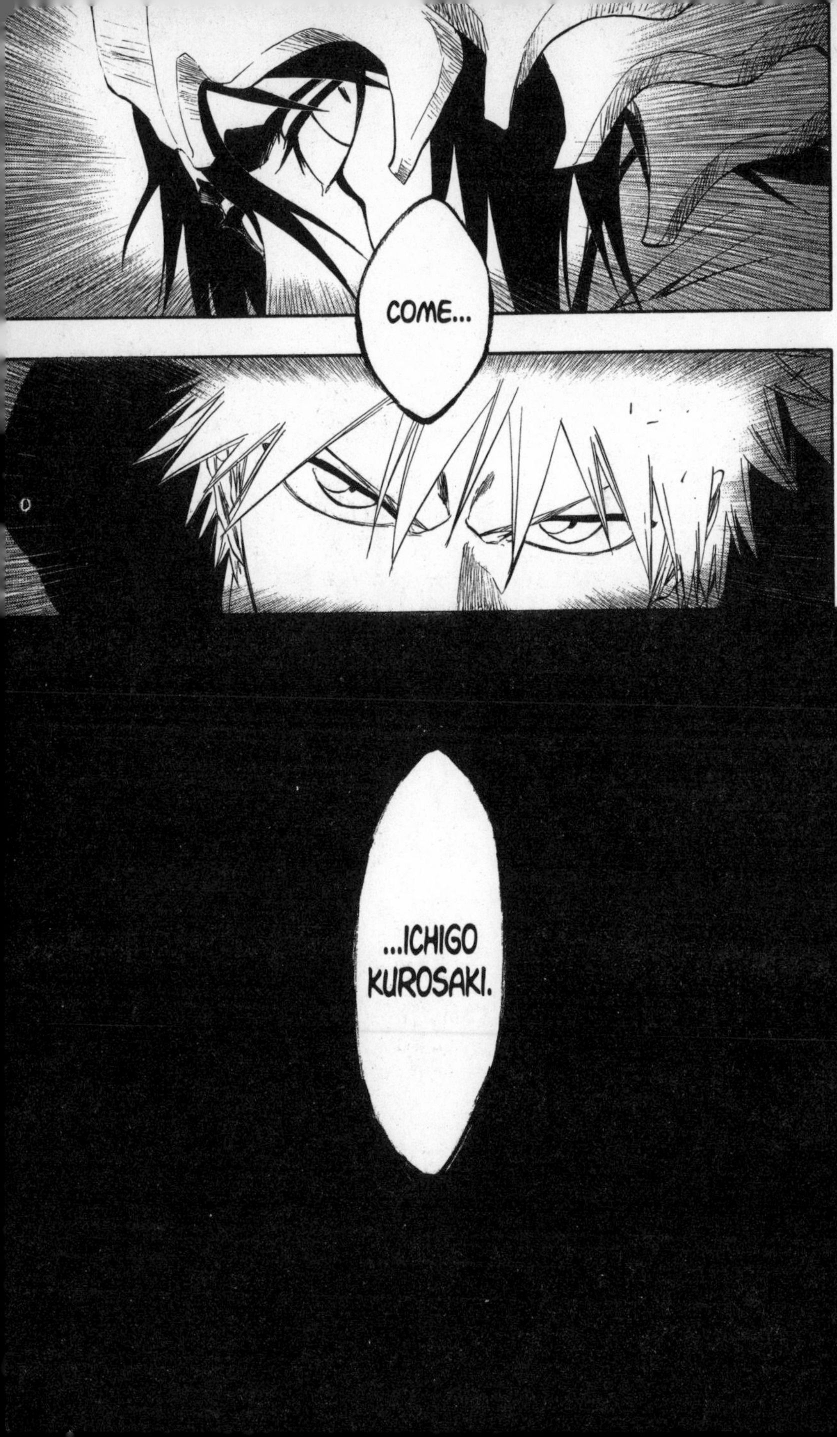
COME...
...ICHIGO KUROSAKI.

CONTI
NUED
IN
BLEACH
...?

Next Volume Preview

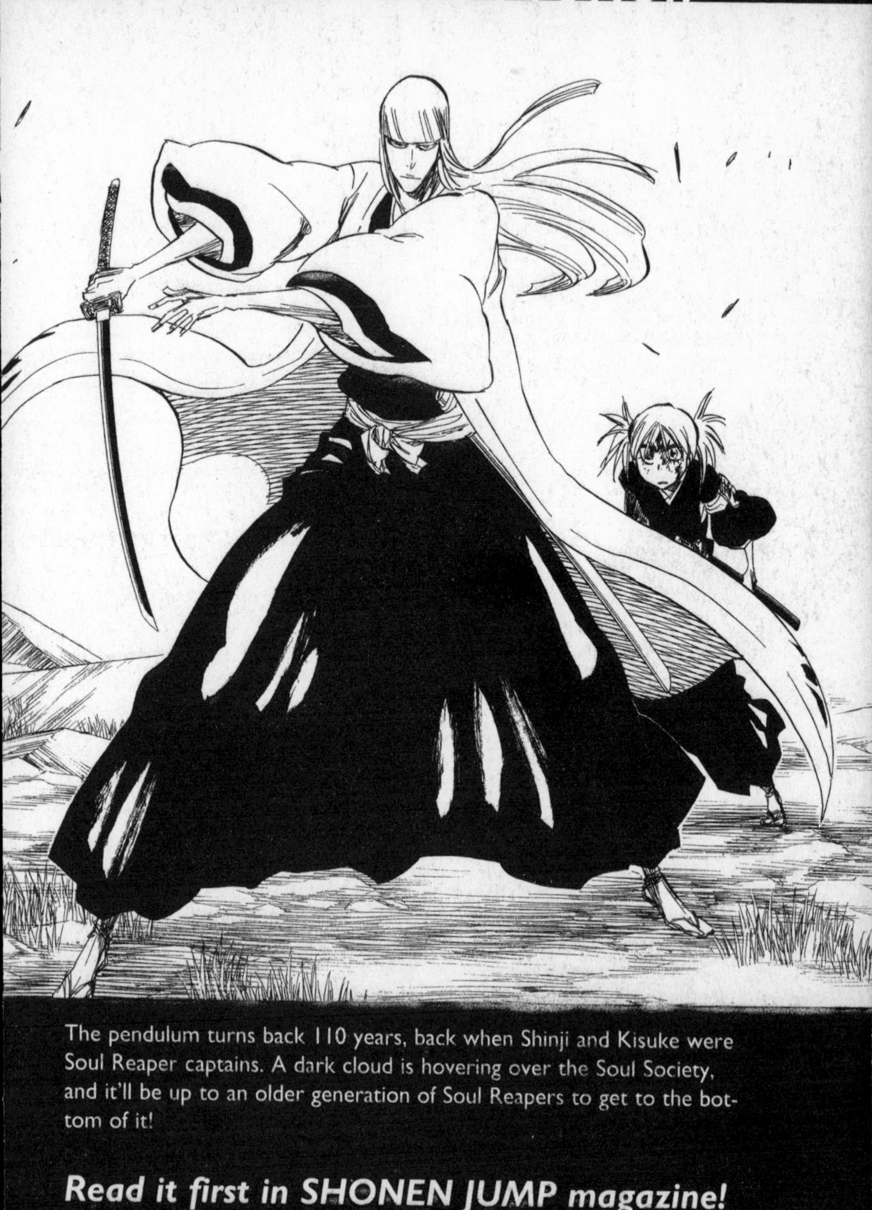

The pendulum turns back 110 years, back when Shinji and Kisuke were Soul Reaper captains. A dark cloud is hovering over the Soul Society, and it'll be up to an older generation of Soul Reapers to get to the bottom of it!

Read it first in SHONEN JUMP magazine!

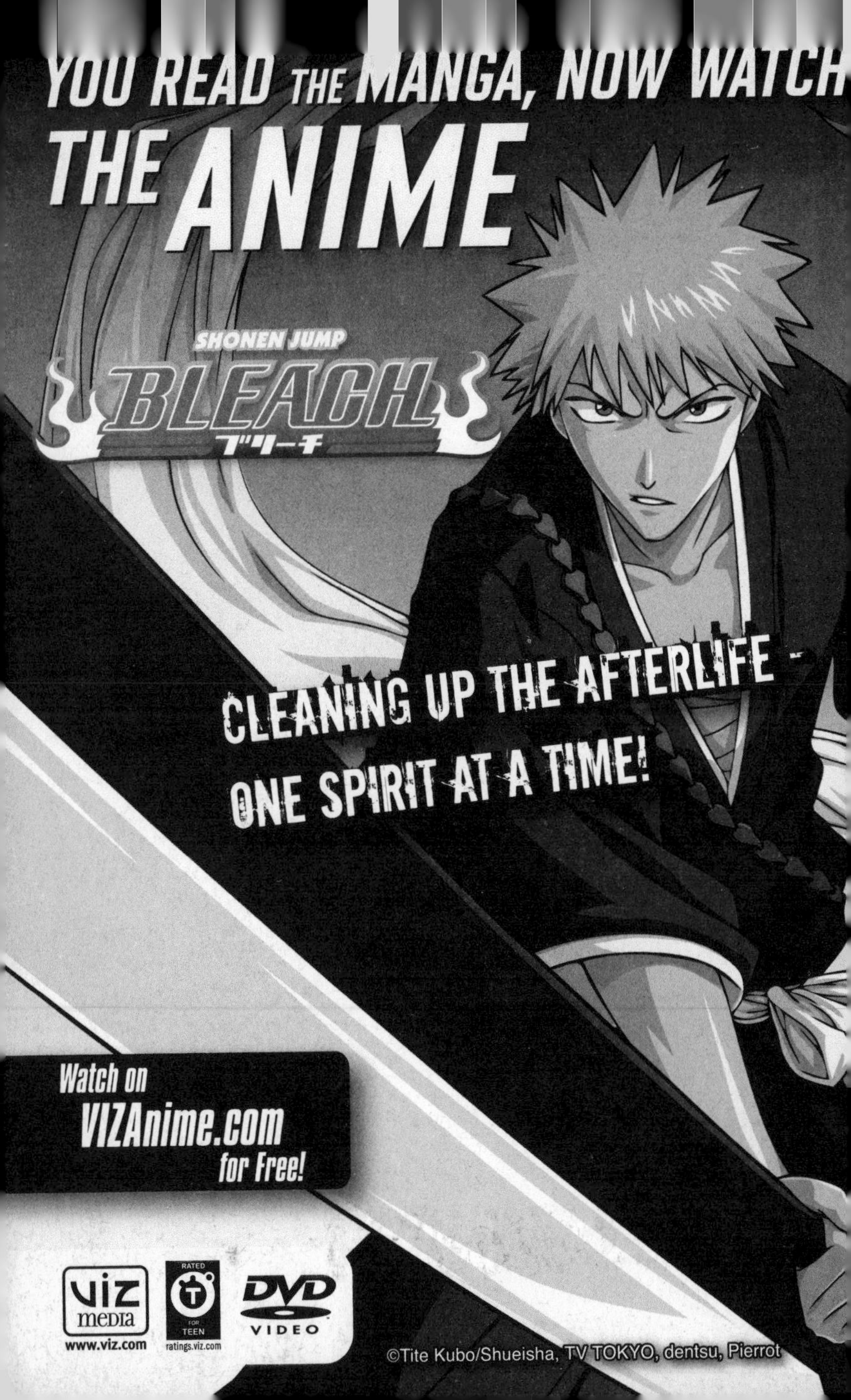

YOU READ THE MANGA, NOW WATCH
THE ANIME
SHONEN JUMP
BLEACH
ブリーチ
CLEANING UP THE AFTERLIFE -
ONE SPIRIT AT A TIME!
Watch on
VIZAnime.com
for Free!
viz media
www.viz.com
RATED
T
FOR TEEN
ratings.viz.com
DVD VIDEO
©Tite Kubo/Shueisha, TV TOKYO, dentsu, Pierrot